Commanding WordStar®
Release 7.0
2nd Edition

Commanding WordStar® Release 7.0

2nd Edition

William Warren Pitts

Windcrest®/McGraw-Hill

SECOND EDITION
FIRST PRINTING

© 1993 by **Windcrest Books**, an imprint of TAB Books.
TAB Books is a division of McGraw-Hill, Inc.
The name "Windcrest" is a registered trademark of TAB Books.

Library of Congress Cataloging-in-Publication Data

Pitts, William Warren.
   Commanding WordStar release 7.0.—2nd edition / by William Warren
Pitts.
      p.   cm.
   Includes index.
   ISBN 0-8306-3970-5 (P)
   1. WordStar (Computer file)   2. Word processing—Computer
programs.   I. Title.
Z52.5.W676P58   1992
652.5'536—dc20   92-27992
                                                                    CIP

Acquisitions Editor: Brad Schepp
Book Editor: Kellie Hagan
Director of Production: Katherine G. Brown
Series Design: Jaclyn J. Boone
Cover Design: Sandra Blair Design, Harrisburg, Pa.   WT1

Contents

8. Writing in the document mode   95

9. Using the Onscreen Format Menu   107

Introduction

The purpose of this book is to put you in command of a writing tool called Word-Star. Its goal is to let you take charge of this tool as quickly and painlessly as possible. This book will speak to you in plain English. Instead of talking over your head, it will attempt to talk directly to you and your needs.

This book assumes that you know how to type and how to turn on your computer. It helps if you know how to run a program—any program—on an IBM-compatible computer. If you've already used another word processor, so much the better. But it really isn't necessary. We'll work together through this book and I'll get you up and running with WordStar.

WordStar is a writing tool, so this book also acts as a writing manual. I want to help every writer get his writing done with WordStar. Although written specifically to explain WordStar, much of the basic principles in this book are applicable to all word processing programs.

Instead of relying on lessons, this book instructs by explaining in detail and by applying WordStar features to specific writing tasks. It has overviews and step-by-step instructions for each feature. Where possible, I've also provided practical tips for using each feature. This book's design takes advantage of WordStar's logical structure.

Who needs this book?

This book is for people who need to write a lot, who want to use WordStar to write, and who don't want anything hindering the writing process. This book assumes that you don't know much about computers and probably don't want to know much more. Like most people, you just want your computer to help you get your work done.

This book contains much information about WordStar—how to use it, what to use it for, and how to customize it so it works the way *you* want it to work. This book is written specifically for writers who are on many different levels of word processing use. There are explanations and information for everyone from an absolute beginner to an experienced professional to even a computer hacker.

How to begin learning WordStar

The first thing to know is *you don't have to understand everything*. Nobody uses everything WordStar has to offer all the time. There's just too much to know and too much to remember. I often use this book to recall features I seldom use. If you forget how to use something, this book can help you find it again fast.

It's important to get an overview of word processing itself. Then you can use this information in order to understand WordStar. Most user manuals begin by assuming that first-time users *already know* what word processing is. I've found that this assumption is most often false.

Accordingly, the first three chapters in this book give a necessary overview of word processing. Following chapters will provide an overview of WordStar—telling you what's old and what's new. Next, you'll start writing with WordStar, using its features to make your documents better.

This book uses calculated redundancy, the philosophy being that it's better to explain repeatedly than risk confusing you or losing you in cross references. Chapters and sections stand alone, providing all the information necessary to use specific features. References to elsewhere will appear only when subjects are too lengthy or too complex to explain without obscuring the section or chapter you're reading.

The most important thing about learning WordStar is understanding its basic logic:

- You begin by running WordStar and then opening a file to work on.
- It's primarily a menu-driven program, meaning you call up a menu and then select a command from it.
- You can issue commands directly, without waiting for menus to appear. You can also command WordStar with a mouse.
- WordStar prints by reading a file from disk and sending it to your printer. This means that you can print one file while working on another.

There it is in brief. Grasp those basic features of WordStar and everything else will fall into place. WordStar uses basic steps over and over and over again. Once you use it enough to become familiar with the following kinds of action it becomes an easy rhythm:

- All commands are issued the same way.
- All embedded printing controls are placed in the document the same way.

- All documents are sent to the printer the same way, despite length or kind.

Take only what you need

WordStar is a smorgasbord of word processing features. Take what you need. This book has information for all kinds and levels of writers. It makes no difference whether you're writing letters, reports, college themes, research papers, theses or dissertations, or The Great American Novel—WordStar doesn't care. To Word-Star, a document is a document, and a rose by any other name . . .

Only *you* know what kinds of documents you have to write. The "plain vanilla" version of WordStar is set up to write and print documents with 66 line pages and 65 spaces or columns per line. You can vary this, however, almost any way you like. Learn to use the features to layout and design, and you'll be able to print documents the way you want them to look.

WordStar has a feature to cover almost every writing task anyone could want or need to use. No one knows your needs better than you. It isn't necessary to learn every WordStar feature before you can use it with satisfaction. Just step up to the smorgasbord and fill your plate.

Once you know basic WordStar features, it's only a matter of finding out what else you need to get your work done. Some features work better in one kind of document, and others better elsewhere. Take what you want or need from Word-Star and leave the rest alone.

Using this book

WordStar is a writing tool, not a toy. It's a craft to master. It isn't a computer game. It applies directly to your real world. Word processing is definitely a skill, not some artistic talent you were born with. Kids learn computers faster because they don't have anything to unlearn. They just take it as it is.

This means that you're going to have to work. It also means that you'll have to remember the basics from one session to the next. This is how you build a foundation of knowledge to fall back on. How much and how fast you learn is strictly up to you.

Don't be afraid of making mistakes. Everybody makes mistakes. You *will* make them no matter what. So just accept it and get on with the work at hand. Word processing mistakes are easy to correct, and are often the best teacher.

Buy a yellow highlighter pen and use it to mark passages as you read. Keep a notepad handy, and make notes about features you need to use. Use post-it notes to make yourself reminders and stick them on your monitor or computer. Put them where you can see them.

Teach yourself to find your way out of problems. Finding your own solution to a sticky situation will give you a confident feeling you won't forget.

What to do if you need help

The number one cause of needing help is when you get ahead of yourself. It happens when you try to use something without reading the explanation, or without following the steps.

I designed this book to serve as both a reference and a resource. Use its table of contents and index to find features and explanations to answer your questions. All explanations and tips have come from many WordStar users' experience, and answer common (and not-so-common) problems and questions.

If you really, really need help, there are several things you can do. Which of them you choose depends on your problem. But one of them should get the job done:

Use WordStar's built-in help feature   It has a help message for most WordStar options or situations. Select Help from the Opening Menu, or use Ctrl−JJ while inside a document. You can print out these messages with Ctrl−PrtSc.

Read the appendix, *Getting help with WordStar*   It tells you how to use the Help feature and translates help and error messages into something you can understand.

Consult your dealer   There might be someone there to help you. If not, complaining will at least make you feel better.

Locate and join a WordStar user's group   Most of these groups publish newsletters and have a hotline to call with problems.

Locate and join a PC users' group   They can help you with anything related to your computer.

Call or write WordStar International Tech Support   They'll help for free if you're a registered user, and charge you moderately if you aren't.

Write to me care of this publisher   If everything else fails, you might have a problem I'd like to hear about.

1
CHAPTER

An introduction to word processing

The first goal of this book is to give a word processing overview. If you're a first-time user, you'll need clear explanations of the principles of basic word processing in order to understand what this book has to teach you. Unfortunately, most user manuals assume that first-time users already know what word processing is and does. The truth is, however, a bit different.

The first three chapters of this book present an overview of word processing for first-time or inexperienced users. These chapters will explain what word processing is and give practical advice about using it. If you're an old hand at WordStar, feel free to skip to later chapters. But even "old-timers" might find useful information here.

What is word processing?

Word processing is writing with a computer. A word processing *program* is a writing toolbox. These tools make a personal computer work like an enhanced typewriter. Toolboxes like WordStar tell your computer to do what you want it to do. These tools can help you write better and faster.

There are many word processing programs available. Each has roughly the same set of options and features. Most programs, unfortunately, insist on using different names for the same options and features. Most have their own way of using those options. Yet all word processors do one thing—let you type words on the keyboard, edit those words on the screen, save the words to permanent storage on disk, and print them on paper. Everything else is icing on the cake.

Computerized writing is based on one thing: text files. A *text file* is the form in which your documents are stored on disk. To write with a computer, you open a text file, give it a name, and write the document inside the text file.

As you type the document, your words are stored *temporarily* in computer memory (also called RAM). When you save the text file, this records a permanent copy of it on a disk. When you close the file, the version in memory is erased, and only the copy stored on disk remains.

Text files are stored magnetically, using the same technology as music recorded on a stereo cassette. Though the disk hardware is different and the recording heads more delicate, it does the same thing as your stereo. Just as recorded music can be played again and again, stored files can be "played," or used repeatedly.

When you need to edit or add to a file, just reopen it. This copies it back from disk storage into computer memory. While it's in memory, make whatever changes or additions you want. When you save the edited file, the new version replaces the old one on the storage disk.

When you type on a typewriter, the words go onto paper as you type them. With word processing, the words go onto the screen. They are sent to paper only as the final step. This is called *printing* the file. Printing the file sends a copy to the printer, with instructions on how to print it. A printed document is called a *hardcopy*, and the version on disk (or in memory) is the *softcopy*.

Getting started

It takes more to get started with word processing than simply turning on the computer. You have to learn how to use the doggone thing. Writing with a computer is distinctly different than writing with a pen or a typewriter. Learning its methods can change the way you think about words themselves, and about how you use them. It can change your attitudes about the process of writing.

Writing is the craft of communicating through the written or printed word. Some writing can become art—but most writing is simply craft. It's meant to get a job done. The more you practice any craft, the better chance you have of getting better.

There are many different kinds of documents, and therefore many kinds of writing that are used to get many different jobs done. As you begin learning Word-Star 7, only *you* know your writing needs—or the kinds of documents you need to write. WordStar 7 can be used to write any kind of document, large or small. This book aims to teach you what you need to get your writing done.

The most important function of any word processing toolbox is how it can take over organizational tasks and free you to concentrate on the things you have to say. Before that can happen, however, you must get familiar with WordStar and the computer running it.

WordStar's rhythm

WordStar's rhythm is made up of the steps you need to follow in order to get your writing done. If you've used other word processing programs before coming to WordStar, you'll find that it does things differently from most other programs. The basic steps for writing a document with WordStar are as follows:

1. Load and run WordStar. It can be run either from your hard-disk drive or from a floppy-disk drive.
2. When the Opening Menu appears, create a new text file, or open an existing one to work on.
3. When the text file is open, write the document inside it. You do this by typing the words on the keyboard.
4. As you write the text file, you can make any changes, additions, deletions, or rearrangements you need in order to complete the document by reading the words on the screen and entering editing commands from the keyboard. Save the text file to disk at regular periods.
5. When the document is completed, only then should you format it with special layouts and fonts. Print intermediate drafts to check your layout and design.
6. When the document is as perfect as it needs to be, print the final draft.

Many ways to do everything

Part of understanding WordStar 7's rhythm lies in its flexibility. With every single feature and option, WordStar gives you two, three, or four different ways to use it. You're never locked into a single, rigid pathway to any solution. No matter what kind of document you're writing or what kind of layout and design you want to give it, you're always free to follow your own whims in getting the job done.

As you become familiar with WordStar 7, you'll discover that some things are easy to do one way, while other methods work best for other things. For some procedures you'll want to use the mouse to activate the pull-down menus, classic menus, and dialog boxes. For others, you'll get in the habit of using Ctrl−key combinations, which allow you to issue commands without lifting your fingers from the keyboard. Sometimes you'll even find it convenient to type the dot commands directly into the document. For those who like to do several things at once, macros offer complex manipulations with only three or four keystrokes.

Ultimately, WordStar's rhythm is *your* rhythm. You'll learn to customize WordStar to make it work exactly the way you want it to work. The number of combinations and custom settings available through WSCHANGE is virtually unlimited. WordStar can become what you want it to be and do everything you want it to.

What is a computer?

Computers are one of the most talked about and least understood components of modern-day life. They seem to be everywhere, are built into more and more kinds of machines, and are doing everything at once. They've invaded our lives and won't ever go away.

If you're reading this book, it means that computers have entered *your* life and are intruding on your workday. You have a computer sitting on your desk—either at the office or at home—and you need to use it to write. You might know how to begin or you might not. But the basics are always the best place.

Your attitude toward the computer

Like most first-time users, you probably have to correct your *attitude* toward computers. Attitude determines how you feel about the computer—and feelings control how you learn. Techies are fond of saying "feelings are unimportant" when using high-technology devices. That is false. Feelings influence you more than anything else—and set the tone for getting your work done.

Since 1980, I've known too many people who bought personal computers and were afraid to touch or use them. Though not as common as it used to be, it still happens. The causes are false notions and nonsense circulated about computers.

As you begin to write with WordStar, take time to understand the computer's quirks and capabilities. It's just a machine. Learn what it's supposed to do. Learn what it can and can't do. Read the manuals that come with your computer. Even if they stink, they might have information you can use. Find someone to explain what those megahertz, megabytes, RAM, ROM, and so on really mean. The more you know, the less mysterious it will seem.

What a computer isn't

Almost everything said about computers in literature, television, and movies is pure baloney. Computers can't do, or won't do, anything but run software. In the real world, computers are mundane and boring. But people are fascinated by the idea of computers, so movies and TV programs often portray them quite differently.

Forget everything television, the movies, and popular fiction say about computers. They don't know what they're talking about. There's so little truth in their stories that it's better to wipe the slate clean and start over.

Get this straight—a computer isn't going to hurt you and, if you practice a little common sense, you can't hurt it. The best way to lose those negative feelings is with hands-on experience. Familiarity will dissipate those awkward, fearful feelings. Fiddle with it. Learn how to make the doggone thing work. Find your way in and out of problems. You don't have to know why something works. Just learn how to use it.

The personal computer is nothing but a tool. It's no more complicated than your television set or your family car. The PC doesn't think. It won't come alive and take over your house—or get jealous of your dog. Compared to your dog, it's actually pretty stupid. It can't do *anything* unless someone tells it exactly and precisely what to do.

Think of it as a totally efficient file clerk who can only go by the rules and obey orders. This clerk has a remarkable memory and the fastest hands in town, but no initiative. If you give it a task, it will work tirelessly. It can file things away and find them faster than blazes. But if you don't tell it what to do it will just sit around looking good. You must spell out what you want it to do in the words it knows and understands. If you give wrong directions, it will refuse to work—or happily do everything wrong. It doesn't care one way or the other.

WordStar and your computer

Every time you write with WordStar, you make the computer obey thousands and thousands of orders. Most computers function invisibly—because everything you do causes thousands of calculations inside the microprocessor (the heart of the computer) *per second*.

If you had all the time in the world, you could issue each command individually. This is called *writing a program*. Fortunately, WordStar is an already-written program, a large set of special instructions used by the computer. WordStar does most of the work for you. Just give it commands, or select options, and WordStar will tell the computer what to do. But WordStar has its own way of doing things—of issuing commands and selecting options—and you must learn it.

You *must* pay special attention to format and spelling when issuing WordStar commands, or typing in filenames or directory paths to use. Computers can't guess. A miss is as good as a mile—or worse. You must use command format and syntax without variation. Typos will result in either nothing or the wrong thing happening.

Like any other complicated tool, a computer can be (and often is) frustrating to learn how to use. But never give up and never panic. If you concentrate, pay attention to detail, and don't give up, you *can* learn to make it work for you.

Even the most versatile tools have limitations. This manual describes how to use WordStar's features and options. When they don't do things the way you want, then do them the way you must. Learn each feature one by one. If you don't get the results you want, back up and try again. You probably made an error issuing the command. Or you were telling the computer and WordStar to do something they can't do. There *is* an underlying logic to it all. Once you learn this logic, it will become easier to use the powerful writing tool called WordStar.

A short history of user manuals

All too often, after people go to the expense and trouble of buying a computer and word processing software to use with it, they get left out in the cold. They don't know how to go about learning to use what they've purchased. They might not even know the difference between hardware and software. What they probably see is a complex, intimidating machine that can do complicated things in mysterious ways. If you're one of these people, read on.

Different methods of instruction

In recent years, many computer stores and various schools have been giving classes in word processing and using MS-DOS. I hear mostly horror stories about inept or bored instructors and badly taught classes. Too many instructors and their textbooks assume that students already understand more than they do—and thus explain over their heads (if they even explain at all).

Most people never take classes. The very *thought* of having to go to a class makes everything seem that much more difficult. So they teach themselves how to use word processing, and they do it the hard way—by trial and error—because most user's manuals are so badly written that most people can't understand them.

Frustrating experiences

Anyone who's ever sat down to a "factory" user's manual for the first time and tried to learn how to use a computer program on his own has most probably come away with feelings of confusion and frustration. The words in that manual *appear* to be in plain English, but the sentences built from those words never really seem to say what you think they do. And when you try to follow the instructions, things never work out right.

Why so many user manuals are unreadable

Most factory manuals don't explain the computer or program they come with. At worst, they appear to be written in Sanskrit. At best, these books assume a prior level of knowledge beyond the real-world understanding of their readers. So they leave out basic concepts and explanations because the authors assume such things are obvious, simple, and easy. The most common phrase I've heard from computer engineers is "don't explain that, it's *obvious*."

Some manuals are even filled with cartoons to show how "user-friendly" everything is. And that just makes people feel like idiots when they can't understand the manuals.

The biggest reason for bad user manuals is that too many manuals are concocted by technicians, engineers, programmers, and people who lack communications skills or professional training in writing. Poorly written documentation, filled with "nonexplanations" that assume everything is obvious can cause people who read it to react in hostile, highly emotional ways. People already intimidated by their computers might get the false impression that if they can't understand what they're reading it's their fault.

Too many people take on this attitude when the fault really lies with books that don't do what they're supposed to do. Too many people give up because word processing seems too difficult to learn. I was almost one of those people myself.

A personal approach to technical writing

I've been writing since I was twelve years old. For several years now, I've earned my living by writing. All my early work was done on a much-battered electric portable typewriter. But I dreamed about computer word processing before there was such a thing. I wanted a keyboard to suck the words from my fingertips.

I'll never forget the first time I tried to make a word processor work. No one should have to live through that. The frustration, anger, and humiliation were totally avoidable—but made inevitable by the so-called user's manual for the program. It was unreadable and patronizing, and was missing vital information.

I've always been a technically minded person, but I realize that many people fear technology. While many high-tech processes and equipment are simpler than they appear, they're most easily understood when explained in plain English.

What about this book?

I wrote this book specifically for folks who want to learn something new. There's no reason that any writer—whether secretary, clerk, journalist, lawyer, or novelist—can't learn word processing and use it to make writing easier. WordStar 7 is a professional-strength word processor, but it can be used for writing the simplest documents.

This book has practical information for even an experienced WordStar user. If you taught yourself to use earlier versions of WordStar, you might have picked up some bad habits. To help you correct those, I've tried to be especially instructive on methods for planning and organizing writing. While those are key elements in all writing, word processing makes them mandatory. If you don't stay organized and keep track of what, when, and where, you can get lost and stay lost.

This book serves as both instructional guide and reference manual. It does this by presenting—clearly and simply—an overview of word processing, of the basic WordStar program, and of WordStar options and features. Where possible, I've provided practical applications. I've tried to meet you eye to eye. If this book fails, it's my fault, not yours.

2
CHAPTER

Planning
and writing
a manuscript

When used correctly, word processing makes it easier to plan and write both small and large documents. Because every word processing program has countless combinations of features and options, there are as many methods for planning and writing as there are writers. But word processing embraces them all.

Incorrectly used, word processing can give you headaches and takes more time than typing documents with a typewriter. The main reason that many people use it incorrectly is that they have an unclear overview of what it can and can't do.

There are basic guidelines that anyone can use to help organize their writing processes. Think of this as "getting the big picture." A word processor can eliminate unnecessary labor and free your writing time for more creative things.

The basic element of word processing

The basic element of word processing is the *text file*. Every document is kept in a text file of its own. In fact, the terms *text file* and *document* are interchangeable. Every text file has a distinct name to keep it separated from other files, and every text file is stored on either a floppy disk or a hard disk. Text files can be copied, moved, merged, edited, deleted, or printed.

Opening a text file means either creating a new one or loading an existing one from disk into computer memory. Then you can type words and use commands in order to move those words around, check their spelling, or lay out and design the document.

Saving a document means issuing a command to copy the text file from computer memory to permanent storage on disk. You can copy the text file to as many disks as you want.

Printing a text file means transferring a copy of the text file from disk to the printer, along with printing instructions to tell the printer how to print the text file. Those instructions include things like margins, line spacing, the type and size font to be used, and so on.

Editing a text file means reopening the file and changing either its content or formatting. Some people consider any changes made to a text file, even during the original writing, to be editing.

Think in terms of a boilerplate

During the 19th century, boilers were at the heart of every steam engine. Boilers came in all sizes, and constantly needed repair. To simplify boiler making, the metal plates were standardized in size, shape, and curvature. To build a certain boiler, you used certain plates from a standard supply. If a boilerplate burst, a ready-made replacement was available for speedy repair.

The printing industry adopted *boilerplate* as a term for typeset blocks of text that were available to be used over and over again. This principle applies to a lot of what you do with word processing. Once you've typed something into a text file and saved it to disk, you never have to type it again.

- You can reuse an entire text file or parts of a text file—by either copying them or merging them into other documents.
- If you open a document in a second window, you can copy directly from one text file to the other.

If you create boilerplate during the planning stage of your documents, you can "cut and paste" it into your documents wherever you need to. By planning ahead, you can have half your document ready before you start to write it.

Different kinds of boilerplates

A boilerplate can be anything you want to use again. It can be a complete letterhead with your return address and signature block already typed—and a blank place to insert the date. It can be a form letter with a blank place to type in the addressee's name and address. It can be a list of names and addresses used for printing mailing labels.

If you work in a law office, you can make a text file for every kind of contract or agreement you use, with blank places for "Party of the first part" and so on. If you write complicated contracts from scratch, keep individual paragraphs and articles in separate files, then merge them in as needed.

If your documents rely on tables, charts, graphs, and spreadsheets, save each to a separate text file. For example, you can make a new table in quick order by using an existing one as a template and then making whatever corrections are needed.

Make preliminary notes

Though important to planning and organizing a document, keeping notes can be the most tedious part of preparing to write anything important. The notes must be carefully revised, updated, sorted, and generally kept organized and available. Word processing can handle this with a minimum of effort. You never have to waste time retyping anything.

Use a word processing program to write and assemble your notes, and all other preliminary writing, on subjects to be included in the document. The sooner you start getting your boilerplate stored on disk, the less time you have to spend rewriting later.

Tip: If you still prefer keeping your notes on index cards, you can buy index cards for tractor feed and print a hardcopy. Set the page size for the size of the card. Set margins at $1/2$ inch inside the page margins, and turn off page numbering.

Organize by writing outlines

One of the hardest parts of writing is getting the printed document to match the one in your mind. Too much is too easily lost during the translation. This can make the difference between success and failure.

Many people use outlines as an organizational tool. Outlines can be good or bad for your writing. The trouble with outlines is they can subconsciously limit you, thus stifling creativity. They're fine if used as an *overview* of the document to be written. They turn on you if used as a rigid mold for the document. Thoughts don't come chiseled in stone. Why should your documents?

The best use for an outline is in *reorganizing* your documents—after you've finished your first draft. An outline written before you have a first draft will show you only where you want to go. An outline made from an existing text file will show you exactly where you are and what you have.

With word processing, outlines are never chiseled in stone. Change it, rearrange it, rewrite it with a minimum of labor. The order of subjects in the outline can be rearranged again and again with WordStar's cut and paste features. Unwanted items can easily be deleted and the space closed up.

This gives you the freedom to rethink and rearrange your document, to make the version on paper match the one in your mind. Every manuscript has an inherent purpose, premise, and best order of presentation. Getting those three things right is crucial to the success of the document.

Using a table of contents as an outline

While there are many programs available to actually write outlines, I've found the best one to be the table of contents generator built into WordStar. Simply remember to embed the TOC commands for chapter, section, subsection, and subsubsection in the text file as you write the first draft. You can then generate a table of contents from that text file. The only difference between a table of contents and an outline is the name.

Keep it simple

Whatever you write, the surest path astray is to make your document more complicated than necessary. Zen Buddhist philosophy has a concept called *Shibui*, which is Japanese for "restrained elegance." You don't have to convert to an eastern religion to understand and use Shibui. It simply means that the simpler something is, the easier it is to it make work. The fewer moving parts in a machine, the fewer things to go wrong.

Every document has a primary goal: to communicate its ideas to its readers. An overly complex style can get in the way. Avoid literary doodads, gimmicks, jargon, and gizmos that replace simple communication. Simplicity is essential when trying to communicate something complicated. The more information you have, the simpler design or style you should use. This always makes writing more effective.

Be sensitive to white space

Although you're a writer and probably not a typesetter, you should still try to think about what the printed page will look like. *White space*, the area of the page with no printing on it, is crucial to communication. Whether in a novel or a business letter, how a page looks often determines how it affects the reader.

You can control white space with more than just typesetting. Paragraph breaks, word length, and sentence structure all contribute to the flow of the page. The longer the page goes without a break, the harder it becomes to read—and the easier to lose your reader.

Writing the first draft

When writing any large manuscript, it takes an average of five drafts to whip the document into an acceptable final form. Careful proofreading, editing, and rewriting are vital to good writing. I've known writers who could cut this to three drafts and writers who insisted on fifteen drafts. The main ingredient is the basic ability of the individual writer. But the most important factor is the care you put into that first draft.

No one should expect a first draft of a business proposal, a research paper, or any other large document to be perfect. No one is that well organized or that good of a writer. But the first draft always sets the quality, direction, and effectiveness of the final document. If you screw it up from the start, you might never get it right.

Always use your word processor to write a first draft. It doesn't matter if the first draft is full of holes or errors. It's always easier to edit, correct, and rewrite a text file than to type consecutive drafts from scratch. If you want to keep all of your drafts for future reference, you can always save them in separate files.

Divide a document into easily handled files

Computerized writing allows dividing the manuscript into easily handled fragments. This keeps you in control while still maintaining an overview of the entire document.

WordStar can handle virtually any size document as a single text file, providing you have room for it on disk. But the larger a text file, the more time the program spends moving through it. When writing long documents, like novels, dissertations, or any kind of book, divide them into parts, chapters, or major sections. This accomplishes several things at once:

- The smaller a text file, the less cumbersome it is. Everything works quicker: opening the text file, saving it, searching and replacing, etc. Saving a 500K text file can take several minutes.
- Dividing the document into workable text files can act as passive protection for the contents of the document. Sometimes clumsy handling can damage or delete a text file you want to keep. The smaller a text file, the less work it takes to recreate it.
- Two of the most common triggers of writer's block are anxiety and frustration. Dividing a document makes it psychologically easier to cope with. Even the most talented writer can hold only so much in his mind at any given moment.
- Dividing a document simplifies backing up your text files. Accidents happen with even the best hard drives. The only complete protection for your work is to make multiple copies on backup disks.

Most computers can take information from and store information on floppy disks that hold only 360 or 720 kilobytes of data. Because of the way WordStar handles files, it's best not to work on floppy disks with text files bigger than 150 kilobytes. WordStar needs more than *twice* as much empty space on disk as the size of the file being worked on. For writing and editing large documents, you should stick to the hard drive. Your hard drive is also going to be several times faster than the floppy drive.

Use find and replace to fill in your blanks

Getting stuck is a form of writer's block. Every writer inevitably comes to places in the manuscript where the right words won't come when he wants them to. These are usually facts you aren't sure of, things on the "tip of your tongue," or descriptions and dialogues that don't quite work. If you break momentum or dwell on them, you risk increasing that sense of being stuck and losing your head of creative steam.

When a journalist who's "on a roll" comes to a passage he can't finish, the traditional thing has always been to type in the letters TK and then keep typing. (TK is a proofreading symbol for *to come*.) When doing the rewrite, the journalist can find the information he needs and type it into the document.

WordStar's find and replace capabilities, however, greatly simplify this kind of situation. When you come to something you can't finish, you can mark the place. When it's time to rewrite, use search and replace commands to track down your place markers and then fill in the blanks.

It also helps if you make up a coding system for gaps you're forced to leave. Make it something distinct like aaa, gap1, or stat1. Plan ahead or make it up as you go along, but be consistent. It helps if the code actually identifies the nature of the gap. It just has to be something unique in the body of the document.

1. At the gap in the document, type the code letters or word into the manuscript. Then, before you continue, take a quick moment to jot down the code word on paper, with a *brief* description of the missing information.
2. Wait until you've finished writing the first draft of the text file. Then look up or figure out the information you need.
3. When you're ready with the missing text, use a find command to locate the code word and type or copy in whatever's missing.

You can use find and replace commands to substitute a word or phrase for a code word. WordStar can find and replace phrases up to 65 characters long. If you have to leave out a company or place name throughout a document, for example, then a global search and replace can make a tedious job a snap.

For example, if date1 equals 1789, then tell WordStar to find and replace all occurrences of date1 with the date 1789.

Print your work daily

It's always best to print a hardcopy of your day's work. Print whenever you finish working for the day—even if the draft you're working on isn't finished. No matter how many words you type into a text file, it isn't real until you print it. There's no feeling of accomplishment until there's a hardcopy in your hands. I've never known a writer yet who didn't need the special satisfaction that comes only from watching the pages stack up.

There's no denying how a word processor like WordStar can help you write better and faster. But for psychological reasons, the document is the *printed* copy, never the text file on disk. Some of the reasons for this are covered later in this chapter.

Reassemble the divided document

There are several different ways to reassemble and print a divided document. You can print each file individually and stack up the pages. Or use Ctrl−KR to read the segments into a single document and then print it. Or use merge printing to assemble the parts into a single printed document. Find the method you like best and use it.

Psychological considerations

Electronic text is psychologically different from printed text. Most of us inevitably think about it differently. This is mainly because people have been reading print, in one form or another, for centuries. So the concept of *physically holding* reading matter is deeply rooted in us. The onscreen document is still too new, too unfamiliar.

The pop philosopher Marshall McLuhan, among others, has insistently predicted the demise of the printed word. He said that electronic media would make printing anything obsolete. From his point of view, paper was good for wrapping fish, but not for communication. But Marshall McLuhan foresaw neither the personal computer nor the kind of word processing it makes possible. Instead of abolishing printed documents, word processing has increased their size and quantity exponentially.

Holding what we read is a customary part of reading. I don't think anything is likely to change this completely. We're accustomed to adjusting our bodies for comfortable reading. We prefer our reading matter to be within arms' reach.

A document on paper has a reassuring *feel* to it. We're happiest when we can "come to grips" with things affecting our lives. We rely on our hands for psychological support, and express ourselves with our hands. We naturally find it frustrating to deal with things kept beyond our grasp.

3
CHAPTER

How to write and edit documents

This chapter gives an overview of procedures and steps for creating word processed documents (rather than specific instructions). It defines and explains concepts used in producing medium to large documents. These include creating text files, writing inside them, editing, saving, and printing hardcopies.

Word processing is a powerful tool, therefore most people need an overview to help them get maximum use from it. And an overview of what word processing can and can't do is a long way toward "getting down to business." Then it's just a matter of picking up the necessary skills.

Understanding text files

A *text file* is an electronic document. This electronic document exists only as digital coding held in computer memory (also called RAM), or in storage on disk. Nothing about a text file is ever permanent until it's saved to disk or printed on paper.

Word processing programs like WordStar make a personal computer work as a glorified or enhanced typewriter. Instead of typing words directly onto paper, you keep your words in text files of coded digital information. Storing text files on a disk is the electronic equivalent of storing file folders in a file cabinet drawer.

The following are things you can do with text files:

Creating   means telling the computer to set aside space in memory for your file, and then typing text into that memory. You see it onscreen, but it's only in temporary memory. Because the document is electronic, parts of it can easily be changed, rearranged, moved, edited, copied, and deleted. The file isn't safe from change until it's been saved.

Saving   means copying, or recording, a file from memory to storage on either a disk or tape. There's no specific limit to the number of files you can store. You're limited only by the size of the storage space on the disk or tape.

Reopening   means copying a text file's data back into computer memory from disk or tape storage. This is also called loading a file into memory. When a text file is reopened for writing and editing in RAM, its contents can be changed and rewritten any way you want, and the revised file saved, or copied back to storage.

Copying   means recording another copy of a file to disk or tape. This is electronically identical to dubbing copies of a music cassette. A text file also can be copied under a different name, either in the same disk or elsewhere.

Deleting   means removing a file's name from a directory listing, and allowing its space on disk to be used by other files.

Tip: Simply deleting a file doesn't erase it from disk. There are utility programs, like Norton Utilities and Mace, that can "undelete" a file. You must use these programs, however, before another file has had a chance to write over the deleted file's space.

Creating and editing a text file

There are five steps to creating and editing documents in text files. Briefly, they are as follows:

1. Load and run WordStar.
2. Open a file in the document mode and type text into it.
3. Use the editing features to customize and correct the file.
4. Save the file to storage on a disk.
5. When desired, print the file on paper.

Load and run WordStar

Loading and running WordStar means giving the computer the command to copy the program into memory. This makes the program active and ready to respond to commands. You do this at DOS prompt (the A>, B>, or C> you see on the screen before you run WordStar) by typing an abbreviation of the name of the program (in this case, WS) and pressing the Enter key.

When WordStar loads and runs, the Opening Menu will appear onscreen. WordStar has 20 major modes or commands available through this menu. Each of these features is described in the chapter entitled *The Opening Menu options*. Simple features are described in detail. Complex features comprise entire sections of the chapter.

Open a document text file

The standard write-and-edit mode for WordStar is the *document mode*. Because WordStar doesn't start up in this mode, you must select it from the Opening Menu, and then create or choose a text file to work on.

When you select the document mode, WordStar will ask for the name of a text file. At this time, you can create a new file or reopen an existing one. This is called *opening a document*. The term comes from the image of pulling a file folder from a drawer and opening it to work on the papers inside. It's the same thing as *loading a file*.

Speed write a new file

Since WordStar 4, you can also open a new document file without first typing in the filename. This is called *speed write*. You begin writing the document at once, and don't name it until the first time you save it. You can use this option to open only a file in the current directory.

Use unlimited editing and correction

Editing a file means correcting and changing anything or everything about the words or layout of the document created by the word processor. Nothing is permanent in memory. You can change everything in the file, or as much as you need to change. Once a text file is in memory, there's no limit to how much of it can be edited, corrected, or rewritten. Keep working on it and revising it until you get it exactly like you want it.

Use the dictionary and thesaurus

WordStar 7 has built-in spell checking, a thesaurus, and a dictionary with definitions. Use these for correcting your spelling and word usage. Nothing makes a document look unprofessional more than misspellings and poor word choice.

Save the text file to permanent storage

Because a file is only a pattern of data in the computer's magnetic memory, it has no more substance than a puff of smoke. It can be easily lost, damaged, or destroyed. If you turn off your computer, a file that you haven't yet saved will disappear. For permanent storage, the data must be copied, or saved, to magnetic disks or tape.

The most common form of storage today is $5^1/_4$-inch or $3^1/_2$-inch disks.

Inside the plastic sleeve of these disks is a plastic disk covered with the same magnetic coating found on magnetic recording tape. In fact, most PCs could use a standard cassette recorder for this purpose. This is all those expensive backup drives really are. Disks, however, are much faster and more convenient to use.

The price of hard disk drives has fallen to the point where they should be considered standard equipment on a personal computer. In fact, the full version of WordStar 7 can only be loaded from a hard drive. If you write a lot, and don't have a hard drive in your computer, then I urge you to buy one. It makes all the difference in the world.

Hard disk drives are three to ten times faster than the best floppy drives, and their storage capacity is many times greater.

By dividing the disk space into directories, you can make a vast archive of your files and boilerplate—where everything you need is at your fingertips. But the possibility of a hard drive crash or failure means you should never rely on it as your sole archive.

For backup or safety purposes, make copies of all your files and directories to floppy disks, and keep those disks in a safe place. If this is done as a part of your regular housekeeping, it keeps loss of work and time to a minimum. So file archiving and backup disks are also part of getting your work done more efficiently.

Print the document

Once the text file is created, edited, the layout designed, and the file saved, the final step is to print the document. For this, you need a printer connected to the computer—and it must be set up for use by WordStar. The printing routine reads the stored file from disk, formats it, and sends it to the printer. This is also called the *print runoff*. The printed document is often called a *hardcopy*.

Using the computer's keyboard

The computer's keyboard works exactly like the keyboard on an electric typewriter, except that the words go to a monitor screen instead of directly to paper. Once a text file has been opened, all you have to do is type. The words appear onscreen as you type them. WordStar automatically formats the words to fit the current margins, line spacing, and justification.

What is the cursor?

The *cursor* is the small blinking box you see on the monitor screen. It marks the location where text appears when typed, or the point where formatting and printing commands take effect when issued. The cursor marks the place where *you* are working in the document. The following are different ways to manipulate the cursor:

- Using the arrow keys, you can move the cursor around onscreen or anywhere in the document, by the following increments: one space, one word, one line, and one page.
- You can do the same thing quicker with commands issued by typing keystroke sequences. These are usually executed by holding down either the Ctrl or Alt key, and typing the letters of the command. Such commands are also called macros, and many of them are assigned to the function keys or hotkeys on the keyboard.
- With the mouse, you can move the cursor anywhere onscreen with a flick of the wrist—pointing to locations and clicking the buttons on the mouse. If you have a mouse, you can select commands and features from the pull-down menus.

Using wordwrap

Wordwrap is a feature that eliminates the need to press the carriage return key at the end of each line of typing, the way you need to with typewriters. Just type normally, and forget about carriage returns—except at the end of a paragraph. When the cursor passes the right margin, wordwrap automatically breaks off the line and starts a new line of text at the left margin.

The first benefit you get from wordwrap is that your typing speed should increase, and your percentage of errors decrease. This results from eliminating the disruption caused by shifting your hand to press the Enter key. Wordwrap gives you one less thing to worry about.

You can toggle the wordwrap feature on and off through the Onscreen Format Menu. With it turned off, the typed line moves past the right margin without breaking off—and continues until you issue a carriage return. This is useful only for extending a line of text past the normal right margin.

If you want these extended lines to remain in the text file, you must protect them by entering a .aw off command above, and a .aw on command below the line. Otherwise, a subsequent reformat of the line with wordwrap on will reshape the document to the set right margin.

Soft versus hard

The factory documentation from WordStar International uses the words *hard* and *soft* quite frequently. It talks about hard and soft carriage returns, and hard and soft spaces. This is just the sort of thing to confuse a new user. In most cases, these terms explain distinctions that don't make much difference to the user.

The difference between hard and soft has been an argument among computer purists for many years. It's also a distinction that most PC users care little about—especially in word processing. At the most basic level, *hard* refers to anything done by the physical equipment or hardware and *soft* is anything done by the program or software.

When you're writing documents with WordStar, it doesn't matter whether something is hard or soft. There's no distinct separation between hardware and software, because neither functions without the other. But just for clarification, I've defined them below:

- A hard carriage return is issued by pressing the Enter key. It puts a less-than symbol ($<$) on the right margin of the text.
- A soft carriage return is the term for what wordwrap does when it breaks off a line and starts a new one. And what wordwrap actually does is controlled by hidden word processing commands.
- A hard space is any space added by pressing the spacebar. This moves the cursor to the right by one column (or fractional unit of measure) at a time.
- A soft space is another hidden word processing command that WordStar uses, for example, when right justification is turned on. Empty spaces are added between words to fill out the line. You have the option of displaying soft space dots onscreen. These show up as tiny dots between words on the screen that don't print in the hardcopy.

Insert versus overtype

There are two different modes for typing text onscreen. These are the insert and overtype modes. When text is inserted, it pushes existing text to the right to make room for itself as it's typed. When text is overtyped, the new text erases and replaces anything in its path.

WordStar's default typing mode is insert. You can toggle between the two modes by pressing the Insert key, or by using the Ctrl−V command. The status line will tell you whether you're in insert or overtype. If the word *Insert* is in the middle of the status line, then insert is active. If you see *Ins-off*, then overtype is active.

It's best to use the insert mode for all normal typing. Don't fall into the bad habit of trying to use word processing with the overtype mode as default. It might seem convenient to overtype because you don't have to use the Delete key to correct mistakes, but you can erase important information much too easily.

Many commands and features are designed to work best in insert mode. They become "quirky" in overtype. For example, turning insert off changes normal Enter and Tab key functions. It also interferes with block movement, unerase, and other word processing functions. In the long run, these are stumbling blocks that will only slow you down.

Typing in overtype is a shortcut to nowhere. To become truly proficient with WordStar, you must get in the habit of using the Delete and Backspace keys, the delete commands, and the editing options to correct your documents. Otherwise, you simply aren't using WordStar to its fullest capacity.

Tip: WordStar can be set up with WSCHANGE to use a different sized cursor to indicate whether insert or overtype is active. I recommend using a small cursor for insert, and the large cursor for overtype. (The large cursor is annoying for normal typing.) At the WSCHANGE Main Menu, type ACEAD for monochrome monitors or ACFAD for all other monitors.

Moving around the document

After you've written a document, the most basic editing function is learning how to move around in its text file. This is done by moving the cursor, or by scrolling the text.

On a typewriter, the Tab key and spacebar are used to move the typehead across the platten. But on a typewriter, you only have one page to work with at a time. On a word processor, you have all pages of the document to move around in—with only 24 to 50 lines of text showing onscreen. So learning to move around is crucial. And it makes a difference whether insert is on or off.

- When insert is on, the Tab key inserts tab commands, and the spacebar inserts spaces into a line.
- When insert is off, the Tab key simply moves across the line a tab stop at a time, while the spacebar deletes text as it moves across the screen.

If you're one of those people who switches on the overtype mode for writing and editing, you must remember these differences. If you keep insert on all the time, and use the cursor movement commands or the scroll bar, it's one less thing to worry about.

Using the cursor-movement keys

All PC keyboards have special keys for moving the cursor. Their exact functions vary from program to program. Their functions with WordStar 7 are as follows:

Arrow keys   move the cursor the direction the arrow points.

The Home key   moves the cursor to the top left of the screen page.

The End key   moves the cursor to the bottom right character onscreen.

The PgUp and PgDn keys   moves the cursor up or down one screen page at a time.

Ctrl−PgUp and Ctrl−PgDn   scrolls the screen page up or down one line for each press, or for as long as you hold them down.

On most monitors, a *screen page* is 24 to 26 lines of text. You can set WordStar to display 46 or 50 lines of text onscreen. (A standard-sized sheet of paper has 66 lines.)

Using Ctrl−key commands to move the cursor

The Ctrl key is the control or command execution key in WordStar. The Ctrl key works like the Shift key: you must hold it down while typing other keys to issue a command. There are nine Ctrl commands to move the cursor around onscreen or through the document.

To issue a Ctrl command, hold down the Ctrl key and type the characters of the command. If you hold down these command keys, the commands will repeat. The different Ctrl commands are:

Command	Cursor movement
Ctrl–S	Moves cursor one space left
Ctrl–D	Moves cursor one space right
Ctrl–A	Moves cursor one word left
Ctrl–F	Moves cursor one word right
Ctrl–E	Moves cursor one line up
Ctrl–X	Moves cursor one line down
Ctrl–I	Inserts one Tab command
Ctrl–QE	Moves cursor to top of screen
Ctrl–QX	Moves cursor to bottom right character

Scrolling through the document

The term *scrolling* means moving the document through the screen window instead of moving the cursor through the document. The scrolling commands are below. If you hold down the keys, the commands will repeat. The scrolling commands are:

Command	Scrolling movement
Ctrl–Z	Scrolls the text up one line
Ctrl–W	Scrolls the text down one line
Ctrl–C	Scrolls the text one screen page up
Ctrl–R	Scrolls the text one screen page down
Ctrl–PgUp	Scrolls the text down one line
Ctrl–PgDn	Scrolls the text up one line

Cutting and pasting documents

Most word processors have the ability to cut text from one place in a document and paste it into another place. The time this can save is incalculable.

To understand this, think of text to cut and paste as a block of text that you need to mark at the beginning with Ctrl–KB and at end with Ctrl–KK. Doing this covers the block with an inverse video highlight. You can mark as big a block as you want, under a 64K limit. If you're using a mouse, just click on the beginning of the block, hold the button down, and drag the inverse highlight over the block to be moved. You can then move, copy, or delete the block, as the following commands show:

Command	Function
Ctrl−KB	Marks the beginning of block
Ctrl−KK	Marks the end of the block
Ctrl−KV	Moves the block to a new cursor location
Ctrl−KC	Copies the block to a new location
Ctrl−KY	Deletes the block from the file

Ctrl−U is the universal abort command for halting a command before it completes execution. But it's also the Unerase command, and can be used to restore a deleted word, line, or block of text.

When text is deleted with Ctrl commands, it's held in the computer's memory buffer until the next delete command. Until then, you can use Ctrl−U to restore that text from the buffer. This means that you can use the command for limited cut and paste functions.

Tip: The limit is the size of the buffer. You can make this buffer bigger by modifying WordStar with WSCHANGE. At the WSCHANGE Main Menu, type CCH and then increase the number of bytes to be allocated to the buffer. The default is 500. Increase this 500 bytes at a time until it's as big as you need. It allocates roughly one byte per character.

To cut and paste a word delete the word with Ctrl−T, move the cursor where you want to paste the word, and restore the word with Ctrl−U.

To cut and paste a line delete the line with Ctrl−Y, move the cursor where you want to paste the word, and restore the line with Ctrl−U.

To cut and paste a block of text mark the text as a block, delete the block with Ctrl−KY, move the cursor where you want to paste the block, and use Ctrl−U to restore the text. (If WordStar tells you the block is too big to restore, don't delete it.)

Deleting or erasing text

Another great convenience of word processing is the ability to delete or erase text from a document at will. Your mistakes can be removed and corrected with a few keystrokes. Typos become a thing of the past.

There are seven Ctrl commands for deleting text from a document, and one to restore it. They're listed below. If you hold down the keys, the commands will repeat.

Command	Function
Ctrl−T	Deletes word to right
Ctrl−Y	Deletes line at cursor
Ctrl−G	Deletes one character right
Ctrl−H	Deletes one character left

Command	Function
Ctrl–QY	Deletes line to right of cursor
Ctrl–Del	Deletes line to left of cursor
Ctrl–QT	Deletes to designated character
Ctrl–U	Restores deleted text

Formatting and reformatting paragraphs

As you type a document, WordStar automatically formats, or shapes the document to fit the current margins and line spacing. This is WordStar's approximation of "what you see is what you get." Within limits, the document onscreen does look like the document on paper. (True WYSIWIG programs actually show you a graphic representation onscreen of what your document will look like. WordStar's Page Preview feature is WYSIWIG.)

WordStar also has *auto align*, which reformats a paragraph if you make any changes. This feature is on by default, and remains on unless you turn it off.

Auto align doesn't always work perfectly when you perform cut and paste procedures; change line spacing, margins, or font type and size; or change the number of columns in the document. This means that you must manually reformat with the commands Ctrl–B or Ctrl–QU to ensure all paragraphs get properly reformatted after any major reformatting changes. The auto-align commands are as follows:

Command	Function
Ctrl B	Reformats a single paragraph
Ctrl QU	Reformats the remainder of the document from the cursor position
Ctrl QQB	Reformats the remainder of the document from the cursor position, when the above doesn't work as well as you like

An introduction to WordStar 7

WordStar is a professional-strength word processing program that can be used by any level of writer. It can be used to write any kind of document. It has applications for professionals, yet can satisfy the simplest word processing needs. WordStar 7 is a much improved version of one of the world's best-selling word processing programs. It was rewritten to take full advantage of MS-DOS 5.0 and to use your computer to its fullest capacity.

WordStar *empowers* you to type, format, and edit text onscreen—and does so by not getting in your way. With a few keystrokes, or the click of a mouse button, you can command WordStar to perform special effects with your text. You can manipulate words in many different ways, as often as you choose, and until you get them exactly the way you want.

WordStar gives you utility features like a thesaurus and a spell checker to correct your mistakes, index and table of contents utilities, and printer drivers for almost any printer you can buy.

What makes WordStar special?

There are many word processors on the market. So what makes WordStar special? Three things stand out:

- its onscreen formatting, layout, and design features
- its many ways of using the command structure
- the fact you can customize it endlessly to meet your needs

Improved onscreen formatting

Many word processing programs now attempt to display the text onscreen as it will look when printed, and use a graphic WYSIWIG (what you see is what you get) feature. WordStar also gives you onscreen formatting, but without resorting to a cumbersome graphic user interface.

Though still not perfect, WordStar 7 has excellent onscreen formatting. With it, the document's appearance changes onscreen as you type, insert, delete, rearrange, change margins, line spacing, and the number of columns. It previews the hardcopy to come.

WordStar also has a WYSIWIG *page preview* feature, which uses the graphics mode to show *exactly* how the document will look when printed. It displays different types and sizes of fonts, and all the special effects you've typeset in with layout and design features. Footnotes, endnotes, headers, and footers are all revealed in the onscreen display. You even have your choice of displaying from 1 to 32 pages at once. Within its limitations, what you see onscreen with WordStar is what you get.

A flexible command system

With the easily accessible command structure, it's simple to tell WordStar what to do. Every system has its limitations, and WordStar is not free of them. But with WordStar, there are two or three different ways to do *everything*.

There are two entirely different sets of command menus to choose from. You can issue commands directly from the keyboard. You can install four levels of commands on each function key. You can use the Macro Menu to create and edit the macros that execute strings of commands. Finally, you can now use a mouse to access all WordStar commands.

Open-ended customization

With the WSCHANGE utility toolbox, you can customize the entire WordStar program. WSCHANGE also lets you create different versions of WordStar for different word processing needs. So your customized version of WordStar will boot up ready to work in special ways.

Every feature of WordStar can be adjusted to your needs. Every WordStar feature and option has at least two settings—on and off—that you can preset as the default. Most others offer multiple choice settings from a list of options. And many features, like margins, tabs, line spacing, and so on, can be preset to any value you choose.

WordStar also offers redefinable paragraph style tagging, which lets you set layout and design, font type and size, and so on, for entire paragraphs, pages, or documents with a single command.

Using other word processors' files

With the StarExchange utility program, you can convert text files from all popular MS-DOS word processing programs to the WordStar format. And you can convert WordStar files to the format of any other major word processor. The newest version of StarExchange is even compatible with Macintosh text files.

Desktop publishing applications

WordStar 7 has many of the capabilities of a true desktop publishing and typesetting program. With a laser printer you can produce professionally typeset, quality, camera-ready hardcopy. Because WordStar text files are in an industry standard format, they can go on disk for easy conversion to mass printing.

You can use WordStar with any of the full-page WYSIWYG monitors like the Princeton Genius. You can use downloadable soft fonts from third-party vendors to give your documents that special look you want them to have. You can also import graphics—illustrations, graphs, etc.—from most graphics programs and use them directly in your documents.

If WordStar's layout and design features aren't enough for you, WordStar text files are fully compatible with every major desktop publishing program. You will have no problems using WordStar text files with Ventura Publisher, PageMaker, Publish It, NewsMaster II, and others.

Many people find desktop publishing programs too complicated and too limited to use for writing documents. Typesetting documents is what a DTP program does best. If you do try to write a document with any of them, you'll find them to be excruciatingly slow. Most DTP programs lack standard word processing features: spell checker, word counting, thesaurus, dictionaries, global search and replace, merge printing, index or table of contents generation, and so forth.

Desktop publishing programs rely on graphic interfaces that make heavy use of your computer's power. So they all work best in high-powered computers with megabytes of memory. Even in the faster computers, there's an inevitable flicker or hesitation as you type and the graphic screen redraws.

Most DTP programs print documents from memory instead of from disk, and this puts a limit on the size of documents you can work with. (It can be no greater than the available RAM in your computer.) And they take *forever* to print if you don't have megabytes of RAM in your printer, or a special printing card in your computer.

WordStar, on the other hand, can't be beaten when it comes to writing and editing basic text files. The entire program, thesaurus, dictionaries, etc., can be loaded into RAM and used at lightning speed. And WordStar is still fully compatible with even the oldest MS-DOS computers. It can be customized to use whatever system you have, and rapidly print whatever size documents you need.

Getting ready to use WordStar 7

If you've already used word processing, you've got some idea of what's going on. You might have prejudices, good or bad, about the whole idea of using word processing instead of your typewriter. Perhaps you have a bad taste in your mouth from an inadequate word processor you tried to use. Or, if you've become proficient using another popular word processor, you might be prejudiced toward doing things its way. Most people develop a devotion to their first word processor, whether they mean to or not—regardless of its limitations. Don't let your prejudices get in the way of learning WordStar.

WordStar is a word processing program that can be used by a novice, yet has fully professional capabilities. It's up to you to learn how to use those capabilities. WordStar is easy to learn once you understand the *way* it gets things done.

Tips to the first-time user

Read this manual carefully, next to WordStar running on your computer. Don't try to go too fast, or get ahead of yourself by trying to learn too much at one sitting. Everything is going to be unfamiliar at first. Go through the features, one by one, until they become second nature. Don't be afraid to make mistakes. You'll make them no matter what. Use this manual as a reference and study guide. The table of contents and the index will direct you to the specific information you need.

Upgrading from earlier versions of WordStar

For those of you upgrading from an old version of WordStar, Release 7 might come as something of a shock to your system. In upgrading it to take advantage of MS-DOS 5.0, the programmers at WordStar International got a little bit carried away. In effect, they wrote a whole new program, and then went back and made it look and work like WordStar.

Many of these changes are internal, and thus invisible to the user (unless you know something about computers and programming). Others are very obvious: both in appearance and how things work.

The most obvious change is to the pull-down menus. They've all been graphically redesigned and are much easier on the eye. Five out of seven have been renamed, all have had their command options rearranged, and a Help menu has been added.

All the dialog boxes have been redesigned and rearranged, and several new ones have been added. Most of these changes have been made to accommodate the new mouse support. Now, most of WordStar's commands and options are available for execution with the click of a mouse.

The most drastic change is to the macro system. A whole new interface has been added, and the old Shorthand Menu is gone. The new macros are much more powerful, and give you access to even the function keys without having to go through WSCHANGE. But they're more difficult to use.

If you're an old-time WordStar user, your first response to these changes might very well be annoyance and resistance. Don't let this prejudice you against WordStar 7. In most cases, the changes really are improvements, and they make WordStar more powerful and work better.

You should have no real problems learning how to use the new features of WordStar 7. Everything you already know from your old version of WordStar still applies to the newest version. All you have to learn are the new features and the companion programs. If you don't need a particular feature, then ignore it.

Learning WordStar

The best way to learn WordStar is with a *hands-on* approach. Don't try to learn by reading this whole book at a sitting. Learn by doing. Start using WordStar to get your work done. Think of it as a box of tools you have to use. Every tool gives you an advantage that otherwise wouldn't exist. This is equally true for hammers and computers. WordStar can help you drive your words straight and true, to build solid documents.

WordStar can give you writing advantages you never thought possible. Its tools can take over most of the drudgery of writing. Their power can free your creativity. But you don't have to learn every tool—just the ones you need.

- Go through this book and find the tools that apply to *your* needs. Grab them and learn how to use them.
- Make sure you understand the purpose of each tool and what it can and can't do before going on to the next.
- Mark useful information in this book with a yellow highlighter pen.
- Take notes about anything especially useful or distinctly confusing. Keep your notes handy until you no longer need them.
- Use post-it notes. They're wonderful for marking places in the book, and for posting reminders directly on the front of your computer and the sides of your monitor.

5
CHAPTER

Commanding WordStar

This chapter describes the command system of WordStar. It tells you what its elements are and how to use them. The information in this chapter applies to every use of WordStar you might find. WordStar has its own logical way of getting everything done, and its own way of issuing commands and providing the computer with the information it needs. When you're familiar with this, you'll know how to use WordStar.

Understanding WordStar's commands

You are in command of WordStar every time you sit down to use it—and never forget it. You're in charge. You run the program. You select the mode and features to use. If the terms *mode* and *features* seem confusing, don't worry. Sometimes the line between modes, features, and commands grows thin. It doesn't matter what something is, as long as you know how to use it. The important thing is that WordStar does what you tell it to do.

Since the release of WordStar 5, an endless argument has been raging over "the best" way to use and work with WordStar. The newest version of WordStar has two independent sets of command menus, an ever-growing number of dialog boxes, a long list of control commands, an even longer list of dot commands, and the addition of full mouse support.

Some people hate a mouse and refuse to own or use one. Some hate to issue Ctrl commands. Some hate the pull-down menus. And some people prefer using dot commands whenever possible. Which is best? It really doesn't matter. All of them get the same job done. The best method is whichever way or combination you feel the most comfortable with.

Command terminology

There's no escaping a certain amount of jargon when it comes to describing how to use WordStar's commands, features, and options. If you're new to computers or word processing, you'll quickly realize that they use special words to describe many things. You'll also discover old and presumably familiar words being used in unpredictable, often contradictory ways. You need to learn these words and remember their special meanings.

Attribute   A property that controls whether a character or font is normal, bold, italic, underlined, double-strike, etc.

Click   To select an onscreen item, menu, command, or option by moving the mouse cursor or pointer to it, and then clicking the mouse button once. Depending on where you are, this will sometimes execute the command or option.

Command   Any instruction you give to either the computer or WordStar to tell it to do something or perform a specific task.

Command-driven   A program that accepts commands typed in from the keyboard. Command-driven programs can be more difficult to learn, because they require memorizing a series of interrelated commands. Once you learn the commands, though, you can use the program faster because your hands never have to leave the keyboard and you can state a request concisely. Contrast with *menu-driven*.

Data file   A computer file that contains a collection of data records. In WordStar, it's a special ASCII text file written either in the nondocument mode or with the MailList program. It contains the raw facts and figures used for printing mailing lists and other merge printed documents.

Dialog box   Similar to a submenu. It appears onscreen when you have multiple choices to make. Each dialog box contains one or more variables to choose from, activate, or toggle on and off. Many have lines where you type in controlling data.

Desktop publishing   Using a computer to produce high-quality camera-ready hardcopy for the printer, and text files usable by a professional typesetter. The key feature of DTP is its ability to merge and manage text with graphics and display it on the screen in a WYSIWYG style. You're able, therefore, to layout, design, and typeset an onscreen document and know exactly how it's going to print.

Double-click   To select and execute an item, menu, command, or option by moving the mouse cursor or pointer to it onscreen and then clicking the mouse button twice.

Feature   A particular capability, function, or option available to be selected and used in writing, editing, typesetting, and printing documents.

Field   A unit of information in a data file, or a point on a dialog box where you specify data or change a variable.

Flag or flag column   A graphic indicator of the status of a paragraph, or dot command. The flag column runs down the right side of the WordStar writing and editing screen.

GUI   Acronym for *graphical user interface*. Also called simply a *graphic environment*. A command interface that's based on using icons, pull-down menus, pop-up boxes, and an electromechanical device called a mouse. Commands, features, and options are represented by a graphic symbol implying its function. They are executed by pointing and clicking with the mouse. Term is often pronounced "gooey."

Icon   A small, graphic representation onscreen of an object, function, or command. It's used in programs with graphical user interfaces (GUIs). Select a command by moving the mouse cursor or pointer to its icon and clicking the mouse button.

Menu   A list of available options and commands displayed onscreen as an interactive method for using a program. You select or execute menu options by typing the number or letter assigned to it, by clicking on it with a mouse cursor, or by moving a highlight to it and pressing the Enter key.

Menu-driven   A program commanded by selecting options from a list that appears onscreen.

Mnemonic   The use of acronyms, keywords, or easily remembered words or abbreviations as names for complicated subjects. The purpose is to assist memory through a methodical use. All WordStar Ctrl and Alt commands are mnemonics. Pronounced "ni-män-ik."

Mode   An operational state that a program or computer has been switched to. There are countless modes for both hardware and software. For example, WordStar has two writing and editing modes: document and nondocument. Each mode in a program has its own set of rules, restrictions, and purposes. A mode is defined by what it does. The product resulting from each mode is distinctly different. A fax mode produces fax files. A printing mode produces printed hardcopy. In all cases, modular definitions reflect different ways of thinking about what a computer does.

Mouse   A hand-sized device connected to a computer and used as a pointing or drawing tool. It got its name from its shape, and the fact its cable resembles a mouse tail. A mouse contains either a roller ball or optical sensor to translate the physical motion of the mouse into linear motion. Software can be written to recognize a mouse pointer and use it to execute commands.

Onscreen   Anything appearing on the monitor screen, or relating to the video display of text or graphics.

Option   Any choice on a menu, submenu, dialog box, or list of variables.

Select   To choose, activate, or execute any command, option, or variable from any menu, dialog box, or icon. You can select by issuing a Ctrl command, using the arrow keys to move the highlight, or clicking with a mouse.

Text file Any computer file that contains only text, or the data of a word processed document. This is the elemental building block of word processing and desktop publishing. Such files are created, edited, saved, stored, and printed.

Toggle commands These are like a light switch: flip it one way to turn it on, and flip it the other way to turn it off. Most WordStar toggle commands insert dot command lines in the document. The first time you embed it, the dot command uses the opposite of what's currently set. The next time, the opposite. . . and so on.

Variables Optional values on a dialog box that can be accepted as a group or changed individually every time you call and use the dialog box. Changing the variables changes the result or product of using the dialog box. On the Printing dialog box, the variables control specific elements of each print run-off. Some variables are set in WordStar as defaults. Others reflect current settings at any particular point in the text file.

Commands that change onscreen formatting

WordStar uses onscreen formatting. This means, within limits, that the soft document displayed onscreen looks like the hardcopy document on paper. When you're writing an electronic document, you basically type it the same way you would on a typewriter. As you type, however, the document will automatically format or shape to fit the preset formatting, like margins and line spacing. And, unlike a typewriter, you can always easily go back and change what you've written.

With WordStar, you use commands and features either to move you around in the document or to control its layout. By your command deleted words disappear, new words are inserted, and paragraphs are reformatted when you make changes to the document. All edits and revisions are immediately reflected onscreen. So when a document looks the way you want it to using the Advanced Page Preview feature, save it and print it.

Eight ways to issue commands

WordStar gives you eight different ways to issue commands and use its word-processing features. You can either pick the one you like best, or use a mix of different methods. No matter how you issue a command, the results are the same. I personally recommend using a mixture of the mouse, Ctrl commands, and dot commands. The different command methods are:

- Classic, or Ctrl command menus, which contain or access all of
  WordStar's basic Ctrl commands.

- Pull-down command menus, which contain or access all of WordStar's basic commands.
- Dialog boxes (or submenus), where you select variables and type in specific information.
- Control commands, which allow you to execute functions without waiting for a menu to appear.
- Programmed function keys with predefined commands, which can execute whatever you define them to do.
- Macros, which can issue multiple commands or insert boilerplate text.
- Pointing and clicking on pull-down menus and dialog boxes with a mouse.
- Dot commands typed directly into the document. These embed permanent commands that take effect on the line they're typed.

Understanding WordStar's menus

To understand how to command WordStar, think of it as being a primarily *menu-driven* program. This means that you "call" menus with a preliminary command or click of the mouse, and then select the command features to use.

Two kinds of menus, and which to use

WordStar has two kinds of command menus: the Ctrl, or classic menus, and the pull-down menus. Both contain and issue the exact same commands. The difference is how the commands are organized and arranged on the menus. Use whichever you like the best, or create your own combination.

- When you first install WordStar 7 in your computer, the pull-down menus are the default. This is help level 4. If you're a first-time user, or you plan to use a mouse with WordStar, then leave this setup alone.
- If you're an "old-hand" with WordStar, and prefer the Ctrl or classic menus, you can use help level 2 or 3 so those menus are the default. However, WordStar 7 doesn't provide mouse support for the classic menus.
- Even if you prefer to use the pull-down menus, the classic menus are always still available in the background. Just call them with the usual Ctrl commands.

Complications in having two sets of menus

Having two sets of menus can, however, cause complications in describing how to use WordStar commands. For experienced users of releases 5 through 6, upgrading is made worse by the fact that the pull-down menus have been completely rearranged.

This means that old-time users are pretty much in the same boat as first-time users wherever pull-down menus are concerned. *Nobody* knows where the pull-down menu commands are anymore. Everyone has to begin from scratch and learn them.

The only consistent link between previous releases and WordStar 7 are the Ctrl or classic command menus. And all WordStar help messages are based on classic menus. Most old-time users still prefer to use Ctrl commands directly and avoid menus altogether. If you're a first-time user, you'll learn that Ctrl commands are always the quickest way of issuing commands.

Because most people upgrading to release 7 still prefer issuing Ctrl commands directly—and because the classic menus are the only link between the old WordStar and the new—the instructions in this book are based on using classic WordStar menus.

Stick with the default

When you install WordStar 7 on your hard drive with WSSETUP, the pull-down menus became the default. (This is help level 4.) These pull-down menus became a part of WordStar with release 5. With every upgrade since, they've been steadily changed, rearranged, enlarged, and otherwise improved.

If you're a new or first-time WordStar user, leave the help level setting alone—even if you don't plan to use a mouse. All the instructions in the user manual assume that the pull-down menus are active. You might confuse yourself if you change the help level and then refer back and forth between this book and the manual. Although this book instructs people how to issue the Ctrl commands directly, I do advise you to buy a mouse to use with WordStar 7.

If you're an experienced WordStar user upgrading to release 7, the new pull-down menus might come as a shock to your system. Five out of seven have been renamed, all have been substantially rearranged, and an eighth, the Help Menu, has been added. Don't change the help level if you plan to use a mouse. No mouse support has been included for the classic menus.

The classic command menus

WordStar has five classic command menus. These menus have been a part of the program since it came on the market. All WordStar 7 commands and options are still available through the classic menus and dialog boxes.

The Opening Menu is what you see onscreen after WordStar has finished booting (see Fig. 5-1). With the help level set to 2 or 3, the classic Opening Menu will appear. This menu contains all the major WordStar options and modes. To select a feature, type the highlighted letter beside it.

```
========================= WordStar =========================
———————————— O P E N I N G   M E N U ————————————
  D open a document              L change drive/directory
  S speed write (new file)       C protect/unprotect a file
  N open a nondocument           E rename a file
  P print a file                 O copy a file
  \ fax                          Y delete a file
  K print from keyboard          F turn directory off
  I index a document             M macros
  T table of contents            R run a DOS command
  X exit WordStar                A additional
  F1 help                        ? display status

Filenames:          Path: C:\WS   45M free
..              \   FAX           \   MACROS          \   OPTIONS          \
ARROW.HP      .3k   BOX         .4k   CHEX.HP       .5k   DBOO.DTB       80k
DB01.DTB     375k   DB02.DTB    84k   DB04.DTB     188k   FILELIST.TXT   27k
FONTID.CTL   7.6k   HP-ENV.LST 1.0k   HP2-ENV.LST  1.0k   ILLUS.DOT      .4k
INDEX.DTB     46k   KEYBOARD.MRG .1k   LIST.DOC     .8k   MAILING.DOC   1.0k
OPENMENU.BAK 2.0k   OPENMENU.FIG 2.2k  PDFEDIT.HLP  35k   PLAYBILL.DOC   .6k
PLAYS.DOC     .9k   PLEAD.HP    .1k   PREVIEW.MSG   10k   PRINT.TST      12k
REVIEW.DOC   3.1k   SHADE.HP    .0k   SHAKE.DOC    6.0k   SPELL.DOC     6.0k
VESA1024.WGD 2.9k   WINSTALL.HLP 32k  WS.DEF        .9k   WSINDEX.XCL   1.5k
```

5-1 WordStar's classic Opening Menu.

Calling and using a classic menu

Calling a classic menu means making it appear onscreen. The other four classic command menus are called with Ctrl commands from inside either the document or nondocument modes. These other classic menus, and their calling commands, are listed below:

Menu	How to call it
Opening	Run WordStar
Onscreen Format	Ctrl−O
Block & Save	Ctrl−K
Print Controls	Ctrl−P
Quick	Ctrl−Q

Once a classic menu appears, find the option or feature to use and then type the highlighted letter beside the option. This will either execute the command, or call a dialog box with further variables.

Each classic menu, including its options and dialog boxes, is discussed in a chapter of its own. Easy-to-use features are described in detail in these chapters. More complicated features and commands have chapters of their own.

The pull-down command menus

Pull-down menus are onscreen menus that are displayed from the top of the screen downward after you select their titles from the title bar. The pull-down Edit Menu is shown in Fig. 5-2. Commands or features of a related function are grouped on these menus. The menu remains onscreen until you use a command or option, or send it away. These menus are normally used for issuing commands with a mouse.

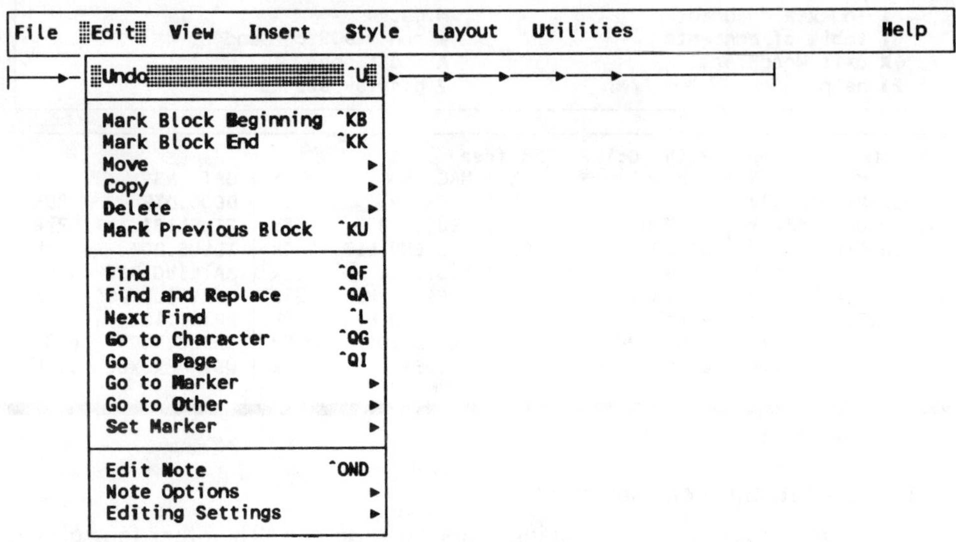

5-2 An example of a pull-down menu, in this case the pull-down Edit Menu.

The following pull-down menus, and brief descriptions of their word-processing functions, are listed below:

File   Contains commands and word-processing features used to open, close, print, and generally work with text files.

Edit   Contains commands and word-processing features used to make changes or corrections to a text file, and to move around in the file.

View   Contains options for changing the onscreen display. Includes using the page preview, and opening or closing a text file in a second window.

Insert   Contains commands to insert dot commands, notes, printing codes, or other special information directly into the text file.

Style   Contains commands to attach character attributes, assign font type and size, and work with paragraph style tags.

Layout   Contains commands that control paragraph justification, newspaper column layout, headers or footers, page and line numbering, and general page layout.

Utilities   Contains options and features for checking spelling, using the thesaurus, sorting blocks of text, reformatting modified paragraphs, inserting merge printing variables, and setting up macros.

Help Provides help messages that describe specific WordStar commands, features, and options. Also permits changing the help level setting.

Calling and using a pull-down menu

Calling a pull-down menu means making it appear onscreen. There are two different ways of "calling" a WordStar pull-down menu. It makes no difference which method you use. You can either click on its title in the title bar at the top of the screen or hold down the Alt key and type the highlighted letter in the title. Once the title bar has been made active by calling any pull-down menu, you can move to other menus with the left and right arrow keys.

There are two different ways of taking a WordStar pull-down menu off the screen without selecting or executing a command. You can move the mouse cursor off the menu and click the button once, or press the Esc key.

WordStar's pull-down menus were added primarily to allow people to execute commands by pointing and clicking a mouse. But these menus all have three different ways of letting you access WordStar's features and options. Use any of these methods, or any combination you find pleasing.

- Call the menu and click on the menu item with the mouse.
- Call the menu, use the arrow keys to move the highlight to the item, and then press the Enter key.
- Call the menu and type the highlighted or underlined letter in the menu item.

Keyboard method for using pull-down menus

Many people don't like using a mouse, and many old-time WordStar users are so familiar with the Ctrl commands that they won't use any other method. People who are fast touch typists often find it annoying to take their hands off the keyboard, even for the convenience of the pull-down menus or a mouse. The following is the "keyboard method" for using the pull-down menus:

- To call a pull-down menu while working on a document, hold down the Alt key and type the highlighted letter in its name on the title bar, or click on it with your mouse.
- To use a pull-down menu option, use the up and down arrow keys to move the highlight to it and press the Enter key, or click on it with your mouse.
- To send a pull-down menu away without selecting and executing a word-processing feature or command, simply press the Esc key.

The above method provides a happy medium for people who like the pull-down menus but hate using a mouse or the Ctrl commands.

Some people prefer the pull-down menus to the classic because their word-processing features are arranged in a more logical order. They're slower to use without a mouse, but they're easier to use for learning WordStar because the tutorial program provided with the program describes and relies on them.

Understanding and using dialog boxes

In WordStar, a *dialog box* is the same thing as a submenu. One will appear onscreen after you select an option from a command menu or issue certain Ctrl commands. It indicates that you have multiple choices.

Changing the variables

Changing the variables is what you do in every dialog box. These are alternatives, or optional values that can be accepted as they are, or changed individually, every time you call and use the dialog box. Changing the variables changes the effects or results of whatever commands the dialog box executes.

Some variables are set in WordStar as defaults. Others reflect current settings at any particular point in the text file. Any variable can always be reset at the dialog box. Sometimes this is multiple choice. Sometimes you can type in a range of alternatives.

For example, on the Printing dialog box, the variables control specific elements of each print runoff. All its variables are defaults, and appear on the dialog box every time you call it. You can customize these default settings using WSCHANGE.

Hot letters

Every dialog box contains *hot letters*. Each field or item on the dialog box has a highlighted letter or letters. You can jump the cursor to any item by holding down the Alt key and typing that letter.

Checkboxes

A *checkbox* is a type of variable on a dialog box. It's indicated by brackets, [ ], beside the variable name. It's active if an X appears between the brackets. To toggle it on and off, put the cursor between the brackets and press the spacebar or click on it with the mouse.

Push-buttons

A push-button is an icon in a dialog box that's drawn to resemble the physical push-button switches commonly found on radios and other electrical appliances. They're part of the new mouse support in WordStar 7. The idea is to graphically remind you of its function—the execution of a command.

To select and use a push-button, click on it with the mouse. You can also use the arrow keys to move to it and then press the Enter key. There are three main types of push-buttons:

OK Tells WordStar to go ahead and execute the commands or functions stipulated in the dialog box.

Cancel Tells WordStar to get rid of the dialog box, without executing any of its commands or functions, and return you to the writing and editing mode. You can get the same effect by pressing the Esc key Ctrl−U.

Continue Means WordStar has either completed a dialog box or macro function, or has done as much as it can. Click on it, or press either the Esc key or the Enter key.

Guidelines to using dialog boxes

The following are general guidelines for using and working with dialog boxes. Every dialog box presents a different set of questions you must answer. The answers you give depend on what you want WordStar to do.

- Many dialog boxes contain one or more variables to choose from, activate, or toggle on and off. Most have lines where you type in controlling data, like margins, line spacing, tab stops, etc.
- Many dialog boxes contain a line where you can type in a range as a variable. For example, when printing, you can type in specific pages or groups of pages to be printed. You can also select only even-numbered or only odd-numbered pages (for back-to-back printing and binding).
- When a dialog box contains preset variables, like the Printing dialog box, you can either accept the default answers or change them one by one.
- The data in the dialog box, when it appears, always represents the current settings at any point in the text file. When you change these settings, they become active from the point you issue the command—either to the end of the text file or until countermanded by other commands.
- To move through the variables on a dialog box, use the Tab key to move forward and Shift−Tab to move backwards. You can also use the arrow keys or click on the variable with the mouse.
- When ready to execute the function of a dialog box, use Ctrl−K or press the Enter key. You can also click on the OK button with the mouse.
- To exit a dialog box without executing its function, simply press the Esc key. You can also click on the Cancel button with the mouse.
- All Insert, Style, and Layout dialog boxes embed dot commands or special data in the text file when you execute the dialog box function. You can always go back and directly edit these dot commands or special data without having to return to the dialog box. To completely remove dot commands or special data, use Ctrl−T or Ctrl−Y.

Universal abort commands

There are two universal abort commands you can use to exit from a menu or dialog box, or to halt most commands before they complete execution: Ctrl−U, which has always been able to halt a command in "mid-stride," and Esc, which you can use to escape from menus and dialog boxes, interrupt Ctrl commands, and halt macro playback before it finishes executing the macro string.

Universal execution commands

The Ctrl−K command can be used to accept any dialog box and execute the commands and variables on it. This is the best habit to get into, providing you don't have a mouse.

WordStar 7 comes with the Enter key set to function as an execution command. This works on some dialog boxes, and not on others. You can use WSCHANGE to undo this, and restore the Enter key to its previous function of merely jumping from item to item on a dialog box. I recommend that you do this.

Beginning with release 5, WordStar began using the F10 key as a universal command-execution key. It has this function whenever you've called a menu or a dialog box. This, however, can be very dangerous. The Save and Exit Document command, Ctrl−KD, is also assigned to the F10 key. If you press F10 twice, or hold it down too long, it will execute the dialog box commands, then save and exit the text file you're working on.

Tip: Don't get in the bad habit of using F10 as the universal executor. If you aren't using the mouse to execute a dialog box, it's better to use Ctrl−K as the universal executor.

Issuing commands directly

WordStar has always been both a menu-driven and a command-driven program. Up until now, however, I've discussed mostly the menu methods. This section will cover ways of issuing commands directly.

Understanding direct-control commands

Being *command-driven* means that WordStar accepts commands issued through the keyboard. It can be more difficult to learn these direct commands because they require memorizing a series of interrelated codes. The pull-down menus are the easiest way to learn how to use WordStar, but they're always going to be the slowest way, and there's nothing you can do to speed them up.

Once you learn the commands, though, you can use the program faster because your hands never have to leave the keyboard and you can state your request concisely. Experienced WordStar users know that the quickest way to execute or use any option and feature is to issue its Ctrl command directly.

The caret symbol

WordStar-issued manuals have consistently used the caret, or ^, symbol to represent the Ctrl key. You'll also find this symbol preceding a two- or three-character code on the Edit Menu (if you use it), and on other menus and dialog boxes. All first-time users find this confusing.

Whenever you see the caret in the manual, or on a menu or dialog box, it means "hold down the Ctrl key while typing the following letters or characters."

Rather than following these confusing manual conventions, I've substituted *Ctrl* when I want you to hold down the Ctrl key. I don't understand why anyone would want it any other way.

Control commands

Control commands are executed by holding down the Ctrl key and then typing the letters of the command. These commands correspond to the options on the classic menus. The *first* letter calls the command menu. The *second* letter selects and executes the command. You don't have to wait for the menu to appear. If you type the command without pausing, its function executes at once.

For further information on Ctrl command, see the chapter titled *Using direct-control commands*.

Using programmable function keys

Function keys are the ones on your keyboard labeled F1 through either F10 or F12. (Some keyboards have ten function keys; others have twelve.) Some keyboards label these keys PF1, PF2, PF3, and so on, but they're still the same keys. They're called programmable function keys because their commands vary depending on the program currently running, and because—depending on the program—you can determine their commands yourself.

WordStar comes from the factory with four different commands assigned to each of these function keys:

- The first level is executed by pressing the function key alone.
- The second level is executed by holding down the Shift key and then pressing the function key.
- The third level is executed by holding down the Ctrl key and then pressing the function key.
- The fourth level is executed by holding down the Alt key and then pressing the function key.

Note: In all previous versions of WordStar, the first two levels of function-key assignments were optionally displayed in key labels at the bottom of the write and edit screen. This has been a WordStar trademark. These key labels aren't available in revision A of WordStar 7, although there is an available patch, but they are displayable in later versions.

What are programmed functions?

Programmed functions are either an individual command or strings and combinations of commands. The factory-installed function key commands control things like character boldface, underlining, italics, centering, and reformatting. Other function keys call dialog boxes and execute direct commands.

Reprogramming function keys

As a major revision in WordStar 7, you can no longer change the function key assignments through WSCHANGE. These key assignments are now part of the new macro system, so you can redefine their functions through the Edit/Create Macro dialog box called with the command Ctrl−MD.

For further information on redefining the programmable function keys, read the following section and the chapter titled *Using WordStar's new macros*.

Executing commands with macros

Release 7.0 of WordStar inaugurates what might prove to be the most powerful macro feature in any word processor on the market.

What happened to shorthand macros?

For long-time users of WordStar, a number-one question is going to be "What happened to the Shorthand Menu?" In upgrading to release 7, the programmers eliminated it completely. They say that it's gone forever. In its place is the all new macro system, with its own Macro Menu, dialog boxes, and, regrettably, a whole new BASIC-like macro language you must learn.

The new macro system is definitely more powerful than the old Shorthand Menu and, with 82 predefined macros, it almost doubles the number previously available. The number of commands and features assignable to a single macro is now practically unlimited. But the new macros are slower and more difficult to use, and editing or creating them is definitely not for the first-time user. In addition, several keys previously available for macro assignment and redefinition, namely F1, F10, and Esc, are restricted in revision A of the program. You can, however, redefine them in later revisions with WSCHANGE.

Because the new macro system is so radically different, and much more complicated to use than the old Shorthand Menu, I'm allocating it a chapter of its own. See the chapter titled *Using WordStar's new macros*.

Using hotkeys

Hotkeys are macro commands that are assigned to mnemonic keystroke sequences. This means you have to press only one or two keys to issue complex strings of commands. You can also record boilerplate words or sentences as macros, and insert them in a document wherever you need to repeat them. If you find yourself typing the same words, phrases, or sentences repeatedly, record them to macros and give yourself a break.

For example, I have the word *WordStar* installed as a macro on the hotkey Alt−W. Instead of having to type it every time I use it, I let the hotkey do it for me.

Default hotkeys

WordStar comes with macros assigned to most of the available hotkeys. You can use these as they are, edit them to better meet your needs, or write new ones from scratch.

As mentioned under a previous section, all the function keys are now hotkeys, and are defined through the Macro Menu instead of through WSCHANGE. The instructions for using, editing, and creating new hotkey assignments are found in the chapter titled *Using WordStar's new macros*. Table 5-1 lists WordStar's default hotkeys, with their associated functions and macros.

Understanding embedded commands

WordStar has two different kinds of embedded commands. The term *embedded* means that the command is inserted into the body of the text file in a very special way. You can see the command onscreen as a command line or symbol, but it doesn't print in the hardcopy. Instead, the command either controls onscreen formatting, or is executed by the printer during the print runoff.

Embedded printing controls

The options on the Print Controls Menu embed commands into the body of the document. These printing controls are represented onscreen by special symbols, and they tell the printer how to format and print a hardcopy.

- Some of these commands control character attributes. These are Boldface, Doublestrike, Italics, Underlining, Subscript, Superscript, and Strikeout. The symbol for this is a single uppercase letter, preceded by a ^ or caret.
- Some of these commands control the type and size of font being used to print the document. When you tag a word, sentence, paragraph, or document with a specific font, a specification indicating the font, like < Courier 10 PC > or < Times PC 12.0 >, will appear at the cursor.

Table 5-1 *WordStar's default hotkey assignments.*

Hotkey	Function executed	Macro name
* F1	Get help with features	HELP
F2	Undo last command	UNDO
F3	Issue Underline command	UNDERLIN
F4	Issue Boldface command	BOLD
F5	Embed a ruler line	RULER
F6	Delete a word DEL_WORD	
F7	Reformat a paragraph	REFORMAT
F8	Mark text for Italics	ITALICS
F9	Insert temporary indent	TEMPINDT
* F10	Execute dialog box/save & close	
F11	(unassigned)	
F12	(unassigned)	
Shift-F1	Toggle command tag display	DISPLAY
Shift-F2	Center a line of text	CENTER
Shift-F3	Check spelling for document	SPL_ALL
Shift-F4	Check spelling of a word	SPL_WRD
Shift-F5	Delete the marked block	BK_DEL
Shift-F6	Hide the marked block	BK_HIDE
Shift-F7	Move the marked block	BK_MOVE
Shift-F8	Copy the marked block	BK_COPY
Shift-F9	Mark beginning of block	BK_BEGIN
Shift-F10	Mark the end of block	BK_END
Shift-F11	(unassigned)	
Shift-F12	(unassigned)	
Ctrl-F1	Call Find dialog box	FIND
Ctrl-F2	Call Find & Replace dialog box	FIND_RPL
Ctrl-F3	Repeat last find command	FIND_NXT
Ctrl-F4	Call Go to Page dialog box	GOTO_PG
Ctrl-F5	Set the left margin	MARGIN_L
Ctrl-F6	Set the right margin	MARGIN_R
Ctrl-F7	Set the paragraph margin .5"	MARGIN_P
Ctrl-F8	Insert a page break	PG_BREAK
Ctrl-F9	Go to left side of line	GOTO_LNL
Ctrl-F10	Go to right side of line	GOTO_LNR
Ctrl-F11	(unassigned)	
Ctrl-F12	(unassigned)	
Alt-F1			DRW_VERT
Alt-F2	-	DRW_HORZ
Alt-F3	┌	DRW_T_L
Alt-F4	┐	DRW_T_R
Alt-F5	└	DRW-B_L
Alt-F6	┘	DRW_B_R

Alt-F7	⊤	DRW_H_DN
Alt-F8	⅃	DRW_H_UP
Alt-F9	⊦	DRW_V_R
Alt-F10	⊣	DRW_V_L
Alt-F11	(unassigned)	
Alt-F12	(unassigned)	
Alt-1	Turns on Page Preview	PRVIEWS
Alt-2	(unassigned)	
Alt-3	(unassigned)	
Alt-4	(unassigned)	
Alt-5	(unassigned)	
Alt-6	(unassigned)	
Alt-7	(unassigned)	
Alt-8	(unassigned)	
Alt-9	(unassigned)	
Alt-0	Selects a paragraph tag	STYLE
Alt-A	(unassigned)	
Alt-B	Creates a bullet list	LIST_BUL
Alt-C	(unassigned)	
Alt-D	Debugs a new macro	DEBUGMAC
Alt-E	Calls the Edit Menu	
* Alt-F	Calls the File Menu	
Alt-G	(unassigned)	
* Alt-H	Calls the Help Menu	
* Alt-I	Calls the Insert Menu	
Alt-J	(unassigned)	
Alt-K	(unassigned)	
Alt-L	Calls the Layout Menu	
Alt-M	Creates a memorandum	
Alt-N	Creates a numbered list	LIST_NUM
Alt-O	Inserts .LM command line	
Alt-P	(unassigned)	
Alt-Q	(unassigned)	
Alt-R	(unassigned)	
Alt-S	Calls the Style Menu	
Alt-T	Creates a daily to-do list	TODO
Alt-U	Calls the Utility Menu	
Alt-V	Calls the View Menu	
Alt-W	(unassigned)	
Alt-X	(unassigned)	
Alt-Y	(unassigned)	
Alt-Z	(unassigned)	

---

* Currently unavailable for redefining.

- These symbols can be deleted like text, either individually or along with the words and sentences they mark.
- The display of these symbols can be toggled on and off with the Ctrl−OD command. They become hidden text and are easy to delete accidentally if you aren't careful.

Use of these print commands is fully explained in the chapter titled *Using the Print Controls Menu*.

Embedded dot commands

The other kind of embedded command is the dot command. Many of the commands on the Insert, Style, and Layout pull-down menus embed dot commands automatically when you click on OK on one of their dialog boxes. These can also be typed directly into a text file.

Dot commands are one of the oldest ways of issuing word-processing commands. They've been around since before there was such a thing as a personal computer. They either control the onscreen display or are executed by the printer during the printing process.

- Each dot command takes up an entire line of its own in an onscreen text file. This command line is not text to be printed.
- The dot command gets it name because it begins with a period.
- Each dot command has two letters, and is often followed by numbers or characters to further specialize the command.
- Each dot command line ends with a carriage return.

Some of these dot commands are used with ordinary documents. Others are specific to merge printing, or for creating indexes and tables of contents. A detailed description of the WordStar dot commands is given in the chapter titled *Using the dot commands*.

Using command blocks

An important use of dot commands is in *command blocks*. These are groups of dot commands placed at the beginning of a text file. As a block, the commands can be used to lay out and design an entire document.

Dot commands for special page and paragraph formatting can be written and stored in individual files. This includes things like templates for section and sub-section headings, blank numbered lists, and so on. With dot commands, you can create a boilerplate archive of ready-to-use commands. When you need them, just cut and paste them into your documents.

As you gain skill with WordStar, you can write command blocks for your special-purpose documents. Then use Ctrl−KW to write each block to a file of its own. When you need to write a similar document, use Ctrl−KR to paste the command block into the text file.

Suggested commands blocks are letterheads, format styles, and blank master documents for merge printing. Some users also call this a file archive, and keep it on a disk of its own.

Pointing and clicking a mouse

WordStar 7 has a rudimentary graphical user interface (GUI). Though not as comprehensive as Windows, or GEM Desktop, it provides full mouse support for all pull-down menus and dialog boxes. Now you can simply point and click, and access virtually all of WordStar's options and features.

It's easier to use a mouse than to describe how to do it. Using a mouse can reduce complex or difficult maneuvers to pointing and clicking. The hardest thing about using a mouse is installing it in your computer. Next comes clearing a place on your desk to put it. The rest you can figure out in a few minutes of trial and error.

Selecting attributes with the style bar

The addition of a style bar across the top of the screen makes it possible to use the mouse for typesetting, layout, and design. All the basic character attributes—Boldface, Italics, etc.—plus justification, margins, and access to paragraph style tags are installed on the style bar. You must have a mouse to use the style bar. The following are different ways to use the style bar:

1. Click on the beginning of the text to get special attributes.
2. Click on the icon of the attribute on the style bar.
3. Click on the end of the text to get special printing.
4. Click on the style bar to embed the command to end the special attribute.

Calling pull-down menus with the mouse

Pull-down menus were initially designed for use with a mouse. This capability has been enhanced in WordStar 7. The menu names are listed on a title bar across the top of the screen whenever the help level is set to 4. Just put the mouse cursor on your selection on the title bar and click the button.

Using the mouse with dialog boxes

You can jump the cursor to any item or field on a dialog box. Just point and click. Dialog boxes also have push-buttons that you can click on to execute commands. There are three main types of push-buttons:

OK Tells WordStar to go ahead and execute the commands or functions stipulated in the dialog box.

Cancel   Tells WordStar to send the dialog box away, without executing any of its commands or functions, and return you to the write and edit mode. You get the same effect by pressing the Esc key or by using Ctrl−U.

Continue   Means WordStar has completed a dialog box or macro function, or has done as much as it can. Either click on the displayed message or press the Esc or Enter keys.

Browsing through the directory tree

You can use the mouse to browse or search through directories without opening them. Do this from the Opening Menu, or any directory listing accompanying a dialog box, without touching the keyboard. Just point and click until you find the directory you're looking for. Then double-click on the filename to select it. The following are guidelines for using the directory tree:

- The subdirectories of the current directory are always shown in any onscreen list of filenames. You can browse through a subdirectory by clicking on its name with the mouse.
- If you're accessing a certain subdirectory, the previous directory is always indicated by the symbol [.. \] in the upper left corner of any onscreen listing of files. You can browse backward by clicking on this symbol.
- By clicking on the directory names and the previous directory symbol, you can browse through any directory or subdirectory on the hard drive.

Use all three hands

It's been said that using a mouse is "like having a third hand." But you won't get the full convenience of your mouse if you rely too heavily on it. A mouse isn't the answer to all your word-processing problems.

As you become experienced with WordStar 7, you'll find that some things are easier to do with the mouse, and some things are easier to do with Ctrl commands, dot commands, and macros. There are many things that are either more difficult or painfully slow to execute with a mouse. Sometimes it's downright annoying to take your hands off the keyboard to use a mouse. Whenever you get annoyed for this reason, you're using the mouse too much.

The best approach is to use all three hands. Find your own most convenient routine for using WordStar's features. Just because you're using one hand with the mouse, it doesn't mean you can't execute another command at the same time with your other hand. You can use a hotkey to run a macro, or press a highlighted key on a dialog box. Two hands, or three, are always quicker than one.

Turning on mouse support

Mouse support for pull-down menus is installed as the default setting by the WSSETUP program. WordStar must be set to help level 4 in order to use a mouse.

No mouse support is provided for the classic menus. If for any reason mouse support has been turned off, use WSCHANGE to turn it on:

1. At the DOS prompt for the WordStar 7 directory, run WSCHANGE.
2. At the WSCHANGE Main Menu, type the letters D, C, H, A, and Y. This toggles mouse support on and off.
3. Type x until you see the message *Are you through making changes?*.
4. Answer Y to save the change you just made, and return to the DOS prompt.

Setting the mouse for the right or left hand

Like most everything else in life, WordStar 7 comes with mouse support set up for right-handed people. But it's easy for left-handed people to change this.

1. At the DOS prompt for the WordStar 7 directory, run WSCHANGE.
2. At the WSCHANGE Main Menu, type D, C, H, B, and Y. This toggles the left-handed mouse support on and off.
3. Type x until you see the message *Are you through making changes?*.
4. Answer Y to save the change you just made, and return to the DOS prompt.

Tip: While you're at the Mouse Support Menu, make sure all the settings are the way you want. Make a note of the default settings before changing them so you can restore them if things don't work out.

6
CHAPTER

Getting
a quick start

This chapter covers some basics and tries to give you a quick start toward writing and editing documents with WordStar. Its directions are sparse, and you'll have to look in following chapters for detailed information. But it will give you essential information you'll need to get yourself up and running.

First things first

As you begin writing with WordStar, it's a good idea to grasp the basics. Learn the rules and the terminology. Most first-time users find computer terminology hard to grasp. But once you know the basics you can avoid a lot of mistakes. In the meanwhile, watch what you're doing, read this book carefully, and take notes on anything you don't understand.

The prime rule in first aid is "First, do no harm." The same rule applies to learning how to use WordStar. Fortunately, it's difficult to do any harm with WordStar. The worst you can do is delete text files or program files from the hard drive. If you're just getting started, it's unlikely that you'll have any important documents on disk you can ruin.

The instructions in this book refer to the generic program name WS.EXE for WordStar. However, most people eventually make a customized version of WordStar and give it a special name to keep it distinct from the "plain vanilla" version that's first installed.

If your version of WordStar has a special name, substitute it wherever WS.EXE (or the corresponding WS to run the program) appears in this book. It doesn't matter what you call the WordStar program file. To learn how WordStar can be customized and renamed with WINSTALL and WSCHANGE, see the chapters *Using Winstall to set up WordStar* and *Customizing WordStar with WSCHANGE*.

The instructions in this book assume that WordStar has been copied to your hard drive, and that it's ready to go. To learn how to install and set up WordStar on your hard drive, see the appendix *Copying WordStar to your hard drive*.

The instructions also assume that WordStar is on the hard drive named C: in the \ WS directory. If you have WordStar in any other drive or directory, substitute them for C: and \ WS.

Basic terminology

Following are some basic terms you'll need in order to understand how to get started:

Currently logged drive and directory   refers to the drive and directory that WordStar is linked with while in the write and edit mode; also referred to as the current directory. The files in this drive and directory will be listed onscreen below the Opening Menu. This is the drive or directory that WordStar will use as source and target for text files you write, edit, and save. You can always change the current drive from the Opening Menu, the pull-down File Menu, or from the Block & Save Menu.

Default drive   For WordStar, the default drive is the drive from which you run WordStar. Though commonly the same drive you booted the computer from, it can be *any* drive in the computer. WordStar always searches the default drive for its program files. The only way to change the default WordStar drive is to exit and run the program from another drive.

Default system drive   The drive containing the MS-DOS system files, and the drive used to boot up the computer. Whenever you or WordStar issue a system command, the computer searches the default system drive for the file it needs in order to obey the command.

Installing   means making a working copy of WordStar on your hard drive or floppy disks.

Set up   means customizing WordStar to run correctly on your computer, and telling it what monitor, drives, and printer you're using.

Log on   Derived from ancient practice of signing into a logbook to make your arrival or entrance official. When you leave, you log off. Computers do this whenever they talk to one another, or to devices like disk drives and fax boards. In simplistic terms, think of the computer and drive "shaking hands." As long as they keep shaking, they're linked for communication.

Opening a document   means selecting the document text file to work on. Either a new file will be created, or an existing one loaded from storage into memory.

Pathname   the route to any subdirectory or file on disk. If the text file CATHY-24.FEB is stored in the C drive and the LETTERS subdirectory of the WORDSTAR program directory, its pathname is C:\WS\LETTERS\CATHY-24.FEB.

Path   The MS-DOS command used to link directories and subdirectories so you can run programs and batch files in one place without having to change to its specific directory. It's normally placed in the AUTOEXEC.BAT file (and thus executed when you log on), and is followed by all the directory paths to be linked.

Printing   The transfer of a text file to the printer, which produces a hard-copy of the document.

Source disk   The disk from which a text file is being opened or copied. It can be any disk on any drive in your computer. It can be the same as the target disk.

Target disk   The disk to which a text file is being saved or copied. It can be any hard disk or floppy disk in your computer. It can be the same as the source disk.

Running WordStar from a hard drive

Depending on how you have your computer system set up, there are a variety of ways to run WordStar from the hard drive. This section covers them briefly.

From its program directory

If you let WSSETUP use the default settings when it copies WordStar to the hard drive, then its program files should be in the C:\WS directory. WS.EXE is the name of the WordStar program file. You can always run WordStar from its own directory.

1. At any DOS prompt, type CD\WS to log on to the WordStar program directory.
2. At the C:\WS directory, type WS and press the Enter key.
3. When the Opening Menu appears, WordStar is ready to use.

From a text-file directory

If the directories on your hard drive are specified in the path, the best way to use WordStar is to change to the text-file directory you're going to use *before* running WordStar. This will save a step, and the DOS command for changing directories is quicker to use than the Change Drive/Directory option of WordStar's Opening Menu. If you don't know how to change directories, or how to use basic path commands, read the chapter *Understanding and using MS-DOS*.

1. At any DOS prompt, type WS and press the Enter key.
2. When the Opening Menu appears, WordStar is ready to use.

Tip: If you've copied the macro and style sheet overlay files to the text-file sub-directory, booting from that directory will cause WordStar to use them as the default—instead of the ones in the \ WS program directory. Then, when you write and edit macros and paragraph style tags, they'll be saved specifically to those overlay files. This lets you create multiple sets of macros and paragraph style tags.

Running WordStar from floppy disks

This section tells you how to run and use WordStar from a working copy on a floppy disk. It also tells you how to create working disks.

WordStar 7 is now too big to install on 360K floppy disks. It can fit only on high-density 3¹/₂" or 5¹/₄" floppies. It also requires two floppy disks to use the program successfully: one for the WordStar program and one for the dictionaries. The WINSTALL, WSCHANGE, and companion programs require additional disks.

Tip: There's a special cut-down version of WordStar for people who use a laptop computer, called the Laptop Collection. It comes with a special bundle of companion programs designed to enhance WordStar on a laptop computer.

Making a working copy

At present, WSSETUP is only for installing WordStar on a hard drive, and doesn't permit you to copy the program to floppy disks. So the only way to make a floppy disk working copy is to manually copy the installed program files from the hard drive to floppy disks.

1. Format two high-density floppy disks, and label them Program and Dictionaries.
2. Put the Program disk into the floppy disk drive and copy the WordStar program files, WS.EXE and all .OVR files, to it with the DOS COPY command.
3. Put the Dictionary disk in the drive and copy all the .DCT files to it.

This creates a minimal working copy of WordStar 7. It takes up 789K of the Program disk, leaving 419K for text files. There's also room for DOS if you want a bootable working disk. If, however, you plan to use the Dictionaries disk for spell checks, use drive B for text files because you'll need to swap disks to check spelling. (After you run WordStar, log on to drive B.)

This working copy will have all the default settings of the version on the hard drive—including the default printer. If you need to change any of these defaults, use either WINSTALL or WSCHANGE.

Tip: Use WSCHANGE to make drive B the default drive. Then WordStar 7 will automatically look to that drive for text files. At the WSCHANGE Main

Menu, type C, E, and E. Set the Initial Directory Logon to B. Don't forget to put the text file disk in drive B before you boot WordStar.

Booting WordStar from working disks

These instructions assume that you have a working copy of WordStar 7 made with the above steps. If you want, you can make the disk bootable and set drive B as the default directory. This lets you boot the computer and run WordStar from the same disk.

1. Boot your computer normally and wait for the DOS prompt to appear.
2. Put your formatted target disk in drive B, and type B: and Enter at the DOS prompt.
3. When ready, type WS and press the Enter key. WordStar will load and run.
4. When the Opening Menu appears, WordStar is ready to use. Put your text file disk in drive B and call up any file you want.

Swapping floppy disks

Many people still prefer using a floppy drive for their text file storage while writing documents—whether or not they have a hard drive installed in the computer. This keeps the hard drive from filling up with extraneous documents, and helps keep everything sorted.

Always remember to "change" the current drive whenever you change floppy disks. Although it's the same drive, the computer is still using the file-allocation table (FAT) information from the first disk. If you swap disks without doing this, you can ruin the FAT file on the second disk the first time you save a file. Ruining the FAT file can trash the disk.

If you want to know what a *file-allocation table* is, see the *Lexicon* at the end of this book, and read the chapter *Understanding and using MS-DOS*. It's simple to change drives when swapping floppy disks. The steps are given below:

1. Close the current text file and return to the Opening Menu.
2. Take out the old floppy disk and put in the new one.
3. Type L for Change Drive/Directory.
4. When the Change Drive/Directory dialog box appears, type in the letter name (A or B) of the drive you're using. (If you've simply swapped disks, it'll be the same drive that's currently specified.)
5. Use Ctrl−K to activate the dialog box.
6. WordStar will log on the new disk, and list its files on the Opening Menu. Now you can safely open those files.

Selecting and opening the document

This section will briefly tell you how to open and name a standard WordStar document text file. There are three ways to select the text file:

- Type the name of a file from the onscreen list, then press the Enter key. If the file isn't in the current directory, simply precede the filename with its pathname.
- Use the arrow keys to highlight the name on the list and hit the Enter key.
- Use the mouse to double-click on the filename in the onscreen list. This will select and open the document without going through the dialog box.

Naming a text file

WordStar 7 uses MS-DOS's rules for giving a name to its text files. The filename can be between one and eight characters long. Leave no blank spaces in the name. You can make the filename longer by adding an extension. To add an extension, type a period after the last character of the filename, and then up to three characters. Extensions are optional, not mandatory. They are primarily used to "code" or identify the file.

There are numerous characters reserved for special purposes. These are the so-called illegal characters. If you try to use any of them in a filename, WordStar will refuse to accept them. They're listed below:

    \ ; : = ? * [ ] . , \

The same characters are illegal for extensions as for filenames. There are also illegal filenames, so-called because they too are reserved for special purposes, so MS-DOS won't let you use them. They're listed below:

    AUX CON PRN NUL

Opening the document

Opening a document means selecting the document text file to work on. Either a new file is created, or an existing one is loaded from disk storage into memory. The term is derived from opening a file folder so you can get to the document inside. The document mode is used for writing and editing standard WordStar text files. When you open a file in the document mode, it's ready to be worked on.

These steps assume that you're accessing (logged on to) the directory containing the files to be worked on. If not, then change to that directory before opening the document.

1. At the Opening Menu, type D for Open Document.
2. At the Open Document dialog box, you can either create a new text file or open an existing one.

3. If you're creating a new text file, type in its filename and press the Enter key. WordStar will say that it can't find it and ask you if you want to open a new file under that name. Answer Y to create the new file.

4. If you're opening an existing file, use the arrow keys to move the highlight to the file of your choice, and press the Enter key. If you have a mouse, then double-click on the filename.

5. WordStar will open your text file document in the standard write and edit mode. Now you're ready to get to work.

Bypassing the Opening Menu to open a document

It's possible to bypass the Opening Menu to run WordStar and open a text file in a single step. You need to be a little familiar with MS-DOS, know the filename, and know exactly where the text file is stored. Also, your computer system must contain the path of the subdirectory containing the text file. If not, you must precede the filename with its pathname.

1. Log into the directory where the text file document is stored.
2. At the DOS prompt, use the following format: WS *pathname**filename*
3. When ready, press the Enter key.

This is the quickest way to get into WordStar. If you haven't yet created the file, WordStar will pause to say it can't find the file and ask if you want to create it. You can open a file this way from any drive and/or directory. Just insert the path statement before the filename.

Warning: If you misspell the name of the file to be opened, WordStar will attempt to open a new file under the misspelled name. Be sure of your spelling before you press the Enter key.

Speed writing a document

Speed Write is the option to open a new document without naming it first. You can use this option to open only a document on the current directory.

1. At the Opening Menu, type S.
2. WordStar will open a brand-new empty file in the current drive and directory.
3. The first time you save this file to disk, you must name it.

This speed-write feature doesn't really save much time. But sometimes it's convenient to have it.

Writing the document

When a text file is open in the document mode, all you have to do is type. When you reach the right margin, don't issue carriage returns. A feature called *wordwrap* will break off the line automatically as you pass the right margin, and start a new line at the left margin. You only need carriage returns at the end of a paragraph or to insert blank lines.

- Special effects are controlled through the pull-down Style and Layout Menus, or through the Print Controls and Onscreen Format menus.
- For best results, always leave Insert turned on. Don't get in the bad habit of trying to write documents with Insert off. The overtype mode interferes with normal WordStar functions.
- Use Ctrl−T to delete words from the cursor position forward. Use Ctrl−Y to delete an entire line at the cursor position. The Backspace key deletes backward a character at a time, as long as you hold it down. The Del key erases characters or spaces at the cursor position forward.
- Use the arrow keys to move the cursor around onscreen. Ctrl−left or right arrow will jump the cursor a word at a time. Home puts the cursor at the top of the screen. End puts the cursor at the bottom of the screen. PgUp and PgDn keys will move you through the document.

Storing the document on disk

This section will tell you how to save your writing and store the text files on disk. It also briefly covers methods for hard-drive management.

When a document is open in computer memory, it exists only as a pattern of digital coding held in a weak magnetic field. This is why you can change it so easily. But the open document depends on the stability of the electric current in the computer. Any sharp dip or surge in voltage can wipe the text file from memory.

Saving the document means recording a copy of it to permanent storage on the hard or floppy disk. The process for doing this is virtually identical to that used to record music on cassettes. You can, in fact, use a standard stereo cassette to store digital information.

Save the document and keep writing

The longer the document, the more time and labor invested, and the greater its value. To protect your document while working on it, you must periodically save it to disk. This keeps the version on disk updated, so it matches the version in memory. Use either Ctrl−KS or Alt−FS with the pull-down File Menu.

Save the document and return to the Opening Menu

When finished working on the document, you must save the text file to disk storage and return to the Opening Menu. This is done with either Ctrl−KD or the Alt−FL command from the pull-down menu.

Save the document and exit WordStar

When you've finished working on a document and plan to run another program or turn off the computer, you can save the text file and exit WordStar in a single step. When you exit WordStar, you go to the DOS prompt of the current directory. Use either Ctrl−KX or Alt−FX with the pull-down File menu.

Hard-drive management

It's extremely important to properly manage your text file storage on the computer's hard drive. The worst thing you can do to yourself is to lose control of where things are in the computer. If you don't keep your work organized, you'll be forced to spend precious time hunting down documents you've misplaced.

Never store text files in the WordStar program directory. It's already cluttered with 140 program files and sample files put there during basic installation. Adding more simply increases the mess. It also increases the likelihood that you'll damage or destroy a program file.

Always create a separate directory for each type or category of text file you write. This means one for personal letters, one for business letters, one for memorandums, and so on. If you write major documents, like novels, screenplays, technical manuals, masters theses, or doctoral dissertations, create a separate directory for each—and don't hesitate to create subdirectories within as needed.

Some people prefer to store their text files in subdirectories of the WordStar program directory. There's nothing wrong with this, and it can often be convenient. But that directory already has five subdirectories in addition to the 140 files. In the long run, you're better off staying out of the crowd.

The least troublesome method is to keep all your text file directories stored in the root directory. This provides the simplest path to any directory and file. Thus, moving back one directory from any major directory takes you to the root. From there, all the other directories are immediately available.

There's another little-known benefit of this storage method. If you copy the WSSTYLE.OVR and HOTKEY.OVR files to each directory, you can have multiple sets of paragraph style tags and macros in the same computer. If you boot WordStar from a directory containing these files, WordStar uses them instead of the version in the \ WS directory. Any changes you make to paragraph tags, or any macros you write, become unique to that directory. So you can have a separate set in each text-file directory.

Previewing the printed document

WordStar has a Page Preview feature to let you see exactly what the printed document looks like—before you send it to the printer. By using a graphics mode,

WordStar gives you a true WYSIWYG display. Actual font types and sizes, margins, line spacing—in other words, full layout and design—are shown. To use Page Preview:

1. Move the cursor to the first page of the text file.
2. Use Ctrl−OP to start Page Preview.
3. Use the arrow keys, PgUp, and PgDn to move through the document.
4. Use the pull-down View Menu to set the page viewing level.
5. Use the pull-down Exit Menu to return to the write and edit mode.

Printing with WordStar

This section gives only a brief overview of printing a text file with WordStar and describes two ways of sending a file to the printer. For complete information, read the chapter titled *Printing with WordStar.*

From the Opening Menu

The following instructions assume that you've already learned how to open and write a document. If you don't know how to do that, go back and read the earlier sections of this chapter. The instructions also assume that WordStar is running, and that you're accessing the directory containing the text file to be printed.

1. Turn on the printer and make sure it's on-line (properly connected to your computer).
2. At the Opening Menu, press P to call the Print dialog box.
3. At the Print dialog box, use the arrow keys to put the highlight on the filename. Then press the Enter key.
4. The file is now selected for printing, with its name appearing in the dialog box. Use the Tab key to move forward through the variables, accepting or changing them individually.
5. When ready to accept the conditions on the dialog box, hold down the Ctrl key and type K.
6. This sends the file to the printer.

From inside the document mode

There's also a quick way to print any text file when you've finished working on it. You can go directly from the document mode to the Print dialog box. Follow these steps:

1. Turn on the printer and make sure it's on-line.
2. Save the text file with Ctrl−KS.
3. Use Ctrl−KP to call the Print dialog box.
4. At the Print dialog box, use the arrow keys to put the highlight on the filename. Then press the Enter key.

5. The file is now selected for printing, and its name will appear in the
   dialog box. Use the Tab key to move forward through the variables,
   accepting or changing them individually.
6. When ready to accept the conditions on the dialog box, hit Ctrl−K.
7. This sends the file to the printer.

7

Opening Menu options

This chapter covers the Opening Menu features and options. Simple-to-use features are described completely. Complicated features requiring lengthy instructions are given "quick start" descriptions here, and covered in depth in chapters of their own.

WordStar doesn't start up in the write and edit mode like some word processors. Instead, a command menu appears from which you select specific modes and features. This is the Opening Menu. WordStar works this way because it isn't just a single program; it's a *package* of programs working together to help you plan, write, and print your documents.

Two kinds of menus

As described in the chapter *Commanding WordStar*, there are two entirely different kinds of menus from which you can give WordStar commands. These are the classic newer pull-down menus.

- To select an option from the classic Opening Menu, type the highlighted letter beside the option. This classic menu is always active when you boot WordStar, even when pull-down menus are used.
- To select an option from the pull-down Opening Menu with the keyboard, type the first letter in its title on the command bar. Then type the highlighted letter in the option name.

99% of all commands are available on both sets of menus. Of the remaining 1%, some are available only through either a classic menu or a pull-down menu. Despite any convenience each may offer, none of this final 1% are absolutely essential to using WordStar.

Though WordStar comes with the pull-down menus as default, most old-time WordStar users prefer the classic menus, and their Ctrl−key commands. Even when the pull-down menus are active, the classic menus are always available if you issue their calling commands.

The classic menus serve best as a means of teaching you the direct Ctrl and Alt commands. Once you know the direct commands for using the features you rely on, you'll use menus only for seldom-used options. For this reason, the directions in this book are based on your using the classic menus exclusively.

If you don't know which kind of menus are which, there's a quick way to find out. If it looks like Fig. 7-1, then the classic menus are active. If the Opening Menu looks like Fig. 7-2, then WordStar is using the pull-down menus. Make sure the default is pull-down menus. If it isn't, use WSCHANGE to permanently change the help-level setting to 4.

```
███████████████████████████ WordStar ████████████████████████████
─────────────── O P E N I N G   M E N U ───────────────────────
  D open a document              L change drive/directory
  S speed write (new file)       C protect/unprotect a file
  N open a nondocument           E rename a file
  P print a file                 O copy a file
  \ fax                          Y delete a file
  K print from keyboard          F turn directory off
  I index a document             M macros
  T table of contents            R run a DOS command
  X exit WordStar                A additional
  F1 help                        ? display status
```

Filenames:		Path: C:\WS 45M free					
..	\	FAX	\	MACROS	\	OPTIONS	\
ARROW.HP	.3k	BOX	.4k	CHEX.HP	.5k	DB00.DTB	80k
DB01.DTB	375k	DB02.DTB	84k	DB04.DTB	188k	FILELIST.TXT	27k
FONTID.CTL	7.6k	HP-ENV.LST	1.0k	HP2-ENV.LST	1.0k	ILLUS.DOT	.4k
INDEX.DTB	46k	KEYBOARD.MRG	.1k	LIST.DOC	.8k	MAILING.DOC	1.0k
OPENMENU.BAK	2.0k	OPENMENU.FIG	2.2k	PDFEDIT.HLP	35k	PLAYBILL.DOC	.6k
PLAYS.DOC	.9k	PLEAD.HP	.1k	PREVIEW.MSG	10k	PRINT.TST	12k
REVIEW.DOC	3.1k	SHADE.HP	.0k	SHAKE.DOC	6.0k	SPELL.DOC	6.0k
VESA1024.WGD	2.9k	WINSTALL.HLP	32k	WS.DEF	.9k	WSINDEX.XCL	1.5k

7-1 Classic Opening Menu.

The pull-down Opening Menu

The pull-down Opening Menu displays only the title bar and the list of files in the current directory. The options on the title bar are File, Utilities, Additional, and Help. Each of these options represents a separate pull-down menu. To call the menu, type the highlighted letter in each menu name.

```
Filenames:            Path: C:\WS  45M free
..                \   FAX              \   MACROS            \   OPTIONS            \
ARROW.HP      .3k      BOX          .4k     CHEX.HP       .5k     DB00.DTB        80k
DB01.DTB     375k      DB02.DTB    84k      DB04.DTB     188k     FILELIST.TXT    27k
FONTID.CTL   7.6k      HP-ENV.LST  1.0k     HP2-ENV.LST  1.0k     INDEX.DTB       46k
KEYBOARD.MRG  .1k      LIST.DOC     .8k     MAILING.DOC  1.0k     OPENMENU.FIG    .3k
PDFEDIT.HLP   35k      PLAYBILL.DOC .6k     PLAYS.DOC     .9k     PLEAD.HP        .1k
PREVIEW.MSG   10k      PRINT.TST   12k      REVIEW.DOC   3.1k     SHADE.HP        .0k
SHAKE.DOC    6.0k      SPELL.DOC   6.0k     VESA1024.WGD 2.9k     WINSTALL.HLP    32k
WS.DEF        .9k      WSINDEX.XCL 1.5k     WSMIN.PAT     .0k
```

7-2 Pull-down Opening Menu.

Opening File Menu options

To call the pull-down Opening File Menu, type F. The menu, shown in Fig. 7-3, contains the following commands and options:

New   Create a new, empty text file in the current directory, without first giving it a name. This option puts you directly into the document write and edit mode. It's the same as Speed Write in the classic menu system.

Open Document   Open an existing text file or create a new one by typing its name or selecting it from an onscreen list. You can open a text file in any directory or subdirectory this way.

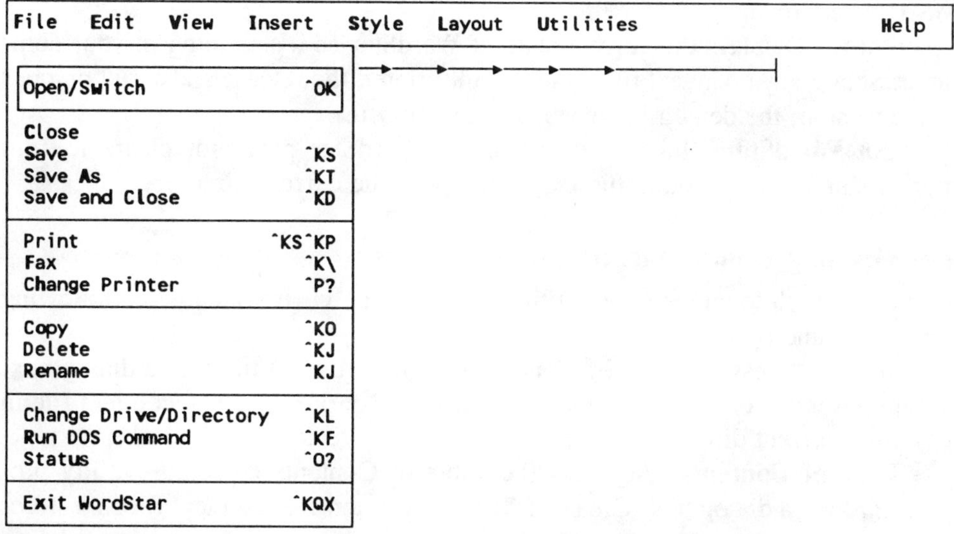

7-3 Pull-down File Menu.

Open Nondocument   Open an existing ASCII text file or create a new one by typing its name or selecting it from an onscreen list. An ASCII text file in any directory or subdirectory can be opened this way.

Print   Select a text file from a directory list, set custom print-time variables, and send the text file to the printer.

Print from Keyboard   Also called *typewriter mode*. Select a template to use for typing text directly to the printer. Can be used for filling out standard forms.

Fax   A utility program for converting WordStar text files to a standard fax file format. Files can then be sent directly through a fax board installed in your computer.

Copy   Accesses the MS-DOS COPY command through a dialog box. Makes a copy of any text file, and stores it in the current directory under different name or in different directory under any name.

Delete   Accesses the MS-DOS DEL command through a dialog box. Deletes any text file in either the current or any other drive or directory.

Rename   Accesses the MS-DOS REN command through a dialog box. Renames any text file in the current or any other drive or directory.

Protect/Unprotect   Safeguards a text file from editing by changing it to a read-only file. Toggles between protected and unprotected. Select any text file from any drive or directory.

Change Drive/Directory   Allows you to change to any drive or directory in your computer.

Change Filename Display   Permits you to control the onscreen display of filename to show all or specific filenames by type.

Run DOS Command   Opens a DOS window through which you can run an MS-DOS command.

Status   Displays the current state of WordStar as it's running in your computer. Shows any open text files, the default printer, the release and serial number of the version, the default language, and memory use.

Exit WordStar   Takes you out of the WordStar program, clears it from memory, and returns you to the DOS prompt of the current directory.

The Opening Utilities menu

To call the pull-down Opening Utilities Menu, type U. It contains the following commands and options:

Index   Accesses the Index Generator utility program through a dialog box. Creates an index of a text file and stores it in a separate file. Select a text file in either the current directory or any other drive or directory.

Table of Contents   Accesses the Table of Contents Generator utility program through a dialog box. Creates a Table of Contents from a text file and stores it in a separate file. Select a text file in the current directory or any other drive or directory.

Macros   Calls the Macros Menu, from which you can Play, Record, Edit, Create, Copy, Delete, or Rename any macro.

Opening Additional Menu options

The pull-down Opening Additional Menu accesses WordStar's companion programs. To call this menu, type U. It contains the following commands and options:

MailList   A utility program for writing mailing lists and other data files. It uses an onscreen template as an interface. The fields on its template correspond directly to the data columns in the data file.

TelMerge   A telecommunications program to link your computer, via a modem, to any of ten standard online services or another TelMerge user. With this program, you can transfer text files and data files directly through your telephone line.

Star Exchange   A utility program used to convert WordStar text files to formats of other word processing programs, or convert other formats into WordStar text files. This utility makes WordStar compatible with 50 major IBM-compatible and Macintosh programs.

The classic Opening Menu

The Opening Menu displays two different things: the available modes and commands and the list of files in the current directory. The available modes and commands is a list of features in the WordStar writing toolbox. To select a mode or command, type the highlighted letter beside it. The list of available files is a list of the text files stored in the current drive and directory. These files are available without having to change drive or directory. If no directory listing appears, either the disk in the current drive is empty, or the directory display is toggled off.

Changing the help level

The instructions throughout this chapter assume that you're using the classic WordStar commands but leaving the pull-down menus active. If the classic menus are currently active, you need to change the help level to 4. Below are the steps for temporarily changing the help level from the classic Opening Menu.

1. Hold down the Ctrl key and type H.
2. Type 4, and press the Enter key (once or twice, depending on how you have WordStar set up to use the Enter key).
3. The help level is now set to display and use the pull-down menus (see Fig. 7-4).

Tip: I strongly recommend that you permanently set WordStar to use the pull-down menus, even if you prefer using only the classic commands directly. Some

```
Help Level:                                          ▮   OK   ▮

 ♦  4  Pull-down Menus                               ▮ Cancel ▮
 o  3  Classic Menus—All Menus On
 o  2  Classic Menus—Edit Menu Off, Submenus On
 o  1  All Menus Off, Confirmations Off
 o  0  All Menus Off, Confirmations Off, Allow Hidden Block Changes
```

7-4 Help Level dialog box.

commands, and mouse support, are available only through the pull-down menus. At the WSCHANGE Main Menu, type DBAA and set the level to 4.

Using the document mode

WordStar doesn't boot up in the write and edit mode. You must activate the document mode and tell WordStar what text file to open. Choose either an old file or a new one. Pick it from the onscreen list or from storage in any other drive or directory.

WordStar calls its standard text files *documents*. As documents are written, WordStar embeds special, hidden word-processing commands in them. These commands tell WordStar how to display the text onscreen and how to print a hardcopy of the file.

Opening a file is like pulling a folder from a file drawer and opening it to work on the papers inside. Here it also means that WordStar is going into the write and edit mode, and is copying the text file from disk into memory.

The routine for creating a new file is the same as for reopening an old one already stored on disk. WordStar must be told a filename before it can go to work. Tell it an old filename, and the document will appear onscreen. Tell it a new filename, and it will ask you if you want to create it.

Opening a document from the current directory

The foolproof way to work with a document is to first change to the drive or directory storing the file. The available filenames will be displayed onscreen, and you can select your file visually.

1. Type D to call the Open Document dialog box.
2. At the Open Document dialog box, use the arrow keys to put the highlight on the filename to be opened, or double-click on the filename.
3. The drive light will come on as WordStar loads the file into memory.
4. When the document appears onscreen, you can begin writing and editing.

Opening a document in another directory

You can open a document in either another drive or subdirectory. If you know how to specify paths, you can load it directly from your current directory.

- To open a text file in another directory, precede the filename with the full directory path.
- To open a text file in another drive, precede the filename with the drive—A:, B:, C: and so on.
- To open a text file in another drive and directory, precede the filename with both the drive—A:, B:, C:—and the full directory path.

Opening a document with a mouse

If using a mouse with WordStar, you can select and open a text file with a double-click on its onscreen filename.

If you're using a mouse, you can change your directory or browse from directory to directory by clicking on one of the directory names listed onscreen. When you get to the directory or subdirectory containing the file you want, double-click on its name.

If WordStar can't find the file

If WordStar can't find the file, the dialog box shown in Fig. 7-5 will appear on the screen. The following are possibilities of why this has happened:

- The filename you typed is a new one. If you want to create a file, answer Y for yes or hit Enter, and a new file will be opened under the given name and path.

```
━━━━━━━━━━━━━━━━━━━━━━━━  Open Document  ━━━━━━━━━━━━━━━━━━━━

                                                       ▓   OK   ▓

   Filename: C:\WS\dogmeat.rgr                         ▓ Cancel ▓

  ───────────────────────────────────────────────────────────
                  ┌─────────────────────────────────┐
  Filenames:      │ Can't find that file.  ▓   OK   ▓│
  ..          \   │                                 │  OPTIONS        \
  ARROW.HP   .3k  │ Create a new one?   ▓ Cancel ▓  │  DB00.DTB      80k
  DB01.DTB  375k  └─────────────────────────────────┘  FIDDLE7.PAT   27k
  FILELIST.TXT 27k  FILENAME   .5k  FONTID.CTL  7.8k │  HP-ENV.LST  1.0k
  HP2-ENV.LST 1.0k  ILLUS.DOT  .4k  INDEX.DTB    46k │  KEYBOARD.MRG  .1k
  LIST.DOC    .8k  MAILING.DOC 1.0k OPENMENU.BAK 5.2k│  OPENMENU.FIG 7.4k
  PDFEDIT.HLP 35k  PLAYBILL.DOC .6k PLAYS.DOC    .9k │  PLEAD.HP      .1k
  PREVIEW.MSG 10k  PRINT.TST  12k  REVIEW.DOC   3.1k │  SHADE.HP      .0k
  SHAKE.DOC  6.0k  SPELL.DOC  6.0k VESA1024.WGD 2.9k│  WINSTALL.HLP  32k
  WS.DEF      .9k  WSINDEX.XCL 1.5k WSMIN.PAT    .0k │
```

7-5 Open Document dialog box with a *Can't find that file* prompt.

- You typed the wrong name or directory path, or you misspelled either the filename or the pathname. Type N or hit Esc to return to the dialog box. Check for errors and correct them. Then try again.
- You don't know what the correct drive and/or path are. Press the Esc key until you return to the Opening Menu.

Telling WordStar the drive name

Drives are named with letters of the alphabet, followed by a colon, so they look like the following:

A: B: C: D: E:

It never matters whether the letter is capitalized or lowercase. WordStar can address up to 26 drives in a computer or network without having to modify its program. This means that all the letters in the alphabet can be used as drive names.

When telling WordStar to open a file from a different drive, add the drive, typed as a prefix to the filename. Following are three typical drive and filename specifications:

A:CHAPTER.01 C:GENEVA24.FEB B:MEMO13.JAN

WordStar establishes a handshaking relationship with the drive as long as the file is open. When the file is closed, WordStar lets go the handshake.

Telling WordStar the filename

There are two ways to tell WordStar the name of the text file. You can type the filename or select it from an onscreen list. To select a filename from an onscreen list, you can:

- Use the arrow keys to put the highlight on it and then press the Enter key.
- Double-click on the filename with the mouse.

Rules for naming a file

Text files are named following standard MS-DOS rules. These rules are simple, limited in flexibility, and must be followed without exception. They are as follows:

1. A filename can be from one to eight letters or numbers long, in any combination, with no blank spaces allowed in the name.
2. A filename can be lengthened by adding an optional three-character extension. Add this extension by typing a period after the filename and then between one and three characters. Extensions are always optional, and are used to make the filename more specific.

3. There are illegal characters you cannot use in any filename or extension. They have been reserved for special use by WordStar and MS-DOS. If you try to use them, WordStar will refuse to accept them.

Files with identical names

MS-DOS doesn't allow you to have two files in the same directory with the same name. You can use the same name in a different drive or directory. Remember to keep files with the same name in their proper directory.

Keep in mind that copying a text file to a disk or directory already having a file with the same name will write over the stored file—destroying it.

Illegal filenames

There are four illegal filenames, reserved by MS-DOS as device names. If you try to use them, MS-DOS will refuse to accept them. They can be used as extensions, however. These illegal filenames are AUX, CON, PRN, and NUL.

Illegal characters

There are some characters that are defined as illegal for use in a filename. This means that they're reserved for special purposes by either WordStar, MS-DOS, or both. The illegal characters are as follows:

\ ; : = ? * [ ] . , \

Nothing bad or harmful happens if you try to use any of these characters in a filename. WordStar will simply pop up a message saying you've tried to use an illegal character.

Using filename extensions

Filename *extensions* are exactly what they sound like. They extend or lengthen a filename. These optional extensions are added by typing a period immediately after the characters of the filename, then an additional one, two, or three characters. You can use either letters or numbers, with the same restrictions about illegal characters.

Program files require special filename extensions so MS-DOS can process them correctly. WordStar text files don't require them. Text file extensions serve only as a personal convenience or as a coding system.

The more text files you write, the more annoying the eight character limit can be. It isn't flexible, and forces you to plan filenames carefully. Eight letters or numbers isn't sufficient for any prolonged use. Sometimes the only way around this limitation is to use filename extensions.

Make your extensions as personal or distinctive as possible. You want them to identify the file or its contents. For example, use .TXT or .DOC for text documents. Use your imagination, and make up your own coding system.

Illegal extensions

There are illegal extensions you cannot use for text files. They're reserved by WordStar and MS-DOS for program files. They are:

.BIN .EXE .BAT .COM .BAK .OVR

Fast-opening a new document

You can open a new document in the current directory without first having to name it. You'll then name it the first time you issue a Save command. In previous releases of WordStar, this was called speed write. It's still called this on the classic Opening Menu. In the pull-down Opening Menu, however, it's called New. There are two ways to open a new text file:

- At the classic Opening Menu, type S to speed write a new text file.
- At the pull-down Opening Menu, type FN to open a new document.

Once the new document opens, you can begin typing at once.

Using the nondocument mode

First-time users are always confused by the term *nondocument*. They ask, "If it isn't a document, then what the heck is it?" What it is is an ASCII text file, which is a text file without any of the embedded word processing commands WordStar uses to control printing or the onscreen display.

For a complete explanation of the nondocument mode, read the chapter titled *Using the nondocument mode*.

Uses for nondocuments

ASCII text files are opened and named with the same rules as documents. They are written and edited much like document files, except that many WordStar editing features are turned off.

The nondocument mode creates files that you can use in merge printing, with a telecommunications program, or with other programs. With it, you can open and edit data files from Lotus 1-2-3, Cyma, or other accounting software.

You can use the nondocument mode as a line editor for writing computer programs. It should also be used for writing and editing batch files—simple programs to execute strings of MS-DOS commands as one.

Opening a nondocument

The foolproof way of opening a nondocument text file is to first change to the directory storing the file. Then open it through the Opening Menu. Below are the basic steps:

1. At either Opening Menu, type N to call the Open Nondocument dialog box.
2. At the Open Nondocument dialog box, use the arrow keys to put the highlight on the filename to be opened, or double-click on the filename.
3. When the nondocument appears onscreen, you can begin writing and editing.

Using other drives and directories

You can open nondocuments in other drives or directories using the same steps as for standard document text files. The only limitation is with a mouse. You can't open a nondocument file with a double-click of the mouse without first typing N or FN—unless you're using a version of WordStar modified to open in the nondocument mode as the default.

Printing a file

Only a "quick start" set of instructions for printing a file are given in this section. This is a complicated enough subject to require a chapter of its own to fully cover it. For complete information on printing with WordStar, see the chapter titled *Printing documents and nondocuments*.

WordStar prints from disk

Some word processors print a document from the copy of the file held in memory. The maximum size file they can print depends on the available RAM in the computer. WordStar prints a text file by copying it from disk and sending it to the printer. There are two distinct advantages to this:

- You can print any size document stored on disk.
- Because the memory is unused, you can work on another text file while one is printing. This is called background printing.

Printing from the Opening Menu

The foolproof way to print a file is to access the directory with the file to printed, then start print run-off through the Opening Menu. When you call the Print dialog box, WordStar looks for the file in the current drive and directory. The files in the current directory appear onscreen below the Opening Menu. WordStar can, however, print any file stored on any drive or directory if you tell it the path to the file.

Before starting the print runoff, make sure your printer is turned on and is online with your computer. Below are the steps for printing a text file through the Opening Menu:

1. At either Opening Menu, type P to call the Print dialog box. It looks like Fig. 7-6.

```
█████████████████████████████████████  Print  ███████████████████████████

        Filename: C:\COMMAND.WS6\OPENMENU.FIG _______________      █  OK  █

    Page Numbers:                          Pages:           █ Cancel █
              ◆  All                          o  Odd
              o  Selected Pages:              o  Even
                 _______________________      ◆  Both

          Copies: 1__
                                           [X] Use Form Feeds
         Printer: LASERJET                 [ ] Pause Between Pages
                                           [ ] Print Unformatted Text
      Redirect To: _________________       [X] Interpret Merge Variables

    ─────────────────────────────────────────────────────────────────────
    Filenames:           Path: C:\COMMAND.WS6   45M free
    ..             \  │ ARCHIVE        \ │ 2COLTAB.RR   .3k │ APPENDIX.01  5.6k
    APPENDIX.02  9.5k  │ AUTHQUES.TAB 8.7k│ AYS          .5k │ BLOKMENU.USE 5.0k
    CAUTION       .3k  │ CHAPTER.01    19k│ CHAPTER.02   25k │ CHAPTER.03   24k
    CHAPTER.04    11k  │ CHAPTER.05  9.1k │ CHAPTER.06   22k │ CHAPTER.07   74k
    CHAPTER.08    46k  │ CHAPTER.09    14k│ CHAPTER.10   79k │ CHAPTER.11   77k
    CHAPTER.12    55k  │ CHAPTER.13    45k│ CHAPTER.14   20k │ CHAPTER.15   18k
    CHAPTER.16    44k  │ CHAPTER.17   7.8k│ CHAPTER.18   33k │ CHAPTER.19   28k
    ─────────────────────────────────────────────────────────────────────
```

7-6 Print dialog box.

2. At the Print dialog box, select the text file to print by typing in its full name and extension. Or select it from the onscreen list by moving the highlight to it with the arrow keys. When ready, press the Enter key.

3. Tell WordStar which pages of the document to print (either all or a selected range of pages).

4. Use the Tab key to move forward through the print-time variables. Change each, or accept each, as needed for this print runoff. The defaults are marked with either diamonds or Xs. Use Shift−Tab to move backward.

5. To delete the dialog box without starting the print job, either press the Esc key or click on the Cancel push-button.

6. When ready to start the printing, use Ctrl−K or click on the OK push-button.

If the file is in another drive or directory, identify it by preceding the filename with the drivename and path. If using a mouse, you can call other directories after pressing P by clicking on the directory names onscreen.

You can always accept as many printing variables as you want. Use Ctrl−K to accept the variables and send the file to the printer. Once started, the printing will run automatically until complete or interrupted.

Pausing or stopping the print runoff

Before starting a document printing, it's good to know how to pause or cancel the printing. This is done through the Printing dialog box (see Fig. 7-7). You call it with the same command used to start the printing:

- If at the Opening Menu, type P to call the Printing dialog box.
- If printing was started inside the document mode, use Ctrl−KP to call the print-time Printing dialog box.

```
────────────────────────────── P R I N T I N G ──────────────────────────────
   P pause                                    ^U cancel printing
   C continue after pausing                   F print at full speed
   B print from background
```

7-7   Printing dialog box.

To pause printing when the menu appears, type P. The printing will pause as soon as WordStar stops sending text to the printer. How long this takes depends on the printer being used. To continue printing after a pause, type C. Printing will resume at once.

To cancel printing when the menu appears, hold down the Ctrl key and type U. This will cancel the print runoff as soon as the printer's buffer clears.

Pausing or stopping printing immediately

When you pause or stop printing through the Printing Menu, the printer will continue to print until its buffer is empty. Depending on the printer being used, this can take from one to several pages.

- To pause printing immediately, use the switch on the printer to take it off-line. If you don't know how to do this, read your printer manual.
- To stop the printing immediately, turn the printer off at its power switch. Call the Printing dialog box and issue Ctrl−U. Wait 10 seconds before turning on the printer. The printer won't print another line of the file.

Background printing

Because WordStar prints from the disk, you can tell it to send one text file to a printer, and then open another file to work on. Or you can send a file to the printer while already working on one. This is called background printing. The more memory your computer has, the better background printing works—especially if you have WordStar set up RAM-resident.

- On a PC-XT computer with only 640K of RAM, WordStar has to share the same memory between the write and edit mode, and the printing mode. This will cause flickers, pauses, and temporary keyboard lockouts.

- On a PC-AT or better with 2+ megabytes of RAM, WordStar has enough memory available to spare each mode its own RAM. The flickers and pauses shouldn't be noticeable.

Setting print-time variables

When you start a print routine, the Print dialog box (see Fig. 7-6) appears. It contains twelve variables that you can use to customize your print job. Each time you begin printing, you can either accept the default answers or change the variables.

These variables include: page numbers; whether to print all pages, even pages, or odd pages; the printer being used; pausing between pages; issuing form feeds; whether to print as a nondocument; setting the number of copies to print; directing the printing to another port; and interpreting merge variables.

Note: The last option—Interpreting Merge Variables—represents one of the more significant changes in WordStar 7 printing. Merge printing is no longer a separate printing routine. It's now merely an option of every print runoff.

Converting text files to fax files

This new utility program converts any WordStar text file to a fax file in the standard .PCX format. Once converted, you can transmit the file directly through a fax board installed in your computer.

This allows you to send faxes of documents that look like they were printed on a laser printer—with all your fonts, layout, and design. Of course, the true resolution of the received fax always depends on the receiving fax machine. But the conversion process lets you control the sending resolution so you can adapt to different machines.

For complete information on using the fax file conversion utility program, see the chapter titled *Converting text files to faxes*.

Printing from the keyboard

Only a description of the Print from Keyboard utility is given below. For a complete explanation, read the chapter entitled *Printing documents with WordStar*.

The Print from Keyboard option lets you use your printer like a typewriter. This is useful for filling out pre-printed forms, addressing envelopes, typing individual mailing labels, and so on. With this option active, a line of text onscreen can be sent to the printer as soon as you press the Enter key.

However, this feature is difficult to use, requires much practice to master, and has many limitations. One problem is that text doesn't word wrap automatically, and can't be reformatted. Another is that the practical use of this feature requires templates and only one general-purpose template comes with WordStar. A third drawback is that this option doesn't work well with laser printers because each press of the Enter key usually issues a form feed.

Creating an index

An *index* is an alphabetical list of words or subjects in a document, with page numbers to indicate where each can be found. When made correctly, an index is a powerful tool for finding specific information in a book.

The Index option in WordStar is a utility program for generating an index from a text file. Indexing is a complicated subject and only an overview is given here. For complete information, read the chapter *Indexing your documents*. It gives detailed instructions on:

- Preparing a file for indexing
- Using WordStar to generate an index
- Editing and formatting an index for printing

Different methods for indexing

WordStar has five different ways to index a file. All get the job done efficiently. Use whichever method you find convenient, or any working combination. The different methods are:

- Index every word in the file and then delete the references you don't want included in the index.
- Use an exclusion file to create a list of words you don't want included in the index. WordStar will then generate an index of all the words not in the exclusion file.
- Embed the dot command .ix in the document. The command line contains a word or phrase to go in the Index.
- Use the print controls command Ctrl−PK to mark key words and phrases included in the index.
- Mix and match the above methods to create your own special system of indexing.

Using the Index program

The steps for using the index-generation program assume that you have a document written and prepared for indexing. If you don't have a sufficient exclusion file prepared, or if the document hasn't been marked for indexing, the only way to generate an index is to index every word (which defeats the purpose of an index).

1. At the Opening Menu, type I.
2. When the Index dialog box appears (see Fig. 7-8), tell WordStar the name of the file being indexed. You can select the file from the list below the menu, or type in a filename from a different drive and path.

Index

Filename: **C:\WS\OPENMENU.FIG** _________________________   ▓ OK ▓

Page Numbers: ♦ All   Pages: o Odd   ▓ Cancel ▓
              o Selected Pages: o Even
                                                    ♦ Both

              [ ] Index Every Word

Filenames: Path: C:\WS   45M free
..   \ | FAX   \ | MACROS   \ | OPTIONS   \
ARROW.HP   .3k | BOX   .4k | CHEX.HP   .5k | DB00.DTB   80k
DB01.DTB   375k | DB02.DTB   84k | DB04.DTB   188k | FIDDLE7.PAT   27k
FILELIST.TXT 27k | FILENAME   .5k | FONTID.CTL   7.8k | HP-ENV.LST   1.0k
HP2-ENV.LST 1.0k | ILLUS.DOT   .4k | INDEX.DTB   46k | KEYBOARD.MRG   .1k
LIST.DOC   .8k | MAILING.DOC 1.0k | OPENMENU.FIG 9.6k | PDFEDIT.HLP   35k
PLAYBILL.DOC .6k | PLAYS.DOC   .9k | PLEAD.HP   .1k | PREVIEW.MSG   10k
PRINT.TST   12k | REVIEW.DOC 3.1k | SHADE.HP   .0k | SHAKE.DOC   6.0k
SPELL.DOC   6.0k | VESA1024.WGD 2.9k | WINSTALL.HLP 32k | WS.DEF   .9k
WSINDEX.XCL 1.5k | WSMIN.PAT   .0k |

7-8 Index dialog box.

3. Accept or change the index options.
4. When ready to start generating the index, use Ctrl−K to begin.
5. The program creates an index file with the same name as the file selected for indexing—but with the extension .IDX to identify it.
6. You can open this .IDX file as a document in order to edit and format it any way you want.

See chapter 15, *Creating an index*, for a more detailed explanation of this procedure.

Writing a table of contents

A *table of contents* is a consecutive list of the divisions in a document, including the page numbers where each can be found. A well-written table of contents is essential for finding usable information in a book. A poorly written Table of Contents can destroy the value of any book.

The Table of Contents option is a utility program that WordStar uses to generate a table of contents from embedded comments placed in a document. The writing and generation of a table of contents is a complicated process, requiring a chapter of its own. Only a quick-start version of the instructions are given here. For complete information, read chapter 16, *Creating a table of contents*. It provides detailed instructions on:

• Preparing a file for the Table of Contents program.
• Generating a table-of-contents file from a prepared document.

- Editing and formatting a table-of-contents file for printing and inclusion with the document for which it was written.

Using the Table of Contents program

The instructions given here assume that you have a file with embedded table-of-contents codes for all divisions in the document. Below are the steps for creating a table of contents from a prepared file:

1. At the Opening Menu, type T.
2. When the Table of Contents dialog box appears (see Fig. 7-9), tell WordStar the name of the file to use. Select it from the list below the menu, or type in a filename from a different drive and path.

```
                        Table of Contents

   Filename: C:\WS\dogmeat.rgr                            █   OK   █

Page Numbers: ♦ All                      Pages: o Odd    █ Cancel █
              o Selected Pages:                 o Even
                                                ♦ Both

Filenames:          Path: C:\WS  45M free
..               \  FAX            \  MACROS          \  OPTIONS         \
ARROW.HP       .3k  BOX          .4k  CHEX.HP       .5k  DB00.DTB      80k
DB01.DTB      375k  DB02.DTB     84k  DB04.DTB     188k  FIDDLE7.PAT   27k
FILELIST.TXT   27k  FILENAME     .5k  FONTID.CTL   7.8k  HP-ENV.LST   1.0k
HP2-ENV.LST   1.0k  ILLUS.DOT    .4k  INDEX.DTB     46k  KEYBOARD.MRG  .1k
LIST.DOC       .8k  MAILING.DOC 1.0k  OPENMENU.FIG  12k  PDFEDIT.HLP   35k
PLAYBILL.DOC   .6k  PLAYS.DOC    .9k  PLEAD.HP      .1k  PREVIEW.MSG   10k
PRINT.TST      12k  REVIEW.DOC  3.1k  SHADE.HP      .0k  SHAKE.DOC    6.0k
SPELL.DOC     6.0k  VESA1024.WGD 2.9k WINSTALL.HLP  32k  WS.DEF        .9k
WSINDEX.XCL   1.5k  WSMIN.PAT    .0k
```

7-9 Table of Contents dialog box.

3. Accept or change the Table of Contents options.
4. When ready to start generating the table of contents, press the Enter key.
5. The Table of Contents program will run, creating a new file with the same name as the file it was generated from—but with the extension .TOC to identify it.
6. You can open this .TOC file as a document in order to edit and format it any way you want.

Changing the current drive or directory

WordStar recognizes MS-DOS path instructions, so you can access any drive or directory in your computer. This section discusses basic information on text files,

MS-DOS directories, paths, and the use of alternative drives while writing with WordStar. Skip over anything you already understand.

WordStar always has one drive in the system it looks to for the main source and target drives for the text files being worked on. This is, in WordStar terminology, the *current drive*, and it can be any drive. Don't confuse this with the *default drive*, which is the drive WordStar accesses when it's first run.

The current drive or directory is where WordStar looks for files. The files in this directory are listed below the Opening Menu. You can change, or log on, to a different drive anytime you want—either from the Opening Menu or with Ctrl−KL. You can specify any existing drive and path combination available in your computer.

As mentioned above, the default drive and directory is where you booted up WordStar. This is where the computer looks for WordStar program files when needed. The only way to change the default drive is to reboot WordStar.

If running WordStar on a dual-floppy-drive computer, the default is commonly the A drive. If running WordStar on a computer with a hard drive, this is commonly the C drive.

Changing to a different drive

You can change to any drive from the Opening Menu with the following steps:

1. Type L to call the Change Drive \ Directory dialog box (see Fig 7-10). The current drive, directory, and available text files will appear.

```
                    Change Drive\Directory

                                                    OK
    Drive\Directory: C:\COMMAND7
                                                   Cancel

    Directories:    C:\WS  45M free
    ..              \ | FAX          \ | MACROS        \ | OPTIONS        \
```

7-10 Change Drive/Directory dialog box.

2. To send the dialog box away without changing the current drive, press the Esc key or click on the Cancel push-button.
3. To access a new drive, type the letter of the drive (A, B, C, etc). The colon is unnecessary here.
4. When ready, press the Enter key.
5. WordStar will change its access to the new drive, and display the files in the drive.

Changing to a different directory

You can access any directory in any drive from the Opening Menu with the following steps:

1. Type L to call the Change Drive \ Directory dialog box. The current drive and directory will appear.
2. To leave this dialog box without changing the current drive, press the Esc key or click on the OK push-button.
3. To switch to a different directory, type in its full pathname. Or, if the directory is in the onscreen list, use the arrow keys to put the highlight on it.
4. When ready, press the Enter key.
5. WordStar will change to the new directory, and display the files in it onscreen.

To change drive and directory at the same time, simply preface the pathname with the drive's full name, for example, C: \ LETTERS.

Browsing through directories with a mouse

Using a mouse with WordStar can add a new dimension to changing the current drive or directory. You can browse through directory after directory from the Opening Menu—without ever touching the keyboard—until you find the file you're looking for.

*   Subdirectories of the current directory are always listed in any onscreen display of filenames. You can access subdirectories by double-clicking on their names.
*   The symbol [.. \ ] represents the previous directory. It appears in the upper left corner of any subdirectory list of files. You can move backwards through directories with a double-click on this symbol. If you keep selecting this symbol, you'll eventually end up in the root directory. From there, you can change to any other directory and its subdirectories.

Using batch files to change directories

You can use batch files to change directories at any MS-DOS prompt. Simply put the command CD (change directory) on a line in the batch file, followed by the pathname of the directory. You can also use these same batch files from inside WordStar.

1. Type R to call the Run DOS Command dialog box.
2. On the DOS command line, type the batch file name and press the Enter key.

3. WordStar will change to the specified directory, and tell you to *Press any key to return to WordStar*.

4. When you press any key, the Opening Menu will return and the file list of the new directory will appear.

Protecting and unprotecting files

WordStar's File Protect/Unprotect utility allows you to shield a text file from writing and editing changes by making it a read-only file. Repeating the command will toggle the protection off. File protection is recommended if you share a computer or use WordStar over a network. Use it to protect final drafts, master versions of form documents, or boilerplate files from unintentional changes or deletion.

Protected files can be opened and read, and can have their contents copied into another file. They just can't be edited or overwritten by an MS-DOS command. Protected files can't be renamed or deleted. When you open a protected document, the word *Prtect* appears on the status line.

1. At the Opening Menu, type C to call the Protect/Unprotect dialog box (see Fig. 7-11).

```
████████████████████████████  Protect/Unprotect  ████████████████████████████


                                                             ▌   OK    ▌
     Filename: openmenu.fig_________________________________
                                                             ▌ Cancel  ▌


     Filenames:              Path: C:\COMMAND.WS6  45M free
     ..              \   ARCHIVE          \   2COLTAB.RR   .3k │ APPENDIX.01 5.6k
     APPENDIX.02 9.5k   AUTHQUES.TAB 8.7k   AYS          .5k │ BLOKMENU.USE 5.0k
     CAUTION      .3k   CHAPTER.01    19k   CHAPTER.02   25k │ CHAPTER.03   24k
     CHAPTER.04   11k   CHAPTER.05   9.1k   CHAPTER.06   22k │ CHAPTER.07   74k
     CHAPTER.08   46k   CHAPTER.09    14k   CHAPTER.10   79k │ CHAPTER.11   77k
     CHAPTER.12   55k   CHAPTER.13    45k   CHAPTER.14   20k │ CHAPTER.15   18k
     CHAPTER.16   44k   CHAPTER.17   7.8k   CHAPTER.18   33k │ CHAPTER.19   28k
     CHAPTER.20  8.3k   CHEK.BOX      .3k   CHEKLIST    1.9k │ CHESS.DOC    36k
     COLUMNS      30k   COM-WS6.PR5   23k   COMANDWS    9.3k │ COMMAND.MSS 449k
     COMPANIO    3.3k   EDITMENU      .4k   EXAMPLE      .3k │ FILENAME     .5k
```

7-11 Protect/Unprotect dialog box.

2. Select the File by putting the highlight on it with the arrow keys or double-clicking with the mouse.

3. WordStar will tell you the current protection status of the file, and ask if you want to reverse it.

4. Answer Y to toggle the protection status or N to exit without changing the protection status.

Renaming files

Renaming a file accesses the MS-DOS REN command through a dialog box. You can rename any file in any drive or directory.

1. At the Opening Menu, type E to call the Rename dialog box (see Fig. 7-12).

```
                              Rename

 Current Filename: C:\COMMAND.WS6\OPENMENU.FIG              ▓  OK  ▓

     New Filename: _______________________________          ▓ Cancel ▓


 Filenames:           Path: C:\COMMAND.WS6  45M free
 ..              \    ARCHIVE          \   2COLTAB.RR   .3k  APPENDIX.01  5.6k
 CAUTION       .3k    CHAPTER.01     19k   CHAPTER.02   25k  CHAPTER.03   24k
 CHAPTER.04    11k    CHAPTER.05    9.1k   CHAPTER.06   22k  CHAPTER.07   74k
 CHAPTER.08    46k    CHAPTER.09     14k   CHAPTER.10   79k  CHAPTER.11   77k
 CHAPTER.12    55k    CHAPTER.13     45k   CHAPTER.14   20k  CHAPTER.15   18k
 CHAPTER.16    44k    CHAPTER.17    7.8k   CHAPTER.18   33k  CHAPTER.19   28k
 CHAPTER.20   8.3k    CHEK.BOX       .3k   CHEKLIST    1.9k  CHESS.DOC    36k
 COLUMNS       30k    COM-WS6.PR5    23k   COMANDWS    9.3k  COMMAND.MSS 449k
 COMPANIO     3.3k    EDITMENU       .4k   EXAMPLE      .3k  FILENAME     .5k
```

7-12 Rename dialog box.

2. Select the filename from the onscreen list by moving the highlight with the arrow keys, and then pressing the Enter key. Or use a double-click of the mouse.
3. On the New Filename line, type the new name for the file.
4. When ready, press the Enter key or double-click on the OK push-button.
5. WordStar will ask you if you really want to rename the file. Answer Y to rename it or N to return to the Rename dialog box, where you can select a different filename. Press the Esc key to exit the dialog box.

Tip: You can rename a file to any name, in any drive and/or directory. In this way, it works like the following Copy option.

Copying files

Copy accesses the DOS COPY command through a dialog box. You can copy any file to any drive or directory. You can't copy a file to itself. If you want to make another copy of a file, you must save it to a different name, drive, or directory.

WordStar adds a layer of protection by checking to see if a file by the same name already exists at the target location. Then you're asked if you want the new file to overwrite the existing one.

```
Existing Filename: CHAPTER.01_______________________          ▓  OK  ▓

  New Filename:  ___________________________________          ▓ Cancel ▓
____________________________________________________________________________

Filenames:               Path: C:\COMMAND.WS6  45M free
..                   \   ARCHIVE           \   2COLTAB.RR   .3k   APPENDIX.01  5.6k
APPENDIX.02   9.5k   AUTHQUES.TAB  8.7k   AYS          .5k   BLOKMENU.USE 5.0k
CAUTION        .3k   CHAPTER.01    19k    CHAPTER.02   25k   CHAPTER.03   24k
CHAPTER.04    11k    CHAPTER.05    9.1k   CHAPTER.06   22k   CHAPTER.07   74k
CHAPTER.08    46k    CHAPTER.09    14k    CHAPTER.10   79k   CHAPTER.11   77k
CHAPTER.12    55k    CHAPTER.13    45k    CHAPTER.14   20k   CHAPTER.15   18k
CHAPTER.16    44k    CHAPTER.17    7.8k   CHAPTER.18   33k   CHAPTER.19   28k
CHAPTER.20    8.3k   CHEK.BOX       .3k   CHEKLIST    1.9k   CHESS.DOC    36k
COLUMNS       30k    COM-WS6.PR5   23k    COMANDWS    9.3k   COMMAND.MSS  449k
COMPANIO      3.3k   EDITMENU       .4k   EXAMPLE      .3k   FILENAME      .5k
```

7-13 Copy dialog box.

1. At the Opening Menu, type O to call the Copy dialog box (see Fig. 7-13).

2. Select the filename from the onscreen list by moving the highlight with the arrow keys and then pressing the Enter key. Or use a double-click of the mouse.

3. On the New Filename line, type in the name for the new file.

4. When ready, press the Enter key or double-click on the OK push-button.

5. If a file by that name already exists at the target location, the following message will appear: *File already exists. Overwrite (Y/N)?*

6. Answer Y to overwrite the existing file. Answer N to return to the Copy dialog box, and select a different filename. Press the Esc key to exit the dialog box.

Deleting files

The Delete option accesses the MS-DOS DEL command through a dialog box. You can use it to delete any text file in either the current or any other drive and directory. Below are the steps for deleting one file from storage in the computer:

1. At the Opening Menu, type Y to call the Delete dialog box (see Fig. 7-14).

2. Select the filename to delete from the onscreen list by moving the highlight with the arrow keys and then pressing the Enter key. Or use a double-click of the mouse.

3. WordStar will now ask you if you're sure you want to delete the selected file.

4. Answer Y to delete the file or N to return to the Delete dialog box, and select a different filename. Press the Esc key to exit the dialog box.

```
                                                           ▮  OK  ▮
Filename: ______________________________________
                                                           ▮ Cancel ▮
```

```
Filenames:              Path: C:\COMMAND.WS6   45M free
..               \  | ARCHIVE           \ | 2COLTAB.RR    .3k | APPENDIX.01  5.6k
APPENDIX.02   9.5k | AUTHQUES.TAB  8.7k | AYS           .5k | BLOKMENU.USE 5.0k
CAUTION        .3k | CHAPTER.01     19k | CHAPTER.02    25k | CHAPTER.03    24k
CHAPTER.04    11k | CHAPTER.05    9.1k | CHAPTER.06    22k | CHAPTER.07    74k
CHAPTER.08    46k | CHAPTER.09     14k | CHAPTER.10    79k | CHAPTER.11    77k
CHAPTER.12    55k | CHAPTER.13     45k | CHAPTER.14    20k | CHAPTER.15    18k
CHAPTER.16    44k | CHAPTER.17    7.8k | CHAPTER.18    33k | CHAPTER.19    28k
CHAPTER.20   8.3k | CHEK.BOX       .3k | CHEKLIST     1.9k | CHESS.DOC     36k
COLUMNS        30k | COM-WS6.PR5    23k | COMANDWS     9.3k | COMMAND.MSS  449k
COMPANIO      3.3k | EDITMENU       .4k | EXAMPLE       .3k | FILENAME      .5k
```

7-14 Delete dialog box.

Tip: The quickest way to delete files is to select Run a DOS Command and then use the MS-DOS DEL command. Just keep in mind that you won't be asked to verify the deletes before making them.

WordStar has no utility for recovering deleted files, but deleted files can be recovered with utility programs like Norton Utilities or Mace. This is possible because deleting doesn't actually erase a file. It removes the first character of the filename, which contains the file's identification and protection codes. Their absence tells MS-DOS that the space used by the file is free to use again. If you use an undeletion program at once, you should be able to recover the file.

- If you've deleted a file you meant to keep, exit from WordStar at once.
- If you're working on a document and you can afford to lose any changes made, abandon the file with Ctrl−KQ.
- Avoid using Ctrl−KS, Ctrl−KX, or Ctrl−KD, and any other command that writes to disk until you've recovered the deleted file.

Toggling the directory display

WordStar's directory display shows the filenames of files in the current directory. It appears below the Opening Menu when you boot up WordStar. You can toggle this directory listing on or off, and also customize it to show only specific filenames or extensions.

- To toggle the directory display off, press the F key. The onscreen list of files will immediately disappear.
- To toggle the directory display on, press F again. This time the Change File Listings dialog box will appear (see Fig. 7-15). It always contains

Change file listings to include only filenames that match: ■ OK ■

????????.???   ■ Cancel ■

Wildcard characters * and ? may be used.

7-15   Change File Listings dialog box.

the wildcard-character specification ????????.??? to display all
filenames. Press the Enter key, and the full list will appear.

- To customize the directory display, toggle it off and then back on again.
  At the Change File Listings dialog box, type in the pattern for the
  display, for example, *.LTR to display only your letters. Press the Enter
  key, and the custom list will appear.

Defining and using macros

WordStar's macro system has been completely revised and rewritten in WordStar
7. Gone is the familiar Shorthand Menu, which has been a part of the program
since release 4. In its place is perhaps the most powerful macro system of any
word processor.

You can use macros to help you write faster, and work more easily with Word-
Star. Only an overview is given here. For complete information and instructions
for macros, read the chapter *Defining and using WordStar's new macros*.

Macros are the assignment of commands to a single key or two-stroke key
sequence. Individual commands, or multiple commands, can be executed at once
by pressing those keys. For example, commands installed on the function keys are
macros. You can program up to 82 macros with the new Macro Menu.

Commands or boilerplate text are assigned to hotkeys. They are executed or
inserted by typing those keys. Below are the Macro Menu options:

Play a Macro   This option executes a macro's functions. The simplest way
to play a macro is to press its hotkeys. A list of the factory-supplied macros is in
the chapter titled *Defining and using WordStar's new macros*. If you don't know
the hotkeys, you can play the macro through the Macro Menu.

Record a Macro   You create a macro by recording its command keystrokes
or boilerplate text, then letting WordStar compile it into a macro file. This is done
without using the BASIC-like macro language required by the following option.
Ctrl−MR starts the recording, then assigns a hotkey. Type the keystrokes of the
macro commands, then use Alt−equal sign to end the recording.

Create/Edit a Macro   This requires learning and using a complex BASIC-
like macro language. The macro opens in a second window, and is written with

this language. Ctrl−MD opens the macro file. Ctrl−KD closes and compiles the macro file.

Copy a Macro   This lets you use an existing macro file as a template for creating or editing a new macro.

Delete a Macro   This option erases a macro file from the Macro directory, and releases the hotkey, if applicable.

Rename a Macro   This lets you give an edited macro file a new name.

Running an MS-DOS command

The Run a DOS Command option opens what is commonly called a *DOS window*. It's also called *shelling out to DOS*. Through the DOS dialog box, you can issue MS-DOS commands directly to the computer. If you're proficient with MS-DOS, you can use this to speed up file movement and directory search procedures. It's usually quicker to issue a DOS command than to wait for a WordStar menu. When inside the document mode in WordStar, Ctrl−KF does the same thing as selecting the Run a DOS Command.

1. At the Opening Menu, type the letter R to call the Run DOS Command dialog box (see Fig. 7-16).

```
■■■■■■■■■■■■■■■■■■■■■■■■■■■■■■■  Run DOS Command  ■■■■■■■■■■■■■■■■■■■■■■■■■■

    Current Drive: C                                          ▓   OK   ▓

      DOS Command:_                                     _     ▓ Cancel ▓

■■■■■■■■■■■■■■■■■■■■■■■■■■■■■■■■■■■■■■■■■■■■■■■■■■■■■■■■■■■■■■■■■■■■■■■■■■■■■■
```

7-16 Run DOS Command dialog box.

2. On the DOS command line, type the MS-DOS command. Make sure that your format and syntax are correct.
3. When ready, press the Enter key until the command executes or click on the OK push-button.
4. When the DOS command executes, the message *Press any key to return to WordStar* will appear.
5. Press any key and the Opening Menu will reappear.

Never use MS-DOS commands unless you know what those commands really do and the correct format and syntax necessary for issuing them. MS-DOS commands can be reissued, but their effects might not easily be undone.

Batch files

You can run batch files through this DOS window, providing they contain no commands to interfere with WordStar's use of computer memory.

A batch file, as explained earlier in this chapter, is a small program containing groups or batches of MS-DOS commands. By running this program, you can execute all the commands at once instead of one by one. Batch files must have the .BAT extension and, if you're writing them in WordStar, you must use the non-document mode.

For more information on writing and using batch files, read the chapter *Using MS-DOS*.

Never run WordStar from an MS-DOS window!

Once you've created an MS-DOS window, never, never, never, under any circumstances run WordStar again. It can be done, and appears to function harmlessly. But any command to write to disk can ruin the file-allocation table on the disk. This can cost you all the files in the disk or directory.

The directory listing will indicate that everything is okay. The damage won't be apparent until you open a file. Then you'll discover that a file is truncated or empty.

If you've done this and lost files, stop at once and exit from WordStar. Norton Utilities' Disk Doctor might be able to repair the damaged file-allocation table and recover your files. If you don't have Norton or Mace, or aren't sure how to use them to repair a FAT file, get experienced help.

Be careful running TSRs

Under most circumstances, avoid running terminate-and-stay-resident programs (TSRs), also called memory-resident programs, through the Run dialog box. It's best to run those programs *before* you run WordStar. Otherwise, you risk causing WordStar to crash.

Some TSRs use specific memory locations *no matter what*. If another program is already using the memory space, the TSR will kick it out. WordStar is smart enough to fit itself around other programs already in memory. Before running a TSR through the dialog box, make sure it doesn't interfere with WordStar.

Running a companion program

Companion programs are a package of utilities you can use to help you work with WordStar. These programs are discussed in the appendix *WordStar's companion programs*. Below are the steps for running these additional programs:

1. At the Opening Menu, type A to call the Additional Menu or dialog box.
2. Use the arrow keys to put the highlight on the companion program to run.
3. Press the Enter key.

Displaying the system status

Typing a question mark at the Opening Menu will cause your system status to be displayed, as shown in Fig. 7-17. This reveals the current state of WordStar as it's running in your computer. It shows any open text files, the default printer, release and serial numbers of version, the default language, and memory use.

This status display can also tell you whether you have sufficient memory to work with additional options or companion programs.

```
━━━━━━━━━━━━━━━━━━━━━━━━━ Status ━━━━━━━━━━━━━━━━━━━━━━━━━

  Current Filename: C:\COMMAND.WS6\OPENMENU.FIG                  ▓ Continue ▓

       Byte count: 25154
      Markers set: (none)
            Inset: Not Loaded
   Current printer: LASERJET

          Release: WordStar for DOS North American Version 7.0 Rev. A
    Serial Number: 632
         Language: United States    (001)

  ┌─ Memory Usage ──────────────────────────────────────────────────────┐
  │                                                                      │
  │       WordStar:    212k      Messages:    2k     Hyphenation:    0k   │
  │   Text and Data:   158k      Printing:    0k      Thesaurus:    0k    │
  │                                                    Spelling:    0k    │
  │                                                                      │
  │   Conventional Memory          In Use:   372k     Available:    96k   │
  │                                                                      │
  │   Expanded Memory (EMS)                   Unavailable                 │
  │                                                                      │
  └──────────────────────────────────────────────────────────────────────┘
```

7-17 WordStar's system status display.

Getting help with WordStar features

WordStar offers help in two different ways. First, it provides helpful descriptions and information on using all of its word-processing features. You can access these while working on a document.

Second, it allows you to temporarily change the display level of the onscreen menus and dialog boxes. This can also be done at any time while writing or editing a text file.

Exiting from WordStar

The Exit WordStar option takes you out of the WordStar program, clears WordStar from memory, and puts you at the DOS prompt of the current directory.

8

CHAPTER

Writing in the document mode

This chapter discusses WordStar's document mode, which is used for writing standard text files. It explains the basic document screen, defines its elements, and tells you how to move around in the text file. Once you understand these things, you essentially know how to write and edit with WordStar.

Understanding the document screen

When you open a text file in the document mode, it is displayed on the *document screen* (see Fig. 8-1). When you begin a new document, all you'll see onscreen are editing tools and blank space. This is where you'll write, edit, run spell checks, and use the thesaurus. This is also where you'll format your document by controlling the layout and design.

The new WordStar 7 document screen might come as a shock to both old and new users alike. The default version you get from a standard WSSETUP installation bears little relationship to any previous version of the program. But once you get past this new look and feel, the WordStar program is still as usable and reliable as ever. But first you need to understand what all this new stuff is and what it does.

What *is* all this stuff?

Figure 8-1 is an illustration of the standard document screen. This is what you see if you run the plain vanilla, or basic, version that WSSETUP installs on your hard drive. If you're an old-time WordStar user, you'll likely think the screen looks

8-1   WordStar's document screen.

cluttered. If you're a first-time user, it will no doubt look confusing. But there's an order and method to the madness.

Everything on the screen has a purpose, and a good use. Most of the changes in version 7 were made to incorporate full mouse support to WordStar for the first time. You can click on almost anything and get some kind of command response. From top to bottom, left to right, the following is what you'll see:

Status information   On the basic version of WordStar, the status information has been split between the top and the bottom of the screen. This tells you the filename and where you are inside it. The entire status line can be moved to the top of the screen if you want.

Menu bar   The names of, and icons for calling, the document pull-down menus.

Style bar   This line contains icons and descriptions of formatting information. Style, in this context, means *design*. Its options control the technique and appearance of the printed document. It can be moved to the bottom of the screen if you want.

Ruler line   An onscreen representation of left and right margins and tab stop settings.

Flag column   Down the right side of the screen, a graphic display of carriage returns and embedded commands status.

Scroll bar   Down the rightmost edge of the document screen, it contains an arrow on the top and bottom, a colored bar, and a small box in the bar. You use it

96   *Writing in the document mode*

to move through the document with the mouse. Just point, click, and drag the box up and down.

Writing area   In the middle of all this stuff is the writing area. Depending on how many onscreen options you display, the line spacing being used, and whether you're using standard display or the special VGA graphics display, there's room for between 21 and 48 lines of onscreen text. This is often called the *screen page*.

Cursor   The small, blinking box you see onscreen. It tells you where you are on the screen. When you type text, it appears at the cursor.

Mouse pointer   If you have a mouse installed, and mouse support is active, the pointer is the unblinking larger onscreen box. Think of it as a floating cursor. You move it around with the mouse, and when you point and click the mouse on icons you're executing commands.

Status-line information and icons

On the basic version of WordStar, the status information is split between the top and the bottom of the screen. This gives you the filename and tells you where you are inside the file.

From left to right, the status line lists the drive, directory, and filename of the text file open in the document screen. Next comes the words *Insert* or *Ins-off*, telling you whether new text will be inserted or if it will overwrite old text. Then comes the page number, the line number, the vertical distance of the cursor from the top of the screen, the column number, and the horizontal distance of the cursor from the left margin.

Tip: If you don't like having the status information split between the top and bottom of the screen, you can change it temporarily with Ctrl−OB. You can change it permanently with WSCHANGE. At the WSCHANGE Main Menu, type DBA. At menu #1, set the Flag Column and Dot Command display on. At menu #2, set the Style Bar Location to bottom and Status Line Location to top.

Notice how most of this information describes the location of the cursor, both onscreen and in the text file. Everything you do onscreen is in relation to the cursor. Without the cursor, you'd be hopelessly lost.

The status-line icons are the places you can click on to execute a command, or to call a menu or dialog box, to change onscreen status and display. They're listed below:

Status icon	What it does
P#	Calls the Go to Page dialog box
Insert	Toggles between Insert and Ins-off
↕#	Calls the Alignment and Spacing dialog box
L	Turns on ragged-right justification *
C	Turns on center justification *

| R | Turns on ragged-left justification * |
| J | Turns on full justification |

*These options are available only if the Return to Classic Editing screen option is set to yes, Style Bar Position is bottom, and Status Line Position is top.

Menu bar information

The menu bar is the second line on the standard document screen. It contains the names of all the document pull-down menus. The icons are the menu names. Click on a name to call the corresponding pull-down menu. These menus contain 99% of WordStar's word-processing, layout, and design commands. The icons are:

Menu icon	**What it does**
File	Calls the pull-down File Menu
Edit	Calls the pull-down Edit Menu
View	Calls the pull-down View Menu
Insert	Calls the pull-down Insert Menu
Style	Calls the pull-down Style Menu
Layout	Calls the pull-down Layout Menu
Utilities	Calls the pull-down Utilities Menu
Help	Calls the pull-down Help Menu

Pull-down menus are the primary way of using WordStar with a mouse. If you don't have a mouse, they're much less useful. But you can still call them by holding down the Alt key and typing the highlighted letter in the menu's name. These menus are described briefly below:

File Contains commands and word-processing features used to open, close, print, and generally work with text files.

Edit Contains commands and word-processing features used to make changes or corrections to a text file, and to move around in the file.

View Contains options for changing the onscreen display. Includes using the Page Preview feature and opening or closing a text file in a second window.

Insert Contains commands to place dot commands, notes, printing codes, and other special information directly into the text file.

Style Contains commands to attach character attributes, and font type and size specifications, and for working with paragraph style tags.

Layout Contains commands that control paragraph justification, newspaper column layout, headers and footers, page and line numbering, and general page layout.

Utilities Contains options and features for checking spelling, using the thesaurus, sorting blocks of text, reformatting modified paragraphs, inserting merge printing variables, and setting up macros.

Help   Provides help messages describing specific WordStar commands, features, and options. Also permits changing the help-level setting.

Style bar information

The style bar is the third line on the standard document screen. It contains 11 icons for directly controlling formatting functions. You can move it to the bottom of the screen if you want.

Click on the Style icons to execute a command or to call a menu or dialog box in order to change onscreen status and display. The style-bar options are:

Style icon	What it does
Paragraph tag	Indicate or select a paragraph tag at the cursor
Font	Display or select font at the cursor
B	Indicate or turn boldface on at the cursor
I	Indicate or turn italics on at the cursor
U	Indicate or turn underline on at the cursor
*	Toggle the print controls display on and off *
L	Turn on ragged-right justification *
C	Turn on center justification *
R	Turn on ragged-left justification *
J	Turn on full justification

* A highlight in the icon means it's currently active.

Ruler line information

The ruler line is the fourth line from the top of the screen. It provides an onscreen presentation of left and right margins, and tab stop settings. If not needed, the ruler can be toggled off with the command Ctrl−OB. You can also turn it off permanently with WSCHANGE, then toggle it on when needed.

The only ruler icon is the ruler line itself. If you click on it, the Ruler Line dialog box will appear. There you can set left and right margins, first-line indent, and tab stops.

Flag column information

The Flag Column runs down the right side of the screen. Flags are status indicators. The column is a graphic display of carriage returns and embedded command status. WordStar displays a flag for each line as a reminder of what's typed on the line. The flags and their meanings are as follows:

Flag	Meaning
<	The line ends with hard carriage return. This usually indicates the end of the paragraph.

Flag	Meaning
space	A blank space in the flag column means the line ends with a soft carriage return (produced by word wrap).
P	Marks a page break. New page below.
F	Marks form feed inserted with Ctrl−PL.
C	Marks a column break.
^	Marks the end of the file.
+	Text extends beyond the screen edge.
.	Dot command that changes both onscreen formatting and the hardcopy.
:	Dot command that changes only the hardcopy.
?	Dot command that's not recognized by WordStar.
1	Dot command that changes onscreen formatting and the hardcopy. The command works best if at the beginning of the file.
-	Line ends with a carriage return but without a line feed. You insert it with a Ctrl−Enter, which causes the next line to overprint.
J	Line ends with line feed but without a carriage return. You inserted it with Ctrl−PJ. The next line will print on the line below, but might not begin at the left margin.

Tip: The flag column is least obtrusive and distracting if you set its background color the same as the background color of standard text. You need to see only the flags, not the column itself. The entire column and flags can be toggled on and off with Ctrl−OB.

Using the scroll bar

The scroll bar runs down the right-most edge of the document screen (outside the flag column). It has an arrow on the top and bottom, a colored bar, and a small box inside the bar.

- It's used for moving through the document with the mouse. Just point and click anywhere on the bar.
- The small box is also called *slider* or *elevator box*. Put the pointer on it, hold down the button, and slide the box up and down.
- The distance between top and bottom represents the length of the entire document, so the distance moved by sliding is relative to the length of the text file.

Tip: The scroll bar is least obtrusive if you set its background color to green or black. The scroll bar can be toggled on and off with Ctrl−OB. You can turn it off permanently with WSCHANGE if you don't have a mouse.

Writing and editing the document

The main thing you'll be doing in the document screen is typing and editing your documents. As you write, you should periodically save your document so the version on disk stays updated. If you aren't sure how to spell a word, you can look it up with the spell checker. If the definition dictionary is active, you can look up the meaning of the word. If you want a better word, you can look it up in the thesaurus.

When the first draft of the document is written, most people go back to the beginning and run a spell check of the whole text file. This catches all those misspelled words you let slip past you. When the spell checker finds a suspect word, it will pause to display suggestions as to the "correct" spelling of the word. The suggestions are often on the money, and you can paste in the correct spelling with a single keystroke. Sometimes the suggestions are so off-base they're good for a laugh.

If this is a long or important document, you might want to print out a hardcopy of the document, and read and correct this copy (in addition to your onscreen editing).

The second draft of the electronic document begins when you start looking through the text file for mistakes. Your marked-up hardcopy can come in handy here. If you've already found most of your mistakes, all you have to do is find them and correct them in the text file.

The more important the document, the more complicated its content, and the more drafts it will probably take to make it as perfect as you can get it. Nobody ever gets it right the first time. No manuscript is worth putting your name on before at least the third draft.

When a document contains all the information it's supposed to have, and you've written it as well as you know how, you're ready to format the document. This means you make all the settings to control how it will look when printed. It doesn't mean, however, that you can't do some formatting as you write. It simply means you shouldn't worry about every single cosmetic feature as you're writing. Don't make the mistake of worrying about appearance until your words are in place. A great appearance never makes up for bad writing.

Cursor movement

After typing the text, the most basic function of word processing is learning how to move the cursor around onscreen. On a treasure map, X marks the spot where important things are found. With a word processor, it's the cursor. The cursor is your real point of contact inside the software. Where it goes, you go.

The cursor is the small, blinking box on the monitor screen. It indicates the point where text appears as typed, where a command takes effect, or where some response is expected on a dialog box. Learning to move the cursor around in a text file is almost as important as writing the document. There are slow ways and and fast ways. You can move a character or word at a time, or jump wherever necessary in a file.

Keys that move the cursor

On a typewriter, you use the Tab and spacebar keys to move across the page. With a word processor, those keys actually add tabs or extra space to a line—pushing already existing text ahead when Insert is turned on. If Insert is off, hitting the spacebar will delete text as the cursor passes over it.

Arrow keys   Every keyboard now has arrow keys. Use them to move left or right, and up or down through the document.

Home   Jumps the cursor to top of the document screen.

End   Jumps the cursor to bottom of the document screen.

PgUp   Jumps the cursor up one screenpage.

PgDn   Jumps the cursor down one screenpage.

Ctrl−Home   Jumps the cursor to beginning of the file.

Ctrl−End   Jumps the cursor to the end of the file.

Tab   Inserts a tab when Insert is on. Moves one tab stop when Insert is off.

Scrolling through the document

Scrolling means rolling the screen up or down, instead of moving the cursor. The following commands are used for scrolling through the document:

Ctrl−PgUp   Scrolls down one line.

Ctrl−PgDn   Scrolls up one line.

Ctrl−Z   Scrolls up one line.

Ctrl−W   Scrolls down one line.

Ctrl−R   Scrolls up one screen page.

Ctrl−C   Scrolls down one screen page.

Commands to move the cursor

There are seven Ctrl commands for moving the cursor to specific places in a document. The function of some Ctrl commands are given below:

Command	What it does
Ctrl−S	Moves the cursor one space left
Ctrl−D	Moves the cursor one space right
Ctrl−A	Moves the cursor one word left
Ctrl−F	Moves the cursor one word right
Ctrl−E	Moves the cursor up one line
Ctrl−X	Moves the cursor down one line
Ctrl−I	Inserts preset tab stop

Ctrl—QP	Moves the cursor back to previous position
Ctrl—QE	Moves the cursor to the top of the screen
Ctrl—QX	Moves the cursor to the bottom of the screen
Ctrl—QS	Moves the cursor to the beginning of the line
Ctrl—QD	Moves the cursor to the end of the line
Ctrl—QR	Moves the cursor to the beginning of the file
Ctrl—QC	Moves the cursor to the end of the file
Ctrl—QG	Moves the cursor forward to unique character
Ctrl—QH	Moves the cursor backward to unique character
Ctrl—QF	Moves the cursor to specific text
Ctrl—QV	Moves the cursor to previous Find position
Ctrl—L	Moves the cursor to Next Find position
Ctrl—QB	Moves the cursor to the beginning of a marked block
Ctrl—QK	Moves the cursor to the end of a marked block
Ctrl—0-9	Moves the cursor to a numbered place marker

Deleting text

What really makes word processing convenient is that it allows you to delete or erase words and paragraphs as you please. You can remove mistakes with just a few keystrokes, so you don't have to worry about making mistakes in the first place—which will increase your typing speed dramatically. The delete keys and commands are as follows:

Command	**What it does**
Ctrl—U	Restores the last deleted word, line, or block
Del	Erases characters at the cursor position
Backspace	Erases characters to the left
Ctrl—T	Erases one word to the right
Ctrl—Y	Erases the line the cursor is on
Ctrl—QY	Erases the rest of the line to the right of the cursor
Ctrl—Q+Del	Erases the rest of the line to the left of the cursor
Ctrl—QT	Erases to a specified character
Ctrl—KB	Marks the beginning of a block
Ctrl—KK	Marks the end of a block
Ctrl—KY	Erases a marked block of text

When words, lines, and blocks are deleted with any command, they're held temporarily in the unerase buffer. The command Ctrl—U calls it back from the buffer and inserts it at the cursor.

Tip: The unerase buffer is normally small, but you can make it bigger with WSCHANGE by setting aside more memory for it. At the WSCHANGE Main Menu, type CCH and set the unerase buffer to at least 1000 bytes. (One byte equals one character.)

Shaping pages and paragraphs

The term *formatting* refers to providing paragraphs and pages with margins, indents, line spacing, different kinds of fonts, and other visual and organizational features. *Reformatting* refers to fitting newly entered text into previously established formatting, or applying new formatting to previously typed text.

Formatting as you type

As you type, WordStar will format the onscreen paragraphs to fit within the current settings of the margins, line spacing, number of columns, and justification. Other formatting, such as fonts, is taken care of when the document is printed. The following is a list of the onscreen formatting that WordStar takes care of when you type:

Wordwrap   Breaks the line of text as it passes the right margin, and moves it down to start the next line. This eliminates the standard use of the carriage return.

Auto-align   Automatically reformats the paragraph when edits, additions, and other changes within a paragraph throw off onscreen format and paragraph alignment.

Manual reformat   With auto-align off, changing a paragraph will distort its appearance until it no longer fits the margins and line spacing. Use Ctrl–B to reformat a paragraph from the cursor position.

Reformat entire text file   The command Ctrl–QU reformats the remainder of the file from the cursor position. Auto-align works only on the paragraph being worked on. When you make changes to margins, line spacing, number of columns, character size, or anything else affecting the entire text file, you must reformat the entire text file.

Splitting the line

The command Ctrl–N inserts a carriage return at the cursor, without moving the cursor. This is called splitting the line. It inserts a new line without moving the cursor down. Everything after the cursor is moved down one line. Use this to split a paragraph and then continue typing.

Getting onscreen help

There are three main ways of getting onscreen help or reminders with WordStar commands and individual features; You can use the Edit Menu, Help Menu, or classic command menus.

Using the Edit Menu

The Edit Menu isn't really a command menu. It's only an onscreen reminder of various commands that are available when you're writing and editing documents.

It appears on the document screen only when help level 3 is active. The Edit Menu fills the top third of the screen, and thus takes up space that can be better used for displaying lines of text.

The Edit Menu is recommended only for new users who need the a constant onscreen reminder of basic word-processing commands. It's much better to keep the space free for displaying lines of text.

Using the Help Menu

WordStar has a built-in help feature that contains information on using every feature of the program. To get a help message on a pull-down menu feature:

1. Call the menu.
2. Put the highlight on the feature in question.
3. Press the F1 key, or use Ctrl−J to ask for help.
4. When finished using Help, press the Esc key.

Calling the command menus

The commands for calling the command menus are listed on the Edit Menu as a memory aid. These other menus can be called only when you're in either the document or nondocument editing modes.

Command	What it does
Ctrl−O	Calls the Onscreen Format Menu
Ctrl−K	Calls the Block & Save Menu
Ctrl−P	Calls the Print Controls Menu
Ctrl−Q	Calls the Quick Menu
Ctrl−J	Calls the Help Menu features

9
CHAPTER

Using
the Onscreen
Format Menu

This chapter covers the commands and options on the classic Onscreen Format Menu. These commands and options will execute many of the functions also found on the pull-down Style and Layout Menus.

Introduction and overview

WordStar has always had onscreen formatting. This means, within limits, that what you see onscreen looks like the printed document. It means that you can set up a document visually, changing it onscreen until it looks the way you want it to look. In addition to onscreen formatting, WordStar's page preview feature gives you WYSIWYG, or "what you see is what you get"—which shows you in advance *exactly* how the printed version will look.

Figure 9-1 is an illustration of the Onscreen Format Menu. Most of its commands and options are also available through the pull-down Style and Layout Menus. These include margin and tab settings, typing mode, and most features with which you can modify the document screen.

Think of the Onscreen Format Menu as a memory aid. Use it to help you learn the Ctrl−O series of commands. Either select these features through the menu or execute them with Ctrl−O commands. In time, you'll find that using the Ctrl−O commands is the quickest way to execute most onscreen formatting.

```
┌─────────────── O N S C R E E N   F O R M A T   M E N U ───────────────┐
│  MARGINS & TABS            TYPING                      DISPLAY          │
│  L left  R right      C center line              P page preview         │
│  G temporary indent   ] right flush line         D turn command tags off│
│  X release margin     V vertically center        B change screen settings│
│  I set/clear tabs     E enter soft hyphen        K open or switch window │
│  O ruler to text      H turn auto-hyphenation on N size current window  │
│  U column layout      J turn justification off   ? status               │
│  Y page layout        A turn auto-align off      Z paragraph number     │
│  F paragraph styles   W turn word wrap off       # page numbering       │
│  S set line spacing   ↵ turn Enter closes dialog on  N notes            │
└────────────────────────────────────────────────────────────────────────┘
```

9-1   Onscreen Format Menu.

Calling and using the Onscreen Format Menu

You can call the Onscreen Format Menu at any time while a document is open for writing and editing. Simply hold down the Ctrl key and type the letter O.

When the menu appears, select any command or feature by typing the highlighted letter beside it. Sometimes this will execute a command. Sometimes it will embed a printing command in the text file. Sometimes it will call a dialog box, where you can type responses or make selections. There are three ways to escape from an onscreen menu without issuing a command:

- Press the spacebar
- Press the Esc key
- Use WordStar's abort command, Ctrl−U

Onscreen Format definitions

There are 27 commands on the Onscreen Format Menu. Following are a list of these commands and options, with brief definitions of what each does or is used for.

OL   Calls the Ruler Line dialog box, where you can set the left margin. Embeds a .LM command at the cursor position.

OR   Calls the Ruler Line dialog box, where you can reset the right margin. Embeds a .RM command at the cursor position.

OG   Temporarily moves the left margin by a tab stop.

OX   Temporarily releases the right margin so you can type text beyond it. Press the Enter key to reengage the margin.

OI   Calls the Ruler Line dialog box, where you can set the tab stop settings. Embeds a ruler line in the document at the cursor position (.RR), with tabs set as directed.

OO   Embeds a ruler line in the document at the cursor position. This ruler line is a dot command that you can edit in order to change the left and right margins and set tab stops.

OU   Calls the Column Layout dialog box. This is used for setting up newspaper or magazine columns. Type in a number of columns or gutter size, and WordStar will calculate the correct column width and embed a .CO command.

OY Calls the Page Layout dialog box. This is used to set top and bottom margins, page offset, header and footer margins, page size, and page orientation.

OF Calls the Paragraph Style Menu. You use this to create, edit, and manage paragraph style tags.

OS Calls the Alignment and Spacing dialog box. You can set the line spacing from 1 to 9.

OC Centers the line of text the cursor is on.

O] Sets the line the cursor is on to flush right alignment.

OV Vertically centers the contents of the page the cursor is on.

OE Inserts a soft hyphen at the cursor position. Used for fine control over hyphenation when auto-hyphenation doesn't work as well as you require.

OH Toggles auto-hyphenation on and off by embedding a dot command at the cursor position. Can be used to protect portions of a text file from hyphenation by auto-align, or a global reformatting.

OJ Toggles full justification on and off by embedding a dot command at the cursor position. Can be used to format portions of a text file in full or other justification, and to protect text from realignment by auto-align or a global reformatting.

OA Toggles auto-align on and off. Lasts for the duration of write-and-edit session.

OW Toggles word wrap on and off. Lasts for duration of write-and-edit session.

O(Enter) O with a bend arrow means to type O and press the Enter key. Changes function of the Enter key on dialog boxes—where pressing Enter will either move you from item to item or execute the dialog box.

OP Turns on page preview. Used for viewing the document in true WYSIWYG graphic display. It can also be used for creating fax files from the currently open document. (These fax files are in correct format for transmission through most fax boards.)

OD Toggles print command tags on and off. Depending on the screen settings, this command can hide or display dot commands, the flag column, and soft space dots.

OB Calls the Screen Settings dialog box. Used to control display of dot commands, flag column, soft space dots, scroll bar, style bar, status line, ruler line, and contents of the pull-down menus.

OK Opens a second window or toggles between two windows if a second one is open.

OM Calls the Change Window Size dialog box. Choose between full screen, half screen, or type in a specific number of lines to display onscreen.

O? Calls the system status readout. Shows the current status of memory use by WordStar and companion programs and the serial number.

OZ Calls the Paragraph Outline Number dialog box. Used to control the level and type of paragraph number inserted at the cursor position.

O#   Calls the Page Numbering dialog box. Used to toggle page number printing on and off. Also controls the number printed and its position on the page.

ON   Calls the Notes Menu. Used to create, modify, and manage five of WordStar's six types of embedded notes.

Setting the layout with dialog boxes

All onscreen formatting features have preset values or defaults. You can change them either by customizing WordStar or by customizing paragraph style tags. WordStar defaults are drawn from the program itself, and can be changed with WSCHANGE or WINSTALL. Paragraph tag defaults are drawn from the style sheet in the WSSTYLE overlay file. This file is also called the library. Those defaults are changed by editing the paragraph tag and saving changes to the library.

The layout and style values you see in any dialog box are drawn from the paragraph formatting assigned to the text at the current cursor position. They change when the format changes.

Modifications through a dialog box apply only to the specific document. WordStar reverts to its default settings the next time you open a new document, or it uses the layout settings in an existing document when you reopen it.

If you find yourself making the same layout changes every time you boot WordStar, you can permanently change the default settings inside the program itself. You're therefore making WordStar more convenient to use by adapting it to your personal needs.

Make permanent changes by customizing a copy of WordStar with the WSCHANGE program. To learn how to permanently customize WordStar, read chapter 34, *Customizing WordStar with WSCHANGE*.

Setting margins

This section discusses document margins, describes and defines options, and tells you how to use margins to format your hardcopy.

Margins are "text boundaries." They set the limits of the printing area. There are eight different kinds of margins to use in your documents. Following is a table of WordStar's default margin settings:

Margin	Default setting
Left	0.0″ or column 1
Right	6.5″ or column 65
Page offset	0.8″ or 8 columns
Top	0.5″ or 3 lines
Bottom	1.33″ or 8 lines
Header	0.33″ or 2 lines

Footer	0.33 " or 2 lines
Paragraph	off (or none)

The above settings are for body text in the standard version as it comes from WordStar International. If the defaults are different in your version of WordStar, someone has changed them with WSCHANGE, or someone has redefined the body text tag in either the document being worked on or in the library of tags in the WSSTYLE overlay file. If you want the factory defaults, simply edit any body text tag and copy it to the library.

Margin restrictions

Obviously, margins must be kept within the physical boundaries of the paper being used. This available printing area varies from printer to printer, and from font to font. WordStar never knows nor cares what size paper you have in the printer. It assumes that the margins are appropriate. If you set your margins beyond what the printer can handle, or beyond the edge of the paper, the excess text simply won't print. Always use page preview before printing.

Tip: Most laser printers have a mechanical margin of $^1/4$ " all around the page. It cannot print outside this margin.

Different units of measure

The standard unit of measure for the U.S. version of WordStar is inches. WordStar also recognizes ruler units (or columns), lines, centimeters, and points as units of measurement. You can change the default for WordStar, or any stylesheet, by using the utility program WSCHANGE.

Use whichever units you understand best. You can mix different units of measure in a single document. For example, if you set line height in points and left/right margins in inches, WordStar will automatically convert these to the current default unit of measure.

To indicate a unit of measure, type the appropriate symbol after its number value. Following is a table of the available units of measure, with the symbols used to indicate them on a dialog box or dot command:

Symbol	Unit of measure
", i, or in	inches (the default)
r	columns (ruler units)
l	lines (line height units)
c or cm	centimeters
p or pt	points ($^1/72$ inch)

Changing WordStar measurement defaults

WordStar's default unit of measure is inches. To change the default to a different standard of measure for vertical and horizontal measurement, run WSCHANGE.

At the WSCHANGE Main Menu, type DAG to get to the menu for setting defaults. Changing the default unit won't affect margins already set with dot commands.

The width of the ruler unit, one space in the ruler line, is set by the horizontal movements index (HMI). To change the default HMI, run WSCHANGE. At the Main Menu, type DNA2 to get to the menu for changing the HMI. The default setting is $180/1800$ or $1/10$ inch. Never change this casually. A wrong setting can wreak havoc.

You can also change the line height unit of measure here. The default for the line height measurement is $240/1440$ or $1/16$ inch. Before changing the default line height measurement unit, be advised that some printers can't support different line height units.

Setting left and right margins

The left and right margins are set on the Ruler Line dialog box (see Fig. 9-2). All other margins (top and bottom, header and footer, etc.) are set with the Page Layout dialog box. See the section later in this chapter, *Setting the page layout*. The steps for calling the Ruler Line dialog box and using it to set the left and right margins are as follows:

1. Place the cursor on the line where you want new margins to take effect.
2. Use Ctrl−OL or Ctrl−OR to call the dialog box, or simply click on the ruler line at the top of the document screen.
3. Type in the new margin(s) and execute the dialog box with either Ctrl−K or by clicking on the OK push-button to execute them.

```
                          Ruler Line
  Left Margin:  .00"    1st Line Indent:          OK

  Right Margin: 6.50"                            Cancel

     Tab Stops: .50" 1.00" 6.00"
```

9-2 Ruler Line dialog box.

The Ruler Line dialog box changes the margins by embedding the dot commands .LM #*n* and .RM #*n* in the document. The # stands for the value of measure, and *n* stands for the unit of measure for the margins. Margins take effect below the embedded command, to the end of the document or until countermanded.

You can set margins for the whole document, or for individual paragraphs and lines. To set margins and tabs for the whole document, make your changes at the beginning of the document. Once familiar with these dot commands, you might find it quicker to type them in directly instead of going through the Ruler Line dialog box.

Tip: To use a particular set of margins over again, mark the dot commands as a block of text, then write the block to a file on disk with Ctrl−KW. Later you can read them into other documents with Ctrl−KR.

Manually embedding left and right margin commands

You can change margins by typing the dot commands .LM and .RM, followed by their respective measurements, directly into a document. Use the following steps:

1. Use Ctrl−N to insert a new, blank line for the command—above the point where you want the new margin to begin.
2. Put the cursor at column 1 on this blank line.
3. For the left margin, type .LM followed by the left margin value. The left margin will shift as you type the number value. For the right margin, type .RM and the right margin value. The right margin will shift as you type the number value.

The new margin will be active below the command line, and will remain in effect to the end of the document or until another left or right margin dot command is embedded. To restore the default style sheet margin, embed either command without a value.

Releasing the margins

The command Ctrl−OX is used to temporarily release both margins on a single line of text. The left margin will default to column 1. Text will extend beyond the right margin, as wordwrap and auto-align are temporarily disengaged. Releasing the margins is useful for printing extra long lines on a page.

The margins will remain released until you end the line with a carriage return. The margins will also be restored if you move the cursor off that line.

Tip: If you're printing part of the document in a smaller font, it isn't necessary to release the margins before typing the text. Just attach the smaller font to the document first. When you type in a smaller font, WordStar will automatically adjust to fit it inside the margins. Don't forget to switch back to the normal font at the end of the text.

A line of text typed with the margin release won't be protected from a reformat command—unless you embed .AW OFF above it, and .AW ON below it.

Automatic paragraph indentation

First Line Indent is an option on the Ruler Line dialog box. The default setting is None. When set to any value, WordStar will automatically indent the first line of every paragraph as you begin typing the paragraph. So you no longer have to use the Tab key for manual indentation. You can also apply this feature retroactively by placing it at the beginning of your document and then reformatting the text file.

Unfortunately, this feature also indents the beginning of every new line you type (except for dot commands). If you're typing a document with section or subsection headings, or other lines you want to start flush left, they'll be paragraph indented as well.

This can interfere somewhat with your use of the temporary indent command in making hanging indentations. If you're writing documents with a complicated layout, you might want to forget about using automatic paragraph indentation. You can't go wrong with a simple tab.

Temporary indentation

The temporary indent command, Ctrl−OG, is used to make paragraphs with hanging indentations. Each time it's issued it indents the left margin one tab stop to the right. It uses the currently set tabs displayed on the ruler line. Its position on the ruler line is marked by a]. Move over as many tab stops as you want. This command works best when installed as a macro on a function key.

Tip: Never use the Tab key to begin any paragraph set for hanging indentation. It embeds a Tab command that you'll have to delete if you decide to reformat the paragraph to different margins.

Below are some guidelines for working with temporary indentation:

- Paragraphs typed after this command align to the temporary indentation as though you had shifted the left margin.
- Existing paragraphs can be reformatted to hanging indentation with this command in combination with either Ctrl−B or Ctrl−QU.
- The command is in effect after and below the cursor position. So put all or part of any paragraph in hanging indentation.
- The command will remain active until you issue a reformat command or a carriage return.
- To remove hanging indentation from a paragraph, use Ctrl−B.
- To protect hanging indentation from reformatting, mark it with .AW OFF above the paragraph, and .AW ON below the paragraph.

Uses for hanging indentation

With hanging indentation you can format all or part of a paragraph away from the left margin. It's quicker than using .LM to change the left margin, but is restricted to preset tab stops. It affects only one paragraph at a time, and the next paragraph typed will revert to the set left margin. You can use this feature to type numbered lists, ordered lists, and unordered lists. It can also be used to leave space for an illustration to be pasted into camera-ready copy.

The hanging indentation command Ctrl−OG is easiest to use when installed on a function key. It's too awkward to issue it through the menu, and only a little better as a Ctrl−command. But as a single-stroke macro, it can brighten every document you write.

Plain indented numbered lists

There are two ways to type indented numbered lists: with the whole list indented, or with hanging numbers and the body of the list indented. The same procedure can be used to format an alphabetical list. To type a list that's entirely indented:

1. Put the cursor on a blank line where you want the list to begin.
2. Use Ctrl−OG to insert a single temporary indent (its position on the ruler line is marked by a]).
3. Press the spacebar once. Then type the number, a period, and two blank spaces.
4. Now type the information that belongs with that list item. (Notice that auto-align reformats the step text to the indented left margin.)
5. At the end of the list item, press the Enter key twice.
6. On this new line, repeat steps 2−5. Continue until you've finished the entire list.

To protect this indented list from accidental reformatting, embed the dot command .AW OFF on a blank line above it, and .AW ON on the blank line below it.

Tip: To really speed this up, type a blank list with the steps above. Mark the blank list as a block, then write it to disk with Ctrl−KW. Then use Ctrl−KR to read it into documents wherever needed. You can type your information into these boilerplate lists with a minimum of effort.

Indented lists with hanging numbers

Many people find it attractive to indent the text of a numbered list, but leave the numbers flush against the left margin. The same procedure can be used to create alphabetical or bulleted lists. To type an indented list with hanging numbers, follow these steps:

1. Put the cursor on a blank line where you want to begin the list.
2. For single-digit numbers, press the spacebar twice, and then type the number and a period.
3. Hold down the Ctrl key and type P. Then release the Ctrl key and press the Enter key.
4. A dash (-) should appear in the right flag column. This indicates you've correctly issued an overprint line command. (If a J appears, you forgot to release the Ctrl key. Delete backward and try again.)

5. Use Ctrl−OG to insert a temporary indent (marked on the ruler line by a]).
6. Now type the information to go under that item in the numbered list.
7. When through typing, press the Enter key twice.
8. Repeat steps 1−7 for each item in the numbered list.

This will produce a numbered list with the text indented one tab stop and the numbers flush on the margin. You'll find this a very attractive way to set up your numbered lists.

To protect this indented list from accidental reformatting, embed the dot command .AW OFF on a blank line above it, and .AW ON on the blank line below it.

Tip: To speed this procedure up, type a blank list with the steps above. Mark the blank list as a block and then write it to disk with Ctrl−KW. Then use Ctrl−KR to read it into documents wherever needed. You can type your information into these boilerplate lists with the minimum of effort.

Indented bulleted lists

A bulleted list contains information in items that are marked by a bullet of some kind in place of numbers. Like numbered lists, they are most attractive when formatted with a hanging indent. The most common bullets are an asterisk, ASCII character 220 (a solid square), or ASCII characters 1−10.

Inserting extended ASCII characters

Due to changes since WordStar 4, your printer might not successfully print the extended ASCII character set. The only way to find out is to insert some in a document and try to print them. If they don't print, contact the WordStar Technical Support department and see if they can send you a better driver for your printer.

There are two ways of inserting extended ASCII characters into your documents. You can use the Extended Character Menu with Ctrl−P0, or you can use the Alt key and the numeric keypad to type in the characters by their number.

Frequently used bullet characters

The most commonly used bullet character is the asterisk (*). Following is a list of ten special ASCII characters that are frequently used as bullets in ordered lists.

ASCII #	Character
Alt−1	☺
Alt−2	●
Alt−3	♥
Alt−4	♦
Alt−5	♣

Alt − 6 ♠

Alt − 7 •

Alt − 8 ▫

Alt − 9 ○

Alt − 10 ◉

Most late-model dot-matrix printers have these ASCII characters in their internal character sets. How well the characters print, however, depends entirely on the printer make and model. If using a laser printer, you should have no difficulty at all, depending on the font set being used.

When using downloadable fonts with WordStar, some font sets have several excellent bullet characters to choose from. To learn how to use them, read the documentation that comes with each package of downloadable fonts.

Using the Extended Character dialog box

If you don't know the ASCII number of an extended character, you can find and insert it from the Extended Character dialog box.

1. Place the cursor where you want the extended character to be inserted. Hold down the Ctrl key and type P0.
2. The Extended Character dialog will appear.
3. Find the extended character on this menu you want to insert in your document.
4. Type its number and press the Enter key. It will be inserted at the cursor.

Typing extended ASCII characters

You can type in extended ASCII characters at the cursor position, but you must use the numeric keypad to do this.

1. Place the cursor where you want the extended character to appear. Hold down the Alt key.
2. On the numeric keypad, type the ASCII number of the character to be inserted.
3. After typing the number, release the Alt key.
4. The extended ASCII character will be inserted at the cursor position.

Paragraph alignment and line spacing

This section explains different types of paragraph and line justification, and describes uses for them. Paragraph alignment is an important element in formatting documents, and makes a great difference in how a document looks and how easy it is to read.

The Alignment and Spacing dialog box

Most elements of alignment and different types of spacing are set up through the Alignment and Spacing dialog box. The remainder can be set individually on the Onscreen Format Menu, or the pull-down Layout Menu. There are three different ways to call this dialog box:

- Click on the double-sided arrow in the status line.
- Use Ctrl–OS
- Select Alignment and Spacing from the Layout menu.

Setting line spacing

A line is a specific row of text onscreen or on a printed page. Line spacing controls how many lines of text a single line, including the space above and below it, occupies in a document. This is set on the Alignment and Spacing dialog box. You can set line spacing from 1 to 9.

Setting leading space or line height

The term *leading* refers to the amount of vertical space a line takes up on the printed page. This is the same thing as line height. Measure it from the bottom of one line to the bottom of the following line.

You can access the Line Height command through the Alignment and Spacing dialog box. Insert the command directly with .LH #*n* (# being a number and *n* being a unit of measurement).

With absolute leading as the default, lines are equally spaced, regardless of font size. Line height can vary between 2 and 255. The smaller the line height, the more lines you can print per page. (For example, a 12-point typeface needs a .LH .17" or .LH 12pt, etc.) Or use .LH A, where A means automatic and WordStar sets the leading automatically.

Setting paragraph justification

Paragraph justification is a simple thing to use, but a complicated subject to talk about. It doesn't help that WordStar documentation, menus, and dialog boxes use the misnomer *justification* for *full justification*, and use the term *alignment* without defining it carefully. Following are the various terms and definitions for justification and paragraph alignment available through WordStar:

Alignment   Horizontal position of text within the left and right margins. This includes justification, which determines how the text fills each line and paragraph.

Full justified   Adds or subtracts spaces between words to make each line exactly the same length, so that both margins are even. Spaces can be either incremental or proportional. You can toggle full justification on and off with the .OJ (output justification) command.

Left justified   The text is lined up against the left margin, to print a smooth left margin and a ragged right margin. Also called *ragged right*.

Right justified   The text is lined up against the right margin, printing a smooth right margin and a ragged left margin. Also called *ragged left*. You can create right-justified paragraphs by using the Alignment and Spacing dialog box. You can also right justify only the current line with Ctrl−O].

Center justified   Each line of text is centered on the space between the set margins, leaving both margins ragged. Also called *output centering*. You can make center-justified paragraphs with the .OC embedded dot command, and the text will be justified as you typed it (called *output centering*). Or you can center only the line the cursor is on with the Ctrl−OC command.

Toggling auto-align on and off

The commmand Ctrl−OA toggles auto-align on and off. This is the feature that realigns paragraphs as you make changes to them. With auto-align off, deletions, additions, and other changes will throw off paragraph alignment. You can realign paragraphs with the manual reformat command Ctrl−B, or realign entire text files with Ctrl−QU.

Turning auto-align off lasts for the duration of the current write-and-edit session, but it'll be back on when you next open a file.

Toggling word wrap on and off

The command Ctrl−OW toggles word wrap on and off. This is the feature that formats paragraphs as you write them. It breaks off lines of text as they pass the right margin, moves them down, and starts new lines below. With word wrap off, lines will continue until you issue a carriage return or use the manual reformat command Ctrl−B.

Turning word wrap off will last for the duration of the write-and-edit session, but it'll be on when you open your next file.

Protecting paragraphs from realignment

Paragraphs that are formatted with special alignment, like hanging indentation, or a different line spacing, can be undone by the next realignment command (which will restore them to the current margins and line spacing).

To protect specially aligned paragraphs and lines for realignment, use the dot command .AW OFF above and .AW ON below the text.

Vertically centering page contents

The command Ctrl−OV will vertically center the contents of an entire page between the top and bottom margins. This doesn't always work, however, especially if the page is too full. It works best on partial pages or pages that have graphics.

Using hyphenation to control spacing

The term *hyphenation* in word processing means inserting hyphens into words at syllabic divisions in order to break words at the end of a line, and thus fit more text on a given page.

Auto-hyphenation is a feature that WordStar uses to hyphenate words, as you type them or reformat them, without you having to specify where the hyphens belong.

The command Ctrl−OH toggled auto-hyphenation on and off. It embeds the dot command .HY ON or .HY OFF in the text, on the line above the current paragraph, or below the current dot command line.

Setting the page layout

From the Page Layout dialog box, you can control such things as the printing offset, top and bottom margins, header and footer margins, page orientation, page size, and paper bin selection.

What is printing offset?

Printing offset is the distance from the left edge of the page to the left margin of your text. WordStar has a default printing offset of 0.8″ (8 columns, so you don't have to move the left margin to print normally. With a 6.5″ right margin, this will print a balanced page on standard $8^{1}/_{2} \times 11$ paper—whatever font you're using.

Setting the printing offset

The printing offset is normally set at the beginning of the text file, and the same offset used for the entire document. The offset serves as a baseline for the left margin, to ensure a consistent appearance to documents.

Tip: Most laser printers, especially the HP LaserJet, have a built-in printing offset of $^{1}/_{4}″$ all the way around the page. It can't print outside this offset, and text outside it will be lost during printing.

Shifting the offset is a device for controlling how much, or how little, text gets printed on a page. Printing offset is simply a margin by a different name. It's controlled through the Page Layout dialog box. Use Ctrl−OY to call it, or select Page from the pull-down Layout Menu.

Printing offset for odd/even pages

WordStar allows you to print odd and even pages as a variable on the Print dialog box. This allows you to create documents with back-to-back pages.

Some people recommend setting the even page offset at .50″ and odd page offset at 1.00″ for standard computer paper. For many printers and uses, however, this is acceptable. If the paper you're using is opaque (preventing you from seeing one side of the page through the other), it doesn't really matter.

For a more precise lineup of left and right pages, especially when printing on an HP LaserJet or compatible, I recommend setting .POO .96″ and .POE .50″ because this seems to achieve the most perfect alignment for pages where the printing shows through.

1. Place the cursor at the beginning of the text file.
2. Call the Page Layout dialog box with Ctrl−OY, or select Page from the pull-down Layout Menu.
3. Set the odd and even printing offsets as desired. Use any unit of measure you want.
4. WordStar will embed the dot commands .POO and .POE at the cursor position, with each command followed by the distance of the offset from the left edge of the paper.

Tip: An undocumented fact about WordStar is its ability to print documents back-to-front. If, for example, you're printing a 50-page document, type in the range of pages as 50−1. Print odd pages first. Then you won't have to shuffle the pages to get them in the correct order for printing the even-numbered pages.

Setting the top and bottom margins

The *top margin* is the distance from the top edge of the paper to the first line of printing in the hardcopy. The *bottom margin* is the distance from the bottom edge of the paper to the last line of printing in the hardcopy. Both these margins are set through the Page Layout dialog box.

The Top and Bottom margins determine how many lines are available on the page for printing text. The smaller the margins, the more lines you can print.

WordStar comes with a top margin default of .50″, and a bottom margin default of 1.33″. I recommend you set the top margin to 1.00″ for a more evenly balanced page layout. This is especially necessary if you intend to print two or more headers.

1. Place the cursor at the beginning of the text file.
2. Call the Page Layout dialog box with Ctrl−OY, or select Page on the pull-down Layout Menu.
3. Set the top and bottom margins as desired. Use any unit of measure you want.
4. WordStar will embed the dot commands .MT and .MB at the cursor position, each followed by the distance of the offset from the edge of the paper.

Header and footer margins

The header margin is the space set aside in the top margin for printing header messages. The footer margin is the space set aside in the bottom margin for printing footer messages.

WordStar can print between one and five header and/or footer messages on any given page. Obviously, you must leave room for all these information lines. The default top margin of .5″ and header margin of .33″ leave only .17″ (one line) for header text.

Tip: Most laser printers, including the HP LaserJet, have a built-in printing offset of 1/4″ all the way around the page. It can't print outside this offset, and text outside it will be lost during printing. You must change the top margin setting accordingly.

To print all five possible header or footer lines, you must allow a header/footer margin of at least .85″, so a 1.00″ top margin is barely sufficient. Don't put the headers or footers too close to the body text or they'll look crowded.

1. Place the cursor at the beginning of the text file.
2. Use Ctrl−OY to call the Page Layout dialog box, or select Page from the pull-down Layout Menu.
3. Set the header and/or footer margins wide enough to contain all the lines of text to be printed there. (Any header or footer you don't leave room for simply won't be printed.)
4. The dialog box will embed the dot commands .HM or .FM, respectively, for header or footer margins. Each command is followed by a number representing the distance from the edge of the body text area to the outer limit of the header/footer line.

The headers and footers themselves can't be set up through this dialog box, nor through the Onscreen Format Menu. Either embed their dot commands manually or do so through the pull-down Layout Menu's Headers/Footers option.

WordStar can print a maximum of 100 characters in any header or footer. This includes carriage returns, extended characters (which each count as three characters), and control characters. This length can be increased with WSCHANGE.

If your headers and footers don't print, and you've set margins wide enough to accommodate their lines, you might be running out of buffer space. You can either reduce the number of header or footer lines, or use WSCHANGE to make the buffer space larger. At the WSCHANGE Main Menu, type CC2A, and enlarge the buffer size.

For complete information on using headers and footers in your documents, see the chapter entitled *Printing documents with headers and footers*.

Setting the page orientation

Page orientation is the way the lines on a page are set up to print along the length of the paper. Portrait orientation is the standard and default. It prints lines of text perpendicular to the length of the page. Landscape orientation prints lines of text or graphics horizontal to the length. WordStar offers both through the Page Layout dialog box.

1. Put the cursor at the top of the document or page to be printed in Portrait or Landscape orientation.
2. Call the Page Layout dialog box with Ctrl−OY, or select the Page option from the pull-down Layout Menu.
3. Set orientation for either portrait or landscape, as desired. (You need to select portrait only to switch back to the default after using the landscape orientation.)
4. The dialog box will embed the dot commands .PR OR=L for landscape, and .PR OR=P for portrait.

Tip: Bear in mind that when you print in landscape the printing is going on the paper sideways. Remember to set the page length accordingly and move the right margin to 9″.

Setting page size

The page size means the page's dimensions. U.S. standard letter paper is $8^{1}/_{2} \times 11$″. Legal paper is $8^{1}/_{2} \times 14$″. If printing on either of these or nonstandard paper, you must tell WordStar the physical size of the page being printed on.

Sheets of labels are a common, nonstandard printing surface. When a printing tractor feeds mailing labels, remember that each label should register as a single page. A 1″ label, then, is a page 1″ high. Set the page length through the Page Layout dialog box, or embed the .PL dot command directly. It belongs at the beginning of the document, or the top of the page getting different orientation.

Selecting a paper bin

A paper bin and a paper tray are the same thing. The only difference is who makes the printer and what they like to call it.

When you select a paper bin through the Page Layout dialog box, WordStar inserts the .BN dot command, followed by the number of the particular bin or tray, in the text file at the cursor position.

If your printer has more than one paper bin, use this option to select the bin a particular page uses for printing. This is especially useful when you're printing on letterhead stationery. The first page of the document goes on the letterhead. The subsequent pages go on blank stationery in the alternative bin.

The paper bin option is equally useful if your printer has an envelope feeder bin. You can print the envelope from one bin and the document from the alternative bin. This lets you do everything for a form-letter mailout in a single print runoff.

Or if you're simply printing documents larger than a single bin of paper, mark the text file to switch bins at the point one runs out of paper. If the second bin doesn't hold enough paper to finish the print runoff, mark the text file to switch bins again. This will keep the runoff uninterrupted, and give you the chance to refill the bins.

1. Place the cursor at the top of the page in the text file where you want it to switch bins.
2. Call the Page Layout Dialog box with Ctrl−OY.
3. Type in the name or number of the paper bin, or select it from the onscreen list.
4. The dialog box will insert a .BN dot command followed by the number of the particular bin or tray in the text file at the cursor position.

Setting and using tab stops

The Tab key can be one of the most useful keys on the keyboard. You can use tabs to indent paragraphs or to set up perfectly aligned columns of words or numbers. WordStar's tabs work just like the ones on a typewriter—except they're much more flexible.

Tip: Never use the Tab key to begin a paragraph set for hanging indentation. It will embed a Tab command that you'll have to delete if you decide to reformat the paragraph to different margins.

What are tab stops?

Tab stops are preset movements of the Tab key. WordStar comes with default tab stops set every half inch, or every five columns out to column 56. Each time you press the Tab key, it moves the cursor over one tab setting.

Standard tab stops are identified on the ruler line by a right-pointing triangle, and decimal tabs are identified by a small dot. When the insert mode is on, the Tab key will insert a tab command (Ctrl−I). When the overtype mode is on, the Tab key will move the cursor across lines of text a tab setting at a time, without inserting a tab command.

Three different kinds of tabs

WordStar has three kinds of tabs: Standard tabs, decimal tabs, and a special eight-column tab inserted with Ctrl−PI.

Standard tabs simply move your cursor to whatever point you set them. Text is inserted flush left against the tab stop when typed.

Decimal tabs are used for typing columns of numbers containing decimals. Numbers typed at a decimal tab are inserted to the left of the tab stop until you type the decimal or a space. Then they're inserted to the right.

Eight-column tabs are primarily used in nondocuments and rarely used in documents. They ignore existing tab stops, and move the cursor by eight columns whether a stop is set at all. The special tab character is assigned to the Tab key in the nondocument mode. You can insert it in the document mode with Ctrl−PI.

Unlike standard tab stops and decimal tabs, eight-column tabs aren't shown on the ruler line at all.

Six ways to set tab stops

There are six different ways of changing the tab stops. Each method gets exactly the same job done. Use whichever you like, or any combination of them.

- Set them with the Ruler Line dialog box
- Embed the .TB command directly in the document
- Edit an embedded ruler line
- Permanently change the default tab settings inside WordStar with WSCHANGE
- Edit the preset ruler lines using WSCHANGE
- Edit the ruler lines in any paragraph tag

Setting tabs with the Ruler Line dialog box

Tab stops can be reset in the Ruler Line dialog box. When you change or set tab stops here, WordStar embeds a .TB command line in the document. The new tabs take effect below this ruler line. They remain in effect until changed, or until the cursor passes another .TB line or embedded ruler line. If you want your tab stops to be in effect for the whole document, put the .TB line at the beginning of the text file.

1. Put the cursor at the point in the document where you want the tab stops to become active.
2. Use Ctrl−OI to call the ruler line dialog box. The cursor will be on the tab setting line when the dialog box appears. You can also click on the ruler line itself.
3. Either edit the existing tab settings or type in a whole new group of settings. The default unit of measurement is inches.
4. When all the tab settings are the way you want them, use Ctrl−K to accept them (or click on the OK push-button) and embed the .TB command. It looks like this:

    .TB.50″ 1.00″ 1.50″ 2.00″ 2.50″ 3.00″ 3.50″ 4.00″

5. The new tab settings become active below this line. If there are any mistakes on this line, you can edit it directly without having to go back to the Ruler Line dialog box.

Embedding the tab command directly

You can embed the .TB command directly in the document. Put the cursor at column 1 on a blank line in the text file, type .TB, and then enter the new tab settings in decimal inches. Be sure to put a blank space between each tab stop. The format is exactly the same as that used with the Ruler Line dialog box.

Set as many tab stops as will fit on the page, at any place you need them. Don't set tabs and margins beyond the edge of the page, or the printout will be ruined from that point on.

Editing the preset ruler lines

WordStar has 10 stored ruler lines you can preset however you want them. To insert a preset ruler line in your text file, type the .RR dot command, followed by the number of the stored ruler line 0−9, at the left margin.

You can edit these stored rulers using WSCHANGE. At the WSCHANGE Main Menu, type DAE, and then set each ruler individually. The format is the same as for typing tab setting at either the ruler line dialog box or on the .TB command line.

Tip: You might want to make a note of what the default settings are for these rulers in the event you decide to restore them later.

Setting tabs on embedded ruler line

The command Ctrl−OO embeds a ruler line dot command at the cursor position. Embedded rulers are discussed at length in the next section.

Setting and using decimal tabs

Decimal tabs are a special kind of tab used to format columns of numbers with decimals. To set one, use any of the six methods listed previously, but precede the tab setting with the pound or number symbol (#). A decimal tab is identified by a small dot on the ruler line.

When you type text at a decimal tab, it's inserted from right to left until you type the decimal or a space. Then the text is inserted normally. This aligns the column of numbers along the decimal, stacking them neatly for easy viewing.

Keeping an archive of tab settings

Tab settings can be a pain to get right. It's a good idea to make boilerplates of them to use when you need them again. You can create and maintain an archive of special tab settings and use them in other documents. Simply mark a .TB or .RR command line as a block of text and write it to a file of its own. Give each an identifying name and keep a written log of what each contains.

Tip: Use the same extension (.TAB or .RR, for example) and copy them to a separate directory or floppy disk. Then you won't have to remember what directory you were in when you made them. When you need one, use Ctrl−KR to read it into the new document.

Using embedded ruler lines

The onscreen ruler line shows the margins and tab stop settings at the cursor position in the document. The highlighted marker on the ruler line moves as you type, and indicates the current column position of your cursor in the body of the text. Whenever you make changes to margins or tab stop settings, the ruler line automatically changes to indicate the new settings.

There's also a dot command ruler line you can embed in the text file itself. And you can edit it to change the format and layout of margins and tabs in your documents.

Four ways to use embedded rulers

There are four different ways to use embedded rulers in your text files. Of these, there's no best method. Try all four, and decide which is best for you.

- Use Ctrl−OO to embed a copy of the current ruler line at the cursor position. Then edit that line as needed.
- Type the dot command .RR directly into the document, followed by a ruler line exactly like you need.
- Use between 0 and 9 predefined and stored ruler lines. (They're defined inside WordStar using WSCHANGE.)
- Save copies of all your embedded ruler lines by marking them as blocks of text, then using Ctrl−KW to write each to an archive file of its own. Next, use Ctrl−KR to read them into the text file where needed.

Embedding a ruler line

The command Ctrl−OO embeds a dot command with a ruler line that's a copy of the current onscreen ruler line. You can edit this embedded ruler line like any other text. But, as you change the margins and tabs on it, your edits become the current margins and tab settings.

Editing embedded ruler lines

The embedded ruler line is very useful for setting up text in a layout where you want to fine-control everything, with as few steps as possible. You can do this by editing or typing in the following characters after the .RR:

Character	Meaning
L	Left margin
R	Right margin
P	Paragraph margin
V	Temporary indent
!	Normal tab stop
#	Decimal tab stop
—	Column between margins

The ruler-line command

The embedded ruler-line dot command .RR can be typed directly into the text file just like any other dot command:

1. Put the cursor on a blank line at the point in the document where you want to embed a ruler line.
2. Type .RR on column 1.
3. After the .RR, type in the ruler line using the characters in the table in the previous section. You can always come back to this line for any corrections or changes you want to make.
4. When finished, move the cursor of the ruler line. The margins and tabs you just created will be active below this ruler line.

Using predefined ruler lines

This is the most difficult method. WordStar comes from the factory with only the first three stored rulers already defined. Before you can use the others, you must define them with the WSCHANGE customization program. However, once defined, they're the easiest to select. If you don't know how to customize and change WordStar with this utility program, read the chapter *Customizing Word- Star with WSCHANGE.*

1. Put the cursor on a blank line at the point in the document where you want to embed a ruler line.
2. Type .RR beginning on column 1.
3. After the .RR, type the number 0−9 of the stored ruler line you want to use. If you type the wrong number, you can always delete it and try again.
4. When finished, move the cursor to the ruler line. The margins and tabs you just created will be active below this ruler line. You should be able to tell, by looking at them, whether you've selected the correct stored ruler.

Making an archive of ruler lines

Embedded rulers, like tab settings, are hard to get right. Fortunately, once you get them right you can save them and reuse them endlessly.

One of the greatest benefits of word processing is that once you type something you never have to type it again. This is called the *boilerplate* concept of word processing. All text files can be used over and over again. Individual paragraphs, tables, graphs, etc., can be saved as individual files and copied in wherever needed. The same is true of embedded ruler lines.

1. Whenever you write or insert an embedded ruler line, it becomes text like anything else. You can mark it above and below as a block of text (with Ctrl−KB and Ctrl−KK).
2. After it's blocked, use Ctrl−KW to write the ruler line to a file of its own.
3. Give the file a name that identifies what it's used for in a document.
4. When you need that ruler line again, use Ctrl−KR to read it into the file at the cursor position.

Keep a backup archive of your ruler lines on a separate floppy disk. Label the disk with the files archived on it. With an archive on floppy disk, you don't have to remember which directory you were working in when you archived a ruler line in the first place. If you give them all the same file extension (for example, .RR), you can use the DOS LOCATE command to find them and the COPY command to archive and retrieve them.

Making tables with tabs

For making tables with special tab settings, you must embed two ruler lines in the text file. The first ruler goes above the table, and contains the margins and tab stop settings for your table. The second goes below the table, and contains the margins and tab settings for body text. This restores normal margins, tabs, etc.

It's standard practice to single-space tables of information in documents with double-spaced body text. This helps the table stand out even more from the body text. Embed a dot command above and below the table to protect it from reformatting.

Tab settings vary from table to table, depending on the number of columns and the width of information in each. After you set your tab stops on the first ruler line, mark both ruler lines as a block of text and write them to an archive file.

Put some blank lines between the two ruler lines to give yourself room to work. To type the table, tab to the first stop and type the information. Repeat this for each column. At the end of the line, issue a carriage return and type the next line.

When the table is finished, delete any blank lines between its bottom and the second ruler line. This will tighten its appearance. If you know you're going to use this table in other documents, mark it as a block of text and write it to an archive file with Ctrl−KW.

Putting boxes around tables

Putting boxes around tables can make them distinctive and more attractive. Word-Star added a box drawing capability as early as release 4. The extended graphics characters and commands to use them are installed on the function keys as Alt−key combinations.

How well these boxes print depends entirely on your printer. It must have the extended graphics character set built in, or use font sets that contain them. Most 24-pin printers have them built in. If you have a Hewlett-Packard LaserJet or equivalent, then you can put attractive boxes around your text. Unfortunately, if your printer doesn't support WordStar's line drawing characters, you're pretty much out of luck.

Line and box drawing characters

WordStar's line and box drawing symbols are installed as Alt−function key macros. The extended character set is available through the Extended Character dialog box, or you can insert them as Alt commands through the numeric keypad. They're listed in Table 9-1.

To insert an extended character, hold down the Alt key, type the character number on the numeric keypad, and then release the Alt key. Before the printer can print these high-bit or extended characters, they must be in the font set the printer is using. The font set can be in either the printer's internal fonts, a font cartridge, or a downloaded soft font.

If the characters aren't in the font set being used, WordStar will interpret and print them as their low-bit ASCII equivalent. This will produce Es and Ds, etc., rather than the line drawing characters.

Creating an archive of boxes

WordStar's line drawing feature isn't complicated, but getting boxes exactly like you want them can be time-consuming. If you're going to use boxes often in your documents, create an archive of boxes to use over and over again. Mark your boxes as a block and write them to a file on disk. Give each a name that identifies size and shape. Give all the extension .BOX and copy them to an archive disk.

Two different ways to put text in boxes

There are two different ways to put text inside boxes. Neither is very convenient, and both involve drawing the boxes first. The text in the boxes must be in the same size font as the box drawing characters.

Table 9-1   WordStar's extended character set, with the Alt-key commands to directly insert them into text.

Keystrokes	Character	Keystrokes	Character
Alt+F1	│	Alt+F6	┘
Alt+F2	─	Alt+F7	└
Alt+F3	┌	Alt+F8	┴
Alt+F4	┐	Alt+F9	┬
Alt+F5	└	Alt+F10	┴
Alt+176	░	Alt+200	╚
Alt+178	▓	Alt+201	╔
Alt+179	█	Alt+202	╩
Alt+180	┤	Alt+203	╦
Alt+181	╡	Alt+204	╠
Alt+182	╢	Alt+205	═
Alt+183	╖	Alt+206	╬
Alt+184	╕	Alt+207	╧
Alt+185	╣	Alt+208	╨
Alt+186	║	Alt+209	╤
Alt+187	╗	Alt+210	╥
Alt+188	╝	Alt+219	█
Alt+190	╛	Alt+220	▄
Alt+197	┼	Alt+221	▌
Alt+198	╞	Alt+222	▐
Alt+199	╟	Alt+223	▀

- Draw your box the size you need it. Place it on the page where you want it, and then use the overtype mode to type the text inside the boxes.
- Draw your box the size you need it. Place it on the page where you want it and format the text into margins small enough to fit inside the box. Then use the Column Mode and Column Replace commands to mark the text as a block and paste it inside the box.

Fooling around with boxes

Figure 9-3 is an illustration of the file TABLE.DOC that comes with the WordStar program. I've modified it slightly. Notice that the table has been boxed in using standard keyboard characters. These are the only ones that work with any printer you might have.

As you can see, the information is displayed in a simple, logical order that allows for rapid access of data. As you can see by this illustration, even a modest line capability can enhance a table of information.

Element #	Maximum g	Minimum g	Average g	Spread in g
1	2.21	1.65	1.93	0.56
	2.20	1.65	1.93	0.5
2	2.48	2.25	2.36	0.23
	2.50	2.22	2.36	0.28
3	3.08	2.59	2.84	0.49
	3.12	2.58	2.85	0.54
4	3.07	2.60	2.84	0.47
	3.10	2.60	2.85	0.50

9-3 TABLE.DOC file with line-draw characters.

Using paragraph numbers

This section covers the Paragraph Numbering feature. It defines terms, and describes how to use the feature.

What are WordStar paragraph numbers?

WordStar paragraph numbers are electronic place markers that attach a consecutive number to a paragraph by its current position in the document. It allows you to attach floating numbers to paragraphs. If you cut and paste a numbered paragraph to a different location in the document, WordStar will automatically renumber the paragraphs accordingly. If you type in a new numbered paragraph at any point, WordStar will automatically renumber the following paragraphs.

Uses for paragraph numbers

Paragraph numbers are useful in documents where precise locations of specific information must be indicated by numbers, so information can be located quickly. This is necessary in proposals and legal contracts where readers are referred to "paragraph number such-and-such" as a way of making things definite (if not always perfectly clear).

They're useful for writing documents with numbered sections when you don't know the final order or number of each section. If you rearrange or reorganize your document, you don't have to go back and manually type in the new numbers.

Different levels of numbering

WordStar allows you to easily use the legal style of numbering. For example, a chapter is numbered 1, the first section is numbered 1.1, and the first paragraph of the section is numbered 1.1.1—and so on and so on.

While most readers find such numbering confusing and difficult to read, it's required in most legal and government documentation. WordStar maintains the numbering system levels for you, and renumbers concurrently if you cut and paste sections and paragraphs. WordStar supports this type of numbering up to eight levels deep, if you're so inclined.

Different characters in numbering

Normally, paragraph numbers contain only numerals, up to eight levels deep. You can change the numbering system, however, to include uppercase and lowercase letters and roman numerals.

The dot command .P# is used to switch to a different numbering system. You can embed it like any other dot command by typing it into the body of the document. Examples of this dot command and their corresponding numbering systems are listed in the following table:

Command	Numbering system
.P# 9	Numerals starting with 0
.P# 1	Numerals starting with 1
.P# Z	Uppercase letters
.P# z	Lowercase letters
.P# Z.z	Mixed case letters
.P# I.i	Uppercase and lowercase roman numerals

You can mix and match these symbols to create as complicated a numbering system as you could possibly want. You can even insert other characters into your numbers to make them as distinctive as possible. For example, you can use the extended character set to add the paragraph symbol (¶) or the section symbol (§). Just bear in mind that the more complicated you make your numbering the more you'll confuse the average reader.

Attaching number to paragraph

Following are the steps for attaching a paragraph number to a specific paragraph or section in a document. A paragraph is defined as *any line or group of lines ending with a carriage return*.

1. Place the cursor at the point where you want to attach the number.
2. Use Ctrl−OZ to call the Paragraph Number Menu.
3. The next available consecutive paragraph number is displayed on this menu. You can accept it, type in a different number, or select a different level of numbering.
4. Press the Enter key to insert the selected number.

Tip: If you find yourself using these paragraph numbers frequently, consider recording a macro to attach them, and install it on a hotkey.

Numbering pages as they print

This section discusses page numbering and its various options. Tight control over a document's page numbers can help give documents a professional look and feel.

Page numbering options

You have the option to number pages as they print, or not use page numbering at all. WordStar comes with default page numbering set on, but you can see it either way. Default page numbering status is set using WSCHANGE.

You can modify the standard page numbering through the Page Numbering dialog box. Use Ctrl−O# to call it. Then set page numbering variables however you want.

You also can start page numbering over again at any point in the text file. This allows you to specify special numbering for chapters and other divisions in the document. You can have standard page numbers centered at the bottom of the page, or at a specific distance from the left margin.

Though not found on the Onscreen Format Menu, page numbering can be set in a header or footer. This means you can place them wherever you want to in the top or bottom margins. This is covered in detail in the chapter *Using headers and footers*.

Setting layout through paragraph tags

WordStar's paragraph style tags allow you to attach specific sets of layout and design instructions to paragraphs with a single command.

This section contains a general overview of paragraph style tags. It also defines the options for using, editing, creating, and managing a paragraph style tag library.

Only a "quick start" set of instructions for using paragraph style tags is given here. For complete information on working with these tags, see the chapter titled *Formatting documents with paragraph tags*.

What are paragraph style tags?

Paragraph style tags, paragraph tags for short, are complete sets of layout and design instructions. Each defines a particular kind of paragraph. While working with WordStar, a paragraph is defined as *any line or group of lines ending with a carriage return*. A paragraph can be one word, a heading, a sentence, or a group of sentences.

Once tagged to a paragraph, the set of layout and design instructions will remain in effect until countermanded by another paragraph tag. If the tag provides special formatting to only selected paragraphs, you must revert to your normal paragraph style.

WordStar comes with eight preset paragraph tags. Each contains 22 different attributes used for defining a particular type or style of paragraph. You can use these paragraph tags as is, redefine them any way you want, or create others for special-purpose layout and design.

When paragraph tags are attached to a document, all 22 attributes defined within are attached to the paragraphs with a single command. This paragraph definition will remain in effect until you countermand it by attaching another paragraph tag—or by using any Onscreen Format dialog box to change layout and design.

All changes made when you edit a paragraph tag apply only to the specific document that contains the edited paragraph tag. All new tags created while working in a document exist only in that text file. This creates a local stylesheet for that particular document. You can make edited paragraph tags and newly created tags global by copying them to the paragraph style tag library (through the Paragraph Style Menu). This will save them permanently to the WSSTYLE overlay file. They're then available for use in other documents.

Using the Paragraph Style Menu

All paragraph tag functions are available through the Paragraph Style Menu, called with Ctrl−OF (see Fig. 9-4). To use an option, type the highlighted letter beside it. This will either execute the option or take you to a dialog box for further selections. Follow the onscreen directions.

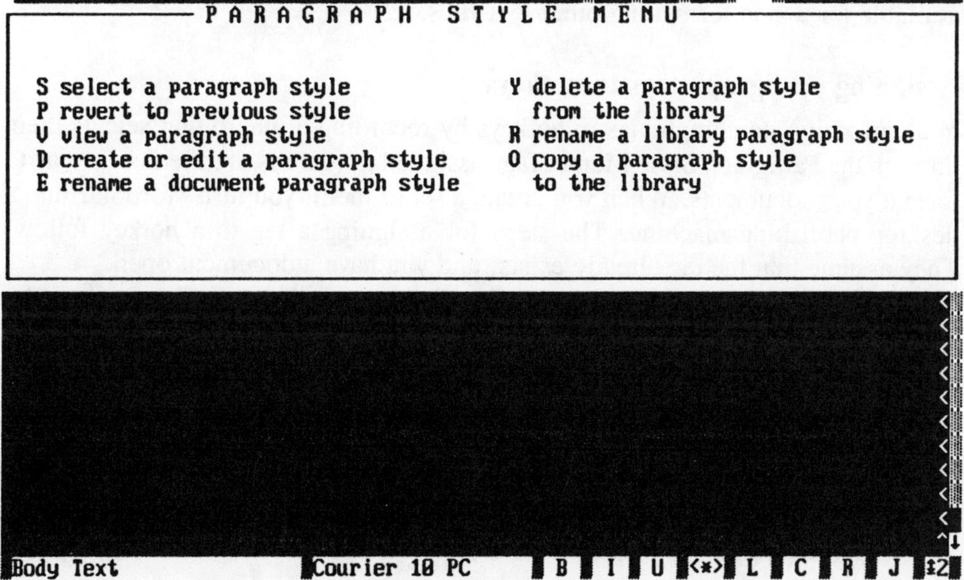

9-4 Paragraph Style Menu.

The Paragraph Style Menu options

The Paragraph Style Menu has eight options for using, creating, and managing your paragraph tags. These same options are available through the pull-down Style Menu. For complete information on working with these tags, see the chapter titled *Formatting documents with paragraph tags*.

Select a Paragraph Style   This option selects and uses an existing tag on the onscreen list.

Revert to Previous Style   This option reverts to the tag used in the paragraph immediately preceding the current tag.

View a Paragraph Style   Used to look at the settings of a tag in the onscreen list to see if it meets your needs or requires editing.

Create or Edit a Paragraph Style   Used to create a new tag, or change the settings in an existing one. The way to create a new tag is to edit one from the list and then save it to a new name.

Rename a Document Paragraph Style   Used to change the name of a tag in the list, presumably so you can use the name over again. If you rename the Body Text tag, WordStar will create a new one with the WordStar default settings.

Delete a Paragraph Style from the Library   Used to remove unwanted tags from the library in the WSSTYLE overlay file. If you delete the Body Text tag, WordStar will create a new one with the WordStar default settings.

Rename a Library Paragraph Style   Used to change the name of a tag in the WSSTYLE overlay file, presumably so you can use the name over again.

Copy a Paragraph Style to the Library   Used to copy a local tag from a document to permanent storage in the WSSTYLE overlay file. The tag is then available for use in formatting other text files.

Assigning paragraph tags to hotkeys

You can assign paragraph tags to hotkeys by recording a macro that selects them through the Paragraph Style Menu. Tags assigned to hotkeys are the fastest way to format your documents. When you create a set of them, you turn WordStar into a desktop-publishing machine. The steps for assigning a tag to a hotkey follow. They assume that the tag already exists, and you have a document open.

1. Place the cursor at the beginning of any paragraph to be given tag formatting.
2. Use Ctrl−MR to start recording the macro.
3. At the Record Macro dialog box, type in the name of the new macro.
4. Move to the Description line, and type in the function of the new macro.
5. Move to the Hotkey line, and select the hotkey you want the macro assigned to.

6. When ready, press the Enter key or click on the OK push-button. WordStar will return to the document, ready for you to begin recording the new macro.

7. Hold down the Ctrl key and type OFS. This calls the Select Paragraph Style dialog box.

8. At the Select Paragraph Style dialog box, type in the name of the paragraph tag you're assigning to a hotkey. When ready, press the Enter key or click on the OK push-button.

9. The paragraph tag will be attached to the text file at the cursor. You're finished recording the macro. Use Alt−equal sign to end recording and save the macro.

Working with WordStar notes

Because this feature is complicated, only an overview of how to use WordStar notes is given here. For complete information, read the chapter titled *Working with WordStar notes*.

WordStar has five different kinds of notes you can attach to your documents: footnotes, endnotes, annotation, nonprinting comments, and index entries. These are all available through the Notes Menu.

With this menu, you can select the type of note you want to use and attach it directly to the document. There's no practical limit to the size of note. Each note can be up to 40K in size—enough room for fifteen pages.

Note options

There are five utility options for working with notes once you've written and attached them to your documents: edit text of note at cursor, convert note type, align text in rest of note, Go to a note, and Spell check rest of note.

Controlling display options

There are eight options on the Onscreen Format Menu you can use to control how the document displays onscreen. These make no changes to the documents; they just control what you see.

Toggling the print control display

The command Ctrl−OD toggles the print control display on and off. The default setting is on. When you attach a print control command to text, the symbol for it will appear in the document. The printing control commands are available through the Print Controls Menu.

Using auto-hyphenation

Auto-hyphenation automatically hyphenates words at the right margin when the line is broken off by either wordwrap or auto-align. Hyphenation can help you improve the appearance of a paragraph. With ragged right margins, it will even up the line length. With justified right margins, it will decrease the number of soft spaces inserted between words. If you don't want your documents hyphenated, toggle this off. If you never want hyphenation, or rarely ever, turn this feature off permanently with the utility program WSCHANGE. You can also permanently change the hyphenation values.

Showing soft space dots onscreen

The command Ctrl–OB toggles the soft space display. When you center a line, use hanging indentation, or justify text, extra "soft" spaces are inserted between words to make the line extend all the way to the right margin. As you edit or align paragraphs, WordStar will add or delete these soft spaces as needed.

Soft space dots are the method WordStar uses to display the soft spaces in a justified line. The default setting is off. The normal character for soft dot display is a pale dot. You can change it to another character with WSCHANGE.

Checking the system status

The system status display shows you how WordStar is currently using the computer's memory for the file you have open. Also displayed are the currently attached printer, the language being used by the keyboard, the version and serial number of the program, the filename and current byte count of the file you have open, and Inset status (see Fig. 9-5).

Using page preview

WordStar's document mode gives a fairly accurate display of the layout and design of "plain vanilla" documents—those that use a standard sized font and standard margins. These include letters, contracts, proposals, and most business documents.

Once you format a document with different font types and sizes, and specify more than eighty columns, however, the onscreen format moves further away from "what you see is what you get." The more you use WordStar's desktop-publishing features, the more this is true.

The command Ctrl–OP is used to call Page Preview. This feature gives you the option of seeing onscreen exactly how your document will look when printed. This preview includes columns, headers, footers, footnotes, endnotes, annotation, fonts, line spacing—everything in your document that will appear in the hardcopy. You must have a graphics monitor to use this option, and it can be used only when a single window is open.

```
========================= Status =========================

Current Filename: C:\COMMAND.WS6\OPENMENU.FIG              █ Continue █

        Byte count: 25154
       Markers set: (none)
             Inset: Not Loaded
   Current printer: LASERJET

           Release: WordStar for DOS North American Version 7.0 Rev. A
     Serial Number: 632
          Language: United States    (001)

  ┌─ Memory Usage ────────────────────────────────────────────────────┐
  │                                                                     │
  │      WordStar:    212k     Messages:    2k    Hyphenation:     0k    │
  │ Text and Data:    158k     Printing:    0k      Thesaurus:     0k    │
  │                                                   Spelling:     0k    │
  │                                                                     │
  │   Conventional Memory        In Use:  372k      Available:    96k    │
  │                                                                     │
  │   Expanded Memory (EMS)               Unavailable                    │
  │                                                                     │
  └─────────────────────────────────────────────────────────────────────┘
```

9-5 WordStar's system status display.

Different views of a document

Once you turn on Page Preview, there are six different ways to look at your document, as follows:

Entire Page Uses the entire vertical height of your monitor to show your pages. The text is usually readable.

Facing Pages Reduces the page display sufficiently to show two even and odd pages, side by side, onscreen. The text is usually readable.

Multiple Pages Reduces the page display sufficiently to show up to six pages onscreen. Text might not be readable, depending on your monitor.

Thumbnail Display Reduces the display to a "thumbnail sketch" of the document. Depending on the monitor being used, this can be up to 144 pages onscreen. The text is unreadable.

2x Zoom Enlarges the onscreen display so it's twice as big as normal. Depending on your monitor, you can see about half a standard page. You can shift the image up and down or left and right with the arrow keys.

4x Zoom Enlarges the onscreen image to four times bigger than normal. Depending on your monitor, you can see about a quarter of a standard page. This is mainly used to zoom in on illustrations, to check alignment, and to verify kerning between characters.

The Go To options

There are five different options you can use to move around in the document while it's in Page Preview, called the Go To commands:

Specified Page Lets you type in a page number and go directly to it.

First Page Lets you go directly to the first page of a document.

Last Page Lets you go directly to the last page of a document.

Next Page Lets you go to the next page of a document and display it onscreen. (It's quicker to use PgDn.)

Previous Page Lets you return to the previous page and display it onscreen. (It's quicker to use PgUp.)

Creating fax files in page preview

In WordStar 7, the option to create fax files is available every time you run Page Preview. This means you can open a document; write, edit, and save it; and then make fax files without exiting the write-and-edit mode.

The fax file conversion routine is found on the Options Menu of the Page Preview screen. The process is streamlined, especially when compared to the Fax dialog box. You're given two choices:

Fax Files for Entire Document Asks you to type in a five-character filename for the faxes, and starts the conversion process when you press the Enter key.

Fax Files for Range Asks you to type in a five-character filename for the faxes, and press the Enter key. Then it asks you to type in the range, and starts the conversion process when you press the Enter key. The range here is limited to Start On Page and Stop On Page.

Note: If you don't type in the five-character filename, fax files created through Page Preview don't use the first five letters of the original filename as the default. Instead, WordStar uses the generic filename F001P001.PCX every time you start the routine.

For further information on Page Preview features and options, read the chapter titled *Using WordStar's Page Preview*.

Working in two document windows

This section discusses WordStar's window feature, and describes how to use it. Because this is a complicated, complex feature, only an overview of it is given here. For complete information on working on documents in multiple windows, read the chapter titled *Working in two document windows*.

A *window* is any rectangular space onscreen set aside to display a program or document. WordStar 7 allows you to open two documents in separate windows and work with both at the same time. Or you can use the file in one window as a source of boilerplate text for the file in the other window.

When you boot WordStar and open a document, its text will appear in a full-screen window. You can open either documents or nondocuments in a second window, work on both at once, and copy or move text directly from one to the other. You can also change window size to full screen, half screen, or a specific number of lines.

Opening a second document window

You can open a second document window from any point inside a text file. The same rules for file and path naming apply to the second document as the first. You can open any text file in any drive or directory in your computer.

1. Use Ctrl−OK to call the Open Document dialog box.
2. Tell WordStar the name of the text file to open in the second window.
3. Use Ctrl−K to load the file, or click on the OK push-button.

Once you've opened it, you can work on the second document the same as any other text file. If the second document screen isn't the size you want, use Ctrl−OM to change it. To close the second window, exit from the text file as you would any other file—use Ctrl−KQ to abandon without saving or Ctrl−KD to save and exit.

Opening a nondocument window

The standard version of WordStar is set up to open documents as the default. When opening a second window, it defaults to another document screen. To open a nondocument window, you must do so from the Opening Menu. To work on a nondocument and document at the same time, the nondocument must be in the first window.

Tip: You can modify WordStar to prompt for either documents or nondocuments after the Ctrl−OK command. Then you can open either type of text file at your discretion. This modification is made with WSCHANGE. At the WSCHANGE Main Menu, type DCGG and set the Window Prompt for Document/Nondoc item to on.

Toggling between windows

As long as two windows are open, you can toggle between them at will. The command Ctrl−OK will move you back and forth each time you repeat it. The cursor will return where you left it each time you toggle.

While in a window, any commands you execute will effect that window alone—except when you move a block from one window to the next.

If you have a mouse, and the windows are displayed at less than full-screen height, you can simply click on whichever window you want to work in. The cursor will jump from window to window as you click.

Temporarily resizing windows

WordStar comes with a default window size of half screen, or 12 lines of onscreen text. But you can change this temporarily with the command Ctrl−OM, which calls the Change Window Size dialog box. The options are Full Screen, Half Screen, or a specific number of lines that you can manually type in.

This screen resizing will last for the duration of the write-and-edit session, or until you close a window. If you close either window, the text file still open will revert to a full-screen display. If you then open a second window, WordStar will use the default sizing.

Permanently changing the size of windows

The default setting of 12 lines per window with two open windows can be changed using the utility program WSCHANGE. At the WSCHANGE Main Menu, type DCGH and set Size of Other Window to 255 (for full screen), or 128 (for half screen).

Formatting newspaper columns

This section discusses the newspaper (also called snake) columns you can use to format documents with a professional look. This feature helps make WordStar a powerful desktop-publishing machine. You can specify multiple columns painlessly with the Column Layout dialog box. Just tell WordStar the number of columns you want, and let it calculate column width. Change the gutter or the right page margin, and it will automatically recalculate your column and gutter widths.

Newspaper columns are the kind of columns you find in a newspaper or magazine. They're commonly called snake columns because the paragraphs wind down the page, and then start over again at the top of the next column. The default number of columns for WordStar's newpaper columns is 1, but you can lay out between 1 and 8 columns for any document or any portion of a document. Either set up the columns before you type the document, or apply them to existing documents and reformat the text file.

Because multicolumn formatting is quirky and complicated to use, I'm providing only a "quick start" set of instructions here. For detailed information, read the chapter titled *Using multicolumn layout*.

Steps for formatting newspaper columns

Below are the basic steps for formatting all or part of a text file in newspaper columns:

1. Place the cursor on a blank line just above the text to be formatted in newspaper column layout. If the entire document is to be formatted this

```
┌──────────────────■ Column Layout ■──────────────────┐
│   Number of Columns: 1            ■    OK     ■      │
│ Space Between Columns:  .25"      ■  Cancel   ■      │
│    Right Page Margin:  6.50"                         │
│        Column Width:  6.50"                          │
└─────────────────────────────────────────────────────┘
```

9-6   Column Layout dialog box.

way, put the cursor at the very beginning of the text file.

2. Use Ctrl−OU to call the Column Layout dialog box (see Fig. 9-6).
3. The default number of columns is 1. Change this to any number from 1 to 8. (Notice that WordStar will immediately recalculate the column width value.)
4. Reset any of the other values on this dialog box. Notice as you do how WordStar immediately recalculates.
5. When all variables are set as you want them, use Ctrl−K to accept the changes and embed the dot commands.
6. You'll be returned to the document. WordStar has embedded several dot commands at the cursor position. The newspaper columns begin below these commands.
7. If this is a new document, just start typing. WordStar will format your text in newpaper columns as you write. If you want to convert an existing document to newspaper columns, you must reformat the entire document with either Ctrl−B or Ctrl−QU.

Warning: Whenever you make additions or deletions to text in newspaper column mode, or change the font being used, you must manually reformat the affected text. Auto-align won't do it correctly. This is the only way to ensure that the proper word processing and printing codes are embedded in the document.

Converting newspaper columns to single column

To convert a newspaper-column document back to a normal, single-column document, use the following steps:

1. Find the column dot commands inserted in your document.
2. Delete the .RM and .CO command lines.
3. Reformat the entire text file with Ctrl−QU.
4. Use Ctrl−OP to view the document in Page Preview to make certain that the entire file has been set up for single column printing. If you find any errors, go to that page and correct the mistakes.

10

Using the Quick Menu features

This chapter covers the Quick Menu features, commands, and options. You'll start out with simple things like deletion, cursor movement, and scrolling commands; progress to global realignment, and search and replace options; and conclude with spelling checks, the thesaurus, and the calculator.

What is the Quick Menu?

Figure 10-1 is an illustration of the Quick Menu. To call the Quick Menu, hold down the Ctrl key and type Q.

The Quick Menu holds WordStar's so-called "quick" commands. The name is actually a holdover from times when things like jumping the cursor around and global search and replace were unusual. Now they're standard features in all writing programs. Quick commands are found under six different headings:

Cursor Movement   These commands allow you to jump the cursor to specific locations in the text file. This is more convenient than moving through the text file with only the cursor or arrow keys.

Find   These commands execute global search and replace functions. They tell the computer to search through the text file for fonts, specific characters, words, and phrases you need to find. You can replace text with other words and phrases. The convenience of this is immeasurable.

Delete   These commands provide enhanced deletion, allowing quick erasure of text. A single command can remove all text to the right or left of the cursor, forward to a specified character, or remove marked blocks of text.

Spelling Check   These will check the spelling of individual words, the entire document, or a word not yet in the text file.

```
,-------------------- Q U I C K   M E N U --------------------,
|        CURSOR              FIND           OTHER           SPELL      |
| E upper left    P previous    F find text    U align rest doc   L check rest  |
| X lower right   V prev find   A find/replace M math   Q repeat    N check word  |
| S begin line    B beg block   G char forward J thesaurus         O enter word  |
| D end line      K end block   H char back                        DELETE        |
| R beg file    0-9 marker      I page/line      SCROLL        Del line to left  |
| C end file                    = next font    W up, repeat      Y line to right |
|                                              Z dn, repeat      T to character  |
'--------------------------------------------------------------------------------'
```

10-1 Quick Menu.

Scrolling These commands move the document up or down continuously onscreen. This allows speed-reading, or scanning for specific lines or paragraphs. You can vary the scrolling speed to suit your preference by pressing the numeral keys 0 through 9. (Zero is the fastest.)

Other These include the thesaurus, global paragraph realigning, a calculator, and a repeat command.

Using the Repeat command

The Repeat command gets lost on the Quick Menu under the Other heading, and is normally explained with those features. You can use this command with many other features and commands, however, so it deserves explanation where it won't be lost.

The repeat command, Ctrl−QQ, can be used to repeat many things. To use it, hold down the Ctrl key, type QQ, and then issue the command to repeat. Once started, the last command will continue until the text file's end, until WordStar reaches the end of the computer's memory capabilities, or when you interrupt the process with Ctrl−U.

One good use for the Repeat command is when drawing boxes with extended graphics characters. The double-line and bar characters are available only through the Extended Character dialog box, or as Alt commands, but you can easily draw a line with these characters using the Repeat command.

Jumping around in the document

The following commands move the cursor to specific locations onscreen or throughout the text file. Most jumps are on the screen page—defined as *the portion of the text file WordStar can display onscreen*. It's what changes when you press the PgUp or PgDn keys. This varies from 26 to 43 to 50 lines—depending on the monitor and on how WordStar is set up for graphic display. If you can afford a full-page vertical monitor, you can display a 66-line screen page.

Many of these commands duplicate the actions of certain Ctrl−directional key combinations (also listed), but it's usually easier to reach letters on the keyboard than to stretch for the directional keys.

Back to where you were

The first jump command I'll discuss is the one to undo all others. When you use any command for cursor movement, WordStar remembers where the cursor was before it moved. The command Ctrl−QP will put the cursor back where it was before you issued your last command. You have to use this command before you issue any other commands, however, or it won't work.

The upper left corner

The command Ctrl−QE (and the Home key) will jump the cursor to the upper left corner of the screen page.

The end of screen page

The command Ctrl−QX (and the End key) will jump the cursor to the bottom of the screen page. The end of the screen page is the bottom line onscreen, one space to the right of the last character—or on the line with the last carriage return—whichever comes last.

The end of the text file

The command Ctrl−QC (and Ctrl−End) jumps the cursor to the end of the text file. The cursor will stop on the last line and last space of the text file.

The beginning of the file

The command Ctrl−QR (and Ctrl−Home) jumps the cursor to the beginning of the file in memory. The cursor will move to line 1, column 1 of the file.

The beginning of a really large file

If you're at or near the end of a really large file, the quickest way to get to its beginning is to save and close the file with Ctrl−KD, and then reopen the document.

When there are two or three hundred pages in a document, Ctrl−Home can take minutes to go from the end to the beginning. With Ctrl−KD, you can save and exit to the Opening Menu in seconds. Because the last opened filename is automatically in the buffer, you can execute this jump with Ctrl−KD, D, and pressing the Enter key.

The end of the line

The command Ctrl−QD jumps the cursor to the right side of the current line, and stops after the last character on the line.

The beginning of the line

The command Ctrl−QS jumps the cursor to the left side of the current line, and stops on column 1.

The beginning of a marked block

The command Ctrl−QB jumps the cursor to the beginning of a marked block of text, wherever it is in the document, whether displayed or hidden. It jumps to the begin block marker, even if no end block marker exists.

The end of a marked block

The command Ctrl−QC jumps the cursor to the end of a marked block of text, wherever it is in the document, whether displayed or hidden. It jumps to the end block marker, even if no begin block marker exists.

A numbered place marker

You can, with the Block & Save menu, insert up to ten temporary numbered place markers arbitrarily through the file. Once placed, WordStar knows where the place markers are, and can go forward or backward to them automatically.

The command to insert a place marker is Ctrl−K followed by a number from 0 to 9. The command to jump to a place marker is Ctrl−Q followed by its number.

You can move and reuse these place markers repeatedly. They don't have to be in any particular order. They last only for the duration of any write-and-edit session, and aren't saved with the document. They're most useful for marking your place when you go somewhere else in the text file, or for marking places for rearranging with Cut and Paste.

A personal marker

There's another way to put permanent markers in a text file—you can use embedded comments instead as personal place markers. These comment lines remain in the text file until deleted, but don't print in the hardcopy. Embedded like dot commands, they hide behind two dots instead of one. They can be deleted, moved, or edited like any other text. Put as many of them in the document as needed. Then use a Find command to locate them.

When using embedded comments as place markers, be as creative and personal as you like. Although they don't take up physical space in the document, it's still best to keep them short and simple. By using a word or two, you can easily remember the marker.

You can use markers to mark where you stop working for the day, a place needing work, a gap left until later, or anything you want. Then use the Find command to search for the comment.

To place a personal marker, use Ctrl−N to insert a blank line, move the cursor to column 1 on it, and type two periods followed by your code words. Each comment takes a line of its own. If you need to say more, add another blank line, type two more periods, and start over.

To jump to a personal marker, use Ctrl−QF to call the Find dialog box; type two periods and the first word or two of your comment, and select the Find options. WordStar will search through the text file for the comment. Make sure to use the G option in order to specify the entire file.

Scrolling

This section discusses scrolling, a method of moving progressively through the document instead of jumping to specific places in it.

The difference between scrolling and jumping around is how the cursor stays in place while the lines of text move up or down onscreen. The term comes from ancient documents written on rolls of paper or skins. To read such a document, you had to unroll it from one spool while winding it up on another. Only the section you were reading was visible at any given time.

Think of the text file as a long roll of paper on spools, with its lines written across the width. This scroll unrolls from top to bottom, or bottom to top. As you roll it off one spool, it wraps around the other—so the same quantity of text is always visible.

- Ctrl−QW starts scrolling upward continuously.
- Ctrl−QZ starts scrolling downward continuously.
- A number from 0 to 9 speeds or slows the scrolling speed.
- Any other key stops the scrolling.

Continuous scrolling up or down

The two scrolling commands, Ctrl−QW and Ctrl−QZ, allow you to move through a document with your hands off the keyboard. Once scrolling begins, it will continue automatically to either end of the file—or until you stop it by pressing any key except a number key. Press any number key to speed or slow the scrolling rate. Zero is the fastest; nine is the slowest.

Scrolling a line at a time

You also can scroll a line at a time, forward or backward through the document. This is best if you want to scroll only a short distance, or simply move onscreen text up or down. There are two commands for scrolling up a line, and two for scrolling down. Holding the keys down repeats the command.

Scroll command	What it does
Ctrl−W	Scrolls up one line
Ctrl−PgUp	Scrolls up one line
Ctrl−Z	Scrolls down one line
Ctrl−PgDn	Scrolls down one line

Using global search and replace

WordStar's Find feature can locate specific words or phrases in the text file. This is commonly called a *global search*—analogous to searching the face of a globe to find specific cities and places. WordStar can search for numbers, words, or phrases up to 65 characters long.

WordStar's Find and Replace feature can locate words or phrases and substitute other words and phrases in its place. The technical name for this is *global search and replace*. This is useful if you used a wrong word or phrase throughout a document. Or you can use it to replace only some repetitions of a word used too frequently. Replacement can be automatic, controlled by options you select, or only on those places you choose.

Finding a word or phrase

WordStar can find any specific word or phrase up to 65 characters long. To escape from any Find command, use Ctrl−U or press the Esc key.

1. At any point in the text file, hold down the Ctrl key and type QF.
2. When the Find dialog box appears (see Fig. 10-2), type the word or phrase you want to locate. Type it exactly as it is in the text file. If you make a mistake, back up and correct it.

```
──────────────────────── F I N D ────────────────────────
Find     dogmeat
         dogmeat
Options (none)
         bug
W whole words    U ignore case    B search backward    ? wild cards
G search entire file

Press F1 for help.
```

10-2 Find dialog box.

3. Press the Tab key to move the cursor to Options. Select the options by typing the bold letters in their names. You can also click on the options with your mouse.
4. When ready, use Ctrl−K to start the search.
5. WordStar will begin searching in the direction selected, and stop on the first occurrence of the word or phrase you typed on the Find line.

The command Ctrl−L will start the search again, and go to the next occurrence. Ctrl−QV will return the cursor to its last found location.

If WordStar can't find the word or phrase as typed, the search will continue to the end of the text file (whichever direction) and then tell you that it wasn't found. If you know the text is in the file, check your spelling and try again in the opposite direction. You might want to ignore case or use wildcard characters.

The Find command options

The Find dialog box has seven options to help you pinpoint the exact word or phrase you're trying to find. Use any combination of these.

At the Options line on the dialog box, type the highlighted hot letter of the option. This will jump the cursor to it, and toggle its current setting. This is quicker than using the mouse because you don't have to take your hands off the keyboard. Remember that an X in a checkbox means it's active. The options in the Find dialog box are as follows:

Search for Next Occurrence   Limits the search to only the next occurrence of the specified text. Allows you to stop after making only one find. The command Ctrl−L can restart the search.

Search Entire File/Global   To search from the beginning of the file, type the letter G on the Options line. Global means the entire file. The default direction of this search is forward; if you search backward with Global, WordStar will go to the end of the file before beginning the search.

Search Rest of File   Though it isn't listed as an option, old-time users will be comforted in knowing that you can still type R in the Options line. This begins the search and replace at the cursor position and moves in the direction stipulated to the end of the text file. It's useful when leap-frogging through a document to make substantive changes. A Ctrl−L will restart the search at the cursor position and continue the last command.

Find *n*th Number of Times   By typing a number in the Options line, you can make the command apply to an certain number of occurrences. For example: specifying 3 or 4 will send the cursor to find the first three or four repetitions of the word or phrase.

Ignore Letter Case While Searching   If you want the search to ignore the letter case of found text, type the letter U in the Options line. WordStar will replace with the text exactly as typed.

Search Backward   The default search direction is forward from the cursor position. To search backward, type the letter B in the Options line.

Use Wildcard Characters in Search   You can use wildcard characters in place of characters you aren't sure of. But you must tell WordStar you're using wildcards by typing ? in the Options line. If unsure about spelling of a word or phrase, substitute the wildcard character ? for the unknowns on the Find line.

Finding print control characters

A print control character is embedded in the text file every time you use a command on the Print Controls Menu. These symbols look like ^B, ^D, or ^Y—and they represent a printing command that the printer executes at print time.

On the Find line, type the command by reissuing it. For example, to indicate the boldface print character ^B, hold down the Ctrl key and type PB. To indicate the italic print character ^Y, hold down the Ctrl key and type PY.

Character to locate	Type the following
Boldface (^B)	Ctrl−PB
Doublestrike (^D)	Ctrl−PD
Italic (^Y)	Ctrl−PY
Underline (^S)	Ctrl−PS
Strikeout (^X)	Ctrl−PX
Subscript (^V)	Ctrl−PV
Superscript (^T)	Ctrl−PT
Indexing (^K)	Ctrl−PK
Footnote, endnote, comment, or annotation	Ctrl−ONG
Font change	Ctrl−Q=
Soft hyphen (end of line)	Ctrl−QF, Ctrl−P, Ctrl−(hyphen)
Soft hyphen (middle of line)	Ctrl−QF, Ctrl−P, Ctrl−6

Finding the next repetition of text

The Find command stops on the first occurrence of a word or phrase, but you don't have to call the dialog box to continue. The command Ctrl−L will repeat the last search command, and look for the next repetition. The last used Find and Replace command always remains in buffer until you exit from WordStar.

Going back to a previous find

WordStar holds the location of the previous occurrence of a word or phrase in buffer memory. To go back to it, use the command Ctrl−QV.

Finding a specific character (forward)

The command Ctrl−QG searches forward through a text file for the next use of any character on the keyboard. You'll probably find this command redundant, as Ctrl−QF can do the same thing.

Finding a specific character (backward)

The command Ctrl−QH searches backward through the text file for any specific character on the keyboard. You might find this command redundant, as Ctrl−QF can do the same thing.

Finding a specific page or line

The command Ctrl−QI can be used to go to a specific page or line number in a text file—depending on the editing mode. In the document mode, the command calls the Go to Page dialog box (see Fig. 10-3). The current page number is displayed, and there's room to type in a five-digit page number. Type in the number and press the Enter key.

```
                              ─── G O   T O   P A G E ───────────────

 Page number   13
               13



 Press F1 for help.
```

10-3 Go to Page dialog box.

In the nondocument mode, which serves mainly as a line editor for data files, batch files, and programs, the command calls the Go to Line dialog box (see Fig. 10-4). The current line number is displayed, and there's room to type in a five-digit line number. Type it in and press the Enter key.

```
                              ─── G O   T O   L I N E ───────────────

 Line number   1
               1



 Press F1 for help.
```

10-4 Go to Line dialog box.

Finding the next font

The command Ctrl−Q= jumps to the next font tag forward in the document. It doesn't call a dialog box, and there are no options. It stops on the next font tag, whether the print command tags display is on or off.

Finding the next paragraph style tag

The command Ctrl−Q< jumps forward to the next paragraph tag in the text file. It doesn't call a dialog box, and there are no options. It stops on the next paragraph tag, whether the print command tags display is on or off.

Find and replace

This section covers the Find and Replace command and options. The command works the same as the simple Find command—except that it replaces the found text with other text. This can be an extremely powerful word processing tool if used correctly.

Finding and replacing a word or phrase

The command Ctrl−QA is used to find and replace any character, word, or phrase with another character, word, or phrase. The limit for both found and replacement text is 65 characters. To interrupt any Find and Replace command in process, use Ctrl−U. The basic steps for using it are as follows:

1. Hold down the Ctrl key and type QA.
2. On the Find and Replace dialog box, at the Find line, type the word or phrase you're searching for.
3. Press the Tab key to go to the Replace line.
4. On the Replace line, type the substitution word or phrase.
5. Press the Tab key to go to the Options line.
6. On the Options line, type in the letters of the options being used. (If you have a mouse, you can select them with a click.)
7. Press the Enter key to start the Find and Replace procedure.

The Find and Replace options

The Find and Replace dialog box has 11 options for customizing the search and replacement. These help pinpoint the exact word or phrase replaced and they control what happens during the replacement. Use any combination.

At the Options line on the dialog box, type the bold hot letter of the option. This jumps the cursor to the option and toggles its current setting. This is quicker than using the mouse because you don't have to take your hands off the keyboard.

Search for Next Occurrence Limits the replacement to only the next occurrence of the specified text, and lets you stop after making only one replacement. The command Ctrl−L can restart the search.

Search Entire File/Global To search from the beginning of the file, type the letter G in the option line. Global means the entire file. The default direction of search is forward. If you search backward with Global, WordStar will go to the end of the file before beginning the search.

Search Rest of File Begins at the cursor position and moves in the direction stipulated to the end of the text file. Type R on the option line. This is most useful when you must stop and start the command repeatedly during the search. A Ctrl−L restarts the search at the cursor position and continues the last command.

Find and Replace *n*th Number of Times By typing a number on the

Options line, you can make the command apply to an *n*th number of occurrences. With Ctrl−QF, specifying 3 or 4 will send the cursor to find the 3rd or 4th repetition of the word or phrase. With Ctrl−QA, the same numbers would replace the next three or four repetitions of the word or phrase.

Realign Paragraph after Replacing   If the substitution text is bigger or smaller than what it replaces, it will throw off paragraph alignment. You can realign paragraphs as replacements are made by typing A on the Options line. (This doesn't reformat paragraphs protected with the dot commands above and below.) Tip: After a global replacement and alignment, use the Find command to locate the commands protecting paragraphs where replacement has taken place.

Replace without Asking   If you want the changes made without you having to do anything further, type N on the Options line. WordStar will make all substitutions without stopping to ask you whether to make them. The default is stopping to ask. Use with G or R to replace without asking throughout the text file.

Replace Whole Words Only   To limit the search to whole words only, type the letter W in the Options line. This is often necessary because many short words, like *the*, *ate*, and *it* can be found as part of longer words, like *theater* and *reiterate*.

Ignore Letter Case While Searching   If you want the search to ignore the letter case of found text, type the letter U on the Options line. WordStar will replace with the text exactly as typed.

Maintain Letter Case of Replaced Text   If you want the substitution text to use the same capitalization status as the replaced text, type M in the Options line. WordStar will replace only with capitals or lowercase, depending on the original case.

Search Backward   The default search direction is forward from the cursor position. To search backward, type the letter B on the Options line.

Use Wildcard Characters in Search   You can use wildcard characters in place of characters you aren't sure of. But you must tell WordStar that you're using wildcards by typing ? on the Options line. If unsure about spelling of a word or phrase, substitute the wildcard character ? for unknowns in the Find line.

Using global find and replace to change the layout

Layout features (margins, tabs, line spacing, etc.) are set by embedding dot commands in the text file. This is done either through dialog boxes, or by typing the command directly into the document. WordStar can find dot commands as easily as anything else. You can change layout typeset with dot commands by finding and replacing them throughout the document.

1. Put the cursor at the beginning of the text file, and use Ctrl−QA to call the Find and Replace dialog box.
2. On the Find line, type in the dot command being changed—exactly as it

is in the document. Type all or part. The more of the command line you include, the more specific the search.

3. Press the Tab key to move to Replace.
4. On the Replace line, type in the new dot command—or at least as much of it being changed. You can replace all or part of any dot command line.
5. Use the option R to specify the scope of the replacements. Use N to make the search and replace continuous.
6. When ready, use Ctrl−K to start the search and replace.
7. WordStar will find and replace the dot command as specified. Repeat the above steps for each dot command needing change.
8. When all layout and design dot commands are replaced, use Ctrl−QU to realign the document to the new settings, from beginning to end.

Finding and replacing a print control character

You can specify print control characters, both to find and to replace, by actually issuing the print control command. See the section *Finding print control characters* earlier in this chapter for specifics.

Finding and replacing the next occurrence

You can use Ctrl−L to restart find and replace after it has been stopped for any reason. This works best if you've typed R as option, as it picks up at the cursor and continues.

Once you issue a Find and Replace command, WordStar holds the complete text and options in memory. They remain in buffer until you issue another Find or Find and Replace command—or until you exit WordStar.

Turning off view of replacements

WordStar's default is to show the replacements as made. This slows down the search and replace. You can toggle this view off by pressing the spacebar after the command begins executing. The toggle works only with global replacements (when you're using G or R as options with N).

Finding and replacing the next font

There's no specific command for finding and replacing fonts. The command Ctrl−Q= jumps forward to the next font tag in the document. It doesn't call a dialog box, and there are no options. It stops on the next font tag whether print controls display is on or off. To replace a font tag, find it, delete it, and insert a new font. (See the chapter *Using the Print Controls Menu*.)

Checking your spelling

You can check the spelling of a document or nondocument any time you have it open. You can check individual words in the document, a specific word before you use it, or the rest of the document. You can also look up definitions, check the spelling in notes, and check for double words.

This spelling checker works best when installed on a hard disk, because swapping disks in and out is a pain. You can still boot up WordStar from high-density floppy disks and use the spelling checker. The computer needs two floppy drives to run WordStar from working disks.

Spell checking the remainder of a file

The command Ctrl−QL starts a spell check for the remainder of the text file—beginning at the cursor position. To check the entire document, place the cursor at the beginning of the document. You can start and stop the spelling check as often as needed, then pick up at the place you left off.

Warning: Since WS4, this command has been a macro installed on Shift−F3 to make it easier to execute. But in WS7, they've added the command Ctrl−QR into the macro. It jumps the cursor to the beginning of the text file before starting the spelling. Once you know how to edit the new macros, you can remove this annoyance.

1. Put the cursor at the point where the spell check is to begin.
2. Hold down the Ctrl key and type QL. This starts the spell check and calls the Spelling Check dialog box (see Fig. 10-5).

```
┌─────────────── S P E L L I N G   C H E C K   M E N U ──────────────┐
│   I ignore, check next word      E enter correction          ^U quit │
│   A add to personal dictionary   G global replacement is off  F1 help │
│   B bypass this time only        X add to exceptions dictionary       │
│                                                                       │
│        Word:     "the" is spelled correctly                           │
│ Suggestions:     1 tee  2 she  3 he  4 th  5 the...                    │
│                  P display previous suggestions                       │
│   Definition:    Definitions not loaded.                              │
└───────────────────────────────────────────────────────────────────┘
```

10-5 Spelling Check dialog box

3. WordStar will begin to check the spelling of the rest of the text file, starting at the cursor position. First it compares words against the main dictionary. If a word isn't there, WordStar will check the personal dictionary.
4. If WordStar can't find the word as spelled in the dictionaries, it will stop

on the word and display a list of suggestions to correct it. The
suggestions match the capitalization and part of speech of the original
word.

5. Sometimes the suggestions are on the mark. Sometimes they're good for
   a laugh. Either accept a suggestion, use an option, or interrupt spell
   checking by pressing the Esc key.
6. To accept a suggestion, type its number. To use an option, type its letter.
   When you quit spell checking a single word, you'll be returned to the
   place where you were writing or editing.

Checking the spelling of a single word

The command Ctrl−QN checks only the spelling of the word the cursor is on.
This feature is simple and easy to use:

1. Put the cursor on the word being checked.
2. Hold down the Ctrl key and type QN. This starts the spell check and
   calls the Spelling Check dialog box.
3. WordStar will check the spelling of the selected word against the main
   dictionary. If the word isn't found, it checks the personal dictionary. If
   the word is found as typed, WordStar says it's spelled correctly.
4. If WordStar can't find the word as spelled in the dictionaries, it will
   display a list of suggestions on how to correct it. The suggestions match
   the capitalization and part of speech of the original word.
5. Either accept a suggestion, use an option, or quit spell checking by
   pressing the Esc key.
6. To accept a suggestion, type its number. To use an option, type its letter.
   When you quit spell checking a single word, you'll be returned to the
   place where you were writing or editing.

Tip: As mentioned earlier, WordStar comes with this command installed as a
macro on Shift−F4—which is much easier to execute.

Spell checking a word not in the file

The command Ctrl−QO lets you check the spelling of a word not in the document. This calls a different, unnamed dialog box. Type in the word being checked
and press Ctrl−K. From here on, it works exactly like Ctrl−QN.

Tip: If there ever was a redundant command, this is it. Rather than memorize
another command, just type the word in the document and check its spelling with
Ctrl−QN.

The Spelling Check options

There are six options on the Spelling Check dialog box to optimize the spell check
and search. They're available whether you're checking the whole document, a

single word in it, or a word before putting it in the document. A seventh option—Add Word to Exclusion Dictionary—is available only when checking a single word. The options are as follows:

Ignore the Word from Now On If you select I, the spell checker will ignore the questioned word for the remainder of the document. (If you use this too frequently while checking large documents, you might fill the ignore buffer. If you have this problem, increase the buffer memory allocation with WSCHANGE.)

Add Word to Personal Dictionary If the spell checker stops on a word, and the word is spelled correctly, you can add the word to your personal dictionary by selecting A. (To remove an unwanted word from the personal dictionary: open its file as a nondocument; find the word; and delete it.)

Bypass This Time Only Select B to skip the word once and continue the spell check. It will stop on the word's next repetition.

Type in Your Correction If the spell checker stops on a word, and you know the correct spelling or would like to substitute a different word, select option E. Type in your correction and press the Enter key. (You might find it convenient to use this with global replacement.)

Replace the Word Throughout the File You must select G for global replacement before other options. When used, it makes the selected correction every time it finds the questioned word.

Add Word to Exceptions Dictionary This option appears only when you're spell checking a single word with either Ctrl−QN or Ctrl−QO. The exceptions dictionary is a list of words you want questioned during any spell check, even if spelled correctly.

Exit from the Spell Checker If you don't want to make a correction, or simply want to escape from the spell checker, use Ctrl−U or press the Esc key.

The spell checker progress display

You can either watch the spell checker in progress or turn it off. WordStar comes from the factory with the display inactive, because it speeds up spell checking.

If you're a fast reader, a global spelling check can let you browse through the document for obvious errors. The Show Spelling Check Progress option must be active. Make on the default with the utility program WSCHANGE. (At the WSCHANGE Main Menu, type DCAK and turn it on.)

If you don't want to watch the spelling check progress, and want to speed up a particular spell check, you can toggle the display off between questioned words by pressing the spacebar. You'll have to press the spacebar each time WordStar stops on a word.

Different kinds of dictionaries

WordStar uses several different kinds of electronic dictionaries for use with documents. Most, like the main, the personal, and the exceptions dictionaries, are for spelling checks. Others are for hyphenation, definitions, and synonyms in a thesaurus.

The main dictionary

WordStar has more than 100,000 words stored in the main dictionary file to use in spelling checks. It compares the words in your text file against those in the dictionary. If WordStar doesn't find the word in the main dictionary, it checks the personal dictionaries.

The main dictionary is the file SPLMN001.DCT in the WordStar program directory. Never attempt to edit this file. It isn't a text file, and editing can damage it. If this file becomes damaged, reinstall it with the utility program WSCOPY.

Personal dictionaries

The personal dictionary contains words not found in the main dictionary—words that you add to it. Each time you spell check a new document, you can add to the personal dictionary.

You might find it convenient to create and use different personal dictionaries for different kinds of documents, especially if you find yourself adding many words. The bigger a personal dictionary, the longer it takes to check spelling.

Tip: Keep an archive of your personal dictionaries by copying them to a floppy disk. It generally takes a long time to get your personal dictionaries exactly the way you want them. Maintaining an archive will protect them from permanent loss or damage.

Editing a personal dictionary

The personal dictionary is the file PERSONAL.DCT in the WordStar program directory. You can add or delete words by opening it as a nondocument. Never open a personal dictionary file as a document. Editing and saving a dictionary file in the document mode will save word processing codes to it. To restore a personal dictionary file that you've accidently opened in the document mode, print it to ASCII and rename it.

Warning: Never open and edit any .DCT file besides personal dictionaries and the exceptions dictionary. The others aren't text files, and can be damaged by attempts at editing.

Personal dictionaries from earlier versions of WordStar can be used with Release 7 if you copy them into the WordStar's program directory. Because WordStar now has a larger main dictionary, your personal words might be in it. To upgrade your personal dictionary:

1. Rename your old personal dictionary PERSONAL.NON so WordStar won't think it's a dictionary file. Then copy it into your WordStar 7 program directory.

2. Run a spelling check on it.
3. Add the words it stops on to your personal dictionary.
4. Your new dictionary will now contain all the unique words from the old personal dictionary, and you can delete the old file from the Release 7 directory.

Tip: If you don't want to go through the above routine, just copy your old PERSONAL.DCT into your WordStar 7 program directory and use it as is.

The exceptions dictionary

The exceptions dictionary holds words you want questioned during a spelling check—even if they're perfectly valid and spelled correctly. Vocabulary differs from genre to genre, sometimes even spelling. Some words are permissible in some kinds of documents, but undesirable in others. You wouldn't use the same choice of words in technical manuals, business proposals, and personal letters.

The option X, to Add to Exceptions Dictionary, copies the questioned word to it. This option is on the Spelling Check dialog box only after you use Ctrl−QN or Ctrl−QO to check the spelling of an individual word.

The exceptions dictionary is the file EXCEPT.DCT in the WordStar program directory. You can add to or delete words from this dictionary by opening the file as a nondocument and following the steps in the previous section.

The hyphenation dictionary

WordStar has a hyphenation dictionary, which contains hyphenated words and hyphenation rules. The auto-hyphenation feature is toggled on and off with the command Ctrl−OH. Hyphenation takes place during the alignment of paragraphs. If auto-align is also on, hyphenation takes place during wordwrap.

The default for hyphenation is on. This default setting can be changed with the utility program WSCHANGE. The hyphenation dictionary is the file HYPMN001.DCT in the WordStar program directory or file. Never attempt to edit this file. It's not a text file, and editing can damage it. To restore a damaged dictionary, reinstall it with WSCOPY.

The definitions dictionary

WordStar has a definitions dictionary so you can look up meanings of words while a spelling check is running. This must be installed using the utility program WSSETUP. The default is that it's turned off, but you can change this default using the utility program WSCHANGE. The definitions dictionary is the file DEFIN001.DCT in the WordStar program directory. Never attempt to edit this file; it's not a text file.

International dictionaries

Foreign-language dictionaries are available from WordStar International. These can be used to check the spelling of documents written in most major languages. If your dealer can't get what you need, contact WordStar directly.

WordStar comes with spelling and hyphenation dictionaries for the current language version you purchased. The default language is American English—unless you purchased WordStar outside the United States.

You can change the default language by using the utility program WSCHANGE. You can change the language in the current document with the .LA dot command, followed by the code for the language being used. Even if a different language is indicated, spelling checks will execute normally. The language codes are in the dictionary's manual and also in the MS-DOS manual.

Medical and legal dictionaries

Medical and legal dictionaries (in some languages) are available directly from WordStar International. These contain the standard dictionary choices plus specialized terms. Instructions for installation come with the dictionaries. Once installed, spelling checks execute normally.

Using WordStar's thesaurus

A *thesaurus* is a dictionary of synonyms. Synonyms are different words with the same meaning. In case you wondered what another word for thesaurus is, it's also called a *lexicon*. The best known is *Roget's Thesaurus*.

WordStar has an electronic thesaurus with 220,000 synonymous words you can use to expand the vocabulary of your writing. You can look up synonyms for a word by putting the cursor on it and calling the thesaurus. The thesaurus is the file THESR001.DCT in the WordStar program directory or disk. Never attempt to edit this file. It's not a text file, and editing can damage it. To restore a damaged dictionary, reinstall it with WSCOPY.

Using the thesaurus

The command Ctrl−QJ starts the thesaurus and looks up synonyms for the word the cursor is on.

1. Put the cursor on the word to check with the thesaurus.
2. Hold down the Ctrl key and type QJ.
3. The thesaurus will begin looking up synonyms for the chosen word, and the Thesaurus Menu will appear.
4. If the thesaurus can't find the word in its dictionary, it will look up synonyms for the root word. If a root word isn't found in the thesaurus,

an alphabetical list will appear, showing the closest words found. The cursor will blink on the word most like the chosen word.

5. When the thesaurus finds the word, synonyms will appear grouped by part of speech and definition. The most commonly used synonyms will be listed first. If you see arrow symbols on the left-most side of the Thesaurus Menu, it means that there are more choices than can be displayed. Use the arrow keys, PgUp, and PgDn to display more choices. You can also click on the arrow symbol to scroll down and then click on your choice.

6. There are six options on the Thesaurus Menu to optimize the synonym search. Use the arrow keys to put the highlight on your choice and either press the Enter key or click on it with your mouse. The selection will replace the original word.

The Thesaurus Menu options

The following are the six options on the Thesaurus Menu that allow you to optimize the synonym search:

Select a Word from the Choices   Use the arrow keys to put the highlight on the synonym and either press the Enter key or click on it with the mouse.

Cross-Reference a Word   If you don't see the synonym you want, you can call up other lists by cross-referencing any word on the list currently displayed. Use the arrow keys to put the highlight on the synonym and type L.

Return to Previous Word   If you cross-reference a word and then decide that the previous selections were better, type P.

Look Up a Definition   You can see the definition of any synonym displayed. Put the highlight on the word and type K. When the definition appears, press N to see the next definition, P to return to previous definition, I to type in another word to look up, or the Esc key to exit.

Type Another Word for a Synonym Check   If WordStar can't find the word at all, you might have misspelled it—or you might think of a similar word. With this option, you can try again or run a synonym check on another word without having to exit and start over. To look up another word, press I, type the word, and then press the Enter key.

Exit without Replacing a Word   You don't have to select a synonym. You can exit the thesaurus and return to the document mode with Ctrl−U or by pressing the Esc key.

If using a dual-floppy computer

If using a dual-floppy disk computer, WordStar will prompt you to insert the disk containing the thesaurus when you issue Ctrl−QJ (or select it from a menu with a mouse). If the computer has enough memory, you can customize WordStar with WSCHANGE to load the entire thesaurus into RAM. Once loaded, it will remain in memory until you exit WordStar. This eliminates the need for swapping disks.

Thesauruses for other languages

Thesauruses in other languages are available from WordStar International. WordStar can use only one thesaurus at a time. The default language is American English—unless you purchased WordStar outside the United States. You can change the default language using the utility program WSCHANGE.

You can specify a different language for a document by using the .LA dot command, followed by the three-digit language code number, to tell WordStar that you're using a different language in a particular document. The language codes are inside WSCHANGE, in the MS-DOS manual, and in the foreign-language thesaurus documentation.

Deleting words, lines, paragraphs

The most convenient feature of word processing must be the fact that you can erase mistakes as easily as you make them. Just delete them and type again. WordStar makes it easy to delete individual characters or words, all or a portion of a line of text, entire paragraphs or groups of paragraphs, and entire sections of a document. The keyboard has special keys for erasing small mistakes, and deletion commands for removing big mistakes.

The Delete key

The Delete key is marked Del on most keyboards and Delete on most 101-key keyboards. Press the Del key to delete the character at the cursor position. Hold down the Del key for continuous character deletion to the right.

The Backspace key

The Backspace key deletes characters backward. Hold down the Backspace key for continuous character deletion backward.

Deleting print control characters

You can embed print control characters in a document with commands from the Print Controls Menu. These are the symbols like ^B and ^Y you see in your documents after marking text for boldface or italic printing. These characters are attached to the word, and are deleted with the word. Individual print controls can be deleted like any other character—with the Del and Backspace keys.

Restoring deleted words, lines, and blocks

Before you delete words, lines, and blocks of text with delete commands, you should know how to unerase them if you either delete too much or simply change your mind.

When you delete text with a command, WordStar holds it in the unerase buffer until the next delete command. You can use the universal command Ctrl−U to unerase the last text erased with a delete command.

Deleting words

The command Ctrl−T deletes a word forward on a line. Repeat the command, or hold down the keys for continuous word deletion.

Deleting lines

The command Ctrl−Y deletes the entire line the cursor is on. Repeat the command, or hold down the keys for continuous line deletion. Be careful, as continuous line deleting can get ahead of WordStar's ability to display what you're deleting—so you can delete more lines than you intend.

Quickly deleting a line to the left

The Quick command Ctrl−Q−Del deletes all the line to the left of the cursor. If auto-align is on, the paragraph will be reformatted to fit the margins.

Quickly deleting a line to the right

The Quick command Ctrl−QY deletes all the line to the right of the cursor. If auto-align is on, the paragraph will be reformatted to fit the margins.

Quickly deleting to a specified character

The Quick command Ctrl−QT deletes all the text from the cursor position to a specified character. The command calls the Delete to Character dialog box (see Fig. 10-6). Type in the character being deleted up to. The command is executed when you type the character.

─────────────── D E L E T E   T O ───────────────

Delete forward to what character __

10-6 Delete to Character dialog box.

- To delete an entire sentence, delete to its punctuation character.
- To delete a phrase, delete to its comma.
- To delete an item in a numbered list, put the cursor on the list and delete up to the next number in the list.

Deleting a paragraph

The quickest way to delete a paragraph is to delete it line by line with Ctrl−Y. But if you have a mouse, you can quickly mark the paragraph as a block and then block delete it.

Deleting a block of text

The command Ctrl−KY deletes a block of text. A block is any portion of your file marked at its beginning with Ctrl−KB and at its end with Ctrl−KK. This puts an inverse video highlight over the text, thus marking it as a block.

There's no limit to the size of block you can mark and delete with WordStar, but there *is* a limit on the size you can restore with Ctrl−U. It depends on the memory allocation for the unerase buffer. If the marked block is too big to restore with Ctrl−U, WordStar will ask you if you really want to delete it.

You can make the unerase buffer bigger by allocating more memory to it with WSCHANGE. WordStar comes from the factory with 500 bytes allocated to the unerase buffer. If you want to use Ctrl−KY for cutting and pasting large sections of text, allocate at least 1 or 2 kilobytes to the unerase buffer.

Tip: At the WSCHANGE Main Menu, type CC2A and change it to 1000 or 2000. Or make it bigger to suit your needs. There's roughly one byte per character, though extended characters count as three. Punctuation, blank spaces, and soft spaces are also characters.

Using Delete and Unerase to cut and paste

You can execute quick cut-and-paste functions by using any delete command with the unerase function of Ctrl−U. This method works best if you have a mouse.

1. Erase the text with any delete command. This cuts the text from its place in the document.
2. Move the cursor to the place in the document where you want to paste in the deleted text.
3. Hold down the Ctrl key and type U.

Realigning an entire text file

WordStar's normal reformat command, Ctrl−B, realigns one paragraph at a time. Realigning an entire text file with Ctrl−B is time-consuming. WordStar has two commands for automatically reformatting an entire text file. These are the quick commands Ctrl−QU and Ctrl−QQB.

When WordStar aligns or reformats a paragraph, it compares the length of the lines to the ruler line. If lines are too long, words are broken off and moved down to the next line, repeatedly to the end of the paragraph. If auto-hyphenation is on, words are hyphenated during alignment.

The term *global realignment* means reformatting either an entire text file or a major section of it—from beginning to end. This allows making major changes in layout, design, and content while making WordStar do much of the repetitive work. Though the command Ctrl−QU is a major part of it, it isn't all. So I've brought together all its elements in a single section.

Why is it necessary to reformat?

To provide onscreen formatting, WordStar aligns every paragraph as you type it, according to the margins, tabs, line spacing, justification, and other design or layout settings. Most of those settings belong to either the stylesheet or the paragraph style tags, or are set with dot commands in the text file. Every one of those settings can be changed for any part of the document, or globally throughout the text file.

Even when you change the stylesheet attached to the document, redefine the layout settings in the style tags, or change the values in dot commands, the text file is still aligned using the old formatting values. Every affected line and paragraph must be realigned to the new layout values.

Another important consideration is the size of the font used to print the document. WordStar automatically readjusts onscreen formatting whenever you change fonts, or change the size of the font. After any font change, the affected text must be realigned to margins, tabs, line spacing, and so on. Failure to reformat will produce a badly aligned hardcopy.

The quick realignment command

The command Ctrl−QU automatically realigns the remainder of the document, beginning at the cursor position. It calls no dialog box, and there are no variables to set. To ensure realignment of the entire document, use Ctrl−QR or Ctrl−Home to jump to line 1, column 1 of the document.

The times to use Ctrl−QU are after you've made global changes to things like fonts, paragraph tags, dot commands, line spacing, and margins.

Automatically repeating Ctrl−B

There might be times when Ctrl−QU won't work exactly like you want it to work. For those times, you can use the repeat command with Ctrl−B. You can issue this as a single command by holding down the Ctrl key and typing QQB. WordStar will repeat the reformat command for the remainder of the text file, beginning at the cursor position.

An important difference between Ctrl−QU and Ctrl−QQB is that Ctrl−QQB can't go past the "alignment and word wrap off" command (.AW OFF), used to protect text from realignment. The cursor stops dead on it. But you can use Ctrl−QU to at least pass through the protected text.

Tips on reformatting text files

There are some tips and quirks you need to know about reformatting entire text files. Both commands reshape the document to currently set margins, line spacing, justification, and other elements of layout status. This can sometimes produce unintended results.

Hanging indentation produced by temporary indentation commands will be reformatted to the current left margins unless protected from reformatting. Embed the format protection command above the temporary margins being protected, and put it below the protected area to turn alignment back on.

The layout and design definitions given to paragraph tags can vary wildly from stylesheet to stylesheet. If WordStar is booted from a directory with a different stylesheet, the boot stylesheet will remain active as long as WordStar is running. Its settings will apply to all documents you open, even those in another directory.

Any text given special layout or design by tags in one stylesheet will be automatically realigned to new stylesheet or paragraph tag changes unless protected.

Using the alignment dot command

To protect text given special layout and design: embed the dot command .AW OFF above the text and .AW ON below the text. When WordStar encounters the first embedded command, alignment is toggled off. After it passes the second command, alignment is toggled back on again.

Using binding spaces

Sometimes, reformatting breaks apart words or phrases you want printed together on the same line. You can protect such text with Ctrl−PO, which inserts a binding space in the text file. A *binding space* prints as a blank space, but locks characters or words together so they don't split to different lines.

The print-time reformatting dot command

There's one last command to use for reformatting a document. It's the dot command .PF, or print-time formatting command. This command should be embedded at the beginning of the text file. Whenever possible, put all major layout dot commands at the beginning of the file. Then you can change them easily, save the file, and send the file to the printer. As the pages go to the printer, WordStar automatically reformats them to your new layout specifications—but the file itself remains unchanged.

This is especially useful for printing different versions of the same text file but with different margins, page offset, or line spacing. Change nothing in the document except the dot commands at the beginning. After printing, simply reopen the text file and restore the dot commands to their original settings.

Using the calculator

The command Ctrl−QM calls the calculator. Of all WordStar commands, this one always seems the most out of place on the Quick Menu—because there's nothing quick about it. WordStar International must be proud of their calculator, because it has remained virtually unchanged since release 4. In my opinion, it's the most poorly designed feature of WordStar.

The Math Menu works like any other WordStar dialog box, although you can't really say that it works like a calculator. What it does do is open a window through which you can access the microcomputer chip's math functions.

- Before you can use the Math Menu, you must understand the principles and relationships of mathematics. Well enough, in fact, to work them out on paper.
- You must correctly type in mathematical equations based on those principles, and use the symbols illustrated onscreen.
- When you have the entire equation typed, press Ctrl−K to calculate the answer.
- WordStar will display the answer below the line Result of Last Calculation.

If mathematically inclined, you might find this easy to use. Otherwise, you're better off using your pocket calculator. You can find the total you need and type it into your text file more quickly than you can use the Calculator dialog box.

Inserting calculator information

For the duration of the current write-and-edit session, WordStar holds the answer to the last calculation in memory. It's easy to insert the results of this math equation into your document. Simply place the cursor where you want to insert the total, press Ctrl−M, and then type the equal (=) key.

WordStar also holds the last equation in the Math buffer until overwritten by another equation, or you exit from WordStar. To insert the last typed equation, place the cursor where you want the equation inserted in your file, press the Esc key, and then type the # key.

You can insert the results of a math equation into your documents as a formatted dollar amount. Place the cursor where you want to insert the total, Press the Esc key, and then type the dollar sign ($). WordStar has a default format for dollar amounts. This format controls the way decimals and commas appear in numbers. Decimal values round off to two decimal places. You can change the default to format numbers and monetary sums by the European standard, which swaps commas for decimals, and decimals for commas with WSCHANGE.

How the calculator works

WordStar's math notation is the same as the basic math order of operations. Equations evaluate from left to right, exponents take precedence over multiplication and division, and multiplication and division take precedence over addition and subtraction.

You can change the order in which WordStar performs its operation by using parentheses to nest, or enclose, operations to calculate first. Be sure to use the parentheses in pairs. Operations inside the innermost set of parentheses always execute first. WordStar always uses its normal order of precedence to perform math functions within parentheses.

Note: The nesting limit is 32, but the equation can become too complicated for WordStar to handle long before then. When the equation is too complicated, an error message will appear when you press the Enter key. Divide the equation into smaller components and calculate them individually.

You can use scientific notation to represent a long number. The answers will be displayed to a maximum precision of 12 digits. When an answer is longer, WordStar will provide the closest answer using scientific notation. For example, the number 1,200,000,000,000,000,000,000,000 can be represented by the exponent 1.23e25. The largest exponential number WordStar can handle is 1e63. This is a 1 followed by 62 zeros. The smallest number is 1e-63, or a decimal followed by 62 zeros and then a 1.

The Calculator dialog box lists symbols and abbreviations you can use. Type them in where needed in a math equation. WordStar will calculate their functions as it processes the equation.

Block math

Although found on a different menu, block math is a related use of the calculator and deserves inclusion here. The command Ctrl−KM can calculate the numbers in a marked block of text, even if the block also has words in it. Block math can work with either standard blocks or column blocks.

To calculate a math block, first mark the block beginning and end of the block, then hold down the Ctrl key and type KM. WordStar will scan the marked block and execute the math calculations contained within it.

You can insert results of block math in your documents through the Macro Menu—the same way you would the results from using the Calculator dialog box.

11

Using the Block & Save Menu

This chapter covers using the Block & Save Menu commands and features. This menu contains all the save commands, file manipulation commands, and all the cut-and-paste commands.

To call the Block & Save Menu while editing a file, hold down the Ctrl key and type K. After a moment, the menu (see Fig. 11-1) will appear. To execute or select any command from the Block & Save Menu, type the letter found to the left of the command. To escape from the menu without executing a command, press the spacebar or the Esc key.

Commands to save your files

The need to protect your work cannot be stressed too strongly. A text file in computer memory exists only as a pattern of digital data. It's vulnerable to loss from moment to moment—at the caprice of any power loss, power surge, voltage spike, or software crash. Don't ignore these minor disasters because they happen infrequently.

Nothing you type, no amount of work, is permanent until you save it to storage on disk. The best protection for work in progress is to save it frequently.

An ounce of prevention is worth a sack full of remedies. Saving regularly keeps a file you're working on updated. When the worst happens—and eventually, it always does—the most you'll lose is the amount done since your last save. There are many good times to save the file:

- Any time you reach a natural break in the document, like the end of a section or subsection.

```
━━━━━━━━━━━━━ B L O C K   &   S A V E   M E N U ━━━━━━━━━
    SAVE                    BLOCK           FILE                    CURSOR
 D save  T save as    B begin block   C copy    O copy         0-9 set
 S save & resume      K end block     V move    E rename           marker
 X save & exit        H turn disp off Y delete  J delete
 Q abandon changes    W write to disk M math    P print            CASE
    WINDOW            ? word count    Z sort    L change drive/dir  " upper
 A copy between       N turn column mode on     R insert a file    ' lower
 G move between       I turn column replace on  F run a DOS command . sentence
```

11-1 Block & Save Menu.

- Whenever you have to leave the keyboard, for any reason.
- When you haven't saved the file in the last fifteen or twenty minutes.

Get into a saving habit, or eventually you'll lose a large part of a day's work. When it happens, don't blame anyone but yourself. Save frequently, and save yourself grief.

Saving and returning to a file

The command Ctrl−KS saves the file to its target disk, and then returns you to writing and editing at the same point you left off. During any save, the Saving message box will appear onscreen. When saving completes, it disappears.

Tip: longtime WordStar users call this "kissing the computer," from the mnemonic KS. Never leave the computer running without kissing the computer first. It will definitely improve your relationship.

Saving a file and returning to the Opening Menu

The command Ctrl−KD saves the file to its target disk, exits you from the document mode, and returns you to the Opening Menu. From there, you can use any of the other WordStar options. Use this command when you're finished working on a document but want to continue working with WordStar. During any save, the Saving message box will appear onscreen. When saving completes, it disappears.

Saving a file and exiting from WordStar

The command Ctrl−KX saves the file to its target drive, exits you from the document mode, and then exits you from WordStar and puts you in the DOS prompt of the current drive (unless you ran WordStar from a third-party menu system). This will clear all the WordStar program files from the computer's memory, and let you use the computer for something else. Use this command when you're finished with WordStar.

Saving a file under another name

The command Ctrl−KT calls the Save As dialog box—the same box you see when you first save a file opened with the Speed Write option of the Opening Menu. It allows you to save an open file to a different name. Use this for creating edited versions, or different drafts, of a manuscript while keeping the previous version intact. You can do the same thing by opening a new file and then copying the old file into it.

You can either save a file to a new name or to an existing filename. If you save to an existing filename, WordStar will overwrite (replace) the existing file. When saving completes, you're returned to the Opening Menu.

1. Hold down the Ctrl key and type KT.
2. The Save As dialog box will appear. Below it are the files in the current directory. Type in a new name, or select one from the list.
3. You can select a filename from another directory by choosing a directory from the onscreen list. Or select from directories outside the current one.
4. After you type or select the filename, press the Enter key.
5. If saving to an existing name, WordStar will ask if you want to overwrite the old file. Answer Y to overwrite or N to return to the dialog box and try again.
6. When saving completes, you'll exit from the editing mode and return to the Opening Menu.

Abandoning a file without saving

The command Ctrl—KQ lets you abandon a file without saving it. This command is called Close on the pull-down File Menu. Below are the steps for abandoning a file:

1. Hold down the Ctrl key and type KQ.
2. If no changes have been made to the file, WordStar will close the file and return to the Opening Menu.
3. If you made any changes to the file since opening it, WordStar will tell you and ask you to verify abandoning those changes. A single inadvertent keystroke is enough to call this message.
4. Answer Y to abandon and N to return to the document.

Caution: Never forget that abandoning a file erases the current version of it from RAM without saving it to disk. You lose all edits made since the last save.

Reasons for abandoning a file

Abandoning a file can be a lifesaver. Unwanted changes to a file are never permanent until you save them to disk. To revert to the last saved version of the file, abandon the file in memory and reload the version on disk.

Sometimes you open a file merely to browse through, or open a file in a window to cut and paste boilerplate text. There's no need to save the file if no changes were made to it. Abandon it and continue with your writing.

Placing markers in a document

You can choose between two different ways to embed place markers. One is using the Block & Save Menu. The other is an offshoot of the dot command structure.

Placing markers with Ctrl–K0 through Ctrl–K9

The command Ctrl–K(0-9) embeds up to 10 temporary place markers in an open document. Once you place a marker, you can jump the cursor directly to it with the command Ctrl–Q(0-9).

Place markers have many practical uses. If you need to find something elsewhere in the document and then come back, embed a marker before leaving. Insert markers at beginning and end of your current work—and anywhere in between. Then use them to jump to specific places in the document.

Large-file manuscripts make place markers especially useful. They help you keep track of important sections—and keep track of where you're working. Place markers also make it easier to use block movements for cutting and pasting:

1. Put the marker where you intend to paste.
2. Find and mark the block to move or copy.
3. Jump back to the place marker.
4. Cut and paste the block.

Setting a place marker

Place a marker anywhere you want one. They don't have to be used in numerical order. Follow any order you like. Use all ten, or the same numbers repeatedly. Put them on a blank line, in the middle of a line, or anywhere you want.

1. Place the cursor at the point you want a marker.
2. Hold down the Ctrl key and type K.
3. Type a number from 0 to 9.
4. A symbol containing the number will appear to mark the place.

Going to a marked place

Use Ctrl–Q(0-9) to jump to any marker. Hold down the Ctrl key and type Q followed immediately by the number of the marker. WordStar knows each marker location, and will go backward or forward to it without further instructions.

Removing a place marker

Remove a place marker with the same steps you used to place it. Either go to the marker and use Ctrl–K(0-9), or simply issue the command twice, wherever you happen to be.

Using embedded comments as markers

I mostly use embedded comment lines as place markers. These comments become a permanent part of the document, or at least until deleted. So if I have to save and exit, they're waiting for me when I come back.

Like a dot command, an embedded comment takes up a line of its own. The line doesn't count toward page length, and doesn't print in the hardcopy.

Place as many embedded comments as needed. Use any word, number, or phrase as a place marker. Use something personal or unique so you can remember them easily. Use your imagination—I use a word I made up years ago.

Place markers can help you keep track of specific paragraphs or sections in any large manuscript. Page and line numbers will shift as you cut, paste, or add to chapters and sections. Place markers are a consistent way to go directly to your work.

Typing in an embedded comment

Don't confuse what I'm talking about with WordStar's nonprinting comment notes available through the Notes Menu. You don't need to call any menu or dialog box to insert these. Just type them into the text file.

A typed embedded comment is more convenient to locate because you can find it with Ctrl−QF. Like a dot command, an embedded comment requires a line of its own in the text file.

1. Use Ctrl−N to insert an empty line in the text file.
2. With the cursor on column 1 of the empty line, type two dots (..) and then the word, number, or phrase of the comment.
3. Notice that a dot will appear on the flag line. This simply indicates that you embedded the comment correctly.

That's all there is to it. The simplest way to make a hidden comment is to type it in this way. The other way to insert a nonprinting comment is through the WordStar Notes Menu—an option on the Onscreen Format Menu.

Going to an embedded comment

Once an embedded comment is in a document, use the command Ctrl−QF to find it again.

1. Hold down the Ctrl key and type QF.
2. On the Find line, type in the complete comment, including the two dots preceding it.
3. Use whatever find options you need, and be sure to tell WordStar the correct direction to send the search.
4. Press the Enter key.

Removing an embedded comment

Embedded comments don't print in the hardcopy, so it isn't mandatory to remove them from the document. To remove an embedded comment, simply find it and delete it.

Block operations

This section covers WordStar's cut-and-paste functions. WordStar has called these *block movements* since its first release. In WordStar, a *block* is *a group of text characters marked for moving, copying, saving, deleting, or other operation, as a unit*. It can be any word, phrase, paragraph, or portion of a text file—up to and including the entire text file. The entire process can be summed up as follows:

1. Mark a block at its beginning with Ctrl−KB
2. Mark a block at its end with Ctrl−KK.
3. Manipulate the marked text with block operation commands.

Using block operations for cutting and pasting

Block operations are WordStar's cut-and-paste capabilities. Once marked, a block can be deleted or copied and moved anywhere in the text file—or to a text file in another window. Write it to a file of its own on disk, or read it back into another file. Cut-and-paste functions make it easier to edit and rearrange documents. Learn them well enough, and they'll become indispensable.

Hotkeys for block functions

These block function commands are installed as Shift−function key combinations. This means hold down the Shift key before pressing the function key.

Keystrokes	Function executed
Shift−F7	Move the marked block
Shift−F8	Copy the marked block
Shift−F9	Mark beginning of block
Shift−F10	Mark the end of block

Marking a block

Mark a block of text using commands to insert block markers, beginning and end. Ctrl−KB marks the beginning of a block and Ctrl−KK marks its end. To mark a block, move the cursor to its beginning and issue Ctrl−KB. Then move the cursor to the end and issue Ctrl−KK. This will cover the block with an inverse video highlight.

Copying a marked block

You can copy a marked block verbatim to any other place in the text file. Copying leaves the original unchanged in its original location. The block remains marked, so you can copy it repeatedly. Follow these steps:

1. Mark the block of text you want to copy.
2. Put the cursor at the place in the document where you want to copy it.
3. Hold down the Ctrl key and type KC. WordStar will copy the marked block to the specified location.
4. Unmark the original block when you're finished with it.

Moving a block of text

Moving a marked block of text cuts it from one place and pastes it into another. The block remains marked, so you can copy or move it again. Use the following steps:

1. Mark the block of text you want to move.
2. Place the cursor in the text file where you want to move the block.
3. Hold down the Ctrl key and type KV. WordStar will erase the marked block from its original location and move it to the specified new location.
4. Unmark the original block when you're finished with it.

Deleting a block of text

The command Ctrl−KY deletes any size marked block. If a block is too big to restore with the Unerase command, WordStar will tell you and ask if you really want to delete it.

Unerasing a deleted block

The command Ctrl−U can unerase, or insert, the last deleted block of text. If the block you used in your most recent block operation was too big for the unerase buffer, only the portion in the buffer can be unerased. Make the buffer bigger by assigning more memory to it with WSCHANGE.

Removing block markers

Block markers cannot be deleted. You must remove block markers with the same commands you used to insert them. Put the cursor on either the <B> and <K> markers and reissue the appropriate command. Removing either tag will unmark the block. Moving the begin block tag, <B>, *after* the end block tag, <K>, will also unmark the block.

Unmarking a block with Ctrl−K<

New to WordStar 7 is the unmark block command Ctrl−K<. This not only removes the block highlighting, but also the block markers. This removes a minor annoyance, but serves little purpose. You don't have to hold down the Shift key to issue this command, so Ctrl−K also works.

Remarking a Block with Ctrl−KU

New to WordStar 7 is the mark previous block command Ctrl−KU. This restores the block markers and highlight to a block unmarked with Ctrl−K<. You don't have to put the cursor on the block to remark it.

Marking or unmarking with a mouse

Using a mouse with WordStar is the easiest way to mark or unmark a block of text. To mark a block, simply click on the beginning of the block, hold down the mouse button, drag the highlight to the end of the block, and then release the button. To unmark a block, click on either end of the block, hold the button down, and then "jiggle" the mouse.

Hiding or displaying block markings

To show a marked block, WordStar covers it with an inverse video highlight. You can toggle this highlight on and off with the command Ctrl−KH. When highlighting is off, the block is hidden. Though still marked, you can only cut and paste it when the inverse video highlight is displayed. This toggle works even when the block highlighting no longer appears onscreen.

Working with column blocks of text

This section describes and defines the column block functions, and tells you how to use them for cutting and pasting columns of text in your text files.

A column block is simply a variation on the standard block mode. In it, you tag vertical columns instead of horizontal lines. This is very useful for rearranging tables of information, and for formatting parallel columns of text in a document. If you've used the Tab key as the delimiter in data files, you can use this mode for rearranging the columns prior to sorting them.

Using the column block mode

The command Ctrl−KN toggles the column block mode on and off. You can tell the mode is on when the word *Column* appears on the status line. With column blocks, the block marking commands earmark the upper left corner and the lower right corner of a column.

A column block can be as wide as the right margin, and any length. Column blocks take longer to move than standard blocks. The bigger the block, the longer it takes. Once a column block is marked, you can copy and move it with the same commands as normal blocks of text. Ctrl−KC copies the marked block.

When copying, moving, or deleting the marked block, only the column of text copies, moves, or deletes. Any dot command lines in the text are left exactly where they are. Use this for rearranging columns in a table, or in a data file where WordStar uses tab stops as the column marker.

When you cut a column from the onscreen page, the text to the right of the missing column will shift left to fill the vacated space. If the text to the right is another column, all is well. If you cut a column from the middle of a paragraph, however, auto-align will scramble the paragraph. You can't paste the missing column back in. You can restore the paragraph only by retyping it.

If you insert a column in a table or another group of columns, the text to the right will shift right to make room for it. If you insert a column anywhere in a column, auto-align will garble the paragraph by merging column text into the paragraph. Again, you can restore the paragraph only by retyping it.

Don't use column mode for cutting and pasting text in newspaper-style columns—use it only with tabbed columns. Be very careful when you have columns within columns.

Marking a column block

Mark a column block, beginning and end, with the same commands as those for marking regular blocks. The difference is that you need to turn on column mode first.

1. Turn the column mode on with Ctrl−KN.
2. Put the cursor on the top left character of the column.
3. Hold down the Ctrl key and type KB.
4. Move the cursor to the point 1 column after the bottom right character of the column. (This can be on a line below the last row of characters if you want.)
5. Hold down the Ctrl key and type KK. The inverse highlight will cover the marked block.

Note: One very important difference in column blocks is how WordStar deals with dot commands covered with a column block highlight. Dot commands belong to their line, never to a column block. When you delete or move a column block, dot commands aren't moved or deleted with it. Remove dot commands when no longer needed.

Using the column replace mode

The command Ctrl−KI toggles the Column Replace mode on and off. Column Replace enhances column block movements. It's active only if the column mode is also on. Column replace is active when *ColRepl* is substituted for *Column* on the status line.

Column replace works like a variation of the insert/overtype feature. When you cut a column block in column replace mode, this leaves a gap in the text. When you insert a column in a table or other group of columns, it will replace, or overwrite, anything in its path. This includes text to the right and below it. So be sure to leave room for it.

Cutting and pasting files or pieces of files

This section covers three major cut-and-paste commands. Learning to use them creatively will make simple work of many difficult writing tasks.

Writing a marked block to disk

The command Ctrl−KW writes a marked block of text to a file on disk. You can use this command to cut any portion of a file in memory and paste it to separate storage. You can send it to any drive or directory in your computer. You can then use the new file later as boilerplate text for other documents.

You can write the block file either to an existing filename or to a new one. Send it to a different drive by typing in the drive name before the filename. To send it to a different directory, use the arrow keys or the mouse to select a directory from the onscreen list.

An important change has been made to Ctrl−KR in WordStar 7. Previously, if a block was written to an existing file it overwrote and replaced the file. Now you have the option of either overwriting the text file or appending the block to it.

Tip: By appending the files, you can cut sections of an existing document or several documents, and paste them together in a single boilerplate file. If you have access to on-line research files, you can use WordStar to assemble all your notes for writing your term paper, business report, thesis, or dissertation.

1. Mark the block of text.
2. Hold down the Ctrl key and type KW.
3. This will call the Copy to Another File dialog box, with space for the filename for the block. Below the dialog box is the list of files in the current directory. Type or select the filename and press the Tab key.
4. The cursor is automatically on Copy to ASCII Format. WordStar is offering you the option of stripping the hidden word-processing codes from the block as it's copied to disk. If you want this option, press the spacebar to mark the checkbox. If not, leave it blank. When ready, press the Tab key.
5. The cursor should now be on OK. Use Shift−Tab if you need to go back and correct mistakes. When ready, press the Enter key.
6. If the filename is new, WordStar will write the block to disk without

further delay. If the filename already exists in that drive or directory, WordStar will ask if you want to overwrite, append, or cancel. Type the first letter of your choice or click on it with the mouse. You can also cancel by pressing the Esc key.

7. WordStar will write or escape, and return to the document screen.

Reading a file into a document

The command Ctrl−KR reads or copies a file from disk and inserts it into your document at the cursor position. It can read a file from any drive or directory in your computer. This form of cutting and pasting makes heavy use of boilerplate text—the ability to use saved text again whenever needed.

The command calls the Insert File dialog box, where you can type in the name of the file to paste in. Below the dialog box are the files in the current directory.

Read a file from the current directory by selecting it from the onscreen list. Read it from a different drive or directory by typing the drive name or path name before the filename.

1. Place the cursor where you want the file read into your document.
2. Hold down the Ctrl key and type KR.
3. This will call the Insert File dialog box (see Fig. 11-2), with a place for the name of the file being inserted. Below the dialog box are the files in the current directory. Type or select the filename, and press the Enter key.

```
━━━━━━━━━━━━━━━━━━━━ I N S E R T   A   F I L E ━━━━━━━━
File   illus.dot
       illus.dot
Press F1 for help.
```

11-2 Insert File dialog box.

4. If found, the file will be copied from disk and inserted at the cursor position. You'll be returned to the document.
5. If not found, WordStar will tell you that it Can't find file on disk. Press the Esc key to return to the dialog box. Correct the spelling or path and try again. Or press the Esc key again to return to the document.

Understanding boilerplates

The term *boilerplate* dates from the Steam Age, when steam engines powered every major machine. The heart of any steam engine is its boiler. When boilers were built, they were assembled from prefabricated metal plates—called boilerplates. When a boiler needed repair, a ready-made plate replaced the damaged one. From a stockpile of boilerplates, a boiler of any standard size could be swiftly built or repaired.

The printing industry borrowed the term to describe blocks of reusable type—like advertisements, notices, handbills, and so on. Instead of resetting type from scratch, they inked the boilerplate and used it again. This saved time and labor.

The ultimate convenience of computerized writing is that once you type something and save it you never have to type it again. With computerized writing and desktop publishing, any portion of any file can serve as a boilerplate.

At its simplest, a portion of a text file can be cut from one place in the file and moved to another. At the next level, portions of a text file can be cut and saved to distinct files, and then pasted into other documents when needed. The third level requires opening two documents in separate windows, cutting boilerplate text from one file, and copying it into another.

The fourth level uses merge printing to join pieces of boilerplate text before you print a document. Merge printing isn't difficult to use, but it is a complicated and complex subject. For more information, see the chapter on merge printing in this book. Everything related to merge printing is an extension of normal cut-and-paste functions.

Building a boilerplate archive

When you build a boilerplate archive, you create a storehouse of reusable text. Other writing programs will call this a *glossary*. The underlying principle is that any portion of any file can be used as boilerplate text in any other file.

Business writing is mostly repetitive typing. Write a hundred business letters, and you'll often type the same things repeatedly. When you aren't mailing enough form letters to make merge printing practical, use boilerplates. Type the first letter and use its file as a template for the others. Copy it into an empty file and change the addressee's name, address, and greeting. You can even keep a separate file containing nothing but mailing addresses—already typed and ready to cut and paste.

Lawyers often use stock paragraphs repeatedly in every contract, proposal, or release agreement. For lengthy documents containing lots of "party of the first part" and "party of the second part" phrases, you can save these phrases to separate files and paste them in when needed. Standard contracts can be saved as boilerplates—simply open a new file, read the boilerplate contract into it, and make the necessary changes.

With an archive of boilerplate text, you can assemble standard documents from reusable pieces—and then type from scratch only those things varying from version to version.

I've used boilerplates every fifteen minutes or so while writing this entire manual. I have template files for section and subsection headings, each with table of contents codes in place. I keep separate files for tips, notes, and warnings—each with dot commands for margin changes.

One file contains a blank numbered list with hanging indentation and another contains a blank bullet list, so all I have to do is type the instructions on the blank lines. I even have the phrases *press the Enter key* and *press the Esc key again to return to the document* saved as boilerplate files. Anything I use repeatedly I store as boilerplate text. The possibilities are endless.

You can store boilerplate text in the same directory as your documents, or keep it in a separate directory on your hard drive. Be sure to keep a backup copy stored on a floppy disk to protect it.

Working in two windows at once

This section discusses WordStar's ability to open and work with text files in two windows at once. With only a few exceptions, working in two windows is the same as working in a single window.

A *window* is the part of the screen where you open and write documents. WordStar 7 allows you to open two windows, with a different document or non-document in window. In the default factory setting, opening a second window splits the screen in half, with a different text file showing in each portion.

The ultimate usefulness of working in two windows lies in the convenience it provides. You don't have to exit one text file to look at or work on another. When text files are open in separate windows, you can switch back and forth, and copy or move text freely between them. This allows you to write one document and easily copy paragraphs or tables into it as boilerplate text.

Opening a second window is like having a second word processor running. If you need to make notes or work on another document, just open it, get your work done, and close it.

Every writer knows that ideas and words don't always come in the right order or in the right place. Sometimes you get an idea belonging to something you're not working on. If you don't write the words down, you might forget them. With a second window, you can always open another text file, new or existing, and write down those words where they belong.

The Windows commands and options

You need to know seven special commands to work with windows. All other WordStar commands can be used in a document open in any window. These seven commands are as follows:

Block command	What it does
Ctrl−OK	Open or switch between windows
Ctrl−OM	Size the current window
Ctrl−KA	Copy block from other window

Block command	What it does
Ctrl – KG	Move block from other window
Ctrl – KW	Write block from active window to disk
Ctrl – KY	Delete block in active window
Ctrl – U	Undelete block in active window
Ctrl – K[	Copy block of text from clipboard
Ctrl – K]	Copy block of text to clipboard
Ctrl – KS	Save the document in a window
Ctrl – KD	Save the document and exit window
Ctrl – KQ	Abandon the window without saving

Opening a second window or switching between windows

The command Ctrl – OK either opens a new window or switches between windows already open. If you're opening another document in the second window, select it just as you would in the first. The same rules and restrictions apply.

Switching between windows with a mouse

There are three different ways to switch between windows using a mouse:

- If the documents are displayed in split-screen mode, point to the window you want and click on it with the mouse.
- The window number of the currently active window is displayed in brackets on the status line. If the documents are displayed in full-screen mode, point to the window number on the status line and click on it with the mouse.
- Click on File on the title bar, then click on Open/Switch. If you're opening another text file from the onscreen list, double-click on it. Otherwise, track it down the normal way.

Working with a document in a second window

While a document is open in a window, all the document mode writing and editing features are available. There are no special instructions for working with a document in a second window. You can do anything with it that you can with any other document.

Opening nondocuments with Ctrl – OK

The factory version of WordStar 7 comes set up to allow you to open documents only in the second window. This can be inconvenient if you want to work on a nondocument and document at the same time. In the factory version, you must open the nondocument in the first window, and the document in the second. If you close the nondocument window first, you can't open another nondocument until you close the document as well.

Tip: You can set up WordStar to prompt you for opening either a document or nondocument in the second window. At the WSCHANGE Main Menu, type DCGG. Set Window Prompt for Document/Nondoc to on. With this setup, you can open documents or nondocuments in either window.

While a nondocument is open in a window, all the nondocument mode writing and editing features are available. There are no special instructions for working with a nondocument in a second window. You can do anything with it you can with any other nondocument.

Sizing the current window

The command Ctrl−OM calls the Change Window Size dialog box. There are three selections on this dialog box to allow you to temporarily resize the window display. When you close either window, WordStar will revert to its default setting. The options are as follows:

Full Screen   If you set window size to Full Screen, only one window will appear at a time, and it will be displayed with as many lines as your monitor setup allows.

Half Screen   The factory default is Half Screen, which is 10 or 11 lines on standard monitors (with style bar, status line, ruler line, etc. all showing). On VGA monitors, Half Screen gives 24 lines for window 1 and 23 lines for window 2.

Specific Number   This allows you to set a specific number of lines for either window. The other window will be displayed in the remainder of the screen.

If you often work in two windows, you'll probably want to switch to full screen display most of the time so you can see as much of the document onscreen as possible. Ten or eleven lines is hardly enough to work in.

Tip: You can permanently change the default window size at the WSCHANGE Main Menu by typing DCGH and setting Size of Other Window to 255. This sets it to Full Screen.

Copying between windows

The window command Ctrl−KA copies a marked block from one window to another. The following steps assume you have two text file windows open.

1. Mark the block you're going to copy.
2. Switch windows, and place the cursor where the copied block is to be inserted.
3. Hold down the Ctrl key and type KA.

4. The marked block will be copied to the cursor location. Because it was copied, the block isn't marked.

Moving a block between windows

The command Ctrl−KG moves the marked block from one window to another. Use the following steps:

1. Mark the block you're going to move.
2. Switch windows, and place the cursor where the moved block is to be inserted.
3. Hold down the Ctrl key and type KG.
4. The marked block will be moved to the cursor location.

Tip: Changes made to a file by moving or copying blocks from window to window aren't permanent until the next time you save the changed file. If you close and abandon the text file, it will revert to the version stored on disk.

Saving, exiting, and abandoning windows

These three things are so elemental that most first-time users find them confusing. They look for something special about them—and there's nothing special at all. What you open in windows are either documents or nondocuments. To save, exit, or abandon a document in a window, use the same commands you would for a single-window document.

- Ctrl−KS saves the file and returns you to editing.
- Ctrl−KD saves the file and closes the window.
- Ctrl−KQ abandons the document and closes the window without saving.

Using the Windows clipboard

This section briefly discusses WordStar's new capability to access and use the Windows' clipboard accessory. For complete information on using the Microsoft Windows clipboard, see the *Microsoft Windows User's Guide*.

WordStar's clipboard commands

There are two entirely new block commands on WordStar 7's Block & Save Menu. These are the commands for accessing the Windows Clipboard feature. These commands are also found on the pull-down Document File Copy Menu.

Clipboard command	What it does
Ctrl−K[or Alt−ECF	Copy block of text from the clipboard
Ctrl−K] or Alt−ECT	Copy block of text to the clipboard

To use the Windows clipboard with WordStar, you must be running WordStar under the Windows program in the 386 enhanced mode. So you must have at least Windows 3.0 and an 80386SX computer.

What is the Windows clipboard?

The Windows clipboard is intended for copying large blocks of text between *different programs*. It does this by setting aside a special buffer in extended memory.

Limitations of the Windows clipboard

Windows application programs make special use of this clipboard buffer. Word-Star 7 doesn't. The only use in WordStar you might have for it is if you have a Windows program that generates ASCII text you want to paste into a WordStar file. If not, don't bother with it. The clipboard has several limitations:

- When you copy a block to it, all WordStar formatting commands are removed, converting it into ASCII text.
- When you copy from the clipboard to a WordStar text file, the text is inserted as ASCII.
- You can't copy a block from the clipboard if it contains graphics or text not in the ASCII format.
- If the block includes a note tag, only the reference number is copied to the clipboard. To copy a note to the clipboard, use Ctrl−OND to display the note text, mark it as a block, and then copy it.
- The Windows clipboard is limited to 64K of data or text. If you try to copy a larger block, only the first 64K will be copied. Depending on the size of the block, WordStar also needs up to 64K of additional memory. So you're talking 128K just to copy one block.

Sorting text in blocks

This section discusses the block sorting command, tells you how to use it, and suggests possible uses.

The command Ctrl−KZ performs an alphanumeric sort of lines in a block, and puts them in either ascending or descending order. Sorts can be performed on standard blocks or on column blocks. In either case, the entire line moves. Use this for sorting data files typed with WordStar or written with MailList.

It would be nice if WordStar offered you the option of choosing between an alpha sort, a numeric sort, and an alphanumeric sort. Because it doesn't, you must be aware of the limitations of a purely alphanumeric sort—and plan ahead.

An *alphanumeric sort* arranges text by number first, and then by alphabet. To sort record lines in a data file, mark all the record lines as a block. WordStar bases sort order, in succession, on all characters in the line, with the first character being the key. Thus, for an ascending-order sort:

- All lines beginning with numerals come before all lines beginning with letters of the alphabet.
- All lines beginning with A come before all lines beginning with B, and so on.
- All lines beginning with AB come before all lines beginning with AC, and so on.

For descending order, the sort is exactly opposite the above examples. An alphanumeric sort is based on the ASCII character set. It sorts columns or lines of numbers and words according to their relative position in this character set. In an ascending order sort, numbers come before letters of the alphabet, which come before the extended characters. Zero is the first numeral, and leading zeros cannot be ignored. Therefore, 011 comes before 10 in an alphanumeric sort.

An ascending-order sort rearranges text or numbers from lowest value to highest. Thus 0-9 and A-Z. A descending-order sort rearranges text or numbers from highest value to lowest. Thus Z-A and 9-0.

Running a block sort

Below are the basic steps for running an alphanumeric sort on a marked block of text. Expect it to take a long time for the sort to complete. The more items being sorted, the longer it will take.

1. Mark the block of text. It can be either lines or a column.
2. Hold down the Ctrl key and type KZ.
3. When prompted, type A for ascending order or D for descending order.
4. WordStar will rearrange the block, moving entire lines.

Sorting text in column blocks

If the column mode is on, WordStar will determine sort order based on the highlighted column. For example: to sort an address list by zipcode, turn on column mode and mark the zipcode column as a block; then sort the text. WordStar will rearrange the addresses according to their zipcodes.

Tip: If spelling checks are getting slower, your personal dictionary might need sorting. WordStar doesn't add words to the dictionary in alphabetical order. They're simply inserted after the last word in the dictionary. Open the file PER-SONAL.DCT as a nondocument, mark the entire file as a block, and sort in ascending order. Then delete superfluous words.

Sorting data files

In data files, the default field (or column) delimiter is the comma. This character tells merge printing where one column of information ends and the next column begins. To use any field column as the key for sorting when the comma is the field delimiter, make it the first column in the record line. For example, put zipcodes first to make them the sort key.

Using WSCHANGE, you can change the delimiter to a tab stop. Then you can replace the commas in your data files with tabs and make neat columns of information in those data files.

Use only one tab to separate each column because each tab specifies a new field of information. Embed a ruler line and set tab stops wide enough for each column. Then you can easily mark any column of information as the key for sorting.

Using MailList to write and sort data files

The MailList companion program is your best bet for both writing and sorting mailing list data files. It's so easy to use that you don't even need to read the documentation for basic features. It's so foolproof that you can hardly go wrong. The data files it creates can all be used by the same master documents. Best yet—you can select any item or field on the template and use it as the key for sorting the data file.

Tip: When writing or editing data file mailing lists with MailList, don't forget to type them in mixed case. If you type them in all caps, the resulting hardcopy form letters or mailing labels will look unprofessional.

Using block math

Block math uses the calculator functions found on the Quick Menu's calculator. Once you master this, it's a much better way to do calculations than through the so-called calculator.

If you know how to use the valid symbols on the calculator, you can write your equation directly into the document. Mark the whole equation as a block and issue Ctrl−KM, the block math command.

The command Ctrl−KM can calculate the numbers and equations in a marked block of text, even if the block also has words in it. Accountants often use this to run a spot check on the numbers in clients' reports. Block math can work with either standard blocks or column blocks. To calculate block math:

1. Mark the block of math functions, beginning and end.
2. Hold down the Ctrl key and type KM.
3. WordStar will scan the marked block and execute the math calculations contained within. If you don't include the valid symbols, WordStar can only add the numbers.

You can insert the results of block math into your documents through the Macro Menu—the same way you would insert results from using the Math Menu.

Macro	What it does
Ctrl−M=	Inserts last math result
Ctrl−M#	Inserts last math equation
Ctrl−M$	Inserts last math as dollar amount

File manipulation

The commands in this section manipulate entire files instead of only pieces of files. These same options are available through the Opening Menu. All are essentially MS-DOS commands, except that they're issued through dialog boxes instead of a DOS prompt.

Copying a file

The command Ctrl−KO calls the Copy dialog box (see Fig. 11-3). It's the same Copy dialog box you get through the Opening Menu.

```
========================= Copy =========================

   Existing Filename: CHAPTER.01______________________      ▌   OK   ▐

        New Filename: ______________________                ▌ Cancel ▐
________________________________________________________________________

Filenames:              Path: C:\COMMAND.WS6   45M free
..                 \    ARCHIVE            \   2COLTAB.RR     .3k   APPENDIX.01  5.6k
APPENDIX.02  9.5k       AUTHQUES.TAB 8.7k      AYS            .5k   BLOKMENU.USE 5.0k
CAUTION       .3k       CHAPTER.01    19k      CHAPTER.02    25k    CHAPTER.03    24k
CHAPTER.04    11k       CHAPTER.05   9.1k      CHAPTER.06    22k    CHAPTER.07    74k
CHAPTER.08    46k       CHAPTER.09    14k      CHAPTER.10    79k    CHAPTER.11    77k
CHAPTER.12    55k       CHAPTER.13    45k      CHAPTER.14    20k    CHAPTER.15    18k
CHAPTER.16    44k       CHAPTER.17   7.8k      CHAPTER.18    33k    CHAPTER.19    28k
CHAPTER.20   8.3k       CHEK.BOX      .3k      CHEKLIST     1.9k    CHESS.DOC     36k
COLUMNS       30k       COM-WS6.PR5   23k      COMANDWS     9.3k    COMMAND.MSS  449k
COMPANIO     3.3k       EDITMENU      .4k      EXAMPLE       .3k    FILENAME      .5k
```

11-3   Copy dialog box.

You can't copy a file to itself. You *can* copy a file from any drive or directory to any other drive or directory. You can even copy the file to a different name. The last saved version of any file in memory can be copied to a different name or location.

The steps for using the copy command can be found in the chapter *Using the Opening Menu features*.

Renaming a file

The command Ctrl−KE calls the Rename dialog box (see Fig. 11-4). It's the same dialog box you get through the Opening Menu.

```
Current Filename: C:\COMMAND.WS6\OPENMENU.FIG                     ▌  OK   ▌

   New Filename: ______________________________________         ▌ Cancel ▌

Filenames:            Path: C:\COMMAND.WS6   45M free
..              \     ARCHIVE          \    2COLTAB.RR    .3k    APPENDIX.01  5.6k
CAUTION       .3k     CHAPTER.01      19k    CHAPTER.02    25k    CHAPTER.03   24k
CHAPTER.04    11k     CHAPTER.05     9.1k    CHAPTER.06    22k    CHAPTER.07   74k
CHAPTER.08    46k     CHAPTER.09      14k    CHAPTER.10    79k    CHAPTER.11   77k
CHAPTER.12    55k     CHAPTER.13      45k    CHAPTER.14    20k    CHAPTER.15   18k
CHAPTER.16    44k     CHAPTER.17     7.8k    CHAPTER.18    33k    CHAPTER.19   28k
CHAPTER.20   8.3k     CHEK.BOX        .3k    CHEKLIST     1.9k    CHESS.DOC    36k
COLUMNS       30k     COM-WS6.PR5     23k    COMANDWS     9.3k    COMMAND.MSS  449k
COMPANIO     3.3k     EDITMENU        .4k    EXAMPLE       .3k    FILENAME     .5k
```

11-4 Rename dialog box.

You can't rename any file open in any window, but you can rename any other file on disk, in any drive or directory. The steps for renaming a file through the Rename dialog box can be found in the chapter *Using the Opening Menu features*.

Deleting a file

The command Ctrl−KJ calls the Delete dialog box (see Fig. 11-5). This is the same dialog box you can call through the Opening Menu.


```
                                                                 ▌  OK   ▌
   Filename: ______________________________________
                                                                 ▌ Cancel ▌

Filenames:            Path: C:\COMMAND.WS6   45M free
..              \     ARCHIVE          \    2COLTAB.RR    .3k    APPENDIX.01  5.6k
APPENDIX.02  9.5k     AUTHQUES.TAB   8.7k    AYS           .5k    BLOKMENU.USE 5.0k
CAUTION       .3k     CHAPTER.01      19k    CHAPTER.02    25k    CHAPTER.03   24k
CHAPTER.04    11k     CHAPTER.05     9.1k    CHAPTER.06    22k    CHAPTER.07   74k
CHAPTER.08    46k     CHAPTER.09      14k    CHAPTER.10    79k    CHAPTER.11   77k
CHAPTER.12    55k     CHAPTER.13      45k    CHAPTER.14    20k    CHAPTER.15   18k
CHAPTER.16    44k     CHAPTER.17     7.8k    CHAPTER.18    33k    CHAPTER.19   28k
CHAPTER.20   8.3k     CHEK.BOX        .3k    CHEKLIST     1.9k    CHESS.DOC    36k
COLUMNS       30k     COM-WS6.PR5     23k    COMANDWS     9.3k    COMMAND.MSS  449k
COMPANIO     3.3k     EDITMENU        .4k    EXAMPLE       .3k    FILENAME     .5k
```

11-5 Delete dialog box.

You can't delete any file open in any window, but you can delete any other file on disk, in any drive or directory. The steps for deleting a file through the Delete dialog box can be found in the chapter *Using the Opening Menu features*.

Printing with the Block & Save Menu

Because WordStar uses background printing, you can send a file to the printer through the Block & Save Menu and continue to work on the file you have open in the document mode. You can execute either standard or merge printing commands while in the document or nondocument modes.

You can print the last saved version of the text file open in the document window. If you've made any changes, WordStar requires you save the file before continuing. You can continue to write and edit the open version—but you can't save it until WordStar is finished printing.

Depending on your computer and your printer, there can be some minor annoyances with background printing. You might have some keyboard lockout while WordStar sends a page to the print buffer. The data transfer to the printer might pause while you type. How much or little it does this depends on the speed of your computer, and the speed or type of printer being used.

Don't use background printing with more than one window open. Don't overload your computer—giving it too much to work on simultaneously.

Printing a file

The command Ctrl−KP sends a file to a printer and lets you continue working on your open file. The Print dialog box (see Fig. 11-6) will appear onscreen, with a list of the files in the current directory below the menu.

```
▬▬▬▬▬▬▬▬▬▬▬▬▬▬▬ Print ▬▬▬▬▬▬▬▬▬▬▬▬▬

   Filename: C:\COMMAND.WS6\OPENMENU.FIG ________       ▌  OK  ▐

Page Numbers:                           Pages:          ▌ Cancel ▐
          ◆  All                          o  Odd
          o  Selected Pages:              o  Even
                                          ◆  Both
             ________________

    Copies: 1_
                                        [X] Use Form Feeds
   Printer: LASERJET                    [ ] Pause Between Pages
                                        [ ] Print Unformatted Text
 Redirect To: ________________          [X] Interpret Merge Variables

 ─────────────────────────────────────────────────────────────────
 Filenames:            Path: C:\COMMAND.WS6  45M free
 ..            \   ARCHIVE         \  2COLTAB.RR    .3k  APPENDIX.01  5.6k
 APPENDIX.02  9.5k  AUTHQUES.TAB 8.7k  AYS          .5k  BLOKMENU.USE 5.0k
 CAUTION       .3k  CHAPTER.01   19k   CHAPTER.02   25k  CHAPTER.03   24k
 CHAPTER.04   11k   CHAPTER.05  9.1k   CHAPTER.06   22k  CHAPTER.07   74k
 CHAPTER.08   46k   CHAPTER.09   14k   CHAPTER.10   79k  CHAPTER.11   77k
 CHAPTER.12   55k   CHAPTER.13   45k   CHAPTER.14   20k  CHAPTER.15   18k
 CHAPTER.16   44k   CHAPTER.17  7.8k   CHAPTER.18   33k  CHAPTER.19   28k
```

11-6 Print dialog box.

Type in the name of the file or select it from the onscreen list by using the arrow keys to put the highlight on its name and then pressing the Enter key. You can also select it by double-clicking on it with the mouse.

You can identify a file in another drive or directory by preceding its filename with the drive name and path. With a mouse, you can call other directories by clicking on the directory names onscreen.

Accept or change the printing variables, and use the Enter key to go from item to item. Use Ctrl−K when you're ready to send the file to the printer. Once started, the printing will run automatically until complete or interrupted.

Merge printing a file

The command Ctrl−KP can also start merge printing a file in the background. Merge printing is now an option of any print run-off. Just be sure that the checkbox for Interpret Merge Variables is checked. For further information, read the chapter titled *Merge Printing with WordStar*.

Converting a text file to a fax file

The command Ctrl−K \ calls the Fax dialog box. This is the same dialog box you get through the Opening Menu. This feature is used for converting your WordStar documents and nondocuments to fax files in the standard .PCX format. Once created, these fax files can be transmitted directly through a fax board installed in your computer.

This conversion program, and the steps for using it, are fully covered in chapter 14, *Converting text files to faxes*.

Changing the current drive/directory

The command Ctrl−KL calls the Change Drive/Directory dialog box (see Fig. 11-7). This is the same dialog box you get through the Opening Menu.

You can change to any drive or directory in your computer. This does not change the drive or directory for the currently open document, but you can use the alternative path for Ctrl−KR and Ctrl−KW operations. And if you exit the cur-

```
━━━━━━━━━━━━━━━━━━━ Change Drive\Directory ━━━━━━━━━━━━━━━━━━━

                                                         ▌  OK  ▌
   Drive\Directory: C:\COMMAND7                          ▌ Cancel ▌


   Directories:    C:\WS  45M free
   ..              \ | FAX          \ | MACROS      \ | OPTIONS      \
```

11-7   Change Drive/Directory dialog box.

rent document without restoring the original drive or directory, the new drive/ directory will become the current one.

The steps and routines for changing the current drive or directory can be found in the chapter *Using the Opening Menu features*.

Running a DOS command

The command Ctrl−KF calls the Run dialog box. This is the same dialog box available through the Opening Menu. It allows you to run any MS-DOS command. Run batch files and other software through this window. Never run another program with this feature unless you know that it won't interfere with WordStar.

Warning: Never, *under any circumstances*, run WordStar again through this DOS window! This will ruin the file allocation table, and truncates your files in the current directory. It may ruin the entire FAT (file allocation table) on the floppy or hard drive, and truncate everything.

Changing the case of text in blocks

WordStar allows you to change the case of text in a marked block. You can change the case to all caps or all lowercase, or capitalize the first word in every sentence. This works on either standard or column blocks.

Changing to all caps   The command Ctrl−K" will capitalize every letter in every word of a marked block. Mark the block normally, hold down the Ctrl key, and type K". WordStar will convert every letter in the block to all capitals.

Changing to lowercase   The command Ctrl−K' will change every letter in a marked block to lowercase. Mark the block normally, hold down the Ctrl key, and type K'. WordStar will convert every letter to lowercase.

Capitalizing the first letter of every sentence   The command Ctrl−K., or Ctrl−K(period), will capitalize the first word in every sentence and put every other letter in lowercase. Mark the block normally, hold down the Ctrl key, and type K.. WordStar will capitalize the first word in every sentence. Tip: Sometimes this just doesn't work unless you first mark the block in all caps and then use the sentence capitalization command.

Counting the words

WordStar allows you to count the words in a document, nondocument, normal block, or column block. WordStar still hasn't upgraded and restored the old, faithful WC.COM counting program. So you have to open each document or non-document individually, and count its words from inside the write-and-edit mode.

The command Ctrl−K? starts WordStar's word counting program. (It doesn't matter whether you type K? or K/ for running the word count.) It counts both the words and characters in an open document or nondocument. The results are displayed in a dialog box when completed.

The document word count always travels from beginning to end, so you can begin a word count anywhere in the file.

You can limit a word count to a specific block of text. It can be either a standard block or a column block. The block doesn't have to be onscreen when you're counting its words.

12

Using the Print Controls Menu commands

This chapter covers the commands, features, and options found on the Print Controls Menu. This classic menu's commands are used to set the character attributes and select font, printing color, and printer being used. Among the miscellaneous commands are five user-definable custom printer codes. See Fig. 12-1 for an illustration of this menu.

- To call the Print Controls Menu, hold down the Ctrl key and type P.
- To use a command or feature in this menu, type the boldfaced letter beside it.
- To escape from the Print Controls Menu without issuing a command, press the spacebar or the Esc key.

Print control basics and guidelines

This section discusses some of the basic features of working with the Print Controls Menu. WordStar 6 users should notice that no changes have been made to this menu except for the graphic display of the menu itself.

One command that should have been added to this menu but wasn't is the Change Printer Codes command, available only through the pull-down Insert Menu or through the command Alt−IH. This command calls a dialog box used to assign values to the user-definable custom printer codes.

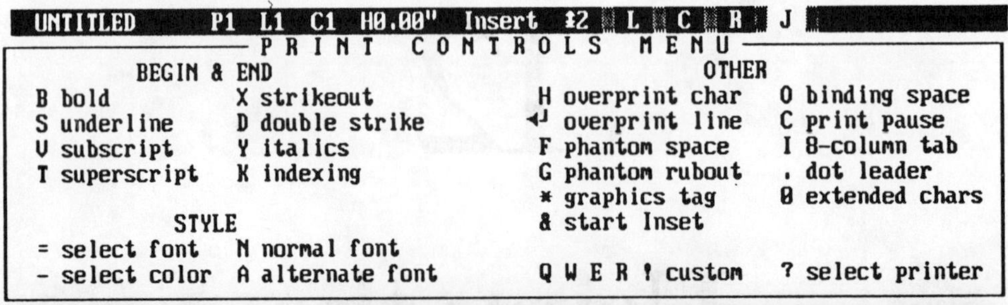

12-1 Print Controls Menu.

The print control commands

There are 29 options on the Print Controls Menu. Eight control character attributes; four select font type, size, and style; one selects a preferred printer and attaches its ID to the document; eleven control the physical aspects of printing lines and graphics; and five are blank, for you to program with custom printing commands.

Note: You'll find that these same commands are split up arbitrarily between the Insert, Style, and pull-down Layout menus.

When issued, the commands from the Print Controls Menu are embedded in the document. This means that, like dot commands, they're visible in the text file but don't print in the document. Instead, they represent a function to be executed at print-time.

When a print control command is embedded, WordStar places a symbol character in the file. This symbol is a caret (^) followed by the letter representing each command. The character can be deleted like any other. When attached to a word or line, it's deleted with the line.

What are print controls?

The printing controls are commands that "tag" words, sentences, or paragraphs with special codes for controlling how WordStar prints something. These printing tags are attached directly and visually to specific text in the document. Some codes tell the printer how to give characters special printing attributes like boldface, italic, underlining, and so on. Others serve to fine-tune the layout of the printed document.

Where do print controls belong?

Printing control commands are placed in the text file at the point where you want them to take effect. Eight commands on the menu are listed under Begin & End. This means that they're placed twice. The first time marks the beginning of the special printing attribute, and the second time toggles it off. The remainder of the standard commands need be issued only once to get the job done.

The user-defined custom commands have no assigned value until you give them one. So they can be either begin & end commands or single-use commands—however you define them.

The print control symbols

When you assign a printing tag, a special symbol will appear onscreen. There's a different symbol for each printing control. These symbols are as follows:

Symbol	What it represents
^B	Boldface text
^S	Underlined text
^V	Subscript text
^T	Superscript text
^X	Strikeout text
^D	Double-strike text
^Y	Italic text
^K	Indexing code
<NORMAL>	Defined normal font is active
<ALTERNATE>	Defined alternate font is active
^H	Overprint previous character
—	Overprint previous line
^F	Phantom space character
^G	Phantom rubout
^C	Printing pause command
~	Binding space
.....	Leading dots
^Q	User-defined custom command
^W	User-defined custom command
^E	User-defined custom command
^R	User-defined custom command

Toggling the print control display on and off

To see these printing code symbols, you must have the print control display toggled on. This is done with the Ctrl−OD command. If you have a mouse, click on the <*> icon on the style bar. This feature is called Command Tags on the pulldown View Menu.

Monochrome monitors On monochrome monitors, the symbols and marked text usually look like all the other characters onscreen. The default monochrome setup at least shows boldface as bold. If your monitor has graphics capabilities, it can also be set up to show underlining onscreen.

Color monitors With color monitors, you can assign each attribute a distinctive color, so you can recognize formatted text at a glance—even with the print control display off.

Tip: Use WSCHANGE to set onscreen colors the way you want them. Color settings have no effect on how anything *works*. If you're worried about about ruining your working copy of WordStar, create a new version of WordStar and tinker with the colors in it. At the WSCHANGE Main Menu, type ABA to select colors individually. Complete instructions are found onscreen.

Print control terminology

Before you continue, you need to understand some print control terminology. Below are the basic print control terms and definitions for all the special printing commands on the Print Controls Menu.

Boldface Text is printed bold, or darker. Dot-matrix printers make two or three passes of the print head to achieve this effect. Daisywheel printers hit the font two or three times. Laser printers usually have a separate bold typeface for each font.

Underline Text is printed with underlining. Dot-matrix and daisywheel printers back up to underline. Laser printers either have a separate underlining font or simply print underlining at the same time as everything else.

Subscript Text is printed slightly below the normal printing line. Daisywheel printers perform a half-roll down to print subscript. Laser printers either have a separate subscript font or simply print subscript at the same time as everything else.

Superscript Text is printed slightly above the normal printing line. Daisywheel printers perform a half-roll up to print superscript. Laser printers either have a separate superscript font or simply print superscript at the same time as everything else.

Strikeout Text is printed with another character, usually a hyphen, printed over it. Used to indicate text that's been deleted.

Doublestrike An obsolete command whose function is similar to Boldface (used when most printers were daisywheels and the only way to achieve bold print was to "double strike" the characters). In most printers, it prints identical to boldface. In printers recognizing it, the print head strikes twice instead of the three strikes used for bold.

Italics   Text prints in slanted, or italic, font.

Select Font   Calls the Font dialog box and displays the list of fonts available for the printer attached to the document.

Select Color   Calls the Color/Shading dialog box, which displays the list of colors or shades of printing available for the attached printer to use.

Overprint Character   Tells the printer to print the following character over the previous character. Commonly used to print accent marks over characters. Is made unnecessary by printers capable of printing the expanded character set.

Overprint Line   Tells the printer to print the following line over the previous line. Is mainly used for printing indented numbered or bulleted lists.

Phantom Space   Tells WordStar to print either the character at the print wheel's hex code 20 position or the special installed character.

Phantom Rubout   Tells WordStar to print either the character at the print wheel's hex code 7F position or the special installed character.

Graphics Tag   Inserts a .PIX graphic into the text file at the cursor position.

Binding Space   Inserts a special space character that binds or locks characters together. Prints as a blank space, but keeps words or characters from being split between lines by wordwrap.

Print Pause   Embeds a command in the text file that pauses printing when processed during print-time. Allows you to change daisywheel or ribbon before continuing.

8-Column Tab   Inserts a special eight-column tab at the cursor location. These tabs are internally set and have nothing to do with tabs set on the ruler line.

Dot Leader   Inserts leading dot characters from cursor position to the next tab stop. Commonly used in tables or indexes.

Extended Characters   Calls the Extended Character dialog box, which provides simple access to the ANSI characters above 128. These include accented letters, drawing characters, and scientific or mathematical notation.

Select Printer   Calls the Change Printer dialog box, where you can select another printer ID to attach to the text file.

Custom Commands   These are user-definable print control commands. The possibilities are limited only to what the printer can do.

What is a font?

A font is a particular style and size of typeface. Fonts normally come in specific sizes, and the measure of font size is points. When you choose a font, therefore, you specify its type and size. For example: 12-point Times Roman, 14-point Helvetica, and 10-point Courier.

For several generations, different font types have been a part of the printing and publishing industry. There are thousands of different kinds of fonts. When computerized writing first came along, you could use only whatever fonts your printer had built in. The average printer—as inflexible as typewriters—normally had only a single built-in font. People thought they were lucky if their printer would do boldface and italic, and print something readable.

Now there are so many font sets that using them can often be confusing. It's bad enough when you have only a letter-quality dot-matrix printer that can use multiple fonts. When you have access to a laser printer, the choices increase exponentially. You're faced with the ultimate tyranny of too many choices.

In addition to style and size, fonts have additional attributes to further customize their printing. The most basic of these attributes are boldface, italic, underline, subscript, superscript, and strikeout.

Many laser printer fonts can also be scalable. This means that they contain the information for font style, but not size. The fonts don't come in specific sizes because you can produce the characters in *any* size. Choose the style and then tell WordStar the size to print it in. The printer will accordingly scale the typeface to the desired size. The range for a proportional scalable font is .25 point to 999.75 points (in .25 point increments).

Fonts are available in different ways. Internal fonts are the ones built into your printer. Cartridge fonts plug into the printer, and are read by the printer during the print runoff. Soft fonts come on a floppy disk and are copied to your computer— which in turn sends them to the printer.

The complete set of information for a printer is kept in the printer driver. When the printer information is copied to WordStar during setup and installation, the driver becomes a part of WordStar. As a part of the same process, the fonts are chosen from a list of available fonts for your printer.

Fonts are grouped in font families of similar characteristics of shape or ornateness. Each family has an identifying name like Courier, Roman, or Helvetica. Kindred fonts are also available in packages or font sets, which come installed in your printer or which you can buy on cartridges or floppy disks.

The font and printer ID attached documents

When you installed and set up WordStar for your computer, you selected one printer as the default. Unless told otherwise, WordStar always expects to print with this printer. When you create a new document, WordStar automatically attaches the ID of that printer to the text file.

Every printer also has a default font, and WordStar automatically uses that font as you type the body text of the document. In most cases, regardless of printer, that's going to be a 12-point Courier font. This is the size and type of screen font that most word processing programs, including WordStar, use in their onscreen display. The ruler line, margins, tabs, and everything else in the display are based on it.

12-point Courier for writing

12-point Courier is a good font to use while writing and editing your documents. This, in effect, keeps you in the draft mode, and keeps everything you write onscreen. Never format anything in another font until the document has been written, proofed, edited, and rewritten to its final draft. There are two good reasons for this.

One is that the document display has one screen font, 12-point Courier. Auto-align fits text between margins based on the printing font. Smaller fonts and proportional fonts, take up less room on a line, so more characters will fit between margins. This will send text off the right edge of the screen. What you see will no longer be what you get.

The second is that fancy layout and printing never make up for bad writing. The most important thing about any document is how well it's written. Concentrate first on making every sentence and paragraph as perfect as you can write them. Don't format until you've thoroughly checked your document.

Print Controls used before and after

There are eight embedded print controls that you can use with WordStar to give characters special printing attributes: boldface, underline, subscript, superscript, strikeout, doublestrike, italics, and index codes.

These commands must be embedded both before and after the characters you want to give special print style attributes to. The first insertion turns the print attribute on; the next insertion turns it off.

Selecting attributes through the style bar

The character attributes commands for boldface, italics, and underlining are available on the style bar. You must have a mouse to use the style bar. This is the slowest way to set character attributes.

1. Click on the first character of the specified text.
2. Click on the icon of the attribute on the stylebar.
3. Click on the end of the specified text.
4. Click on the icon of the attribute on the stylebar.

Assigning character attributes from the keyboard

Following are the steps for inserting all beginning and ending print attribute commands from the keyboard:

1. Put the cursor on the first character of the text to receive the special attribute.
2. Hold down the Ctrl key and type the two letters of the command.

3. The symbol for the attribute will appear at the cursor—telling the printer to begin printing in the special character attribute.

4. Move the cursor to the space after the last character to be printed in the attribute, and repeat the attribute command.

5. The symbol for the attribute will appear at the cursor—this time telling the printer to stop printing in the special character attribute.

Setting attributes with function keys and the mouse

The fastest way of setting character attributes is to use the mouse to place the cursor, and the function keys to assign the attributes.

WordStar comes with boldface assigned to the F4 key, and underlining on the F3 key. If you use any of the others frequently, especially italics, I recommend that you install them on function keys. The factory macros installed on F5, F6, F8, and F9 either aren't very useful or are downright dangerous to a new user. If you install your commonly used attributes on these keys, you'll find that it will noticeably quicken your writing.

Boldface

The command Ctrl−PB, beginning and end, inserts the boldface marker ^B at the cursor position. How your printer executes boldface depends on the printer and how you have it installed. Most dot-matrix printers make a triple pass; daisywheel printers strike the character three times.

The font used is another factor. When a printer can use fonts from cartridges, or downloadable fonts, there are separate fonts for boldface in each type size and style. This is especially true of inkjet and laser printers.

To remove boldfacing from text, delete both inserted characters. If your dot-matrix or daisywheel printer doesn't print boldface as you like it, set it darker or lighter with the utility program WSCHANGE. As a stopgap solution, mark it as both boldface and doublestrike.

Doublestrike

The command Ctrl−PD, used beginning and end, inserts the doublestrike character ^D at the cursor position. Dot-matrix printers normally execute doublestrike by making two passes, and daisywheel printers strike the character twice. For available on cartridges, and downloadable fonts, there is usually no doublestrike font. The printer uses the boldface font. Doublestrike is installed on the hotkey Alt−SOD.

Italics

The command Ctrl−PY, used beginning and end, inserts the italic symbol ^Y at the cursor position. Italic text is slanted and resembles cursive writing. It gives words and phrases special emphasis. The more you use it, however, the less special it becomes.

With daisywheel printers, italics either is an alternative font on the wheel or is located on a separate wheel. Most dot-matrix printers simply scale the text into italics. Other printers, especially laser printers, have separate italic fonts.

Underline

The command Ctrl−PS, used beginning and end, inserts the underline text character ^S at the cursor position. The default setting is to underline only words and not blank spaces between words. You can set WordStar to underline the blank spaces with WSCHANGE. The underline command is normally a macro on the F3 key. Pressing F3 or selecting it from the style bar are the easiest ways to use it.

Tip 1: To get double underline, change the strikeout character to an underscore character with the .XX_ dot command. Then mark the text for both underscore and strikeout.

Tip 2: To get triple underline, mark the text for underlining. Below the text to be underlined, use the Overprint Line command to print a line of equal signs marked as subscript.

Subscript

The command Ctrl−PV, used beginning and end, inserts the subscript text character ^V in the body text. Subscript prints slightly below the normal line of text, and it's mainly used for scientific annotation, for example, H_2O or H_2SO_4.

Subscript varies from printer to printer. Daisywheel printers do a half-line roll down from the normal printing line, then roll back to the normal line when done. Dot-matrix and laser printers simply print the subscript where it belongs.

You can reset the subscript roll inside the document with the .SR dot command, followed by a number that specifies how far below the normal line the printing rolls, in 48ths of an inch. The default is $3/48$. For example, use .SR 5 to change the roll to $5/48$ or .SR 2 to change roll to $2/48$.

Some dot-matrix printers and most laser printers, have a special half-height font available specifically for subscript or superscript. If your printer has this special font, leave the roll set to zero.

You can manually select a smaller subscript font. Use Ctrl−P= to call the Font dialog box and choose the font from the onscreen font list. In the following order—turn on subscript, select the font, type the text, revert to normal font, and turn off subscript.

Superscript

The command Ctrl−PT, used beginning and end, inserts the superscript text character ^T in the body text. Superscript prints slightly above the normal line of text, and its main use is in scientific and mathematical notation. For example: 2×10^{23}.

Different printers print superscript the same way they print subscript; see the previous section for information. You can reset the superscript roll inside the document with the .SR dot command, also specified in 48ths of an inch. An .SR 2 would change the roll to $2/48$.

Strikeout

The command Ctrl−PX, used beginning and end, marks text to be struck out while or after being printed. This is used in standard contracts and agreements forms to show an exception made to the norm, and also with edited text. The symbol ^X appears in the file.

The default strikeout character is the hyphen. You can change this to any other character by customizing WordStar with WSCHANGE. You can also change the strikeout character inside the document without having to customize Word-Star. Use the dot command .XX followed by the new character to use.

Strikeout text printing varies from printer to printer. Some printers print a word, then move back to strike over it with the hyphen or other character. Other printers print an entire line, then strike out the text in another pass. Laser printers simply perform both simultaneously.

Embedded index codes

The command Ctrl−PK, used beginning and end, marks text to be used in an index generated from the text file. There's no limit to the size of an index item, but practicality should restrain you to a word or two.

These index codes are printing codes, because the index generator is actually a print-to-disk routine. After it starts running, the indexer can be paused, continued, or aborted with the same commands found on the Printing Menu. For complete information on indexing a document, see the chapter titled *Writing a useful index*.

Tip: When indexing large documents, this command is especially useful when installed as a macro on a function key (F11 or F12, if you have them). Then you can jump from the beginning to the end of an item and mark it with two keystrokes. Make sure that EXTKB is set to On.

Selecting font, color, and printer

This section discusses the five commands used to select the printer, the specific font to use, and the color or shading of the font. These give you individual control over specific words or paragraphs in a document, and can override settings in text marked with paragraph tags.

Different kinds of fonts

There are many different kinds of fonts—too many, in fact, to describe them all here in detail. So I've discussed only a handful. The kinds of fonts available to you depend largely on the kind of printer you're using. Read the user manual for your printer.

Built-in fonts   Any font permanently stored in the read-only memory of a printer. Also known as a resident or hardware font.

Fixed fonts   Fonts in preset, unchangeable sizes. They always print in the same point size and character width. Also called bit-mapped fonts, they usually include the bold and italic variations, but each variation is considered a separate font. A different font is maintained for each size and variation.

Fixed space fonts   Each character in a fixed space font family takes up the same amount of space on the printed page. They're measured in pitch, or characters per horizontal inch. Also called monospaced and nonproportional fonts.

Proportional space fonts   Each character in a proportional space font takes up a different amount of space on the printed page, depending on its individual size and shape. (An I, for example, takes up less space than an M.) Proportional fonts are measured in points.

Sans serif   This term literally means *without serifs*, those short lines stemming horizontally out of the upper and lower ends of the strokes of letters in serif fonts (like Times Roman). Helvetica fonts are noted for their attractive simplicity and lack of serifs.

Scalable fonts   Fonts existing as outlines to be sized or scaled on demand. Scalable fonts contain instructions on how to make the shape of the font, and they're drawn to the size needed by the computer and the printer. They usually take longer to print because the fonts are created with every print session.

Screen fonts   This is an onscreen raster font designed to replicate onscreen a printer font. The term *raster* means a picture represented as a matrix of dots. The rendition isn't always accurate, simply because there are too many different printer fonts to keep screen counterparts for in your computer. There are hardware and software solutions available to make onscreen fonts look exactly like the printed ones. These are available from your printer manufacturer or dealer. WordStar uses 12-point Courier nonproportional as the raster font in the document screen.

Soft fonts   A font stored in a file that's copied to the printer's memory whenever it's needed to print a file. The file is either stored on a floppy disk or copied to your hard drive. Also called a *downloadable font*.

Changing fonts

The command Ctrl−P= calls the Font dialog box, shown in Fig. 12-2. The name of the currently active font is displayed in the dialog box. A list of the fonts avail-

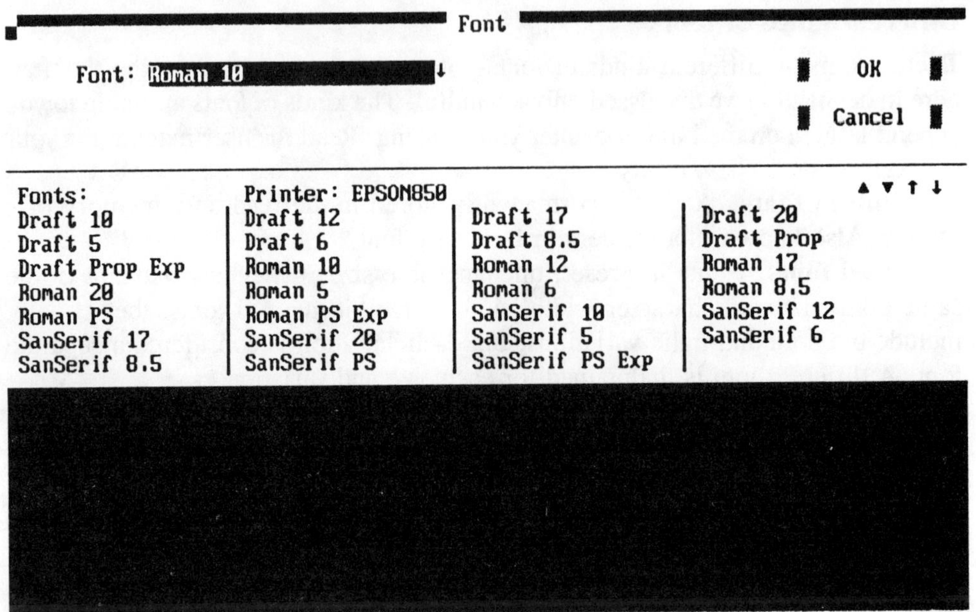

12-2 Font dialog box.

able (for the current printer) will appear onscreen. Use the arrow keys or the mouse to make your selection.

Tip: The font symbol is like any other print control character. It can be deleted, copied, or moved—either with the text or independently. To see the font characters onscreen, to avoid deleting them accidentally, the command tags display must be on. Use Ctrl−OD or Ctrl−OB to control the screen settings.

Below are the steps for selecting a specific font with which to print:

1. Put the cursor on the first character of the text to print in the selected font. (If the entire document is to be printed in this font, then place the cursor on the first line of text in the text file.)
2. Hold down the Ctrl key and type P = .
3. The Font dialog box will appear. Below it are the fonts available for the currently attached printer.
4. Either use the arrow keys to move the highlight to the font of your choice and then press the Enter key, or double-click on the font with the mouse.
5. Now one of two things will happen, depending on the kind of font you're tagging to the text. If it's a fixed font, WordStar will embed its tag with no further delay. If it's a scalable font, WordStar will ask for the point size you want. Type in the point size and press the Enter key. Now WordStar will embed the font tag at the cursor.

6. If the font applies only to specific text, put the cursor at the end of it and revert to the former font.

These font tags look like <Courier 10 PC>, <Univers PC 12.0>, or <Line Pr 17 PC>. The new font becomes active on the first character after the tag. It remains active to the next font tag, paragraph tag, or the end of the text file.

To see these font tags, the command tags display must be on. If using font tags throughout a text file, you should leave this display on. The paragraph tags are nonprinting text and can be deleted like any word or character. Use Ctrl−OD or Ctrl−OB to control the screen settings.

Normal and alternate fonts

You can define WordStar to use one font as your normal font, and another as the alternate or substitution font. Then you can toggle between them with the commands Ctrl−PN and Ctrl−PA. This overrides the font assignment made by any paragraph tag. The normal font is commonly the same as the font assigned by the body text paragraph tag.

If you use these key combinations, instead of changing fonts with paragraph tags, they're most convenient when installed on macro hotkeys. Ctrl−PA embeds the symbol <ALTERNATE> at the cursor. The font defined as the alternative font will become active from this point to the end of the text file, or until countermanded by another font selection command. Ctrl−PN embeds the symbol <NORMAL> at the cursor. The font defined as the normal font will become active from this point to the end of the text file, or until countermanded by another font selection command.

These two commands are very useful if you write documents where you switch back and forth between two fonts continuously. Any font available to the printer can be defined as either normal or alternate.

Tip: Use WSCHANGE to define the normal and alternate character fonts. At the WSCHANGE Main Menu, type BC to call the Printing Defaults Menu #1. Then type G to set the normal font, and H to set the alternate font. The list of available fonts will appear. Follow the onscreen directions.

Switching between the normal and alternate fonts

The command Ctrl−PN automatically selects the normal font, and Ctrl−PA selects the alternate font—whatever they happen to be. Place the cursor on the first character of the text to be printed in either font, and issue the appropriate command.

The normal font is usually the default font of your printer (usually 12-point Courier). However, you can install any available font as the normal one. To do this, use the utility program WSCHANGE.

WordStar now comes with no font currently installed as the alternate. The common practice is to install either a larger- or smaller-than-normal font as the alternate (for titles and level heads).

Setting fonts with paragraph style tags

One option on every paragraph style tag is to select a font. Different kinds of paragraphs often need to be printed in fonts different than standard body text. For example, long quotations are often printed in a slightly smaller font or a different font type. If your documents contain different kinds of paragraphs, it's far simpler to edit or create a paragraph tag to include font changes. If you use paragraph tags for all your formatting, you don't have to remember to change fonts.

Different colors or shading

The command Ctrl−P- is used to select the color of ink used or shading given to fonts and graphics. This can be used only if you have a color printer, or one that can do gray-scale shading or other patterns and font enhancements. The latter includes such special effects as outline, shadow, and reverse (white on black). Dot-matrix, inkjet, and laser jet printers are capable of this.

1. Place the cursor on the first character of the text being printed in a different color or shade.
2. Hold down the Ctrl key and type P- (P and a hyphen).
3. The Color/Shading dialog box will appear, listing the available colors and shades.
4. Use the arrow keys to put the highlight on the selection and press the Enter key, or double-click on it with the mouse.
5. If the command tags display is on, you'll see a tag appear at the cursor. It contains the name of the color or shading just selected.

Text or graphics following this Color/Shade tag will print in the selected color or shading until you change it again—or until the end of the text file. The tag is non-printing text, so you can delete it like any other text in the file.

Setting colors with paragraph style tags

One option on every paragraph style tag is the selection of color. If you have specific kinds of paragraphs that need to be printed in a different color, then edit or create a paragraph tag to include this color. When you tag the special paragraph with this tag and then return to body text, you won't have to remember to change back the color as well.

Selecting a different color

If you're using a color printer, the command Ctrl−P- lets you select colors with which to print the text or illustrations in your documents. To see a print color character onscreen, the print controls display must be on. If you're not using a color printer, marking text in a different color can cause documents to misprint—especially if you've specified gray tones or white on black.

1. Place the cursor where you want the new color printing to start.
2. Hold down the Ctrl key and type P- to call the list of colors.
3. The Colors dialog box will appear, with a display of the color currently in effect. The available colors are: black, red, dark gray, light red, blue, magenta, light blue, light magenta, green, brown, light green, yellow, cyan, light gray, light cyan, and white on black.
4. Use the arrow keys to put the highlight on the new color to be used for printing.
5. When ready, press the Enter key.
6. The color character will appear at the cursor. This color will remain in effect either to the end of the document or to the next color character.
7. If only specific text is to print in that color, put the cursor at the end of it and revert to the former color.

Selecting the printer

The command Ctrl−P? changes the printer assigned or attached to the text file you have open on the document screen. This is where you select the printer used to print your document.

Whenever you create a text file with WordStar, it automatically attaches the ID of the default printer description file to that text file. The first time you save the file, the PDF becomes a permanent part of the file. This is how WordStar always knows what fonts are available to use in the document. This is also where WordStar gets the information it needs to execute WYSIWYG display with Page Preview.

This feature allows you to format documents for printing on a printer to which you have only limited access. Select the printer and use Page Preview to view your work onscreen. Then you need to print it out only once because you already know what it'll look like.

If you change the physical printer for any reason, you must also change the PDF attached to the text file. Otherwise, WordStar will continue formatting text for the old printer, and try to send the text file to it when you start printing.

1. Place the cursor on the first blank line of the text file.
2. Hold down the Ctrl key and type P? (you don't have to hold down the Shift key—just hit the slash mark key).
3. This will call the Change Printer dialog box. Below it are the names of all the printers currently installed for WordStar to use. (This list will vary.)
4. Use the arrow keys to put the highlight on the printer name you want to

use and press the Enter key until it executes. (Or double-click on it with the mouse.)

5. The new printer PDF is now attached to the text file. The change will become permanent the next time you save the file, and stay in effect until you change the PDF again. It's a good idea to use Ctrl−QU when changing PDFs.

Inserting extended characters

This section discusses extended characters and explains how to insert and print them in your documents.

There are 256 characters in the ANSI character set. ANSI is the acronym for the American National Standards Institute's 8-bit character set. The ASCII set uses only the first 128 (0−127) of those characters. Only 68 of these are installed on your keyboard. These are the letters of the alphabet, the numerals, and the punctuation keys.

The remainder of the ANSI characters is called the extended character set. These include graphics characters, Greek letters, and letters with accent marks. WordStar recognizes all codes between 0 and 255. WordStar lets you insert them in your documents, and Page Preview will display them in a screen font. Whether or how well your printer can print them depends on the printer.

Before your printer can print these characters, they must be contained in the printer's built-in character set, in a downloaded font set, or on a print cartridge. This includes most 24-pin dot-matrix printers and laser printers. The only way to be sure your printer can print them is to read the manual that comes with your printer.

There are two ways to insert extended ANSI characters in your WordStar documents. You can use the Extended Character dialog box or you can type them in directly. The former gives you an onscreen memory aid so you don't have to remember what they are. The second is the quicker way.

Using the Extended Character dialog box

The command Ctrl−P0 (zero) calls the Extended Character dialog box (see Fig. 12-3), which contains an onscreen display of the characters and a box where you can type in the number of the character to insert.

1. Place the cursor at the point where you want to insert an extended character.
2. Hold down the Ctrl key and type P0.
3. The Extended Character dialog box will appear. On it is a chart of the extended characters.
4. Find the character you want to insert. Add its column number to the number at the beginning of the line.

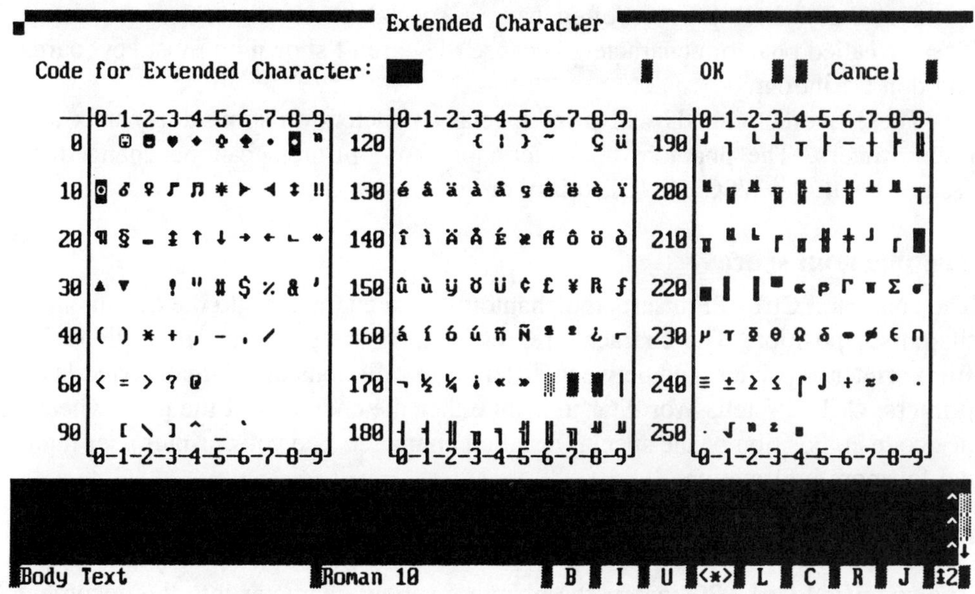

12-3 Extended Character dialog box.

5. Type the resulting number into the small box at the cursor.
6. When ready, press the Enter key.
7. The extended character will be inserted and you're returned to the document.

Typing extended characters directly

The Extended Character dialog box is a great memory aid, but a slow method for inserting extended characters into your documents. If your keyboard has a numeric keypad, you can type these extended characters directly on the page. You can't use the number keys on the top row of the normal keyboard.

1. Place the cursor where you want the extended character to be inserted.
2. Hold down the Alt key and type the decimal number of the extended character on the numeric keypad.
3. Release the Alt key and the character will be inserted.

Tip: These characters, and their decimal numbers, are listed on the character conversion chart in the back of this book. They can also be found in the back of your MS-DOS users manual.

Using phantom characters

The Print Controls Menu has two commands used especially for daisywheel printers. These are the phantom space and the phantom rubout. The print wheels on most daisywheel printers often have a special character or two on them. They're called phantom characters because they aren't shown on most keyboards and don't print out.

These two commands will print special characters on some dot-matrix and laser printers. The phantom characters for those printers can be changed or assigned with the WSCHANGE utility program.

The phantom space

The command Ctrl−PF inserts the phantom space character into the document at the cursor position. The character represented by the phantom space ^F varies from printer to printer, and between different installations of dot-matrix and laser printers. Ctrl−PF tells WordStar to print either the character at the print wheel's hex code 20 position or the special installed character. See your printer user manual for more information.

The phantom rubout

The command Ctrl−PG inserts the phantom rubout character into the document at the cursor position. The character represented by the phantom space ^G varies from printer to printer. Ctrl−PG tells WordStar to print either the character at the print wheel's hex code 7F position or the special installed character. See your printer user manual for more information.

The following printing controls deal with only a single character, line, or space. They're embedded once before the affected text, and their function is executed only once.

Overprinting a character

The command Ctrl−PH inserts the Overprint Character printing command, and allows two characters to be printed in one space. This is commonly used to produce accented letters when your printer can't handle the extended character set. How well this works depends entirely on the printer and font being used. The command is placed between the first character and the character it's to overprint.

Tip: If there are characters you use only for overprinting, you can set up WordStar to automatically overprint those characters whenever you type them in a document. They must be added to the auto backspace table with WSCHANGE.

Overprinting an entire line

The command Ctrl−P and Enter tells WordStar to print two or more complete lines on top of each other. This has too many uses, both practical and obscure, to list them all here. The most common is for printing numbered lists, with the number flush against the margin and the text all indented.

1. Type the first line of text. Don't let it wrap to the line below.
2. Hold down the Ctrl key and type P.
3. Release the Ctrl key, and press the Enter key.
4. Look at the flag column down the right edge of the screen. A hyphen (-) should appear after you press the Enter key. If a J appears, you inserted a line feed instead of overprint line. (This will happen if you don't release the Ctrl key before pressing the Enter key.) Delete backwards until the J disappears and repeat steps 2 and 3.
5. Type the second line that is to overprint the first. It doesn't matter if wordwrap takes subsequent text to lines below. Only the first line will be overprinted.
6. To overprint more than two lines, repeat steps 2 and 3 between each line.

Inserting a line feed

The command Ctrl—PL is no longer shown on the Print Controls Menu, but it's still very much available. It inserts a line feed at the cursor position. This is most useful with older printers that don't feed correctly.

Embedding a print pause command

The command Ctrl—PC tells WordStar to pause the printing at a particular point in a document. The printer will then wait until you make whatever change you need to make. When the printer reaches the command, the message Print Wait will appear on the right side of the status line.

To continue the printing, you must call the Printing Menu. This is done by repeating the same command you used to start the printing. Type P from the Opening Menu. Or type Ctrl—KP from inside the document or nondocument modes.

Tip: This is one way you can print parts of a document in a different color, even when your printer isn't a color printer. Embed a print pause at the beginning and end of a part of text. When the printer pauses, change to a different color printer ribbon. When it pauses again, change it back.

Inserting a binding space

The command Ctrl—PO inserts a binding space between letters or words. This is used to bind, or keep, words together on the same line when wordwrap would otherwise split them apart. To use this, issue Ctrl—PO instead of pressing the spacebar. When the print control display is on, the binding space will appear as the extended character 254 (~) between the words. But it will print as a blank space.

Inserting leader dots

The command Ctrl−P. (period) inserts leader dots from the cursor position to the next tab. This is most often used in a table of contents, between the end of an item and its page number. The name is derived from the fact that the dots "lead" the eye across the page.

Tip: The best place to use these leader dots is on the dot command line .TC used for marking a table of contents item. For detailed information, read the chapter titled *Writing a table of contents*.

Inserting an eight-column tab

The command Ctrl−PI inserts a special eight-column tab at the cursor location. These tabs are internally set and have nothing to do with tabs set on the ruler line, the Margins & Tabs dialog box, or with the .TB dot command. They're set every eight columns, beginning at column 1.

Changing the size of font characters

The size of a character in a nonproportional font is determined by pitch and character width. The commands described in this section are used to control both.

Dot commands to change character pitch

The term *pitch* refers to the number of characters printed per inch on a line, and is also a factor in the size of monospaced, or nonproportional, fonts. Thus, fonts with different pitches will print either more or fewer characters on a line.

Dot command to change character width

The term *character width* is closely related to pitch, and refers to the amount of horizontal space taken up by each character in a nonproportional font set. In a proportional font set, character width is only an average because each character takes up varying space. The simplest way to change character width is to use a font having the desired width.

You can also use the .CW dot command, followed by a number specifying character width in $^1/_{120}$ inch units, to change width. With some dot-matrix printers, this command tells the printer to make the same font wider or narrower. In other printers, especially laser printers, the command tells the printer to use a different font entirely. When using this command with proportional fonts, WordStar uses the font that most closely matches the width requested.

Character width is inversely proportional to pitch. The smaller the width, the bigger the pitch. See the following table:

Character width	Pitch
.CW 6	20
.CW 7.5	16
.CW 10	12
.CW 12	10
.CW 15	8
.CW 24	5

Notice that a character width of 10 is 12-pitch, and a width of 12 is 10-pitch. They're easy to confuse. These are the two most commonly used sizes of type in regular text printing. An elite typewriter gives you 12-pitch type, or 12 characters per inch; a pica typewriter uses 10-pitch type, or 10 characters per inch.

User-programmable commands

WordStar has five print control commands that come with no values assigned to them. You can use these to access abilities of your printer that WordStar isn't programmed to use.

Programming with Alt–IH

The command Alt–IH calls the Changer Custom Printer Codes dialog box. Here you can define any or all of the custom printing commands. The place for this is at the very beginning of the text file. Once you define them for a text file, you should leave them alone for the remainder of the document. In fact, you should be very consistent with how you define them throughout all your text files. Otherwise, you can confuse yourself and easily lose track of what is defined where.

13
CHAPTER

Printing documents with WordStar

This chapter covers methods for printing documents with WordStar. It begins with basics and ends with detailed specifics. Simply find information at the level you need it, and don't worry about the rest.

Introduction and overview

This chapter covers only normal printing with WordStar. Although merge printing is now an option on every print run-off, it's still as complicated to use as ever, and requires several chapters of its own.

How do most people print with WordStar?

Most people print files from the Opening Menu, and pick text files from the current directory. This is the least confusing and most foolproof way. Unless told otherwise, WordStar will look for the file to print in the current drive and directory. A list of those files appears below the Opening Menu. The same list appears when you call the Printing dialog box. Yet WordStar can print any file stored on any drive or path location if you tell it the location.

Many people are used to printing a file, and leaving the computer alone until the printing is complete. All WordStar printing functions, however, are accomplished *in the background*. This means that it isn't necessary to escape from the write and edit mode to print a file. WordStar can print one file while you work on another. This is called *background printing*.

How does WordStar print?

Some word processors print files directly from memory. This is a quick way to do it, and avoids several steps. Other programs print a file by drawing it from disk storage. WordStar does the latter. The print routine copies text files from disk storage into memory, formats the file page by page, and then sends it to the printer. It also sends instructions your printer uses to control printing.

Printing from disk allows you to work with any size document. When printing from memory, documents can be no larger than available RAM. By printing from disk, WordStar keeps memory free for other functions. This means that you can use the computer to work on one document while printing another.

Specifically, you can tell WordStar to send one file to a printer, and then open another file to work on. Or you can send a file to print without exiting the document you're working on. Windows, OS/2 Presentation Manager, and DeskView all allow you to leave WordStar printing and then run and use other programs. There are three different ways to print with WordStar:

- From the Opening Menu, by typing the letter P
- From inside the document or nondocument mode with Ctrl−KP.
- From the keyboard directly to the printer (commonly called "typewriter mode")

Steps in the printing routine

Whenever you print a document, you go through the same basic routine. It's always simplest to change to the directory containing the file(s) to be printed before starting the print routine. The most common way to start printing is through the Opening Menu:

1. Issue the command to call the Print dialog box (see Fig. 13-1).
2. Select a text file to print. If you aren't currently accessing the directory or drive containing the text file, you'll have to specify this information.
3. Select the printer (if more than one is connected to the computer), or alternative printer driver.
4. Accept or change the print-time variables (how many copies, what pages to print, etc.).
5. Tell WordStar to send the file to the printer.
6. Either wait for the document to finish printing or go on to something else.

Terminology

This section provides some of the basic terminology for printing documents in WordStar:

Alternative printer   Any printer other than the currently specified one

═══════════════════ **Print** ═══════════════════

```
        Filename: C:\COMMAND.WS6\OPENMENU.FIG              ▓  OK  ▓

Page Numbers:                              Pages:          ▓ Cancel ▓
            ♦  All                            o  Odd
            o  Selected Pages:                o  Even
                                              ♦  Both
            ___________________

         Copies: 1_
                                           [X] Use Form Feeds
        Printer: LASERJET                  [ ] Pause Between Pages
                                           [ ] Print Unformatted Text
     Redirect To: _______________          [X] Interpret Merge Variables
```

```
Filenames:              Path: C:\COMMAND.WS6   45M free
..               \    ARCHIVE          \   2COLTAB.RR    .3k   APPENDIX.01  5.6k
APPENDIX.02    9.5k    AUTHQUES.TAB  8.7k   AYS           .5k   BLOKMENU.USE 5.0k
CAUTION         .3k    CHAPTER.01     19k   CHAPTER.02     25k  CHAPTER.03    24k
CHAPTER.04      11k    CHAPTER.05    9.1k   CHAPTER.06     22k  CHAPTER.07    74k
CHAPTER.08      46k    CHAPTER.09     14k   CHAPTER.10     79k  CHAPTER.11    77k
CHAPTER.12      55k    CHAPTER.13     45k   CHAPTER.14     20k  CHAPTER.15    18k
CHAPTER.16      44k    CHAPTER.17    7.8k   CHAPTER.18     33k  CHAPTER.19    28k
```

13-1 Print dialog box.

whose printer description file, or PDF, is available for WordStar to use. If you installed WordStar to use two or more printers, one is set up as the default and the others are alternatives. The special printer drivers ASC256, ASCII, Draft, Fax, and WS4 are always available as options.

Attribute   Any property of a font that changes its appearance. Some attributes are: normal, boldface, underlined, italic, subscript, superscript, and strikethrough.

Background printing   Printing one document while writing and editing another document. You can also return to the Opening Menu and use any feature on it.

Current drive   The drive WordStar uses as both source and target for text files. When you boot up WordStar, it initially accesses the directory you were in when you ran it.

Current directory   This is the specific directory on the current drive where WordStar stores files you're working on. Initially, this is whichever directory on your hard drive you used to boot WordStar. Any directory can be the current directory.

Default printer   The printer set up as the primary printer. This is done during the initial installation of the software, or later with WINSTALL. WordStar uses this printer every time you print, unless told otherwise. If you installed WordStar to use two or more printers, one is set up as the default and the others are alternatives.

Font   This is a set of characters in a specific design and size, usually organized in groups or families (Courier, Helvetica, Roman).

Hardcopy   The version of the document printed on paper. The version in the computer is the softcopy.

Access a directory   Means to "handshake" with a specific directory or subdivision on your disk drive, so data and text files can be transmitted to and from it. Dividing a hard disk into directories and subdirectories allows you to store specific files in specific places.

Access a drive   Link or "handshake" with a specific disk drive electronically, so data and text files can be transmitted to and from it.

Print   To convert computer data into a printed document.

Printer   A device that converts computer data output into printed images. Printers are defined by the communications port they use and their type of printing head. The two main types of communications ports are serial and parallel. The four main types of printing heads are daisywheel, dot-matrix, inkjet, and laser.

Printer buffer   A memory storage device for accepting data from the computer and then transmitting it to the printer. This allows the computer to release the data as soon as possible, and free itself for other tasks. There are external printer buffers between the computer and the printer, and internal buffers built into the printer itself.

Print run-off   A term used to describe the entire printing routine—from selecting the file to print, through sending it to the printer, to waiting for the printer to finish with the hardcopy.

Print time   A term for the indefinite period between the moment you call the Print dialog box, and the moment the printer finishes the last page of the document.

Printing from the Opening Menu

The easiest and most common way to print a document is from the Opening Menu. Before starting the print run-off, make sure your printer is on and that it's online with your computer.

1. At the Opening menu, type P to call the Print dialog box.
2. The Print dialog box will appear onscreen (see Fig. 13-1). Below the dialog box is a list of files in the current directory.
3. Select a file to be printed from the onscreen list using either the arrow keys or your mouse to highlight its name. You can also type in the filename if you're accessing a file in another drive or directory. Remember to precede the filename with the drive and path names.
5. Use the Tab key to move forward through the print-time variables. The

settings shown are the defaults. Change or accept each in turn. Use Shift − Tab to move backward and make corrections.

6. When ready to begin printing, hold down the Ctrl key and type K. You can use Ctrl − K at any point on the Print dialog box to accept all the defaults or changes already made. If you have a mouse, you can accept the variables and start printing by clicking on the OK push button.

7. WordStar will begin formatting the file, and then send it to the printer. You'll be returned to the Opening Menu.

Once you complete these steps, the print run-off will run automatically. If you do nothing further, the file will print as directed. If you need to halt or pause the print run-off, type P again to call the Printing dialog box.

Printing from the document mode

There are two ways of printing a text file while in the document write-and-edit mode. One is the command Ctrl − KP, which allows you to specify a file. The other is the command Ctrl − PrtSc, which saves and prints the file you have open.

Printing with Ctrl − KP

Background printing allows you to send a text file to the printer while working on another. This is easy and convenient to do. You can print either the file you're working on or any other file stored in the computer. The command to print from the document mode is on the pull-down File Menu, or the Block & Save Menu. You can issue it directly with Ctrl − KP.

1. In the document mode, hold down the Ctrl key and type KP to call the Print dialog box.

2. The Print dialog box will appear onscreen. Below the dialog box is a list of files in the current directory.

3. Select a file to be printed from the onscreen list using either the arrow keys or your mouse to highlight its name. You can also type in the filename if you're printing a file in another drive or directory.

5. Use the Tab key to move forward through the print-time variables. The settings shown are the default. Change or accept each in turn. Use Shift − Tab to move backward and make corrections.

6. When ready to begin printing, hold down the Ctrl key and type K. You can use Ctrl − K at any point on the Print dialog box to accept the current settings. If you have a mouse you can accept the variables and start printing with a click of the OK push button.

7. WordStar will begin formatting the file and then send it to the printer. You'll be returned to the Opening Menu.

The print run-off will now run automatically. If you do nothing further, the file will print as directed. If you need to halt or pause the print run-off, type P again to call the Printing dialog box.

Quick printing with Ctrl−PrtSc

A quick way to print a file you've been working on is with the command Ctrl−PrtSc. This command will save the file to disk, exit the document mode, and send the text file directly to the default printer. All the default print-time variables are used for this printing.

Changing print-time variables

The Print dialog box has twelve print-time variables you can use to customize the print run-off. You can change any or all these variables every time you print a document. The values in these variables come from the printer driver attached to the file, and thus will change from printer to printer.

The Print dialog box's print-time variables control the nature of the print run-off. They include printing all or selected pages, the number of copies, printing odd/even/both pages, using form feeds, pausing between pages, printing unformatted text (nondocuments), and using merge printing information.

Page numbers

This variable specifies what pages to print. The default is to print all pages in the document. You can also print selected pages as a range or group of pages. You can specify any single page, range, or group of ranges within the document—thereby printing only the pages you want. Following are sample formats for specifying ranges (notice how commas and spaces are interchangeable):

    1,3,7
    1 3 5 7 9
    5-6
    1-9

You have 27 spaces to type in the range. WordStar recognizes wildcards in page number ranges. To begin printing on any specific page and continue to the end of the text file, type the page number, a dash, and the wildcard asterisk character, for example, 9-* 47-*.

An undocumented fact about WordStar is its ability to print text files, or portions of text files, from back to front. Simply specify the range of pages in reverse order:

    7,3,1
    9 7 5 3 1

Number of copies

This variable allows you to tell WordStar how many copies to print. The default is 1, but you can print from 1 to 999 copies of any file. Don't print multiple copies of very large documents on a dot-matrix printer, however, because the ribbons in most of these printers are good for only between 200 and 300 pages.

Selecting a printer

This variable displays the name of the printer description file attached to the text file. If you have only one printer installed, this is also the default printer name. When the cursor is on this variable, the directory of available printer drivers will appear below the dialog box. To send the file to another printer, use either the arrow keys or your mouse to highlight the printer name.

Tip: If a text file was written on someone else's computer, the attached PDF might be different than what you're using, or even unavailable. Don't forget to watch for this. If you don't have this PDF in your directory, WordStar will abort the printing when you try to start it.

WordStar's default installation copies five special printer drivers to the hard drive: ASC256, ASCII, Draft, WS4, and Fax. These are in addition to default printer and any alternative drivers. Some of these options change the way the document prints. Some convert the file to another format—rather than actually printing out a hardcopy. The latter is called *printing to disk*.

ASCII   This PDF converts your text file into a new file on disk, in the same directory as the text file, but in ASCII or nondocument format. All word processing commands, dot commands, soft carriage returns, extended characters, and fonts are stripped. You can then open and edit it as a nondocument or use it with other programs.

ASC256   This PDF does the same thing as the ASCII PDF, except the extended ANSI character set is supported.

Draft   This sends the text file to the default printer. At the same time it turns letter-quality printing and alternative fonts in dot-matrix printers off and specifies the default font of laser printers (normally Courier 12pt).

WS4   This PDF converts your text file to a new file on disk, one in the WS4 format. You can open and edit it using all versions of WordStar, from release 4.0 backward.

Fax   This is a special PDF to help give faxes their best possible appearance. It supplies fonts similar to the HP LaserJet III internal fonts, include Courier, Line Printer, and the scalable Times and Univers fonts. You can add internal fonts, soft fonts, and card fonts using PRCHANGE or WINSTALL.

Two special printer drivers   There are two other ways to send text files to disk instead of hardcopy. They aren't part of a standard installation, and must be set up using PRCHANGE or WINSTALL. These two special drivers are PRVIEW and XTRACT. Sending a file to PRVIEW creates and saves a file named PRVIEW.WS, which looks as much like an actual printout as possible. It includes headers and footers and has inserted data if you're using merge printing. It begins with the page length command (.PL) so page breaks fall at the correct places in the document. Sending a file to XTRACT creates and saves a file named XTRACT.WS. It's very similar to what you get from PRVIEW, only it doesn't have headers and footers, and has soft carriage returns.

Redirecting printing output

You can send a text file to another printer connected to a different communications port by specifying the port on the Redirect To command line. The default is (none). Direct the file to any communications port installed in your computer, for example:

    COM1:   COM3:   LPT1:   LPT2:   DISKPRNT.DOC

This lets you connect as many printers to your computer as you have communications ports. You can also print more than one file at a time on different ports. This feature is especially useful for using printers on a network.

Printing odd, even, or both pages

You can specify different printing parameters for odd and even pages when printing out a text file, including different margins, headers, footers, etc. You can, therefore, print documents for double-sided, or back-to-back, binding by first printing odd pages, then flipping the hardcopy and printing the even pages on the backs. The default is to print both odd and even pages of every document.

Using form feeds

Most dot-matrix and laser printers automatically issue a form feed at the bottom of the page. Other printers must be told to automatically move the paper forward. WordStar draws this default from the PDF attached to the document. If your paper doesn't feed correctly during printing, try changing this setting. If this corrects the problem, you should use WSCHANGE and change the default form feed setting.

This is a checkbox item on the Print dialog box, meaning that it's active if an X appears between the brackets. To toggle it on or off, put the cursor between the brackets and either press the spacebar or click on it with the mouse.

Pausing between pages

This variable specifies whether or not the printer pauses after each page completes. The default answer is inactive. Leave it inactive when you're using automatically-fed paper (bin or fan-fold). Make it active for printing on manually-fed single sheets of paper. When printing pauses, put in a new sheet of paper and ready the printer before continuing.

This is a checkbox, meaning that it's active if an X appears between the brackets. To toggle it on and off, put the cursor between the brackets and either press the spacebar or click on it with the mouse.

Printing unformatted text (nondocument)

With this variable, WordStar asks if you want to print the file as a nondocument. The default is inactive. Make it active if you're printing a hardcopy of data files, other nondocument text files, or ASCII files from another word processor. When you print a WordStar document as a nondocument, all dot commands and hidden comments will be printed in the hardcopy.

This is also a checkbox, meaning that it's active if an X appears between the brackets. To toggle it on and off, put the cursor between the brackets and either press the spacebar or click on it with the mouse.

Interpreting merge variables

This variable tells WordStar whether or not to do merge printing. On previous versions, merge printing was started as a separate routine from the Opening Menu. Now it's an option of every print run-off, which means you can merge or insert data in a document while it's printing. This data can come from dot commands, data files, or the keyboard. The default is active. There are few reasons for making it inactive.

This is a checkbox, meaning that it's active if an X appears between the brackets. To toggle it on and off, put the cursor between the brackets and press the spacebar. For more information on using merge printing, read the chapter titled *Using WordStar's merge printing*.

Using the Printing dialog box

Print time is the interval between the moment you send a file to the printer and the moment the printer finishes. While a file is printing, there are five options you can use to modify the run-off. These are found on the Printing dialog box.

Calling the Printing dialog box

The Printing dialog box (see Fig. 13-2) is where you stop, pause, or continue printing once it has started. You must use this dialog box if Pause Between Pages is active in order to start the printing after putting in a new sheet of paper.

13-2 Printing dialog box.

Call the Printing dialog box with the same command you used to start the printing. If at the Opening Menu, type P again. If working on another document in the write and edit mode, use Ctrl−KP. Then select any of the following options:

Esc   Sends a cancel order to the printer. Printing will continue until its print buffer is empty, which will vary from printer to printer.

Ctrl−U   This isn't listed, but is still the universal abort command. It also sends a cancel order to the printer. Printing continues until its print buffer is empty (see Esc, above).

P   Sends a pause order to the printer. The printing will pause when the printer buffer empties.

C   This continues, or restarts, the printing after a pause.

B   Starts background printing and sends the Printing Menu away. You return where you were before starting print run-off.

F   Starts printing at full speed if the printer has more than one printing speed—even if WordStar is set to use the slower speed. It toggles any special inhibitors your printer might be installed to use off.

Pausing or Stopping the printer immediately

Pausing the printer through the Printing dialog box merely halts the printer when the printer buffer is empty. Depending on the printer, and the size of the printing buffer, this can mean two or more pages.

To pause the printer at once, take the printer offline by pressing the Online button on the printer. This holds printing until you put it online again. To stop the printer at once, turn it off at the power switch. Turning the printer off will erase the print buffer. Leave it off for at least 10 seconds. Don't turn it on again until you've canceled printing with Ctrl−U or Esc—or you'll get printing gibberish.

Background printing

The term *background printing* means printing while doing something else with the computer. If you're printing a document while writing another, you can continue writing. If printing from the Opening Menu, you go back to that menu and use any other options on it. Open another text file, generate an index or table of contents, create fax files, and so on.

With DeskView, Microsoft Windows, OS/2 Presentation Manager, or any other system set up for multitasking, you can leave WordStar running and use another program. This book, however, doesn't cover multitasking applications. See your operating system manuals for information on this.

On a PC-XT computer with only 640K of RAM, WordStar must share the memory between the write-and-edit mode and the printing mode. This can cause flickers, pauses, and temporary keyboard lockouts when you're using the background printing facility. On a PC-AT or better with 2+ megabytes of RAM, WordStar has enough memory available to spare each mode its own RAM. Flickers and pauses shouldn't be noticeable.

Full-speed printing

This option won't be active unless you've used PRCHANGE to set a slower printing speed for your printer. If no slower speed is set, selecting Full Speed will have no effect on printing.

Some printers can't print (or receive data) as fast as WordStar can send it. The smaller the printer buffer, the more this is true. This can cause periodic keyboard lockout as data transfers to the printer. You can fix this by customizing WordStar for slow printing.

When set up for it, selecting Full Speed tells WordStar to send text out as fast as possible. You might need to use this when sending a file to a printer not the default. This is especially true if the default printer is dot-matrix and the other is a laser printer.

Using the mouse to select a file

Using a mouse adds a new dimension to WordStar. Most complex or difficult transactions are reduced to pointing and clicking. Most are easy to execute, but often difficult to describe. This is true of using the mouse to select a file for printing.

File in current directory   To select and print a file from the current directory, type P and then double-click on the filename in the onscreen list.

File from a subdirectory   At the Print dialog box, double-click on the subdirectory name in the onscreen list. This will change the current directory only for the current file selection. Use the mouse to search through all subdirectories of the current directory until you find the specific file to be printed. Then double-click on the filename.

File in directory outside current   At the Print dialog box, double-click on the [.. \ ] symbol in the upper left corner of the list. This puts you in the previous directory. If you're in the directory C: \ LETTERS, for example, you'll go to the C: \ , or root, directory. You can search forward and backward through directories until you find the specific file to be printed. Then double-click on the filename.

Selecting files this way doesn't change the current directory. When you send the text file to the printer, WordStar will return to the directory in which you began.

Using the printer as a typewriter

The Print from Keyboard features lets you use your dot-matrix or daisy-wheel printer as a typewriter. You can use this to address envelopes or to fill out pre-printed business forms. Admittedly, learning to fill out business forms takes time, plus much trial and error, but if you work in an office where you must fill out many forms it can be worth the trouble. The Print from keyboard command is issued from the Opening Menu.

Note: If you're using a laser printer, you must set WordStar's default setting for Use Form Feeds to inactive. This will prevent it from issuing a form feed after the first line you type.

The factory documentation describes Print from Keyboard as simple to use, but once you get beyond simply using it to address envelopes it becomes a complex, highly advanced feature. It's not for the WordStar beginner.

Using Print from Keyboard to fill out standard forms means you must have a template file for each form you're using. KEYBOARD.MRG is the only template file supplied with WordStar. If you can't get by with this default file, you must either custom write your templates or find some from a third-party supplier.

Writing a template file is a complex procedure, requiring advanced knowledge of WordStar, and it must be done in the nondocument mode.

How to print from the keyboard

It's a bit difficult to explain this, so bear with me. Before you start, turn the printer on and make sure it's on-line. Then put the envelope or preprinted business form into the printer as you would into a typewriter.

Tip: Use a 12-point nonproportional font (1 line equals .17″ for that type font). Proportional fonts are too difficult to use, and require a lot of pre-planning and experience.

1. At the Opening Menu, type K to call the Print from Keyboard dialog box (see Fig. 13-3).
2. With the cursor on Template Filename, select the template file of the business form or envelope to use. (KEYBOARD.MRG is the default, and is the only one available unless you write others.)
3. Use the Tab key to move to the Printer line. If using other than the default printer, select it from the onscreen list.
4. Use the Tab key to move to the Redirect Output To line. If sending the printing data to a communications port other than the default, type in its name. Examples are COM1:, COM2:, LPT1:, and LPT2.

```
┌─────────── P R I N T   F R O M   K E Y B O A R D ───────────┐
│ Template file  C:\WS\KEYBOARD.MRG                            │
│                C:\WS\KEYBOARD.MRG                            │
│                                                             │
│ Printer name              STAR-NX1 STAR-NX1                 │
│                                                             │
│ Redirect output to port    (none)                          │
│                                                             │
│ Press F1 for help.                                          │
└─────────────────────────────────────────────────────────────┘
```

13-3 Print from Keyboard dialog box.

5. Use Shift−Tab to move backward and make corrections, if necessary. Otherwise, Tab forward to the OK push button and press the Enter key.
6. WordStar will ask for the first line of information. Type it in. If you make a mistake, use the Backspace key to go back and correct it. This line won't print until you press the Enter key. Use the Tab key to move to other blank items on the line.
7. Repeat for all lines in the preprinted form.
8. When finished addressing the envelope or filling out the form, use Ctrl−U to end printing. This also issues a form feed to eject the form from the printer.

Practice using this on computer paper before trying it out on expensive preprinted forms. It's likely to take time getting used to it. In fact, it's a lot easier to use your typewriter.

What's in the KEYBOARD.MRG template file?

The contents of KEYBOARD.MRG—the default template file—are listed as follows:

```
.RP 65000
.IF &START& < > 1
.MT 0
.MB 0
.OP off
.EI
.SV START,1
.DM Line to print?
.AV " ",LINE
&LINE&
```

This is what you'd see if you opened KEYBOARD.MRG as a nondocument. All but two of these dot commands are merge printing commands. Don't attempt to use merge printing until you have a basic knowledge of WordStar. Here is a table of this file with explanations beside each dot command:

Dot command	What it does
.RP 65000	Lets you repeat instructions up to 65,000 times
.IF &START& < > 1	Conditional statement plus "generic name"
.MT 0	Sets top margin to 0
.MB 0	Sets bottom margin to 0
.OP off	Turns page numbering off
.EI	Ends the conditional statement
.SV START,1	Sets the values to be used in generic name
.DM Line to print?	Displays message *Line to print?*
.AV " ",LINE	Lets you type in a line of text at cursor
&LINE&	Generic name for the line to be typed

If the above makes any sense to you, you're ready to go on to the chapter titled *Using WordStar's merge printing*. If not, don't worry about it and keep reading.

Writing template files

If you're going to write template files, then you need to learn how to use merge printing, especially embedded conditional commands. They're discussed at length in the chapter titled *Using WordStar's merge printing*.

The template file sets up everything needed by WordStar for filling out blank standard forms. This includes margins, line height, character width, whether to use letter quality or proportional space printing, and so on.

Merge printing is a time-consuming process. What you must do is set up a master document for each form you use. This involves measuring the printed form to determine its length, width, and the precise location of every blank line and space on it. The template defines all this for the Print From Keyboard routine.

Other sources for templates

Ask your standard business forms supplier to see if they stock template files for the forms you use. Whatever they cost, they'll be worth the time and labor you'd spend writing them. If you buy template files from someone else, you only have to learn how to use them.

Another possible source for template files is a WordStar users' group. They might have some you can easily modify to work with your blank forms. Or someone might offer to write some for you at a reasonable price.

14
CHAPTER

Converting text files to faxes

This chapter walks you through the steps and process of making a text file to fax file conversion. If it seems confusing, don't worry. All you really have to do is tell WordStar the name of the text file to convert and a location to send the fax file to—then sit back and let it do the rest. You'll get usable fax files every time.

The newest addition to WordStar is the fax utility on the Opening Menu. This utility program takes any WordStar text file and converts it to a fax file in the standard .PCX format. Once converted, you can transmit the file directly through a fax board installed in your computer.

Tip: If you have text files in other word processing formats, first use StarExchange to convert them to the WordStar format. Then you can use this fax utility to convert them to fax files.

What about other fax formats?

If you can't successfully transmit a WordStar fax file with your fax board, it might require a different fax file format. To learn what format your fax board uses, read its user manual.

The .PCX fax file format is an industry standard, and most fax boards can transmit it with no trouble. If your fax board doesn't support the .PCX format, you must convert the .PCX fax files to whatever format is supported by your board.

The utility program for converting .PCX files to your board's format should be on the software disk that comes with your fax board. If it doesn't have a con-

233

version utility, consult your dealer. If they can't help you, call the technical support department of the fax board's manufacturer.

Three ways to use fax file conversion

There are three different ways to use the fax file conversion routine. All do the same job. The method you use depends on your personal choice, and the way you prefer to work with WordStar. These methods are:

- Select Fax from the Opening Menu and then follow the onscreen directions on the Fax dialog box.
- Open a document, run Page Preview, and use the fax file generation options.
- Combine the first two methods. Select Fax from the Opening Menu and then use the Fax dialog box and its Page Preview options.

Whichever of these methods you use, the results are always the same—fax files ready for transmission through the fax card installed in your computer.

Overview and housekeeping

This section contains an overview of what goes on during a fax file conversion. It also discusses alternatives for managing the fax files you create, and methods for dealing with unwanted fax files.

What happens during conversion?

During this conversion, WordStar creates a separate .PCX fax file for each page of the text file. Unless you specify otherwise, WordStar gives each fax file the first five characters of the filename, a three-letter sequential number, and the .PCX extension. Remember to transmit all of these fax files in order to send the whole fax document.

These .PCX files are stored in your \ WS \ FAX subdirectory. WordStar automatically creates this subdirectory the first time you convert a text file to a fax file. You can specify an alternative drive or directory if you want.

Tip: If using WordStar on a network system, you can use WSCHANGE to set up an alternative directory as the target for the fax files. At the WSCHANGE Main Menu, type CD4I and follow the onscreen directions.

Like the table of contents and index generators, the Fax conversion utility is really a variation of the print-to-disk routine. In this case, it's printing a fax file to disk.

Managing your fax files

Because the fax conversion routine creates a separate fax file for each page of the text file, it won't take long to fill the \ WS \ FAX subdirectory if you're creating faxes on a regular basis. You need to put some extra thought into managing these files on your hard disk drive.

Each time you create new fax files, the conversion adds a certain amount of data to each fax file—in addition to the text in the original document. How much is added depends on the resolution selected, the amount of text per page of document, and the quantity of formatting, font types and sizes, and other layout information in the document.

When converting a 9K, seven-page text file, I found that WordStar created seven fax files of 71K, 66K, 80K, 64K, 46K, 50K, and 35K respectively. This totals 412K, for an average size of 59K per file. Converting a larger file with more information per page can create fax files averaging 75K per file. It's easy to see how fax file conversion can use gluttonous quantities of precious computer storage.

Deleting unwanted fax files

If you don't want to keep your fax files, you'll want to periodically clean out the \ WS \ FAX subdirectory by deleting all the fax files from it. You can either delete them manually or write a batch file to do it for you. You can write such a batch file by opening a nondocument named DELPCX.BAT and typing the following commands into it:

```
ECHO = ON
REM Deleting all fax files from \ WS \ FAX subdirectory.
ECHO = OFF
DEL  \ WS \ FAX \ *.PCX
ECHO = ON
```

Store one copy of DELPCX.BAT in your WordStar directory, and one in your root directory. Then you can delete your fax files by typing DELPCX at any DOS prompt. Or you can run the batch file through WordStar's DOS window with Ctrl−KF.

Maintaining a fax file archive

If you intend to reuse fax files later, or simply want to maintain a record of what faxes you've created and sent, keep an archive of those files. Whatever you do, however, you should always delete them from your hard drive. They simply take up too much valuable storage space.

It's simple to copy fax files to a floppy disk before clearing the fax subdirectory. You can archive manually, or write a batch file to do it for you. Open a nondocument called ARCFAX.BAT and type the following commands into it:

```
ECHO = ON
REM Archiving all  \ WS \ FAX fax files to Drive A.
```

```
ECHO = OFF
COPY \ WS \ FAX \ *.PCX A:
ECHO = ON
```

Store one copy of ARCFAX.BAT in your WordStar directory and one in your root directory. Then you can archive the fax files by typing ARCFAX at any DOS prompt. Or you can run the batch file through WordStar's DOS window with Ctrl−KF. Just remember to put a formatted floppy disk into drive A before running the archive.

Creating fax files using the Opening Menu

The most direct way to convert documents to fax files is through the Opening Menu. Because this is a brand-new feature, there's no standard way to make conversions. But going through the Opening Menu is the most direct way to create faxes.

Steps for converting text files to fax files

Below are the steps used for converting WordStar text files to fax files with the Fax option on the Opening Menu:

1. Run WordStar and change to the directory and drive containing the document(s) to be converted to fax files.
2. At the Opening Menu, select the Fax option by either typing FF or pressing the \ (backslash) key. The Fax dialog box (see Fig. 14-1) will appear. Below it are the files in the directory. You can exit this routine at any time before starting the conversion by pressing the Esc key.
3. Select the file to be converted by using the arrow keys to move the highlight to it and then press the Enter key, or click on it with the mouse. You can also type in the filename. When ready, press the Tab key to move to the next variable.

```
▬▬▬▬▬▬▬▬▬▬▬▬▬▬▬▬▬▬▬▬ Fax ▬▬▬▬▬▬▬▬▬▬▬▬▬▬▬▬▬▬▬▬

   File to Fax: C:\COMMAND.WS6\OPENMENU.FIG        ▌  OK  ▐

 Fax File Location: C:\WS\FAX                     ▌ Cancel ▐

  Name of Fax File: OPENM 001.PCX      Resolution:  ▌ View ▐
                                         o  Low
  Fax Page Numbers:                      ◆  High
     ◆  All                             o  Special 300 dpi
     o  Selected Pages: ______________  o  9-pin Dot Matrix
                                         o  24-pin Dot Matrix
```

14-1 Fax dialog box.

4. The cursor will jump to the line Name of Fax File. Type in a five-letter fax name. Use any combination of characters. When ready, press the Tab key to move to the next variable.
5. The cursor will now move to the 001. WordStar uses this to number the individual fax files sequentially. You can change or accept this number sequence. When ready, press the Tab key.
6. Now the cursor is on Fax Page Numbers. Use the arrow keys here to choose to convert either all the file or selected pages. When ready, press the Tab key to move to Resolution.
7. The Resolution variable sets the clarity of the fax being sent. The default is High, which most fax machines can deliver. Select the resolution your fax board uses. Either use the up and down arrow keys to select a resolution or click on the resolution with the mouse.
8. Check the information in the dialog box for errors. When ready, press the Tab key.
9. Now you can execute the conversion, preview the text file, or cancel the routine. Use the arrow key to make your selection and press the Enter key. Or double-click on it with the mouse.

Aborting the fax file conversion

While the conversion routine is running, WordStar turns on Page Preview and displays the pages as each is converted. If left uninterrupted, the conversion will continue until a fax file is created for every selected page of the document file. There are two ways to halt the fax file conversion before it completes:

Use the universal abort command Ctrl−U   This halts the conversion as soon as WordStar finishes the page it's working on. You're returned directly to where you were when you began the conversion—either to the Opening Menu or to the write-and-edit mode.

Press the Esc key   This halts the conversion as soon as WordStar finishes the page it's working on. An error message box will appear, telling you that the conversion is halted. Press the Enter key and you'll be returned directly to where you were when you began the conversion.

Previewing the text file

Selecting View from the Fax dialog box turns on Page Preview. This is the same Page Preview you get in the write-and-edit mode, with all of its features and options.

The primary reason for using Page Preview before creating fax files is to pick the pages from the document you want to fax. If you've written and formatted a document specifically for faxing, you don't need to view it again. Just select All Pages on the Fax dialog box and convert the entire file.

For further information on Page Preview, read the chapter titled *Using Advanced Page Preview*.

Guidelines for naming fax files

When you specify a text file to be used during fax file conversion, the default name WordStar uses is always the first five letters of the original filename, three sequentially generated digits (001, 002, 003, etc.), plus the .PCX extension.

- If you don't want to use the default, you can type in any five characters you prefer.
- You can type in a different numbering sequence if you want. This allows you to print different test runs of the same document.
- If the filename you use is the same as an existing fax file series, WordStar will ask you if you want to overwrite the existing fax files before making the conversion. Answer Y to overwrite the existing fax file and N to return to the dialog box and use a different name.
- It's best to always use a unique or distinctive name when creating fax files. Because you have only five characters to identify a fax file series, it's easy to get confused or to overwrite a fax file you wanted to keep.

Converting selected pages

You're never restricted to using an entire text file when creating fax files. You can always specify any range of pages in the Fax dialog box.

- The format for selecting a range of pages is the same as for printing a range of pages from a document. For example, to select pages 1 through 5 and pages 7 and 9, type 1-5 7 9.
- If you've reassigned page numbers using dot commands, you must specify the physical number of the actual page inside the text file. For example, if you used the .PN command to start page numbering over again on page 5, the physical number is still 5, even though the page number prints as 1.
- If you aren't sure about the physical page numbers, use Page Preview to check the document. This will display the physical page numbers at the top of the screen. If more than one page is displayed, the page numbers are above each page.
- For purposes of converting documents to fax files, it's best to avoid reassigning page numbers with dot commands. The more you do it, the more you'll risk confusing yourself and WordStar. The best rule is to always keep things simple.

When drawing selected pages from large text files for fax file conversion, you might find it a complicated procedure to convert only selected pages from the document.

It's simpler to open a large text file as a document, mark the selected pages as a block, and use Ctrl−KW to write them to a file of their own. Then just run the conversion on the whole special file. In most cases, this is a lot quicker than having WordStar run through an entire large text file and pull out the pages to be faxed.

Setting the fax file resolution

The Resolution variable on the Fax dialog box sets the clarity of the fax being sent. Select the resolution your fax board uses. If you aren't sure, read the documentation packed with the fax board. If this setting doesn't match the setting in your fax board's software, the fax might not look right when sent.

High resolution This is the default setting, and creates fax files with a 200×200 dpi resolution. Most fax machines can deliver this level of resolution. Of course, high resolution fax files produce better looking faxes than ones created with low resolution.

Low resolution This creates fax files with 200×100 dpi clarity. If you have trouble sending a fax to an older fax machine that can't handle high resolution, you might want to try using the low resolution setting of your fax board.

Special 300 dpi resolution This setting creates fax files with super-high resolution for fax boards that can use it. This works best when sending faxes to the newer model fax machines that can deliver 300 dpi resolution. If the target fax machine can't print at 300 dpi, you gain nothing by sending in this mode. It takes WordStar twice as long to create these fax files, however, and they're twice as big as high-resolution files.

Dot-matrix resolution The 9-pin and 24-pin dot-matrix settings aren't intended for creating files to be sent to a fax machine. They create .PCX files to be sent to other computers with installed fax boards. These fax files are intended for printing on dot-matrix printers. The print driver or utility program for doing this should be on the software disk packed with the fax board. It doesn't come with WordStar 7. Select the printing resolution of the target printer. If you aren't sure what it is, use 9-pin. Tip: Be sure to always use the same resolution for sending the fax file as creating it. If the settings don't match, the fax might not look right.

Using SHOWPCX to view fax files

The SHOWPCX utility program is used to view and identify fax files—and to verify they've been created correctly. The file SHOWPCX.EXE is found in the WordStar directory.

Note: How well SHOWPCX displays the fax files always depends on the monitor being used, and the resolution specified before creating the fax file. You get the best results on VGA or better. On lesser monitors, the image might not have the right proportions.

1. Run WordStar and change to the \ WS directory.
2. At the Opening Menu, type R to **Run a DOS Command**.
3. At the Run dialog box, type \ WS \ SHOWPCX \ WS \ FAX \ *filename* and press the Enter key.
4. The fax file will appear onscreen in the half-size format. Use arrow keys, scrolling commands, and PgUp and PgDn keys to move around on the page. Press the plus and minus keys on the numeric keypad to change the viewing size.
5. When finished viewing the fax file with SHOWPCX, press the Esc key. You'll be returned to where you were when you ran SHOWPCX.

Tip: For convenience sake, copy this SHOWPCX.EXE program file to your fax subdirectory. Then access the fax directory before running it. When you run SHOWPCX from the same directory as the fax files, you don't have to type the pathname before the filename.

Creating fax files

Following are some basic guidelines for creating and working on fax files with WordStar. To learn how to send fax files with your fax board, you need to study the documentation packed with the board.

What is a fax file?

Fax files are graphic representations of document pages (and are therefore graphic files, as opposed to text files). This is why .PCX files are so much bigger than the WordStar documents they're drawn from.

The process used to create fax files with WordStar is very similar to what happens when you use Page Preview. This is why WordStar cycles through Page Preview when making fax files, and why fax file generation is also a part of Page Preview. The important difference is that the Fax utility creates permanent files and saves them to disk.

Using the View option

WordStar recommends using Page Preview in 4x zoom as the best way to tell how a fax will look. This depends on the quality of the monitor being used.

All the limitations and features of Page Preview apply to the routine for creating fax files. Colors other than white are always changed to black. The same fonts are available for viewing the fax file, and a 72-point font is the largest size WordStar can display.

Page Preview doesn't display system variables like date and time, and it doesn't display merge printing variable information drawn from generic or variable names and data files.

Using FAX.PDF

WordStar has a special printer definition file it recommends using to help give your faxes their best possible appearance. This is the FAX.PDF and it was installed in your WordStar directory when WSSETUP copied the program files to your hard disk. If your faxes aren't coming out with the resolution you want, attach FAX.PDF to your text file like any other printer definition file.

Tip: If for any reason the FAX print driver isn't in your WordStar directory, find it on the master disks and copy it to the directory with the DOS COPY command. You must use COPYWS.EXE to retrieve the driver from the master disk.

1. Run WordStar and open the document.
2. Use Ctrl−P? to call the Change Printer dialog box.
3. Use the arrow keys to put the highlight on Fax in the onscreen list of drivers, and then press the Enter key.

This print driver supplies fonts similar to the HP LaserJet III internal fonts. They include Courier, Line Printer, and the scalable Times and Univers fonts. You can also install additional internal fonts, soft fonts, and card fonts by using the PRCHANGE utility program or by running WINSTALL.

Memory requirements

Memory problems encountered while using WordStar and its fax conversion program will vary, depending on the computer and video graphics adapter being used. How much RAM you have is also a factor. If you have a newer computer with 1 or more megabytes of RAM and a VGA monitor, you shouldn't have any problems.

During the fax file conversions, the utility program uses up to 27K of RAM in addition to WordStar's requirements. If your computer has 640K or less, always check the system status before running the fax conversion routine. You can either press the ? key to check status at the Opening Menu or use Ctrl−O? to check status inside the document mode.

If using memory-resident software with WordStar, you might need to free some memory before running the fax file conversion. This is especially true if there's less than 512K of memory free before you run WordStar. The directions for clearing specific TSRs from memory are found in the user manuals packed with those programs.

Tip: Unless memory-resident software is loaded by AUTOEXEC.BAT during bootup, the quickest way to remove all TSR programs is to reboot the computer. If your TSRs are loaded during startup, copy AUTOEXEC.BAT to the file USEREXEC.BAT and then remove the TSRs from the boot file. Then always load the memory-resident software with USEREXEC when you're sure you won't need the memory free.

Insufficient memory can cause many fonts, especially large fonts, to look blocky when fax files are viewed with SHOWPCX. When it's not a case of using an inadequate monitor, you might be able to correct it by clearing memory. Then run DELCRT to delete the blocky fonts before creating the fax file again.

If clearing memory still doesn't provide enough memory for WordStar to use the fax file conversion properly, you might be able to use WSCHANGE to free some more memory. A better solution is to add more memory to the computer. WordStar 7 has been rewritten to take advantage of EMS or expanded memory. Many of its other features, like wordcount, rely on EMS memory, and don't work well when it's not available.

If your fax board software is a TSR program, you might need to exit WordStar before transmitting your faxes.

Creating fax files in the document mode

In WordStar 7, the option to create fax files is available every time you run Page Preview. This means you can open a document; write, edit, and save it; and then make fax files without exiting the write-and-edit mode.

The fax file conversion routine is found on the Options Menu of the Page Preview screen. The process is streamlined, when compared to the Fax dialog box. You're given two choices:

Fax files for the entire document Asks you to type in a five-character filename for the faxes, and starts the conversion process when you press the Enter key.

Fax files for a range Asks you to type in a five-character filename for the faxes and to press the Enter key. It then asks you to type in the range, and starts the conversion process when you press the Enter key. The range here is limited to Start on Page and Stop on Page.

Note: If you don't type in a five-character filename, fax files created through Page Preview don't use the first five letters of the original filename as the default. Instead, WordStar uses the generic filename F001P001.PCX every time you start the routine.

For further information on Page Preview features and options, read the chapter titled *Using WordStar's Page Preview*.

15

CHAPTER

Creating an index

This chapter covers everything you need to know about creating indexes for WordStar document text files. An *index* is an alphabetical list of subjects in a document. These include topics, words, and phrases, accompanied by the page numbers where each can be found in the document. WordStar's index generator can take a prepared text file and generate an index from codes embedded in it.

There are four different ways to prepare a text file for indexing. The first three require you to mark the file with embedded index codes. The fourth way is to create an exclusion list of words you want omitted from the index.

If you're using index codes to create your index (the more common indexing method), the following is a general overview of the process: Once all the words and phrases are marked in a document, you can generate an index of this text file by running the indexer from the Index dialog box (see Fig. 15-1). Start it by pressing the I key at the Opening Menu and then specifying the text file being indexed in the dialog box. The indexer will read the text file, find the index codes, and generate a new text file containing the alphabetized subjects and the page numbers of each referenced subject. This text file will have the same filename as the original file scanned, but with the extension .IDX to identify it as an index file. If you want to keep this file, rename it so a subsequent index generation won't overwrite it.

Marking a text file for indexing

The first task of indexing a document using embedded index codes is to place those codes into the text file. This can be tedious work. The larger the document, the longer it takes and the more mind-numbing it can be. I recommend that you don't try to do it all in one sitting.

```
▄▄▄▄▄▄▄▄▄▄▄▄▄▄▄▄▄▄▄▄▄▄  Index  ▄▄▄▄▄▄▄▄▄▄▄▄▄▄▄▄▄▄▄▄▄▄

  Filename: C:\WS\OPENMENU.FIG ________________        █  OK  █

Page Numbers: ♦ All                      Pages: o Odd   █ Cancel █
              o Selected Pages:                 o Even
                                                ♦ Both

              [ ] Index Every Word
─────────────────────────────────────────────────────────────────
Filenames:          Path: C:\WS  45M free
..             \    FAX            \    MACROS         \    OPTIONS          \
ARROW.HP     .3k    BOX          .4k    CHEX.HP      .5k    DB00.DTB       80k
DB01.DTB    375k    DB02.DTB     84k    DB04.DTB    188k    FIDDLE7.PAT    27k
FILELIST.TXT 27k    FILENAME     .5k    FONTID.CTL  7.8k    HP-ENV.LST    1.0k
HP2-ENV.LST 1.0k    ILLUS.DOT    .4k    INDEX.DTB    46k    KEYBOARD.MRG   .1k
LIST.DOC     .8k    MAILING.DOC 1.0k    OPENMENU.FIG 9.6k   PDFEDIT.HLP    35k
PLAYBILL.DOC .6k    PLAYS.DOC    .9k    PLEAD.HP     .1k    PREVIEW.MSG    10k
PRINT.TST    12k    REVIEW.DOC  3.1k    SHADE.HP     .0k    SHAKE.DOC     6.0k
SPELL.DOC   6.0k    VESA1024.WGD 2.9k   WINSTALL.HLP 32k    WS.DEF         .9k
WSINDEX.XCL 1.5k    WSMIN.PAT    .0k
```

15-1 Index dialog box.

The least painful way to do it is as you write the document. Mark paragraphs, pages, or sections one at a time, after you write them. Then you get it done as you go, and are finished marking when you finish writing the document.

If you wait until the document is complete before indexing it, don't try to mark everything at once. Mark words globally. This means using Ctrl−QF to locate unique words or phrases throughout the text file, and index tagging each occurrence before moving to the next unique word. You can even use Ctrl−KC or Ctrl−KR to block copy the reference tag. This ensures consistency throughout the document.

Three different index markers

WordStar has three different commands to mark a file for indexing. The first, Ctrl−PK, is a print-control command embedded at the beginning and end of a phrase you want included in the index. The second is the dot command .IX followed by the word or phrase you want in the index. The third, Ctrl−ONI, uses the Notes Menu to place an index note in the file.

Marking words or phrases in the text file

Use the command Ctrl−PK to mark the beginning and end of words or phrases in the body text of your document. With this command, you don't have to type anything extra. Simply scan through the text file, and mark anything in any paragraph you want included in the index. This works best if you're consistent with terms.

1. Place the cursor on the first character of the word or phrase you want included in the index.
2. Use Ctrl−PK to embed the print-control code.
3. Place the cursor after the last character of the word or phrase you want included in the index.
4. Use Ctrl−PK to embed the print-control code.

The codes embedded by Ctrl−PK create a simple index, without cross references or subreferences. The maximum length of any phrase marked for indexing is 50 characters. WordStar will ignore any extra characters and truncate the item in the index file. The Ctrl−PK command embeds a ^K at the cursor. To remove the index entry, delete it like any other embedded print-control command.

Tip: Because it's monotonous to type these key combinations repeatedly, try recording Ctrl−PK as a macro and installing it on a hotkey. Then you can insert it with a couple of keystrokes.

Using .IX to mark index items

You can also use the dot command .IX to embed and write an index code in the body of a text file. Unlike Ctrl−PK, this command marks words and phrases on a single line, not run into other text in the file. You therefore need to mark only the beginning of the line. This command begins with a period at column 1, followed by the letters *IX*, and then the word or phrase of the index reference. The formula for this is as follows:

.IX *words to index, subreference*

The maximum length of any phrase marked for indexing is 150 characters. Word-Star will ignore any extra characters and truncate the item in the index file.

Tip: To quickly add entries for every occurrence of a specific word, type the first entry and mark the .IX command line as a block. Then use the Ctrl−QF to find every other occurrence, and copy the marked block to each location.

Using .IX to mark index subreferences

A subreference is always optional. When you add a subreference, it prints on the line below the main reference, indented two spaces. Even if you add more spaces in the command line, or tabs, it will still indent only two spaces. The command line:

.IX *words to index, subreference*

will print as follows:

words to index
    subreference, 1

You must insert the .IX command *on every page containing the information you want indexed*. You can put it anywhere on the page. It's common to either place them in a group at the top of the page or directly above the paragraphs to which they refer, but it makes no difference.

- The .IX command has the advantage of allowing you to cross reference and subreference.
- The .IX command has the disadvantage of requiring you to develop an unvarying system for identifying the topics you're indexing.
- The maximum length of a phrase in a .IX command line is 150 characters. If you use more, WordStar will ignore the extra characters and truncate the reference.

You must plan ahead and be consistent with the words or phrases you index with the .IX command. Make a written list of your index codes as you go, and refer to it often so you can keep the spelling and syntax exactly the same. If you use many different words or phrases for the same subject, you'll wind up with a cluttered index. Such an index will contain multiple listings for the same subject under several different headings, scattered randomly through the document.

1. Put the cursor on column 1 of any blank line on a text file page. Type .IX followed by one blank space.
2. After the blank space, type the word or phrase of the index item.
3. If you're adding a subreference, type a comma, one space, and then the subreference text. Don't type commas in the command line unless you're adding a subreference.

Tip: Record the command line as a macro and install it on a hotkey. Then you can insert it with a couple of keystrokes and have it ready to type in the word or phrase.

Automatic boldface numbers in indexes

WordStar offers automatic boldfacing for page numbers in an index list. You can use this for all index codes, or to mark references for special attention. For example, the command line:

    .IX + *words to index, subreference*

will print as follows:

    words to index
        subreference, 1

Using commas and addition and subtraction signs in references

In order to use commas, the plus sign, or the minus in .IX reference lines, you must insert a backslash (\ ) in front of the character. For example, the index code:

.IX \ + *words to index, subreference*

will print as follows:

+ words to index
    subreference, 1

As you can see, the plus sign prints as part of the reference, rather than marking
the page number for boldface.

Use .IX for cross references

The .IX command allows for cross references in the index. To indicate a cross
reference, just put a hyphen (-) before the word or phrase on the command line, as
follows:

.IX -Naming Files, see Files

When printed in the index, it will look like the following:

Naming Files
    see Files

The only difference between a cross reference and the standard index item is that
no page number follows the cross reference. Cross reference items are commonly
printed in italic, as in this example:

Naming Files
    see Files

Using boilerplates to mark index items

It isn't necessary to type these .IX command lines from scratch every time you
need to use them. Just type one for each level of reference, subreference, or cross
reference you intend to use. Then mark them as blocks and write each to boilerplate files. You can use Ctrl−KR to read them into any text file, any time you
need them.

Using the Notes Menu index codes

The command Ctrl−ONI calls the Notes Menu and selects Create an Index Entry
from it. This in turn calls the Notes Entry dialog box, where you can type in up to
50 characters of an index note reference.

When you insert an index note reference with Ctrl−ONI, the first 15 characters (including spaces) will appear onscreen between brackets. This is an index
note tag very much like a paragraph tag or font tag described elsewhere. You can
delete an index tag as a single character, and edit or correct index note tags
through the Notes Menu.

Tip: To quickly add index note tags for every occurrence of a specific word, insert the first tag and then mark it as a block. Use Ctrl−QF to find every occurrence of the word, and copy the marked block to each location.

Marking index items with a macro

The new macro system allows you to easily record the samples in a previous section as macros and install them on hotkeys. Then you can read them into the text file with a couple of keystrokes. This is the fastest possible way to use any of the commands described previously.

Making and using exclusion lists

An exclusion list is a nondocument text file containing an alphanumerical list of words *not* to be included in an index file. It becomes active when you tell Word-Star to index every word.

While the index utility program is running, WordStar automatically looks for two exclusion lists, one named WSINDEX.XCL and another you can create specifically for the document. It compares the words in the text file with the words in the exclusion lists. Any word found in an exclusion list is omitted from the index file.

The WSINDEX exclusion list

The exclusion file WSINDEX.XCL comes with WordStar, and is copied to your WordStar directory as a normal part of setup. At 1.5K, it's a very small exclusion list; it contains a mere 231 words to exclude from an index. If you want, you can open this file as a nondocument and add words to it. Just be sure to keep them in alphabetical order, and use only the nondocument mode.

Tip: Use the column block control Ctrl−KN and block sorting command Ctrl−KZ to keep your exclusion lists sorted in ascending, or alphabetical order.

If you open WSINDEX as a nondocument, you'll see that it contains English words that almost never appear in indexes, including articles, pronouns, prepositions, conjunctions, and so forth. Obviously, these are very common words. By using an exclusion list, you're telling WordStar to index only the unique words it finds in the text file.

It isn't a good idea to make this WSINDEX exclusion list too big. It's far better to create another exclusion file specific to the type of document you're indexing.

Exclusion lists for specific documents

The second kind of exclusion list is one you make up expressly for a specific kind of document. Obviously, the topics in the index relate to the content of the document. Medical documents have medical terms in their indexes, legal documents have legal terms, software user manuals have computer terminology, and so on.

A method for making an exclusion file

There's a way of creating an exclusion list that makes WordStar do most of the work. It requires generating an index for every word in a document and then deleting all unique words from the resulting index file.

1. When preparing the text file for indexing, mark only phrases you want included in the index file. Don't worry about individual words at all. Use Ctrl−PK to tag existing phrases, and .IX to include other phrases. If your index is to contain topics with numbers in them, you need to mark these as well.
2. Start the indexer from the Opening Menu.
3. Select the prepared file for indexing, and tell WordStar to index every word. Then use Ctrl−K to start the indexing routine.
4. Open the resulting index file as a nondocument.
5. Scroll through the index file. Use Ctrl−Y to delete every unique word you want included in the final index. There should be lines with nothing but page numbers on them. Delete these as well.
6. Now use Ctrl−QA, the Global Search and Replace command, to find all numbers and commas, and replace them with nothing. This will delete them from the index file. You must repeat Ctrl−QA once for the commas, and once for each numeral 0−9. How long this takes will depend on the size of the document and the speed of your computer.
7. Now delete all blank lines from the file, but leave one blank line between each alphabetical group in the list.
8. Save and close the file. Rename it, giving it the .XCL extension.

You can use this exclusion list repeatedly. Just rename it to match the file being indexed, and copy it to the same directory as that text file.

You can use this method to make exclusion files for general use, or for specific kinds of documents. You might think that it's a bit tedious, but it requires far less effort than embedding index codes one by one throughout the document. And you have to do it only once for every specific kind of document.

Generating the index file

Once you have the text file prepared for indexing, and any exclusion lists ready, you're ready to generate an index file from your document. Simply start the indexer running, and WordStar will do the rest for you. When it finishes, a new file will be saved to the same directory as the indexed document.

WordStar creates an index file with the same name as the document file, but with an .IDX extension. Then it creates an alphabetized list of the index terms, and includes the page numbers where each is located in the document. So it's important for the document to be in its final printing form, with all editing and formatting complete. If you make substantive changes after generating the index, you must generate a new index. Otherwise, the index page numbers might not match up with the printed document.

Running the indexer

The following steps for using the indexer assume that you have a document written and prepared for indexing. They also assume that you know how to run WordStar and change to the directory you need to use.

1. Run WordStar your normal way. At the Opening Menu, type I. This calls the Index dialog box.
2. At the Index dialog box, tell WordStar the name of the file you want indexed. You can select the file from the list below the menu, or type in a filename from a different drive and path.
3. Use the Tab key to move to the index variables. Accept or change them as desired.
4. When ready to start generating the index, press the Enter key.
5. The indexer will run, creating an index file with the same name as the file selected for indexing, but with a .IDX extension.
6. You can open this .IDX file as a document to edit and format it any way you want.

Pausing, stopping, restarting, and canceling the index

Because the indexer is really a print-to-disk routine, you can use any of the Print Menu options while the utility is running.

Ctrl−U   The universal abort command will cancel the index runoff before it completes.

Esc   Pressing the Esc key will cancel the runoff before it completes.

P   Pressing P key will pause the runoff.

C   Pressing C key will continue the runoff after any pause.

Index variables

The Index dialog box has six variables. Every time you generate an index, you can accept the default answers or selectively change any of them.

All Pages   The default answer is to automatically index every page of the selected text file.

Selected Pages   If you want, you can index only a selected range of pages within a text file.

Odd/Even/Both Pages   The default is to automatically index both odd and even pages throughout a document (or range within the document). If you want, you can opt to index only odd numbered pages or even numbered pages.

Index Every Word   The default is to not include every word in the index. This is a checkbox. Put an X in it to make it active. Don't use this if you're indexing only specific words or phrases marked with indexing codes. Making it active tells WordStar to look for exclusion files. If there are no exclusion lists, WordStar will create an index of every word in the text file.

Creating an index by indexing every word

One very simple way to create an index is to tell WordStar to index every word in it, open the resulting index file, and delete everything you don't want in it. This can be time-consuming if the document is large, but it does eliminate the need to mark the text file with indexing codes. You have to tag specific words and phrases in the text file only once, and you can use Ctrl−QF to locate every occurrence of them.

If you don't have a sufficient exclusion list file prepared, or if the document hasn't been marked for indexing, the only way you can generate an index is to index every word.

Indexing a master document

A little known fact of WordStar's indexer is that you can use it with merge printing variables. You can generate an index of an entire document without having to first join all its component sections or chapters into a single text file. All you have to do is create a master document containing a list of files you want merge printed with the File Include command. A sample is given below:

```
..filename  = merge.mss
..purpose   = to merge print the MS of filename.tst
.fi frontmat.ter
.fi introduc
.fi chapter.01
.fi chapter.02
.fi chapter.03
.fi chapter.04
.fi chapter.05
.fi chapter.06
.fi chapter.07
.fi chapter.08
.fi chapter.09
.fi chapter.10
```

This master document can be used to merge print any document whose respective files are named and numbered as the ones above. It can also be used to generate an index of the document.

Keep this master document in the same directory as your section or chapter text files. To generate an index, simply select the master document for indexing. If your document has more files than the above, simply add more .FI command lines. Substitute your filenames for the the names I've listed. Be sure to keep them in the same order as the desired hardcopy.

Proofreading and printing the index

Once you've generated the index file, you can open and edit it like any other document text file. Print a hardcopy first, and make your corrections there.

One of the first things to do is to check the spelling. If there are many misspellings, you might want to correct them in the document, and then generate the index again. This will also track down any unique words not yet in your personal dictionary. You can add them either automatically or individually to the exclusion dictionary.

It's common to format an index in a different or smaller font than the body text of your document, but there are no hard and fast rules for doing this. If your table of contents is in a different font from the body text, you can use that same font for your index. Don't use a fancy font. The object is to make the index utilitarian. A sans serif font is always practical for your indexes and tables of contents.

It's also common to format the index in two or more newspaper columns. Index topics seldom take up more than a word or two, so there's usually room for several columns on a standard page. This will put more index information per page, and help the reader find what he needs at a glance. It also uses fewer pages in the hardcopy.

Keep the index topics separated visually by arranging them in alphabetical order. Be consistent in using things like boldface, underlining, and italics. (For example, you can put cross-references in italics and major topics in boldface to distinguish them from subreferences.) Remember that the index is supposed to provide quick access to specific information throughout the document. Think of it as a version of the table of contents—which also directs you to specific information in a document.

You can number an index any way you want—or not at all. Just be consistent. If the document is consecutively numbered, beginning to end, then number the index as part of the document. If you use chapter numbering (numbering begins over at the start of each chapter, and code letters identify the chapters), then use this method in your index. The index can also be considered as being "outside" the document, and given either no page numbers at all or Roman numerals.

If you want, you can append the index to the document text file, so that the whole thing prints as one hardcopy. Or just print it separately and put it on the bottom of the document pile.

16
CHAPTER

Creating a table of contents

This chapter covers using the Table of Contents option on the Opening Menu. It tells you how to create table of contents files from WordStar document text files, and provides detailed instructions on:

- Preparing a file for the table of contents program.
- Generating a table of contents file from a prepared document.
- Editing and formatting a table of contents file for printing and inclusion with the document for which it was written.

A *table of contents* is a consecutive list of the divisions in a document, including the page numbers where each can be found. A well-written table of contents is essential for finding usable information in a book. A poorly written table of contents can destroy the value of any book.

WordStar can generate a table of contents from embedded comments you've included in a document. There are two ways to write a table of contents with WordStar. You can print a hardcopy of the document and use it as a reference for typing another text file containing a table of contents, or you can embed .TC dot commands in the document file and use the indexing utility to generate a table of contents file.

Marking a text file with TOC codes

This section tells you how to mark a text file with codes to generate a table of contents.

Using .TC to mark the text file

The command .TC is used to mark the different division titles in your text files, and is embedded in the text file just like any other dot command. What makes it different is that you include the division titles on the command line. The basic format for this .TC dot command is:

1. Place the cursor on column 1 in a blank line directly above a division heading.
2. Type .TC and one blank space. (It doesn't matter if the dot command is capitalized or lowercase.)
3. If the division is a main heading (for the entire file, for example), don't tab; if it's a section, tab once; if a subsection, tab twice.
4. Now type the heading on the command line, exactly as it is on the following line. Include any print control commands if you want to print in boldface, double-strike, italics, or underline.
5. Type a number sign (#) and then backspace the cursor onto it. WordStar will substitute the correct page number for this symbol, during both printing and TOC generation.
6. Type Ctrl−P to insert leader dots to a predetermined tab stop setting.

Repeat the above steps for every division heading in the text file. You don't have to retype the heading every time; you can mark it as a block and copy it to the command line with Ctrl−KC.

Using tabs to design the TOC

You can use tabs on the .TC command line to indent progressive levels of division headings in a table of contents. Use either the default tab settings, or create your own to give the TOC a custom look

In order to make this convenient to use, you must embed a special ruler line at the beginning of the text file. This ruler line has only three tab stops, set to format the table of contents. The ruler line has a left margin of .00″, a right margin of 6.50″, and tabs set at .50″, 1.00″, and 6.00″, and can be used for documents printed on standard $8^1/_2 \times 11$ inch paper.

You can use this ruler line to easily insert leader dots to a preset tab, with plenty of space remaining between the last character of the TOC heading and the page number of the heading.

- Main headings get no tab indentation on this ruler line. They're flush against the left margin.
- Section headings get one tab stop on this ruler line, so they're indented .50″ from the left margin.
- Subsection headings get two tab stops on this ruler line, so they're indented .50″ from the left margin.

- If you need other subdivision headings in your table of contents, simply add more tab stops to the ruler line.

To keep the table of contents file correctly formatted, you must copy the above ruler line to the very beginning of the file. Otherwise, the leader dots won't align to the same column.

Using leader dots

The command Ctrl−P is used to insert leader dots from the cursor position to the next Tab stop. They get their name from the fact they lead the eye across the page from one point to another. In a table of contents, they are used to bridge the distance from the last character in a TOC item, to the page number column. A sample .TC command line with leader dots is:

```
.TC ←Using Leader Dots← . . . . . . . . . . . . . . #
```

WordStar inserts these leader dots in the index file it creates. Using leader dots can produce an attractive, easy-to-read table of contents with a professional appearance. Without them, the reader's eye can easily wander offline while glancing from the heading to its page number.

To keep the table of contents file correctly formatted, you must also copy the special ruler line into its beginning. Otherwise, the leader dots won't align to the same column.

Tip: If you find it awkward to use Ctrl−P, record it as a macro and install it on a hotkey.

Using boilerplates to mark TOC divisions

It isn't necessary to type these .TC command lines from scratch every time you need to use them. Just type one for each level of division head you intend to use. Then mark them as blocks and write each to boilerplate files. You can use Ctrl−KR to read them into any text file, any time you need them. Following are sample TOC markers for three levels of division headings:

```
.TC document title . . . . . . . . . . . . . . . . . . . . . . #
.TC ←SECTION 1: heading. . . . . . . . . . . . . . #
.TC ←          ← : heading. . . . . . . . . . . . . . #
```

If you prefer to get even more detailed use of boilerplate text, you can format an entire blank heading and save it to a file of its own. Now I'm going to give you examples of complete section and subsection headings. The following is a standard section heading you can use in any standard document:

```
.CP 4
.TC ►section : #
^Bsection : ^B
```

Mark it as a block and write it to a boilerplate file named SECTION. The following is is a sample of a standard Subsection heading you can use in any standard document:

```
.CP 4
.TC ►        ►#
^B^B
```

Mark it as a block and write it to a boilerplate file named SUBHEAD. Both of the above samples mark off a distinct amount of space for their headings in the body of the text file. The .CP 4 is the conditional page dot command, telling WordStar to break to a new page if there aren't four lines remaining before the bottom of the page. This keeps the heading tied to the paragraph directly below it, so you don't have to manually insert a page break above division headings.

Marking TOC items with a macro

The new macro system allows you to easily record the samples in the previous section as macros, and install them on hotkeys. Then you can read them into the text file with a couple of keystrokes.

Generating the TOC file

Once the document text file is prepared, the next step is using the Table of Contents utility program to create the TOC file.

The Table of Contents program scans the prepared text file, reads the .TC commands, and uses them to create a new file containing the headings given in the commands. This new file has the same filename as the original file, but WordStar gives it the .TOC extension to identify it as a table of contents file. If you want to keep this file, you must rename it—or the next TOC generation will overwrite it. Once you've created this file, you can open and edit it like any other document.

Using the table of contents program

The instructions given here assume that you have a file in which you've embedded the table of contents codes for all divisions in the document. The steps for creating a table of contents from a prepared file are as follows:

1. At the Opening Menu, type T. This calls the Table of Contents dialog box, shown in Fig. 16-1.
2. At the Table of Contents dialog box, tell WordStar the name of the file you're going to use. You can select it from the list below the menu, or type in a filename from a different drive and path.
3. When ready, use the Tab key to move through the TOC variables. You can accept the default answers, or change each of them every time you generate a table of contents. (Use Shift−Tab to move backward.)

16-1 Table of Contents dialog box.

4. When ready, use Ctrl−K to start generating the table of contents. (Or click on on the OK push button.)
5. The table of contents program will run, and create a new file with the same name as the file it was generated from, but with the extension .TOC.

The table of contents variables

The Table of Contents dialog box has five variables. Every time you generate an index, you can accept the default answers or selectively change any of them.

All Pages The default answer is to automatically scan every page of the selected text file while generating a table of contents.

Selected Pages If you want, you can scan only a selected range of pages within a text file to generate a table of contents.

Odd/Even/Both Pages The default is to automatically scan both odd and even pages throughout the document (or range within the document) while creating a table of contents. If you want, you can scan only odd numbered pages or only even numbered pages.

Pausing, stopping, restarting, and canceling a TOC

Because the Table of Contents utility is really a print-to-disk routine, you can use any of the Print dialog box options while the utility is running.

Ctrl−U The universal abort command will cancel the TOC runoff before it completes.

Esc Pressing the Esc key will cancel the TOC runoff before it completes.

P   Pressing P will pause the TOC runoff.

C   Pressing C will continue the TOC runoff after any pause.

Multiple TOCs from one text file

It's possible to generate up to nine separate tables of contents, at once, from the same text file. This is useful when writing large, complicated documents that are divided into major sections or parts. Each of the nine divisions can have its own separate table of contents. This variation requires adding a number from 1 to 0 after the .TC dot command. The format for this is as follows:

```
.TC1 division heading
.TC2 division heading
.TC3 division heading
.TC4 division heading
.TC5 division heading
.TC6 division heading
.TC7 division heading
.TC8 division heading
.TC9 division heading
```

When you add numbers to the command this way, WordStar gathers items for the numbered .TC commands and puts them into separate text files. These text files all have the same filename as the original text file, but are assigned .TO1, .TO2, .TO3, .TO4, and so on as extensions.

Tip: You will probably find it monotonous to type this dot command over and over again as you mark the text file for multiple TOCs. For greater convenience in embedding this command, install it as a macro, and assign it to a hotkey.

Proofreading and printing the TOC

Once you've generated the table of contents file, you can open and edit it like any other document text file. You might want to print a hardcopy first, and make your corrections there.

One of the first things to do is to check the spelling. If there are many misspellings, you might want to correct them in the document and then generate the table of contents again.

Like the index, it's common to format a table of contents in a different font or type size than the body text in your document. If your index is in a different font from the body text, you can use that same font for your table of contents.

Keep the table of contents headings and topics separated visually by sections and subsections. Put the same number of blank lines between each division. Be consistent in using things like boldface, underlining, and italics. Remember that the table of contents is supposed to provide quick access to the subjects in a document. Think of it as a complement of the index—which directs you to specific information throughout the document.

The table of contents is commonly considered as being "outside" the document, and either given no page numbers at all or Roman numeral page numbering. Just be consistent.

File-specific numbering is a good way to number certain types of documents. In this method, numbering begins over at the start of each file, and code letter prefixes identify the specific file. This kind of page numbering can be used for manuals or books—just about any kind of document that's divided into chapters or major sections. It allows you to revise the individual files, or chapters, without having to reprint the entire document.

If you want, you can append the table of contents to the document text file, so the whole thing prints as one hardcopy. Or just print it separately and put it on the top of the document pile.

17
CHAPTER

Using WordStar's new macro system

This chapter discusses and explains WordStar's new macro system. Macros were first added to WordStar 4, and the Shorthand Menu became an old and familiar face. It's gone now—forever—say the folks at WordStar International. With WordStar 7, the macro system is completely revised and rewritten. It's now perhaps the most powerful macro system of any word processor.

At their base level, macros are the assignment of commands to a single key or two-key sequence. In other words, you can string WordStar commands together so they execute as a group, instead of individually. These groups of commands create a small macro program that you run inside WordStar. You can then attach macros to specific keystroke sequences, called hotkeys, which allows you to run the macro by typing or pressing those keys. For example, commands installed on the different function keys are essentially macros. There are 82 valid hotkeys available.

At a basic level, you can use macros to insert boilerplate or reusable text into your documents. Much business or technical writing is repetitive. If you write business letters or user manuals you'll probably find yourself typing certain words, phrases, or sentences again and again. Now all you have to do is record them to a macro, assign them to a hotkey, and you can insert them with one or two keystrokes.

At a higher level, macros work like batch files. For those not familiar with them, a batch file is a DOS program that's written in ASCII; you can create one in WordStar by opening a nondocument file and typing in a string of DOS commands. When you run the batch file, all the commands you've typed in are executed at once, in sequential order, to perform a series of tasks.

261

Although WordStar's new macros work like batch files, they're not nondocuments. They're created with a macro editor. When you record or edit a macro and save it, WordStar compiles the macro—adding the necessary programming codes to make the macro execute its functions. When a macro is open in the macro editor, it resembles an ASCII text file—because it is an ASCII file. You must edit these files with the macro editor to get usable macros.

You can record any series or string of commands that you would normally execute through the keyboard or the pull-down menus as a macro. And once they're recorded and saved you can play them back whenever you need them repeated.

Old macros and new macros

There are two main criticisms of the new macro system when compared with the old shorthand macros. First, the new macros are so radically different from the old ones that they place even experienced WordStar users in the same boat with first-time users. In fact, the new system has turned six years of habitual use on its ear. The three keys placed permanently off limits are ones heavily used by the old system. In fact, the Esc key can't be used for macros at all.

Second, the new macros run noticeably slower than the shorthand macros. This is, no doubt, because the old macros were stored in the WSSHORT overlay file, and thus ran at machine speed. The new macros are each stored in individual files, and are run much like batch files. In fact, they seem to run at about the same speed as batch files executed through the Ctrl−KF DOS window. WordStar pauses while it locates the macro file, then runs each command statement stored in the file. The bigger the macro, the longer it takes.

Third, there are definitely intimidation and annoyance factors to consider when learning the new macros. Old-time users will be reaching for the Esc key for some time to come, and it's awkward to run a macro if it isn't attached to a hotkey. It's easy to record a new macro, but first you have to swallow a new way of thinking about macros. And to write a macro from scratch with the macro editor takes hours of study and practice.

But there's good news with the bad. Though intimidating at first glance, the Record Macro feature is fairly simple to use. And it's easy to record strings of commands and store lines of boilerplate text. Once you grasp the logic of the system, it's also easy to attach or detach macros to dedicated keystrokes, called hotkeys. And there are more of them available than before. There's a grand total of 82 possible hotkeys, instead of the 36 letters and numbers available through the Shorthand Menu. Even better is the fact there's essentially no limit to the number of macros you can write. You can fill the hard drive with them if you're so inclined. The ones you can't install on hotkeys you can simply play through the Macro Menu.

You can use the new macros to help you write faster and work more easily with WordStar. But it takes more time for the average person to understand them. To learn how to convert your Shorthand Menu macros to the new WordStar 7 macro format, read the section *Upgrading Shorthand Menu macros*, later in this chapter.

Macro hotkeys

WordStar uses the term *hotkey* to describe the keys you type to trigger a macro. In some cases, this is a single key. In others, it's two or three keys. You can assign a macro to hotkeys either when you first create it or when you edit it. You can detach the hotkeys at any time, inactivating the macro. There are 82 hotkeys available for you to use; they are:

- The function keys F2 through F9, plus F11 and F12 (F1 and F10 are reserved) for revision A—as of revision B, all function keys can be used
- Shift−F2 through Shift−F9
- Ctrl−F2 through Ctrl−F9
- Alt−F2 through Alt−F9
- Alt−A through Alt−Z and Alt−0 through Alt−9

You can assign and reassign all the above keys to macros whenever you want. There are several things to remember about macros and their hotkeys:

Changing the FEVISLUH keys

The pull-down menus are installed on hot key combinations of Alt plus the letters F, E, V, I, S, L, U, and H. If you install other macros on the FEVISLUH keys, you can't use them to call the pull-down menus. If you use the mouse exclusively to call the pull-down menus, then it really doesn't matter.

Which macros get hotkeys?

It isn't necessary to install a hotkey to every macro you write or record. You can always play the macro with the Ctrl−MP command. Save the hotkeys for macros you intend to use all the time.

Assigning hotkeys to macros

If you want to assign a hotkey to a macro that doesn't have one, use Ctrl−ME, the macro rename command. Don't use the macro record command Ctrl−MR unless you plan to erase the macro and write a new one.

Predefined macro hotkeys

WordStar 7 comes with macros already assigned to all the function keys, and to many other hotkeys as well. The choice of commands in these macros is intended mainly to show off both WordStar features and macro capability. You aren't obliged to leave these as they are if you have something more useful to install on them.

Macro files and directories

Each macro is stored in a separate file. It's assigned a filename when it's written, recorded, or renamed. All macros have the .WSM extension.

As mentioned previously, although macro files appear to be nondocuments when you edit them, you must only write or edit them with the macro editor.

On most computers, all the macro files are stored in the default \ WS \ MACROS directory. You can change this with WSCHANGE. At the WSCHANGE Main Menu, type CD2G.

Running a macro when you boot WordStar

You can run any of your macros at the same time you're booting up WordStar. This requires using the /M key in the following way:

    WS /Mmacro name

This option is for the control freaks among us, who like to do a dozen things at once every time they run WordStar.

You can, for example, create a macro named LETTER, which changes to a specific directory, opens a new text file, and copies in a boilerplate file containing a letterhead, a date, and formatting instructions—all in the blink of an eye. Then all you have to do is type WS /Mletter and press the Enter key.

Personally, I don't think most people really need or want this much automation. And this is really making a macro do something you can do more easily with boilerplate files.

The Macro Menu options

This section describes and discusses the options on the Macro Menu, shown in Fig. 17-1. These options let you create, edit, and use WordStar macros. There are seven options for calling dialog boxes on the Macro Menu, and nine simple macros you can use to insert special data into your documents.

The seven Macro dialog boxes

The seven Macro Menu dialog boxes are listed and described in the following paragraphs. You can use them to select, play, create, edit, and generally manage your macro archive. WordStar 7 comes with about 48 macros already written. Use them as is, edit them, or custom write your own.

Play a Macro   To *play* a macro means to select and run it so it executes its

```
 ───────────────────────── MACRO MENU ─────────────────────────

   MACRO FUNCTIONS                             INSERT
  P play          E rename         a today's date          * current filename
  R record        O copy           ! current time          : current drive
  D edit/create   Y delete         = last math result      . current directory
  S single step                    # last math expression  \ current path
                                   $ last math as dollar
```

17-1   Macro Menu.

defined functions. The simplest way to play a macro is to press its hotkey. But there are only 82 valid hotkeys and you can write an unlimited number of macros. Use Ctrl−MP to select and run any macro not assigned to a hotkey.

Record a Macro   To *record* a macro means to create it by executing commands or typing boilerplate text, and then copying it all into a macro file. It works exactly like you think it should. You don't have to know anything about the BASIC-like macro language. Just turn on the recorder with Ctrl−MR, give the new macro a name, and assign a hotkey. Type the WordStar commands, and use Alt−equal sign to end recording.

Create/Edit a Macro   At this dialog box, you can either write a new macro from scratch or edit an existing one. This requires learning, understanding, and using a complex BASIC-like macro language. The macro is opened in a second window, and it's written in this language. Ctrl−MD opens the macro file. Ctrl−KD closes and compiles the macro file.

Copy a Macro   This dialog box lets you select and copy an existing macro to a new name and file. Once copied, you can edit and customize the macro through the Edit/Create a Macro dialog box. So your existing macros can serve as templates for new ones.

Delete a Macro   This dialog box allows you to select and delete an existing macro. This will remove its macro file from the \ WS \ MACROS subdirectory.

Rename a Macro   This dialog box allows you to select an existing macro and give it a new name.

Nine simple macros

There are nine simple macros on the Macro Menu that you can use to insert special data into your documents. WordStar draws this data from either the computer system or buffer memory. They are as follows:

Ctrl−M@   This macro inserts today's date at the cursor. It draws the date from the system clock.

Ctrl−M!   This one inserts the current time at the cursor. It draws the time from the system clock.

Ctrl—M=   This inserts the last result of a calculation on WordStar's calculator. It draws the information from buffer memory.

Ctrl—M#   This inserts the last equation used in the calculator.

Ctrl—M$ This inserts the last result of a calculation on WordStar's Calculator. The number is formatted as a dollar amount.

Ctrl—M*   This inserts the name of the file open in the current document window.

Ctrl—M: This inserts the name of the current drive.

Ctrl—M.   This inserts the name of the current directory.

**Ctrl—M **   This inserts the name of the current drive, directory path, and file.

I don't know why the programmers bothered creating most of these. Only the first two of these macros—date and time—are useful on a day-to-day basis. The second three are helpful if you take the time to learn how to use the so-called calculator. The final four are useful mainly to programmers. But remember the symbols attached to them; you can use them in headers, footers, and other merge printing situations.

Playing or running a macro

Playing a macro means the same thing as playing a record album or cassette. The same way you can play music whenever you want to, you can play a macro whenever you need it.

The command Ctrl—MP is used primarily to play a macro not assigned to a hotkey. The command calls the Play Macro dialog box. Below the dialog box are the available macros, listed alphabetically.

Tip: You can also call this dialog box with Alt—UMP, or through the Opening Menu by typing UMP.

You can play a macro through the Opening Menu, or from any document or nondocument screen. The following steps assume that you have a text file open, and need to play a macro for this text file.

1. Place the cursor at the point in the text file where the macro's commands are to take effect.
2. Use Ctrl—MP to call the Play Macro dialog box. Use Ctrl—Z and Ctrl—W to scroll the list up and down.
3. Use the arrow keys to put the highlight on the macro you need to play. Then press the Tab key to select it, and use Ctrl—K to tell WordStar to run the macro. If you have a mouse, just click on the macro name and then click on the OK push button.
4. WordStar will return to the file you have open, and will execute all the macros commands.

Macros that don't need hotkeys

Macros that don't need hotkeys are those that you use only occasionally, or only once per document. The macros that you *do* install on hotkeys should be the ones you need to use over and over again—in every kind of document you write.

WordStar comes with two macros, TODO and MEMO, which are prime examples of macros that don't need hotkeys. TODO creates a list of things to do, which is similar to what you find in a DayTimer-type organizer book. MEMO creates a standard, blank memorandum, with a fancy font headline and all the subheadings in place. The factory documentation further recommends writing a macro named LETTER, which opens a new document text file, and copies in a boilerplate file containing a letterhead and formatting instructions.

It's all too easy to press the wrong keys when using a macro. It can happen any time. Faster computers, like 386s and 486s, will execute macros so fast that you'll seldom have time to stop them before they finish running. If you have a macro like TODO, MEMO, or LETTER installed on a hotkey and run it accidentally, it will insert a page of gibberish into the middle of whatever you happen to be writing. Then you have to delete all this junk before you can get back to work. If you're unfortunate enough to have Insert turned off, a macro like this will write over and erase an entire page of text.

Recording a macro

Fortunately, recording a macro is as easy as it sounds. Unfortunately, for the new WordStar user, you must have a fairly detailed understanding of how to use WordStar and execute its commands. There's no way to get around this.

The command Ctrl−MR calls the Record Macro dialog box. There you type in the name of the new macro, assign it a hotkey, and turn on the macro recorder. This will return you to the document or nondocument screen. Until you turn off the macro recorder, WordStar will "remember" every command you execute and every character you type. When you end the recording, WordStar will save all the information you've entered into the macro recorder to a macro file.

You can record a macro through the Opening Menu, or from any document or nondocument screen.

1. Place the cursor at any point in a text file. A blank line is the best place for a simple macro. The top of a blank page is best for a lengthy, complex macro.
2. Use Ctrl−MR to call the Record Macro dialog box (see Fig. 17-2). The existing macros are listed below the dialog box. Use the Tab key to move forward through the fields, or Shift−Tab to move backward.
3. With the cursor blinking on the Macro Name field, type in the new macro's name (1−8 characters). When finished, press the Tab key.

================= **Record Macro** =================

Macro Name: ________↓   Hot Key: __________↓   ▤ **OK** ▤

                                                             ▨ Cancel ▨

Description: ____

              To stop recording, **press Alt+=**

____

                                                          ▲▼ ↑↓
```
Macro:      Hot Keys:
BK_BEGIN  Shift+F9      BK_COPY   Shift+F8     BK_DEL    Shift+F5
BK_END    Shift+F10     BK_HIDE   Shift+F6     BK_MOVE   Shift+F7
BOLD      F4            CENTER    Shift+F2     DEL_LINE  F5
DEL_WORD  F6            DISPLAY   Shift+F1     DRW_B_L   Alt+F5
DRW_B_R   Alt+F6        DRW_HORZ  Alt+F2       DRW_H_DN  Alt+F7
DRW_H_UP  Alt+F8        DRW_T_L   Alt+F3       DRW_T_R   Alt+F4
DRW_VERT  Alt+F1        DRW_V_L   Alt+F10      DRW_V_R   Alt+F9
FIND      Ctrl+F1       FIND_NXT  Ctrl+F3      FIND_RPL  Ctrl+F2
GOTO_LNL  Ctrl+F9       GOTO_LNR  Ctrl+F10     GOTO_PG   Ctrl+F4
MARGIN_L  Ctrl+F5       MARGIN_P               MARGIN_R  Ctrl+F6
MUDDBONE  Ctrl+F7       PG_BREAK  Ctrl+F8      PREVIEW   Alt+1
REFORMAT  F7            RULER     F8           SAVE      F9
SPL_ALL   Shift+F3      SPL_WORD  Shift+F4     STYLE     Alt+0
UNDERLIN  F3            UNDO      F2
```

17-2 Record Macro dialog box.

4. If a macro by this name already exists, WordStar will tell you so and ask if you want to rerecord it. Answer OK to write over the existing macro, or Cancel to type in a different name.

5. If no macro by this name exists, or you choose to write over an existing macro, the cursor will jump to the Hotkey field and the onscreen list will display the valid hotkeys.

6. You don't have to assign a hotkey to the macro. You can bypass this field by pressing the Tab key. The cursor will jump to the Description field.

7. If you want to assign a hotkey to the macro, use the arrow keys or the mouse to select it from the onscreen list. Or just type it in exactly as it appears on the list. When ready, press the Tab key.

8. The cursor will jump to the Description field. Here you can type in a 48-character description of what the macro is and does. You don't have to assign a description to any macro. When ready, use Ctrl−K to start the recording.

9. WordStar will return to the text file you have open, but the macro recorder is now turned on. Anything you type, any command you execute, any cursor movement at all, will be remembered and recorded. Type the macro exactly the way you want it to execute. You can include any combination of WordStar commands, any layout and design instructions, any word, sentence, or paragraph you want to store and replay. Just use the commands as you would normally.

10. When you're finished typing all the text and executing all the commands, use Alt—equal sign to tell the macro recorder you've finished. WordStar will now compile the macro and save it to a macro file in the MACRO subdirectory.

Once the macro is recorded and saved, you can repeat your commands or insert your boilerplate text by playing the macro.

Naming a macro

A macro name can be from 1 to 8 letters or numbers long, in any combination. You can also use any character not set aside as illegal by WordStar or MS-DOS. The macro recorder won't accept any illegal character in a macro's name. You can't give it an extension; WordStar gives all macros the .WSM extension automatically.

What not to record as a macro

You can record any command executed through the keyboard and any boilerplate word, sentence, or paragraph—plus any combination of commands and boilerplate—as a macro. The macro recorder remembers and stores every keystroke you make and every character you type—even your mistakes and corrections. You can always edit out the latter, but that isn't the point. The point is that there's virtually no limit to what you can record as a macro. The only limit is your imagination.

There is a point of diminishing returns, however. TODO and MEMO are prime examples of macros that are more complicated to write and edit than the benefit provided. They represent word processing functions that are more easily and quickly accomplished with the cut-and-paste commands Ctrl—KW, Ctrl—KY, and Ctrl—KR. When you need a blank memo form, to-do list, or letterhead, you don't need a macro. You only need to keep each in a boilerplate file, and use Ctrl—KR to paste them into new documents whenever needed.

The new macros can be fun to play with, and it's easy to get carried away with their power. But they're often a complicated way to accomplish things that already have simple solutions.

Recording a macro through the Opening Menu

Macros recorded through the Opening Menu tend to be the sort like TODO or MEMO. In other words, they are the complicated kind intended to affect entire documents instead of merely individual paragraphs or sections of a document.

The more complicated a macro is the more you must plan ahead to ensure that the macro works exactly like you intend. You can, for example, record a macro that opens a business letter and copies in a boilerplate file (containing a letterhead with a graphic image and instructions for footnote page numbering, font to be used, selection of paragraph tags, and so on) that completely sets up the letter automatically.

Before you record the macro, you must first create the boilerplate file it's to use. Then you have to work out the best order for the various other commands. Make a list of the commands and check them off as you record them in the macro.

Assigning paragraph tags to hotkeys

You can assign individual paragraph tags to hotkeys by recording a macro that selects them through the Paragraph Style Menu. Tags assigned to hotkeys are the fastest way to format your documents. The steps for assigning a tag to a hotkey are as follows:

1. Place the cursor at the beginning of any paragraph to be given tag formatting.
2. Use Ctrl−MR to start recording the macro.
3. At the Record Macro dialog box, type in the name of the new macro.
4. Move to the Description line, and type in the function of the new macro.
5. Move to the Hotkey line, and select the hotkey you want the macro assigned to.
6. When ready, press the Enter key or click on the OK push button. WordStar will return to the document, ready to begin recording the new macro.
7. Hold down the Ctrl key and type OFS. This calls the Select Paragraph Style dialog box.
8. At the Select Paragraph Style dialog box, type in the name of the paragraph tag you're assigning to a hotkey. When ready, press the Enter key or click on the OK push button.
9. The paragraph tag will be attached to the text file at the cursor. You're finished recording the macro. Use Alt−equal sign to end recording, and save the macro.

Running and using the macro editor

You open and run the macro editor through the Macro Menu. First, select or name a macro through the Edit/Create Macro dialog box. When you open the macro in the macro editor screen, you can modify an existing macro or write a new macro from scratch.

The macro editor is what you get when you open a macro file through the Edit/Create Macro dialog box. You get a screen that looks identical to the document screen. If you open the macro file while working on a document or nondocument, the macro will be opened in a second window.

All of the document mode editing tools and features are available for working on a macro. You can write and edit the macro as though it were a text file, but it isn't a text file. You're limited to the specific terms, commands, and formats of the BASIC-like macro language.

You can save the macro with Ctrl—KS while working on it. You can close the macro file through the pull-down menu or with Ctrl—KQ. When you use Ctrl—KD, however, WordStar will run the macro compiler. On the surface, this appears to work identically to saving and closing. But the macro compiler adds the special programming codes necessary to make the macro function. It will look for errors in spelling, format, and usage, and won't close the file if any are found.

Calling and using the Edit/Create Macro dialog box

The command Ctrl—MD calls the Edit/Create Macro dialog box (see Fig. 17-3). Most people use this dialog box to select and edit an existing macro. You can write a new macro from scratch through this macro editor, but you must understand the macro format and know how to use the macro language.

```
                                Edit/Create Macro

     Macro Name: _______↓           Hot Key: _________↓              ▓▓ OK ▓▓

     Description: _________________________________________      ▓ Cancel ▓


  Macro:      Hot Keys:                                                    ▲▼ ↑↓
  BK_BEGIN  Shift+F9      BK_COPY   Shift+F8      BK_DEL    Shift+F5
  BK_END    Shift+F10     BK_HIDE   Shift+F6      BK_MOVE   Shift+F7
  BOLD      F4            CENTER    Shift+F2      DEL_LINE  F5
  DEL_WORD  F6            DISPLAY   Shift+F1      DRW_B_L   Alt+F5
  DRW_B_R   Alt+F6        DRW_HORZ  Alt+F2        DRW_H_DN  Alt+F7
  DRW_H_UP  Alt+F8        DRW_T_L   Alt+F3        DRW_T_R   Alt+F4
  DRW_VERT  Alt+F1        DRW_V_L   Alt+F10       DRW_V_R   Alt+F9
  FIND      Ctrl+F1       FIND_NXT  Ctrl+F3       FIND_RPL  Ctrl+F2
  GOTO_LNL  Ctrl+F9       GOTO_LNR  Ctrl+F10      GOTO_PG   Ctrl+F4
  MARGIN_L  Ctrl+F5       MARGIN_P                MARGIN_R  Ctrl+F6
  MUDDBONE  Ctrl+F7       PG_BREAK  Ctrl+F8       PREVIEW   Alt+1
  REFORMAT  F7            RULER     F8            SAVE      F9
  SPL_ALL   Shift+F3      SPL_WORD  Shift+F4      STYLE     Alt+0
  UNDERLIN  F3            UNDO      F2
```

17-3 Edit/Create Macro dialog box.

You can use the macro editor either from the Opening Menu or when in the document and nondocument modes. You cannot edit a macro if you also have a file open in a second window. You can escape from the dialog box at any time with Ctrl—U, by pressing the Esc key, or with a click on the Cancel push button.

1. Use Ctrl—MD to call the Edit/Create Macro dialog box. Below it will appear the list of available macros.

2. To edit an existing macro, select it from the onscreen list. Use Ctrl−Z and Ctrl−W to scroll the list up or down. Use the arrow keys to put the highlight on the macro's name, and press the Tab key (or click on the macro with the mouse). To create a new macro from scratch, simply type in its name and press the Tab key.

3. The cursor will jump to the Hotkey command box. The onscreen list will change to display the available hotkeys. If one is already assigned to the macro, it's displayed here. You can use the current hotkey, select an unused one from the onscreen list, or deselect the hotkey entirely. (A hotkey is currently used if a macro name appears beside it on the list.)

4. When ready, press the Tab key. If the hotkey is already assigned to another macro, WordStar will display an error message. You can then accept the hotkey or select another. Press Esc to cancel or the Enter key to accept it.

5. When you attach or detach the hotkey, the cursor will jump to the Description line. You can type in a description of the macro's function, or leave it as is. When ready, press the Tab key.

6. The cursor will jump to the OK push button. You can click on it with the mouse or use Ctrl−K to open the macro editor.

7. The macro editor will open the macro in a second window. Now you can edit, correct, or change it with any WordStar command. Delete mistakes and type in corrections—whatever's necessary. (To make additions, you need to understand the macro language.)

8. If writing a new macro, you can check it by running the macro debugger. Unless someone has changed it, this debugger is a macro installed on Alt−D; if not, it's named DEBUGMAC.

9. When you're finished editing or writing the macro, use Ctrl−KD to save it and exit from the macro editor. This automatically uses the macro compiler, which inserts the necessary codes. If you've used any illegal commands or procedures, the compiler will halt and tell you what they are. Correct them and try again. If you don't know how to correct them, use Ctrl−KQ to abandon the changes and close the macro file.

Deleting nonessential instructions

When you record a macro, WordStar also records information about many onscreen display settings. These become a part of the macro file, and are expressed as commands in the macro language. Seven of the most common are:

```
AutoRestore(ON)
SetHelpLevel(4)
Insert(ON)
CmdTags(ON)
```

        HideDots(OFF)
        ColMode(OFF)
        ColReplace(OFF)

The on and off values in these macro language commands are taken from the current settings at whatever time you happen to record the macro, but whenever the macro is played the commands automatically reset the onscreen display. The settings in them are purely arbitrary. These commands also visibly increase the time it takes for the macro to complete playing. If you find this annoying, you can edit the macro and delete the commands, which will make the macro execute at full speed.

For a full explanation of these macro language commands, and what they do, read *Using the macro language*, later in this chapter. To learn how to convert your shorthand menu macros to the new WordStar 7 macro format, read *Upgrading shorthand menu macros*, also in this chapter.

Checking a macro, step by step, for errors

Single Step is a method for checking a macro for errors. After you write or edit a macro, you can play it back, step by step, to identify any problems. This is most helpful when a macro works partially, but doesn't work exactly as you intended. Just run through the steps until the error occurs; then stop the playback and correct the error.

You can run the Single Step command from either the Opening Menu or from a document or nondocument screen. These instructions assume that you have a document open, and are correcting a macro to use in that document. Note: You can't edit a macro with a file open in a second window.

1. Use Ctrl−MS to call the Single Step dialog box, as shown in Fig. 17-4.
2. Below this dialog box is the list of available macros. Select the macro to play by using the arrow keys to highlight it.
3. Press the Tab key twice and press the Enter key.
4. WordStar will run the first step of the macro and pause.
5. Press the spacebar to continue to the next step, and each following step, until the macro has finished running. You can stop running the macro by pressing Esc or Ctrl−U.

Renaming a macro

The command Ctrl−ME is used to change the name of a macro. It calls the Rename Macro dialog box (see Fig. 17-5), which contains a list of the available macros. A macro name can be 1−8 letters or numbers, in any combination. You can also use any character not set aside as illegal by WordStar or MS-DOS. The macro recorder won't accept any illegal character in a macro's name.

━━━━━━━━━━━━━━━━━━━ **Single Step** ━━━━━━━━━━━━━━━━━━━

Macro Name: _______↓   Hot Key: _________↓   ▓▓▓ OK ▓▓▓

Description: ▓ Cancel ▓

Macro: Hot Keys: ▲▼ ↑↓
BK_BEGIN Shift+F9   BK_COPY Shift+F8   BK_DEL   Shift+F5
BK_END   Shift+F10   BK_HIDE Shift+F6   BK_MOVE Shift+F7
BOLD   F4   CENTER   Shift+F2   DEL_LINE F5
DEL_WORD F6   DISPLAY Shift+F1   DRW_B_L Alt+F5
DRW_B_R Alt+F6   DRW_HORZ Alt+F2   DRW_H_DN Alt+F7
DRW_H_UP Alt+F8   DRW_T_L Alt+F3   DRW_T_R Alt+F4
DRW_VERT Alt+F1   DRW_V_L Alt+F10   DRW_V_R Alt+F9
FIND   Ctrl+F1   FIND_NXT Ctrl+F3   FIND_RPL Ctrl+F2
GOTO_LNL Ctrl+F9   GOTO_LNR Ctrl+F10   GOTO_PG Ctrl+F4
MARGIN_L Ctrl+F5   MARGIN_P   MARGIN_R Ctrl+F6
MUDDBONE Ctrl+F7   PG_BREAK Ctrl+F8   PREVIEW Alt+1
REFORMAT F7   RULER   F8   SAVE   F9
SPL_ALL Shift+F3   SPL_WORD Shift+F4   STYLE   Alt+0
UNDERLIN F3   UNDO   F2

17-4 Single Step dialog box.

━━━━━━━━━━━━━━━━━━━ **Rename Macro** ━━━━━━━━━━━━━━━━━━━

┌─ Current ──┐
│   │   ▓▓▓ OK ▓▓▓
│   Macro Name: _______↓   Hot Key: _________↓   │
│   Description: │   ▓ Cancel ▓
└───┘

┌─ New ──┐
│   │
│   Macro Name: Hot Key: │
│   Description: ________________________________   │
└───┘

Macro: Hot Keys: ▲▼ ↑↓
BK_BEGIN Shift+F9   BK_COPY Shift+F8   BK_DEL   Shift+F5
BK_END   Shift+F10   BK_HIDE Shift+F6   BK_MOVE Shift+F7
BOLD   F4   CENTER   Shift+F2   DEL_LINE F5
DEL_WORD F6   DISPLAY Shift+F1   DRW_B_L Alt+F5
DRW_B_R Alt+F6   DRW_HORZ Alt+F2   DRW_H_DN Alt+F7
DRW_H_UP Alt+F8   DRW_T_L Alt+F3   DRW_T_R Alt+F4
DRW_VERT Alt+F1   DRW_V_L Alt+F10   DRW_V_R Alt+F9
FIND   Ctrl+F1   FIND_NXT Ctrl+F3   FIND_RPL Ctrl+F2
GOTO_LNL Ctrl+F9   GOTO_LNR Ctrl+F10   GOTO_PG Ctrl+F4

17-5 Rename Macro dialog box.

You can rename a macro through either the Opening Menu (type UMN), the write-and-edit screen (Ctrl−ME), or the pull-down Utilities Menu (Alt−UMN).

1. Use Ctrl−ME to call the Rename Macro dialog box. Below it is a list of available macros. Use Ctrl−Z and Ctrl−W to scroll the list up and

down. Use Tab to move forward to the fields, and Shift−Tab to move backward.

2. With the cursor on Current Macro Name, select the macro to rename from the onscreen list. Use the arrow keys to put the highlight on the macro, and then press the Enter key.

3. The cursor will jump to Current Hotkey. You can't change the hotkeys here. When ready, press the Tab key.

4. The cursor will jump to New Macro Name. Type in the macro's new name and press the Tab key. (You can leave the name unchanged, and select a new hotkey.)

5. The cursor will jump to New Hotkey. Select a hotkey from the list or leave this field unchanged.

6. Check the dialog box for errors. Correct any you find, and use Ctrl−K to tell WordStar to complete the name change.

Copying a macro

Ctrl−MO is used to make a copy of an existing macro to a different name. Then you can open and edit the copy, and create a new macro from it. Or you can simply copy macros to backup disks or drives. This works very similarly to the block-and-save command Ctrl−KO.

The Ctrl−MO command is convenient because WordStar won't display the macro filenames if you change to the \ WS \ MACROS subdirectory normally. WordStar considers them to be program files and so keeps them hidden.

1. Use Ctrl−MO to call the Copy Macro dialog box (see Fig. 17-6). Below it is the list of available macros. Use Ctrl−Z and Ctrl−W to scroll the list up and down. Use Tab to move forward to the fields, and Shift−Tab to move backward.

2. At the Macro Name field, type in the name of the macro you're copying, or use the arrow keys to highlight it and then press the Tab key.

3. The cursor will jump to the Hotkey field. Either leave this unchanged or select a hotkey from the onscreen list. When ready, press the Tab key.

4. The cursor will jump to the Name of Copy field. The macro name selected is also displayed here. You can type in a new name or preface the filename with a different drive or directory.

5. Check the dialog box for errors and correct any you find. When ready, use Ctrl−K to tell WordStar to complete the copy routine.

Deleting a macro

Ctrl−MY is used to delete macros when you no longer want or need them. This works similarly to the block-and-save command Ctrl−KJ, except that it can delete only a macro file, and it automatically accesses the \ WS \ MACROS directory.

```
████████████████████████  Copy Macro  ████████████████████████

   Macro Name: _______↓        Hot Key: _________↓          ▦ OK ▦

   Description:                                        ▦ Cancel ▦

   Name of Copy: _______________________________________________

   Macro:     Hot Keys:                                      ▲▼ ↑↓
   BK_BEGIN Shift+F9      BK_COPY   Shift+F8    BK_DEL    Shift+F5
   BK_END   Shift+F10     BK_HIDE   Shift+F6    BK_MOVE   Shift+F7
   BOLD     F4            CENTER    Shift+F2    DEL_LINE  F5
   DEL_WORD F6            DISPLAY   Shift+F1    DRW_B_L   Alt+F5
   DRW_B_R  Alt+F6        DRW_HORZ  Alt+F2      DRW_H_DN  Alt+F7
   DRW_H_UP Alt+F8        DRW_T_L   Alt+F3      DRW_T_R   Alt+F4
   DRW_VERT Alt+F1        DRW_V_L   Alt+F10     DRW_V_R   Alt+F9
   FIND     Ctrl+F1       FIND_NXT  Ctrl+F3     FIND_RPL  Ctrl+F2
   GOTO_LNL Ctrl+F9       GOTO_LNR  Ctrl+F10    GOTO_PG   Ctrl+F4
   MARGIN_L Ctrl+F5       MARGIN_P              MARGIN_R  Ctrl+F6
   MUDDBONE Ctrl+F7       PG_BREAK  Ctrl+F8     PREVIEW   Alt+1
   REFORMAT F7            RULER     F8          SAVE      F9
   SPL_ALL  Shift+F3      SPL_WORD  Shift+F4    STYLE     Alt+0
   UNDERLIN F3            UNDO      F2
```

17-6 Copy Macro dialog box.

Before you delete a macro, you might want to make a copy of it to a backup disk. Just because you don't want it now doesn't mean you won't ever need it again.

1. Use Ctrl−KJ to call the Delete Macro dialog box (see Fig. 17-7). Below it is the list of available macros. Use Ctrl−Z and Ctrl−W to scroll the list up and down. Use Tab to move forward to the fields, and Shift−Tab to move backward.
2. The cursor is on the Macro Name field. Use the arrow keys to put the highlight on the macro you're deleting. When ready, press the Tab key.
3. The cursor will jump to the Hotkey field. It won't do any good to change the hotkey at this time. Just press the Tab key.
4. The cursor will jump to the OK push button. If you're sure you want to delete the macro, press the Enter key.
5. WordStar will delete the macro from the \ WS \ MACROS directory.

Upgrading Shorthand Menu macros

This section tells you how to upgrade your Shorthand Menu macros to WordStar 7 by converting them to the new macro format. These instructions assume that you already know how to use the new macros, and that you at least understand how to rename them and assign them to hotkeys. The utility program WS6MACRO.EXE is a compiler that will convert your old macros to the new format.

```
████████████████████████████████  Delete Macro  ████████████████████████████████

    Macro Name:                    Hot Key:                      ██ OK ██

    Description:                                                 ▓ Cancel ▓
________________________________________________________________________________

    Macro:     Hot Keys:                                                  ▲▼  ↑↓
    BK_BEGIN Shift+F9      BK_COPY  Shift+F8      BK_DEL   Shift+F5
    BK_END   Shift+F10     BK_HIDE  Shift+F6      BK_MOVE  Shift+F7
    BOLD     F4            CENTER   Shift+F2      DEL_LINE F5
    DEL_WORD F6            DISPLAY  Shift+F1      DRW_B_L  Alt+F5
    DRW_B_R  Alt+F6        DRW_HORZ Alt+F2        DRW_H_DN Alt+F7
    DRW_H_UP Alt+F8        DRW_T_L  Alt+F3        DRW_T_R  Alt+F4
    DRW_VERT Alt+F1        DRW_V_L  Alt+F10       DRW_V_R  Alt+F9
    FIND     Ctrl+F1       FIND_NXT Ctrl+F3       FIND_RPL Ctrl+F2
    GOTO_LNL Ctrl+F9       GOTO_LNR Ctrl+F10      GOTO_PG  Ctrl+F4
    MARGIN_L Ctrl+F5       MARGIN_P               MARGIN_R Ctrl+F6
    MUDDBONE Ctrl+F7       PG_BREAK Ctrl+F8       PREVIEW  Alt+1
    REFORMAT F7            RULER    F8            SAVE     F9
    SPL_ALL  Shift+F3      SPL_WORD Shift+F4      STYLE    Alt+0
    UNDERLIN F3            UNDO     F2
```

17-7 Delete Macro dialog box.

This shorthand macro compiler is simple to use—yet not as simple as most users would probably want. Almost nothing is automatic. You need to know how to copy a file from one directory to another, how to change directories, and how to run a program through the Ctrl—KF DOS window. (Or you can exit WordStar and do it all with DOS commands.) After the old macros are converted, you need to know how to rename them, and how to assign them to hotkeys.

The shorthand macros are stored in a WordStar overlay file. The file is named WSSHORT.OVR and is kept in the WordStar program directory. Hopefully, you kept a backup copy of this overlay file before you installed WordStar 7 on your hard drive— because that's the only way you can transfer your macros over to WordStar 7.

Steps for converting shorthand macros

During the conversion, WordStar will check for any Escape characters in the old macros. If any are found, the conversion will pause and display the following warning message:

> Warning—The original shorthand macro contains an Esc character. If Esc was used to call another macro, "Esc" and the called macro name need to be changed in the new macro. Edit the converted macro and specify the new command to replace "Esc" and the new name for the called macro.

Make a note of any macro names resulting in the above error message. You must edit them after conversion before you can use them.

1. Copy the WSSHORT.OVR file to the WordStar 7 macro subdirectory. If you've done a basic installation of WordStar 7, the path to it is C: \ WS \ MACROS.
2. Change to the WordStar 7 macro subdirectory.
3. At the C: \ WS \ MACROS prompt, type WS6MACRO and press the Enter key. (You can also run this through the WordStar DOS window opened with Ctrl−KF.)
4. The WS6MACRO compiler will read the old macro overlay file, and create a separate macro file for each shorthand macro in it. There is a maximum of 36 old macros per WSSHORT.OVR file.
5. The new macros will be stored in the MACROS subdirectory. They all begin with ESC- and are followed by the letter or number key they were installed on in the older version of WordStar, for example, ESC-1.WSM, ESC-2.WSM, ESC-1.WSM, and so on.
6. Use Ctrl−MD to call the Edit/Create Macro dialog box. Select these ESC macros one by one, and edit them as necessary. Rename them, if you want, and assign them to hotkeys so you can use them quickly.

Multiple sets of shorthand macros

Though it wasn't documented by WordStar International, releases 4−6 could have multiple sets of shorthand macros. Many people caught onto this either accidently or by word of mouth. There were two ways to do it; you could either keep different versions stored under different names, or keep a WSSHORT.OVR file in each document directory and boot WordStar from the directory you wanted to work on.

If you used either method, you probably have as many sets of shorthand macros as you have different types of documents. You can convert all of these sets with the WS6MACRO compiler, but WordStar uses the same set of names for each conversion. You must do one set at a time, and rename the resulting macros before going on to the next set. Otherwise, the next set will overwrite the previous.

18
CHAPTER

Writing macros
from scratch

This chapter discusses the macro language, and tells you how to use it with the macro editor to write complicated macros from scratch. This isn't a chapter for first-time users, nor even for users who want to use WordStar macros only occasionally.

The new macros and the macro language

This section describes WordStar's macro language and tells you how to use each of its individual elements.

The macro language logic

When you write a macro, you're essentially writing a small computer program. These macro programs can be run only through WordStar, as they use WordStar commands and features. They're designed to speed up word processing chores. Each macro program can execute a simple function or complete a series of complicated tasks. So macros can be as powerful as any small, independently running program.

The structure of a WordStar macro is very similar to a program written in BASIC. It requires you to write subroutines, each with a series of command statements and arguments. Each subroutine performs a specific word processing task. You can string together as many subroutines as are necessary to get the job done.

An overview of a macro file

Most WordStar macros contain one or more subroutines, in addition to the mandatory main subroutine. A *subroutine* is a series of command statements to execute a specific task. Each command statement contains a specific command or function. It can have a label to identify it. When required, it also contains arguments or variables, and a modifying clause, or conditional.

Macro commands generally control the macro's flow of execution by indicating which command statement to execute next. Some basic commands are Call, GoTo, Return, Stop, and PlayMacro. *Macro functions* perform specific tasks. Some are Key, SetHelpLevel, Insert, and PauseForInput. The Key function is the most important of all because it tells WordStar what characters to insert and what command keystrokes to execute.

To get an idea of how the macro structure and the elements of the macro language fit together, you can open and view the macros that come with WordStar—especially TODO and MEMO. Unless you're familiar with BASIC programming, however, expect to spend time studying and practicing before this system makes sense.

Understanding the macro structure

The following is a simple macro:

```
Sub Main
    Key("press the {F4}Enter{F4} key.")
End Sub
```

This macro inserts the phrase "press the Enter key." Every time you see those words in this book, they were inserted with this macro. You can speed up much of your writing with boilerplate macros like these. Here's another simple macro:

```
Sub Main
    Key("{CTRL-A}{CTRL-T}")
End Sub
```

This one deletes a word backward by jumping the cursor to the beginning of the previous word with Ctrl-A and then deleting the word with Ctrl-T. It's a very simple macro . . . yet a very powerful tool.

The first line, Sub Main, tells you that the subroutine MAIN begins here. The last line, End Sub, ends the subroutine. The lines in between identify keystroke sequences replicated by the macro. Key is a command. Everything between the parentheses that follow this command is a statement. The specific terms of the statement and their order define the argument.

These are the basic elements of a WordStar macro. You can write complex macros by including multiple statements and multiple subroutines. So learning to write and edit complex macros means learning the macro building blocks and how to use them.

Writing complex macros

Writing complicated macros is a lot like writing paragraphs. The building blocks of a paragraph are its sentences. A sentence is just a group of words used to express a complete thought. If you write a group of sentences to express a more complicated idea, this group is called a paragraph.

In a macro, the paragraphs are called subroutines. The sentences in a macro are called statements and the statements contain special words to make up an *argument*—which is a value or group of values to define a function or task. These are also called *variables* and *parameters*.

When writing a subroutine, you're putting together a group of statements to express or execute a specific task—"do this, do this, and do this." And then you get this result. The next subroutine executes a different task and gets a different result, and all the subroutines together complete a complex task.

You don't want to try and make one subroutine do too many things at once. As an essay has many paragraphs, a complicated macro should contain subroutines that divide up the tasks.

A sample macro

WordStar comes with LIST_BUL, a macro for making an ordered or bulleted list. The macro, followed by an explanation of its elements and what they do, follows:

```
REM   This macro is for creating bulleted lists.
Sub Main
        AutoRestore(ON)
        SetHelpLevel(4)
        Insert(ON)
        CmdTags(OFF)
        HideDots(ON)
        ColMode(OFF)
        ColReplace(OFF)
        Key ("{Ctrl-O}FSHanging indent 1{Enter}")
          CALL Input
End Sub
Sub Input
INPUT_LOOP:
        Key ("  ■{Tab}")
        PauseForInput("{ENTER}",'Type the line and press ENTER.')
         IfException
```

```
        NCM: Goto INPUT_DONE 'User typed nothing
            End IfException
                KEY("{Enter}")
            GoTo INPUT_LOOP
    INPUT_DONE:
        Key ("{Ctrl-Q}{Del}")
        Key ("{Ctrl-O}FP")
        Stop
    End Sub
```

The LIST_BUL macro has two subroutines: MAIN, which contains the instructions for making the bullet list, and Times12, which selects the font used by the list. The process is automatic. The macro creates list items, one by one, as you type. When you press Enter, it inserts another bullet and waits for you to type. The macro ends when you press Enter on a line without typing anything.

The macro has comments to remind you what it's doing. The first is the REM line at the beginning of the macro. The second is the phrase *User typed nothing* to describe the situation in which the line takes effect. The third is *Type the line and press ENTER*. These comments display on the status line.

Command statements using the macro commands AutoRestore, Insert, Cmd-Tags, SetHelpLevel, and HideDots are located at the beginning of the MAIN subroutine. The specific settings each command is to use are contained in the parentheses after each command.

The first function, Key, calls the Paragraph Style Menu, and selects the paragraph tag Hanging Indent 1 from the onscreen list. The Call command runs the Times12 subroutine, which calls the Font dialog box and selects the Times 12-point proportional font from the onscreen list. (If you don't have this font, you'll have to edit the macro so it selects a font your printer can use.)

After the font is changed, the Return command takes you back to the MAIN subroutine, and the next function is executed. If you want to make a simpler macro, you could include the font change instructions within the MAIN subroutine, and eliminate the second subroutine.

INPUT_LOOP is a label. A *label* marks or identifies a specific place in a macro, so you can go directly to it and execute subsequent commands. In this case, the label lets you return to the same place repeatedly, creating a *loop*. The Key statement tells WordStar to type two blank spaces, insert the bullet character, and issue a Tab.

PauseForInput tells WordStar to pause the macro while you type in the word or sentence for the list item. In this case, WordStar displays the message *Type the line and press ENTER* on the status line.

In this macro, the Enter key is the input termination character. When you type the line and press the Enter key, the IfException command is ignored and the next

Key statement issues a carriage return. Then the GoTo command moves back to the INPUT_LOOP label and repeats the bullet character and the Tab.

IfException is a conditional command, and begins a conditional clause. EndIfException marks the ending of the clause. Between them are the instructions telling WordStar what to do if you don't give it the expected response, i.e., type in a line of text. The condition here is NCM (for no cursor movement). It tells Word-Star to end the macro if you don't type in anything before pressing the Enter key. When the condition is met, it tells WordStar to go to the INPUT_DONE label.

This conditional statement is your escape clause. If the macro didn't have this clause written into it, you'd have to cancel the macro with Ctrl−U or by pressing the Esc key. Otherwise, you'd just keep on typing a bullet list forever.

The INPUT_DONE label is followed by two Key command statements. The first, Ctrl−Q Del, deletes everything on the line to the left of the cursor (removing the last bullet inserted). The second, Ctrl−O FP reverts to the paragraph tag being used before you started the bullet list. The macro is ended, and you can continue writing the document.

All the indentation and blank lines in the macro are optional. They serve mainly to give you visual separation between the elements. If you record a macro and then open it with Ctrl−MD, you'll see that the recorder doesn't bother inserting them.

Tip: This macro uses Ctrl commands to get the job done. You can also use Alt commands, which call the pull-down menu functions.

Understanding and writing subroutines

This section explains what a subroutine is and tells you how to write one.

The subroutine format

Every subroutine uses the same format: a command beginning it, the functions or tasks it executes, and a command ending it. The format is as follows:

```
Sub name
    command statements (arguments)
    command statements (arguments)
    command statements (arguments)
End Sub
```

Each macro must have a MAIN subroutine, and it must always appear and be executed first. You can have as many additional subroutines in a macro as you need to get the job done. You can repeat the same command statements in other subroutines. You can repeat subroutines to perform a task again. Or you can call a subroutine to use it whenever needed.

Command statements must be contained within a subroutine, i.e., between the Begin and End commands. Subroutines function as distinct groups of commands. A subroutine can call another subroutine, but you can't have a subroutine within a subroutine. Only the MAIN subroutine executes automatically. You must call any other subroutine to execute it.

Use the Call command at the location you want to run a specific subroutine.

Beginning and ending a subroutine

The first line of a subroutine identifies and begins it. The format is:

Sub *name*

A subroutine name must begin with a letter. It can contain up to 31 alphanumerical characters, and you must use the underline character in place of blank spaces. The last line of a subroutine is always the same. It tells WordStar that the subroutine is ending. This line is:

End Sub

All macro functions, statements, arguments, commands, etc. must go between the Sub *name* and End Sub lines.

Indicating key functions

The Key function is the most important element of a macro. It tells WordStar what keystrokes the macro is to execute. It uses the following format:

Key("*keystrokes {special keys}*")

The whole line is called a statement. The first word is the function and the part between parentheses is the argument. The keystrokes within the argument must be enclosed with quotation marks. Special keys, like Enter and Tab, must be enclosed between braces, for example, the following:

Key("press the {F4}Enter{F4} key")

would insert the text *press the Enter key*. The special key {F4} executes the macro installed on the F4 key. In this case, it's the boldface command Ctrl−PB. Braces are also used with special key combinations, as in {Alt+F1} and {Ctrl−P}.

It doesn't matter whether you type in uppercase, mixed case, or lowercase letters. The macro editor doesn't recognize case. The caret symbol (^) can be substituted for the Ctrl key. Braces are not required when using this symbol. For example {Ctrl−U} executes the same function as ^U. The macro editor uses the braces. Whichever you use, just be consistent.

You can insert print controls characters in a macro by executing Ctrl−P and typing the control character. For example, Ctrl−PB will insert a ^B at the cursor.

For keystroke combinations in braces, use a plus sign, a blank space, or a hyphen to separate the keystrokes. For example: {Ctrl+B}, {Ctrl B}, and {Ctrl-B} are equal. You can insert extended characters with either Ctrl−P0 or by holding down the Alt key and typing the character's decimal number on the numeric keypad.

To insert an actual quotation mark, braces, or caret in the macro, just double the character. For example: type ″″, {{, }}, or ^ ^ on the Key function line. For calling dialog boxes and marking checkboxes, you can use the plus and minus signs in a key function line. For example: the Key function line:

```
Key("{Ctrl-O}S{Tab}{Tab}{Tab}+{Ctrl-K}")
```

tells WordStar to call the Alignment and Spacing dialog box and turn hyphenation on. Substituting a minus sign would turn it off.

Using other command functions

There are 10 other command functions you can use in a macro. The tasks they perform are logical and easy to remember—as each is identified by its name. The first two pause the macro to let you type text or answer a question. The remainder set editing conditions used while the macro executes.

Pausing the macro while you type something

When WordStar receives the PauseForInput command, it pauses the macro execution so you can type in words, phrases, or sentences. The format for this is:

```
PauseForInput("input termination key",'message text')
```

The PauseForInput command must be typed inside a subroutine. The input termination key must go between parentheses; it's the key you'll use to tell the macro to resume execution. This is commonly the Enter or Esc key, but it can be any keystroke combination you prefer. It must be enclosed in quotation marks. This key is optional if no message is included, but it does help you customize the macro. If you don't specify a keystroke, the default Alt−hyphen is used.

The message text is the prompt you want displayed on the status line while the macro is paused. It must be enclosed between apostrophes. The message is optional, but also helps customize the macro. If you don't type in a custom message, WordStar will use the default message *Paused. Press {Alt -} to continue*. If you do type a message, the input termination key argument is required. If you use a termination key other than the default, remember to mention it in the message.

Tip: When you record a macro, WordStar uses the default Alt−hyphen as the termination key. You can always edit the macro later and change this.

Pausing to answer a question

The PauseForKey command is used to pause macro execution in order to type a single keystroke. This keystroke is usually Y or N (for yes or no) in answer to a question, but it can be any keystroke. As soon as this key is typed, the macro execution will resume. The basic format for this function is:

PauseForKey(*"macro continuation key"*,*'message text'*)

The PauseForKey command must be typed inside a subroutine. The macro continuation key must go between parentheses; it's the key to tell the macro to select between options and then resume execution. This can be any keystroke you prefer. It must be enclosed in quotation marks. It's optional if no message is included, but it does help you customize the macro. If you don't specify a keystroke, the default Alt−hyphen is used.

The message text is the prompt you want displayed on the status line while the macro is paused; it must be enclosed between apostrophes. The message is optional, but helps you customize the macro. If you don't type in a custom message, WordStar will use the default message *Paused. Press {Alt -} to continue*. If you do type a message, the input termination key argument is required. If you use a termination key other than the default, remember to mention it in the message.

The editing condition functions

The following eight functions set editing conditions for playing back the macro. These affect how the commands in the macro work. It's best to include the functions unless you're sure the editing conditions won't affect macro execution.

For example, if a macro is written assuming that Insert is turned on, and it's actually run while Overtype is active, any text the macro should insert will overwrite anything in its path. If a macro is written at help level 4, but played back at help level 3 or 2, the pull-down menus won't be available. So some of the commands in the macro might not execute as planned.

When you record a macro, WordStar automatically includes all the functions—with their current settings—in the macro file. Let's assume you're in the document mode with pull-down menus available and all the edit settings normal. If you recorded a macro to insert the sentence *Over the rooftops . . . Ireland forever!*, then WordStar would create a macro file containing the following:

```
Sub Main
    AutoRestore(ON)
    SetHelpLevel(4)
    Insert(ON)
    CmdTags(ON)
    HideDots(OFF)
    ColMode(OFF)
    ColReplace(OFF)
    Key("Over the rooftops . . . Ireland forever!")
End Sub
```

The settings are enclosed between the parentheses. To change these with the editor, delete the current setting and type in the new.

SetHelpLevel(1-4)   Type a number between the parentheses from 1 to 4. This sets the help level for use during macro execution. If you never change the help level, this is superfluous—and you can delete it to make the macro run faster. If someone else is going to use your macros, then leave it in.

Insert(on or off)   Type either on or off between the parentheses. You might want to always leave this on. If you run a macro that inserts boilerplate text and Insert is off, then the inserted text will write over anything in its way.

CmdTags(on or off)   Type either on or off between the parentheses. This sets the Command Tags Display status while the macro is running. This can be annoying either way you set it, and you may wish to delete it.

HideDots(on or off)   Type either on or off between the parentheses. This sets the soft space dots display status while the macro is running. This can be annoying either way you set it, and you might want to delete it.

ColMode(on or off)   Type either on or off between the parentheses. This sets the column block mode on or off while the macro is running. Leave this in only if the macro's function marks, moves, copies, or deletes a block of text, and if you need to control the column block mode.

ColReplace(on or off)   Type either on or off between the parentheses. This sets the column replace mode on or off while the macro is running. Leave this on only if the macro's function marks, moves, copies, or deletes a block of text, and if you need to control the column replace mode.

AutoRestore(on or off)   Type either on or off between the parentheses. This sets the functional status of AutoRestore. If any of the above functions change the editing conditions, having AutoRestore on will set the affected changes back to whatever they were before the macro ran.

SingleStep(on or off)   Type either on or off between the parentheses. This sets the functional status of the single step option on the Macro Menu. By using SingleStep(OFF) above a subroutine, and SingleStep(ON) below it, you can run single step through only selected portions of a macro file. This is useful when writing a large, complex macro and need to test run sections of it.

WSQuiet(on or off)   This is a menu suppression command or function. It keeps the classic and pull-down menus from appearing onscreen while the macro is running, but doesn't suppress dialog boxes. Turn it on at the beginning of a routine with commands that call a menu. Turn it off after the commands. This is only a cosmetic command to make your macros look better while running.

Delay(*time*)   The Delay function is used to pause a macro for a given period of time. The unit of time is one hundredth of a second, where $100 = 1$ second. The function can be used anywhere in a macro. One use for the Delay function is at the beginning of a macro like TODO or MEMO to pause the macro before it begins and give you a time to cancel it if desired.

The macro commands

This section discusses the six macro commands, defines them, and tells you how to use them in subroutines.

Selecting and running specific subroutines

The Call command (Call *subroutine*) executes the indicated subroutine in the current macro. After the subroutine finishes running, the macro execution will return to the statement after the Call statement—unless the called subroutine happens to include the Stop command.

The Call command is used to create loops of repeating functions within a macro. In other words, "do this and then do it again when the stipulations are met."

Telling a macro to execute another macro

The PlayMacro command (PlayMacro *'macro'*) tells WordStar to run another macro. The macro's name must be enclosed between a pair of apostrophes.

If the macro isn't in the same directory as the macro playing it, don't forget to include the path name. It's not necessary to include the .WSM extension. To include an apostrophe in the macro name or path, double the character.

When this macro completes running, WordStar will revert to the original macro—to the statement after the PlayMacro statement in the original macro. But it won't do this if the alternative macro contains the Stop command.

Executing a chain of macros

The ChainMacro command (ChainMacro *'macro'*) also executes another macro from within the original. The macro's name must be enclosed between a pair of apostrophes (*' '*).

What happens after the alternative macro completes depends on the subroutine from which the ChainMacro command is executed. If the ChainMacro command isn't in the MAIN subroutine, WordStar won't revert to the original macro. If the ChainMacro command is in any other subroutine, WordStar will revert to the original macro.

Terminating a macro

The Stop command is all you need to bring a macro to a halt. Place it as the last command in the subroutine; it will complete the job being executed by the macro.

It's common to put a Stop at the end of the MAIN subroutine and then write the additional subroutines as referrals, gotos, and alternatives of the MAIN. Thus the MAIN subroutine directs and controls the final result, while using the other subroutines to perform specific, individual tasks.

Returning to a previous subroutine

The Return command will stop the current subroutine and return execution to
either the calling subroutine or the calling macro. If there's no calling subroutine
or calling macro, the macro will terminate.

Going to a specific label in a macro

The GoTo command (GoTo *label*) sends WordStar to the named label, and the
functions identified by the label will be executed. The macro will continue from
this location. The label must be in the same subroutine as the GoTo command.
You can use a label to go to a specific location in the macro, and to repeat a set of
instructions in a loop.

A *label* is a name identifying a statement or location in a macro. A label
name must begin with a letter. It can have up to 31 alphanumerical characters, and
the underline character must be used in place of blank spaces. A colon must end
the label.

You can use the GoTo command to create loops of commands within a subroutine. An example of this is in LIST_BUL, the sample macro file. WordStar
inserts a bullet, issues a tab, and waits until you type text and press the Enter key.
Then it repeats these functions until you tell it to stop. You can write a loop to
execute any repetitive function.

A sample loop

Following is a loop named INPUT_LOOP, used in the sample macro earlier in
this chapter. It's the heart of the MAIN subroutine, and in fact does most of the
macro's work. This loop actually creates the ordered or bullet list.

The first line is the label, which identifies the loop. Notice that the two words
in the label are separated by an underline, and that the label ends with a colon.

```
INPUT_LOOP:
   Key ("  ■{Tab}")
   PauseForInput("{ENTER}",' Type the line and press ENTER.')
     IfException
       NCM: Goto INPUT_DONE 'User typed nothing
     End IfException
       KEY("{Enter}")
   GoTo INPUT_LOOP
 INPUT_DONE:
```

The Key line inserts two blank spaces, types the bullet character, and then executes a tab stop. You can use any character as a bullet character. In this case, the
macro is using extended character 254 (■) as the bullet. Some other common bullets are the asterisk (*), extended character 16 (►), and extended character 248
(°).

The PauseForInput line uses the Enter key as the input termination key, and contains the comment *Type the line and press ENTER*. This tells the macro to wait as you type the text to go after the bullet.

The macro is ready to process the IfException clause, which is a conditional statement. In this case, the condition is NCM, which stands for *no cursor movement*. This statement sets up the circumstances for ending the macro's task. As long as you keep typing anything after each bullet, pressing the Enter key will result in the creation of a new bullet line. The macro will keep looping back to the beginning of the subroutine, and thus repeating it.

```
IfException
    NCM: Goto INPUT_DONE      'User typed nothing
End IfException
```

The NCM conditional statement line tells the macro what to do when the condition is met. In this case, GoTo sends the macro to the INPUT_DONE label, which marks the termination subroutine. When you press the Enter key on a line without anything typed, the macro will delete the last line and return you to the document mode.

You can use more than one conditional command in a subroutine, and thus give a macro alternative tasks to choose between when it pauses.

Using IfException clauses

IfException clauses are used to set up and execute conditional functions within a macro. This is a powerful tool for making a macro select between one or more alternatives in response to a specific query set by the macro.

It might help if you think of IfException clauses as (referring back to my earlier analogy) the question inside of a subroutine paragraph. The question being asked is, "If such and such happens, what do I do?" The macro knows how to answer this question because you've programmed in the circumstances and the resulting course of action. Here is a sample IfException situation from the sample macro earlier in this chapter.

```
IfException
    NCM: Goto INPUT_DONE       'User typed nothing
End IfException
```

This conditional statement provides an alternative action when one of two situations can occur. In this case, the macro runs, the Key function inserts keystrokes, and the macro pauses for you to respond before it can go on to the next function.

You can follow any Key function command with an IfException clause. This clause can handle three types of exception conditions: user acknowledgement required, user clarification required, and no cursor movement made.

User acknowledgement required subclause

The conditional acknowledgement specification is ACK. This condition occurs when WordStar displays a message in response to a command issued by a macro, and you must type a key to acknowledge it. Common acknowledgment keys are Y and N, the Enter key to execute something, and Esc to exit from a dialog box or macro routine.

User clarification required subclause

The conditional clarification specification is QRY. This condition occurs when WordStar presents a dialog box in response to a command issued by the macro— and you must either type in some form of information or choose one of several options.

For example, if a macro is supposed to insert a file, but gives a nonexistent filename, you need to either type in the correct filename or escape the dialog box.

Sometimes, when they're appropriate, the macro recorder will include ACK conditions when recording a macro.

No cursor movement response subclause

The conditional no cursor movement specification is NCM. This is used in macros where a subroutine repeats some cursor movement indefinitely. An example of this is used in the LIST_BUL macro.

```
IfException
    NCM: Goto INPUT_DONE        'User typed nothing
      End IfException
```

The LIST_BUL macro inserts blank bullet list lines indefinitely, as long as you type anything after the bullet. This IfException clause sets the condition for ending a keystroke repetition.

NCM looks for any cursor movement as a condition for executing or not executing further action. Anything you type, any command to move the cursor, will trigger it. You can use it to execute any macro command or function.

This condition is also met when no user input is made before the input termination key is pressed *after* a PauseForInput statement.

The IfException clause format

To include the IfException clause in your subroutines, use the following format for all of its conditional clauses:

```
IfException
    ACK: (clauses)
        command statements or subclauses
```

```
QRY: (clauses)
    command statements or subclauses
NCM: (clauses)
    command statements or subclauses
DEF:
    command statements or subclauses
End IfException
```

The ACK, QRY, and NCM subclauses handle the three conditions described by the IfException clause. The DEF statement defines the default exception procedures for each IfException clause.

IfException, End IfException, and each subclause must begin on a new line. The indentations shown are optional. Use blank spaces or Tabs to indent the subclauses when desired.

You can use any or all these exception subclauses in a macro. The IfException clause becomes active only when one of the subclause conditions is met. If the subclause for the exception is defined, WordStar will execute the defined statements in this subclause.

WordStar will execute the defined functions in the DEF clause if none of the other subclauses are defined. The exception must be an ACK or QRY type, and the DEF must be defined. Otherwise, the clause will remain inactive.

If no IfException clause is included in an ACK or QRY condition, or if an appropriate subclause isn't defined, the macro will display a message on the status line and pause for you to respond to the dialog box or the onscreen message. The macro will resume execution only when the appropriate response is given. When there's an NCM condition, but no IfException clause, WordStar will ignore the condition and the macro will proceed.

When you record a macro, WordStar automatically inserts ACK and QRY IfException clauses when the exception conditions are encountered as you record. It won't insert NCM clauses.

Sample use of ACK

The following macro is a sample of ACK used as an exception in an IfException clause.

```
Sub Main
    WSQuiet(ON)
    Key(" {Ctrl – Q}A")
    WSQuiet(OFF)
    Key("that{Tab}")
    Key("which{Tab}")
    Key("GAM")
    Key(" {Ctrl – K}")
        IfException
```

```
        ACK: Key("{Esc}")
      End IfException
   End Sub
```

This macro uses the Ctrl−QA command to call the Find and Replace dialog box. It instructs WordStar to find *that* and replace it with *which*. It uses the variables G, A, and M—to search the entire file, maintain the case of the replaced text, and realign every paragraph in which a replacement is made.

The {Ctrl−K} starts the search-and-replace process going. The IfException clause, with ACK as a subclause, sets up the condition under which the macro will return automatically to the write-and-edit mode.

During the search and replace, the macro pauses every time it finds *that*, and prompts for verification. The user must respond with a Y or N for the replacement. If you substitute NAGM for GAM as the variables in the macro, WordStar will replace without pausing.

When the macro runs to completion, the *All replacements complete* message will trigger the ACK IfException clause, which supplies the Esc keystroke to automatically clear the screen and return to the document mode.

Sample use of QRY

The following macro is a sample of QRY used as an exception in an IfException clause.

```
   Sub MAIN
      Key("{Ctrl−P} = ")
      Key({"Times 10 PC"})
         IfException
           QRY: Key("{Esc}")
              Key("Courier 10 PC{Enter}")
         End IfException
   End Sub
```

This macro selects the Times 10 PC font, but defaults to the Courier 10 PC font if the Times font is unavailable. The QRY subclause sets the condition and the alternative.

The Ctrl−P equal sign calls the Font dialog box, and displays the list of available fonts for the currently attached printer. The keystrokes tell WordStar to select the Times 10 PC font.

If the Times 10 PC font is unavailable, the error message *Not in the directory* will trigger the QRY IfException. The exception subclauses issue the Esc command to remove the error message, and select the Courier font as the alternative.

Tip: When a macro changes variables in a dialog box, use a separate Key statement for each variable. This lets you set up IfException clauses to correct problems with each variable.

Placing comments in a macro

There are three different ways to place a comment in a macro file as you write or edit it: remarks, which go at the beginning of the macro; statement line comments, which display on the status line; and hidden comments containing information only visible when you open the macro in the macro editor.

Remarks

Remarks are primarily intended to identify the function of a macro to anyone opening the macro for editing. Remarks display on the status line as the macro runs, but they appear too briefly to read.

Each REM takes up a line onscreen. Use REM at the beginning of the line. You can precede REM with tabs and blank spaces. All text typed on this line, after the REM, is in the comment. The following sample is the remark line from the LIST_BUL macro supplied with WordStar.

    REM This macro is for creating bulleted lists.

Comments to display on the status line

You can also include statement line comments, which will display on the status line as the macro is running. You can change the message displayed, depending on the function executing or the response required by the user. The following is the PauseForInput statement from the LIST_BUL macro discussed earlier.

    PauseForInput("{Enter}", 'Enter the text')

The comment must go between apostrophes and be contained in the parentheses of the argument. As above, type a comma after the second quotation mark, a blank space, and an apostrophe. Then type the message and close it with a second apostrophe.

Hidden comments as notes to yourself

You can place hidden comments in a macro, containing information only visible when you open the macro in the macro editor.

You can start a hidden comment anywhere in a macro by typing a slash and an asterisk (/*), and end it anywhere with an asterisk and a slash (*/), as follows:

    /*This is a hidden comment*/

Shortcuts for writing macros

The following are tips and shortcuts you can use to streamline the process of writing complex macros. Use any combination you find convenient.

Use the macro recorder whenever possible

Obviously, it's quicker to record a macro than to write one from scratch. Unfortunately, you can record only commands and keystrokes issued through the keyboard and menus.

But you can also use the recording feature as a time-saving device. When preparing to write a complex macro, always use the macro recorder to store the keystrokes and WordStar commands you want the macro to execute.

You can then open the resulting macros with the macro editor, and write all the complex subroutines as needed. Or you can leave them unchanged and have the complex macro call them when their functions are needed.

Use boilerplate subroutines and statements

You can also use reusable boilerplate text when writing complex macros. Once you have any macro written or recorded, and its file saved to disk, you can use all or any part of it in writing another macro.

Subroutines, command statements, and conditional clauses are the most reusable elements of any macro. You can open a macro in the macro editor, mark any portion of it as a block of text, and use Ctrl−KW to write it to a boilerplate file on disk. Just remember to copy in ASCII format so the file doesn't contain any hidden word processing commands. The file will be stored in whatever directory was current when the macro was opened.

I recommend that you keep a written record of what subroutines or statements you have and their filenames. With these boilerplate files, you can paste together new macros from work done previously.

Use the Windows clipboard

If you have at least a 386SX computer, MS-DOS 5.0, and Windows 3, you can use the Windows clipboard with WordStar. The clipboard is a Windows utility that sets aside space in memory. You can copy text from one program to this memory, and then copy it from memory into another program. Ctrl−K] copies the marked block of text to the clipboard, and Ctrl−K[copies the stored block of text from the clipboard.

Open the source macro in the macro editor. Mark the subroutine or statement as a block. Copy it to the clipboard. Exit the source macro. Reopen the macro being written, and copy the subroutine or statement from the clipboard.

Before you can use the Windows clipboard, WordStar must be running through Windows 3 and Windows must be running in the 386 enhanced mode.

Use nondocuments as a clipboard

You can use a nondocument as a permanent clipboard for holding subroutines and command statements to use in other macros. This lets you cut the reusable stuff directly from the source macros and paste it into the nondocument in the exact order it needs to be executed.

1. Open the clipboard nondocument through the Opening Menu.
2. Open the source macros one by one. Mark the reusable subroutines and comments as blocks, and copy them to the nondocument.
3. As you paste the boilerplate into the nondocument, try to place it in the same order you want the new macro to execute it.
4. When you have all the boilerplate subroutines and statements collected, open the new macro you're writing. Copy all the boilerplate from the nondocument to the new macro.
5. Close the nondocument and finish writing the new macro.

You can keep the nondocument for future use as boilerplate, or delete it from your hard drive.

Open the source macro in a second window

You can open a source macro only in a second window if the first macro was opened through the Opening Menu. WordStar will open the second macro as a nondocument. When the two macros are opened this way, you can cut and paste between them as though they were normal text files.

Ctrl−KA Copies marked block from one window to the other.
Ctrl−KG Moves marked block from one window to the other.
Ctrl−OK Switches between windows.
Ctrl−OM Sizes the windows.
Ctrl−KQ Closes the window and abandons any changes.
Ctrl−KS Saves the macro in the window and compiles it.
Ctrl−KD Saves, compiles, and closes the macro.

Never use macros in place of boilerplates

The most elementary shortcut is to never use macros in place of boilerplate text. If you have something written and stored to disk, you don't have to write a macro to use it. This would be a complete waste of time.

It takes time to record a macro and it takes a long time to write a complex macro from scratch. But boilerplate text saved in text files already exists. The time it takes to write it has already been spent. Now all you have to do is copy it from disk to whenever you need it.

The macros MEMO, TODO, and LIST_BUL are prime examples of complex macros that were clearly a waste of time to write. Their only true justification is to show off the capabilities of the new macro system.

If you write a lot of memorandums and if your office uses a format different than what MEMO produces, it would be much easier to write a blank memo form and store it in a boilerplate file on disk than to edit the MEMO macro to your office style.

The type of ordered or bullet list created by LIST_BUL isn't the only way to create such a list. For one thing, it doesn't put blank space between the items in a list. Rather than edit it, it would be simpler to write a blank bullet list and save it to disk. Then just copy it in where needed and fill in the blanks. The same can be done for the different styles of numbered lists, to-do lists, and so on.

Don't waste your time writing macros when there's an easier method available. Save macros for those things you can't accomplish any other way.

Avoid writing "gadget freak" macros

When I started learning how to use the new macro system, it became immediately clear these new macros have a strong appeal to folks who love gadgets. The macro recorder can store and play back anything you can type or execute through the keyboard. With the macro editor, you can open a macro and rewrite it to do a practically unlimited variety of things with WordStar, and to a text file.

The power of this macro system offers more possibilities than it presents practical uses. All the macros you can't record are included in this reservation. The more complex a macro, the more things it does, the greater likelihood that there's an easier way to do it.

19
CHAPTER

Using Inset
with WordStar

This chapter discusses basic and detailed use of the Inset companion program packaged with WordStar 7. Inset uses graphics files from many different sources, however, and this chapter can't cover every circumstance of its use. For specific information on files from other graphics programs, read their documentation.

An overview of Inset

This section provides an overview of Inset, discussing basic capabilities of the program, hardware and software requirements, and its use with other programs.

Inset is a *memory-resident* program. Such programs load into memory and remain dormant in the "background" until you need to use it. With Inset in memory, you can invoke and use it any time you need it.

Inset, working within WordStar, allows you to capture and attach graphics files to WordStar text files, then print them both in the same document. Thus, you can print documents that merge text and graphics on the same page.

Inset creates graphics primarily by capturing onscreen images and storing them in graphics files. You can also use clip art files provided by Inset (see Fig. 19-1 for some examples) or other graphics programs. Capturing and customizing graphics is very simple; the basic procedure is as follows:

1. Display onscreen the graphic image you want to use in your document.
2. Capture this onscreen image by storing it in a special .PIX file.
3. After capturing and saving the .PIX graphic, use Inset's modify-and-edit commands to change the image to fit your printing needs.

19-1   Some example clip art provided by Inset for use in WordStar documents.

Inset also has its own graphic-generation capabilities, allowing you to blank the screen and create your own images from scratch. Use line-or box-drawing features, or use the mouse to draw freehand. Type text directly onto the graphic, and position it where it belongs. Clip and paste in portions of other graphics to make new images from old ones. The only limits are your skill and your imagination.

Store the image in a .PIX file and then open a WordStar text file and add a PIX tag to it—at the place where you want it to print in the document. You can view the image using Page Preview to ensure that your layout is correct. When you're ready, print the WordStar document normally. The graphic image will be inserted automatically during printing.

Hardware and software requirements

Inset doesn't have exotic hardware and software requirements. To run it with WordStar, you need a computer with at least 512K of RAM. To print an Inset graphic, you need any printer supported by Inset. This includes most dot-matrix, inkjet, and laser printers supported by WordStar. If you're using any printer more than five years old, you probably don't have the equipment necessary to perform modern graphics printing.

To use all Inset capabilities, you need a graphics board in your computer. This is standard issue in all computers with CGA, EGA, and VGA monitors. If you have a monochrome monitor without a graphics adapter, you can't display graphics, so you won't be able to view or edit them. But you can capture simple graphs and charts created in text mode, and insert them into your hardcopy.

Using Inset with other programs

Although Inset is a "companion" program to use with WordStar, it can capture images from many programs, including AutoCAD, Diagraph, Dr. Halo, Ener-Graphics, Lotus 1-2-3, PC-Paint, Symphony, and Windows programs. Inset can capture images from almost any program that produces a graphic image onscreen. I've used it to capture graphic images even from computer games. Following are the basic guidelines for using Inset with programs other than WordStar.

- Because it's a memory-resident program (also called TSR, for *terminate and stay resident*), you must load Inset into your computer's memory before each session.
- When loaded from the DOS prompt, Inset stays in memory until you remove it or reboot the computer. When loaded through WordStar, it stays in memory until WordStar removes it.
- When using Inset with other memory-resident software, always load Inset last. This is mandatory if you want to remove Inset from memory when you're finished using it. A utility program to remove Inset from memory, RI.COM (for remove Inset), is in the C: \ WS \ INSET subdirectory.
- With Inset in memory, run the program displaying or producing the graphic image being captured.
- Once Inset is resident in memory, you can make it active in any directory from either the DOS prompt or inside the other program.
- To invoke Inset when it's resident, hold down the left Shift key and press the Ctrl key. (These are its "pop-up keys," which cause Inset's opening screen to pop up.)

Installing and customizing Inset

This section discusses what you have to do to copy Inset to your hard drive, and to customize its setting to work with your computer and printer.

Installing Inset with WSSETUP

If you haven't yet installed WordStar on your hard drive, use WSSETUP to copy the Inset program files at the same time you install WordStar. Just select Inset from the list of options, and let WSSETUP do it all for you.

Installing Inset with WINSTALL

If you didn't install Inset at the same time as WordStar, then you must use WIN-STALL to copy its program files to your hard drive. WINSTALL is a utility pro-

gram used to customize and modify major segments of WordStar and its
companion programs.

1. Boot your computer and change to your WordStar program directory.
   (Type CD \ WS and press the Enter key.)
2. At the C: \ WS DOS prompt, type WINSTALL and press the Enter key.
3. When the WINSTALL menu appears, use the down arrow key to put the
   highlight on Add or Remove a Feature. Then press the Enter key.
4. When the Add or Remove a Feature dialog box appears, use the down
   arrow key to highlight Inset. Then press the F10 key to start the
   installation.
5. Once you start the Inset installation, it will automatically continue until
   complete. All you have to do is swap floppy disks as directed.
6. When the installation is completed, exit WINSTALL. You now need to
   set up Inset to work with your particular computer, monitor, and printer.

First-time setup for your computer

WSSETUP or WINSTALL merely copies the Inset program files to the hard
drive. You can't use Inset until you run the SETUP program to tell it what monitor
and printer you're using. (And if you ever change the monitor or printer, you have
to change the setup to match the new equipment.) Below are steps for a first-time
setup of Inset. If it's previously been set up, you need to change the setup values.

1. Boot your computer and change to the Inset subdirectory. At the DOS
   prompt, type CD \ WS \ INSET and press the Enter key.
2. At the Inset subdirectory DOS prompt, type SETUP and press the Enter
   key.
3. Follow the onscreen directions and begin selecting the graphics board
   and printer.
4. At the Screen Driver Installation Menu, use the up and down arrow keys
   to select your type of monitor from the onscreen list. When it's
   highlighted, press the Enter key.
5. At the Printer Driver Installation Menu, use the up and down arrow
   keys to select your printer from the onscreen list. When it's highlighted,
   press the Enter key.
6. At the Color Printer dialog box, tell Inset whether you're using a
   black-and-white or color printer. Highlight your choice and press the
   Enter key.
7. After you make your choices, the Hardware Configuration Setup Menu
   will appear (see Fig. 19-2), displaying all the current values. You don't
   have to change any of these unless you want to. You can always come
   back later and change the setup. If your printer uses any port except
   LPT1, you can change the port setup.

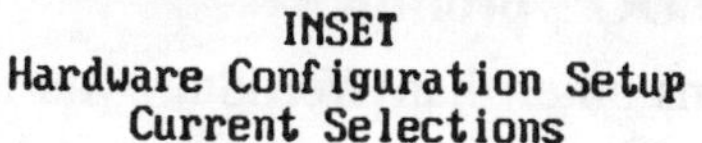

19-2 Hardware Configuration Setup Menu.

8. When ready, press the F10 key to save the setup and exit to the DOS prompt. (These changes don't take effect until you run Inset again.)
9. At the DOS prompt, type RI (for *remove Inset*) and press the Enter key. This clears Inset from memory. Now Inset is ready to use.

Using Inset

After you set up Inset for your monitor and printer, it's ready to use. You can run it from a DOS prompt or use it independently of WordStar. You also can run it from inside WordStar with the command Ctrl−P& or through the pull-down Utilities Menu.

You don't have to run Inset before a WordStar printing session. If Inset is installed on your hard drive, WordStar will use it automatically when processing a graphics tag during printing.

Starting Inset inside WordStar

To use Inset inside WordStar, you must be working on a WordStar document. Then use the Inset commands on either the Print Controls Menu or the pull-down Utilities Menu.

Use Ctrl-P&, the control command to run Inset. You can also use Alt−UI. Memorize these commands if you intend to use Inset frequently.

Starting Inset from the DOS prompt

To use Inset with programs other than WordStar, you must run it from the DOS prompt.

1. Change to the WORDSTAR \ INSET program subdirectory. (At the DOS prompt, type CD \ WS \ INSET and press the Enter key.)
2. At the DOS prompt, type INSET and press the Enter key.
3. Inset will be loaded into memory, and instructions for invoking it will appear onscreen.

The first time you run Inset this way, the SETUP utility program runs automatically. Follow the onscreen instructions to complete setup and customization of Inset. Once it's complete, you must again run Inset with the above steps.

Warning: Don't run Inset through the DOS window opened with Ctrl−KF. Never run memory-resident software from inside WordStar. Some TSRs use specific memory locations. If one tries to use memory already used by WordStar, it can cause serious problems. When you run Inset with Ctrl P&, WordStar knows what to do.

Using the Inset command menu

Inset has its own command menu, which appears across the bottom of the monitor screen whenever you run or invoke it. The appearance of this menu tells you that Inset is active and ready to use. The Inset command menu displays in black-and-white and is very simple to use.

- When you call the menu, the View option is automatically selected in the displayed first-level menu (the word is between angle brackets, e.g., < View >).
- Use the arrow keys to move these angle brackets to the option you want to use, and press the Enter key. If you have a mouse, use it to move the brackets and then click the mouse button.
- The Inset command menu also has built-in hotkeys you can use to select commands and options. At any menu, simply type the capitalized letter of the option or command to execute it.
- Selecting a command or option calls its own submenu of further choices. Use the arrow keys or the mouse to make your selection, and follow the onscreen directions.
- Use the Esc key to move back through the menus. Keep pressing until you exit Inset. When you exit Inset, you'll return to wherever you were before running or invoking Inset. But Inset remains memory-resident until the next time you need it.
- If you've made modifications to any graphic file, Inset will ask whether

or not you want to save the changes before exiting. Answer Yes to save the changes. Answer No to exit without saving the changes.

Using Inset with a mouse

Although Inset is simple to use with keyboard commands and arrow keys, it's definitely easier with a mouse. This is especially true for marking a graphic with cross hairs and using Inset's graphic drawing capabilities. Below are the standard assignments to the mouse buttons:

Mouse button	Function
Right	Same as the Enter key
Middle	No assigned function
Left	Same as the Esc key

Inset requires no adjustments or special support to use a mouse. Just connect your mouse and run its driver. Inset will use it. The mouse slides the angle brackets left and right along the Inset command menu. When the brackets are on the command or option, click on it with the mouse.

Occasionally, Inset seems to interfere with certain mouse drivers. When you exit from Inset, the mouse pointer will disappear but the mouse support will remain active. This is especially true if you run Inset inside WordStar, then later use the left Shift−Ctrl key combination to reinvoke Inset. The remedy is not to use the pop-up keys while working with Inset in WordStar. You can use Ctrl−P& to run Inset again, view a graphic, and then exit Inset. Or, if the above doesn't restore the mouse pointer, open a DOS window with Ctrl−KF—then reset your graphics mode. (Simply repeat the same mode setup command used in your AUTOEXEC.BAT file.) If you don't know how to do this, read the documentation packaged with your computer or graphics board.

Exiting Inset

To exit from any Inset menu, submenu, or command prompt, simply press the Esc key. Pressing the Esc key at the Inset Main Menu will throw you out of the program. You'll be returned to the DOS prompt or to WordStar.

When you exit Inset after making changes to a graphic image, you'll be asked whether you want to save the changes. Answer N to abandon the changes or Y to save the changes. You can save the changed graphic to a different name.

Removing Inset from memory

When you run Inset through WordStar (with Ctrl−P&), it isn't necessary to remove it from memory. WordStar will remove it if you don't use it periodically. However, if you run Inset first from a DOS prompt, WordStar won't automatically remove it. So if you need to use the memory for some other program, you must clear Inset with the RI.COM or remove inset utility program.

Once loaded into memory from DOS, Inset stays in memory until you either remove it or turn off the computer. If you need the memory for another program, you must remove it. To remove Inset from memory with RI.COM, Inset must be the last program loaded. You can't run RI.COM through the DOS window provided by Ctrl−KF. You must be at the DOS prompt.

1. Change to the WORDSTAR \ INSET program subdirectory. (At the DOS prompt, type CD \ WS \ INSET and press the Enter key.)
2. At the DOS prompt, type RI and press the Enter key.
3. The utility program will wipe Inset from memory, and display the message *Ok*.

If Inset wasn't the last program loaded, you'll get an error message. Remove the intervening program and try again. If all else fails, reboot the computer.

Using graphics tags

A graphics tag is embedded in text files like a WordStar note or comment. It doesn't print as text in the hardcopy. Instead, it marks the place where a graphic image should be inserted during printing.

Inserting a graphics tag

Use the following steps to place a graphics tag in the body of your WordStar text file:

1. Place the cursor where you want the graphic to appear in the document.
2. Hold down the Ctrl key, and type P*.
3. The Insert Graphic dialog box will appear. Below it are listed the graphics files stored in the \ WS \ INSET subdirectory.
4. Use the arrow keys to highlight the graphic being used.
5. When ready, press the Enter key.
6. You'll be returned to the document mode, with the graphics tag inserted at the cursor.

Deleting a graphics tag

The graphics tag is embedded in the text file like a note or comment. Though it doesn't print as text in the hardcopy, you can delete it like text—with any delete command.

Moving or repositioning a graphics tag

A graphics tag is embedded in a text file like a note or comment. You can move it anywhere on the page or in the text file. The position of the graphics tag determines the position of the printed graphic in the document. The important thing is to place it correctly and leave space above and below it. The best way to check the position of an inserted graphic is to view it with Page Preview.

* Add or delete blank lines to move the tag up or down in the document.
* Mark the tag as a block and move or copy it anywhere in the text file.
* Delete the tag with Ctrl−T and paste it back in with Ctrl−U.
* Use Ctrl−OC to horizontally center the graphics tag between the left and right margins. (This also centers the graphics tag within a newspaper column.)
* Use Ctrl−OV to vertically center the graphics tag between the top and bottom margins.

Graphics tags in headers and footers

You can use graphics tags in headers or footers as though they were text. The layout and design of the header or footer determines where the graphic will print in the hardcopy, so set up the header or footer normally and check it with Page Preview to see if you have it set up correctly.

Graphics printed in headers or footers aren't restricted to a single line, to the header/footer margin, nor even to the top/bottom margins. Instead, they print as whatever size they're set to print. If the graphic you want to use is too big for normal top or bottom margins, the graphic will overprint everything in its way. The solutions to this problem are fundamental:

* Use a graphic small enough to fit in the standard margins.
* Increase or decrease your top/bottom margins to accommodate the graphic.
* Use Inset Modify options to clip the graphic to a smaller size. Save it to a new .PIX file, and use it instead.

Use the sample footer format .fo as a test of this capability. It uses the MAN.PIX graphic, which comes with WordStar. The graphic is small enough to print within a 1-inch top or bottom margin. Try shifting its vertical position by using .f1, .f2, .f3, or .f4 instead of the generic .fo footer command.

Capturing and using graphics with Inset

Once Inset is loaded into memory, the screen-capture process is fairly straightforward. The steps for capturing a graphic image with Inset are listed as follows:

1. With Inset resident, load and run the program containing the graphic image you want to capture.
2. With the image onscreen, invoke Inset with the pop-up keys (either left Shift−Ctrl or Alt−left Shift−I).

3. When the Inset Main Menu appears at the bottom of the screen, you can use any of its options to modify, edit, or control its printing output.

4. When you have all the capture options set the way you want, save the captured image to a .PIX file on your hard disk. (Be sure the file goes to the INSET subdirectory if you plan on printing the graphic with WordStar.)

5. Repeat the above steps for all graphic images you want to capture from this particular program. When ready, exit from Inset by pressing the Esc key.

6. Now you can run WordStar and attach the graphics tags where you want their image to print in your documents.

Naming a .PIX graphics file

The rules for naming a .PIX graphics file are the same as for any other MS-DOS file:

- Use 1−8 letters or numerals.
- Don't use any of the illegal characters.
- You can use the hyphen and underline characters for spacing in a filename.
- It isn't necessary to type the extension. Inset will automatically add the .PIX extension.

In addition to the above guidelines, Inset provides space for you to type in a directory path. So you can direct a .PIX file to any directory, subdirectory, or disk drive in your computer.

Modifying a captured graphic

When you capture a graphic image with Inset, you grab everything on the monitor screen. This is usually too much, and the graphic might not print correctly without first modifying it. So you need to make it fit your needs.

1. Run WordStar and open the document you want to attach the graphic to.
2. Use Ctrl−P& to run Inset.
3. When the Inset Main Menu appears, the highlight will automatically be on < View >.
4. Press the Enter key to view the .PIX file you need to modify and edit.
5. WordStar should be looking for the file in the Inset subdirectory. If it isn't there, exit WordStar and copy the .PIX file to this directory.
6. If the .PIX file is in this directory, either type in its name or select it from the onscreen list. When ready, press the Enter key. (If the list isn't displayed, type * on the command line and press the Enter key.)
7. You can now customize the graphic to meet your needs.

8. When ready, save the graphic image. You can either save it to the same name (overwrite the old version), or save it to a new name and keep the old version intact.

Viewing a graphic

Step one in working with any .PIX graphic is to load it into memory and view it with Inset. The following steps assume you're working with Inset from inside WordStar 7. As long as WordStar is running, you can view a graphic at any time.

1. Use Ctrl−P& to load and run Inset.
2. The Inset Main Menu will appear at the bottom of the screen, with View selected.
3. Press the Enter key.
4. The View command line will appear, displaying the C: \ WS \ INSET path. If no filename is on the line, then an asterisk follows the path. The asterisk produced a list of available .PIX files in the given directory. (To make this list appear, delete the filename, type * and press the Enter key.)
5. Type in the name of the file being viewed and press the Enter key, or use the arrow keys to put the angle brackets on your choice and press the Enter key.
6. Inset will load the file into memory and display it onscreen.

Saving a captured or modified graphic

The Save command saves whatever is onscreen at the time you issue the command. So you must be viewing or capturing a graphic with Inset before using the Save command.

1. With the graphic you want to save onscreen, select the Save option from the Inset Main Menu.
2. The Save command line will appear, with the current drive and directory displayed. If a graphic is being viewed, its filename will also be displayed. There's room on this command line to specify almost any filename, drive, and directory in your computer.
3. Type in a new filename or accept the default, and then press the Enter key.
4. If a file by this name already exists, Inset offers you the option of overriding it with the new name or canceling the save. If you replace it, the old version will be destroyed. If you cancel the save, you can try a different filename.
5. When you save or cancel the save, you're returned to the Inset Main Menu. You can now exit Inset by pressing the Esc key, or use any other feature.

If you've captured or made any modifications to a graphic screen, Inset always lets you save or abandon your changes when you exit from Inset. Don't save the file unless you really want to keep the graphic or the changes to it. When you save or print a graphic after modifying it, the new settings will become the defaults for the graphic. You can check some but not all of these changes by selecting Status from the Modify Menu.

Tip: Until you become familiar with Inset, and what effect each of its options has on modifying and printing graphics, you should make only incremental changes to your graphics. Save the changes and then exit Inset and view the graphics in Page Preview. This way you can preview the changes in order and undo them if they don't work like you want.

Using the Modify options

There are eight options on Inset's Modify Menu. They control basic changes to the graphic image itself.

Clip   This means cropping the image. You reduce the boundaries of the graphic by clipping off everything you don't want to print.

Rotate   This turns the graphic image 90 degrees to the right or left. The rotation doesn't show onscreen, except when you preview the text and graphic with Page Preview.

Expand   This lets you print the graphic bigger than its normal size. It's especially useful when printing clip art or images created by other graphics programs.

Ink   This option controls how the graphic actually prints. You can select from the following options: Standard, Invert, B&W, Color Table, Contrast, and Display Color Palette.

Pass   This lets you select between single (draft) or double (higher quality) printing passes when the graphic is being printed.

Border   This tells Inset whether or not to print a box border around the graphic at the same time the graphic is printing.

Status   This displays the current status of the modifications made to the .PIX graphic.

NoMenu   This option temporarily turns off the Inset command menu. This lets you view the portion of the graphic screen covered by the menu.

Clipping or cropping a graphic

To *clip* a graphic means to crop the image, like a photograph, before printing it. You cut off everything you don't need in the printed version. When you capture a graphic, Inset grabs everything onscreen. Unless you plan to use the image as is, you must clip away everything you don't want printed.

1. Run Inset and view the graphic you want to crop.

2. At the Inset command menu, select Modify Clip.

3. You now have two sets of cross hairs to bracket the portion of the graphic you want to keep. Use the arrow keys plus the PgUp, PgDn, Home, and End keys to move these cross hairs onscreen. If you have a mouse, use it instead.

4. The first set of cross hairs moves the upper left corner of the image. Use it to mark the upper left corner of the portion being clipped. (Don't worry, you can always reposition it.) When it's in place, press the Enter key.

5. The second set of cross hairs moves the bottom right corner. Use it to mark the bottom right corner of the portion being clipped. When it's in place, press the Enter key.

6. The image is now clipped. Press the Esc key once. You can now use any other Inset options to customize the image.

7. After making all necessary modifications, press the Esc key once. Inset will ask you if you want to save the changes you just made.

8. Answer No if you want to exit without saving the changes. Answer Yes if you want to save the changes before exiting. When you exit, you'll be returned to wherever you were before invoking Inset.

Tip: Always save clipped art to a new file, and leave the original untouched. It's "good housekeeping" to maintain a separate .PIX file for each graphic you use, which reserves originals as a future resource.

An alternative way to clip

There's an alternative way to clip a graphic. First, use the Edit Erase command to remove everything you don't want. Then use Modify Clip to put the clipping brackets around the final image, and save it to a new filename.

Viewing and changing a clipped graphic

You can view a clipped graphic like any other graphic. Unfortunately, Inset doesn't automatically erase the unwanted portion of the original when you clip and save it. So when you view a clipped file, you'll still see all of the original file. The clip marks simply tell Inset or WordStar to print only the portion inside the marks.

You can always reopen any clipped file and make further changes, modifications, or corrections. It isn't necessary to give the clipped file a new name each time you save it. Save it to a new name only when you want to create a new .PIX file.

Rotating a graphic image

To *rotate* means to turn a graphic image 90 degrees to the right or left. This rotation takes place at printing time. The image isn't rotated when you view it through

Inset. The only way to view the rotation is to print the document, use Inset's Preview command, or to view the document with WordStar's Page Preview. The Rotate Left selection turns the image 90 degrees counterclockwise during printing. Horizontal prints the graphic without rotating it, exactly as it appears onscreen. And Rotate Right turns the image 90 degrees clockwise during printing.

Printing the graphic larger or smaller

The Expand command tells Inset to print a graphic image bigger or smaller than its captured size. This is especially useful when printing clip art or images created by other graphics programs. Inset grabs the contents of the whole screen when it captures a graphic, so it's common to clip out most of the screen to get the image you need. The Expand feature lets you size the clipped portion to fit your needs. Available sizes include $1\times$, $2\times$, $3\times$, $4\times$, $5\times$, $6\times$, Columns, and Inches. Only the last two require detailed explanation.

Columns sets the graphic size by columns and rows. You provide the specific dimensions in column units, controlling width, aspect ratio (height as a ratio of width), and height. Inches sets the graphic size by inches. You provide the specific dimensions in standard inches, with increments to the hundredth of an inch, and can control width, aspect ratio (height as a ratio of width), and height.

These two options require a more comprehensive knowledge of layout and design than merely letting Inset do most of the work for you. You should avoid using them except when the standard features won't produce an image that meets your needs.

Changing the ink

The Ink option allows you to change the way the graphic image itself prints. In other words, you control what the printing head does when it passes across the paper. The following options are available:

Standard   Uses standard inks and gray scaling.
Invert   Reverses colors; black prints white and white prints black.
B&W   Eliminates colors from the image. All colors print black—except for black, which prints white.
Color table   Sets and changes color table settings for gray-scale printing.
Contrast   Allows you to control the contrast by selecting a pattern for black, white, and gray scale. Random uses original patterns from the graphic. Gray uses halftone patterns (best for printing gray scales). High uses high-contrast patterns (best for printing text).
Display   Shows the color palette options, and lets you select among them.

Setting the printing pass

The Pass command lets you select between single or double printing passes when the graphic is being printed. A single pass produces a draft-quality graphic, sometimes with wavy lines and indistinct detail. A double pass prints the graphic twice as dark.

Printing a border around graphic

The Border command tells Inset whether or not to print a border around the graphic image. This border is a simple line box used to make the graphic stand out from anything else around it.

Displaying the modification status

The Status option displays the current status of the modifications you've made to the .PIX graphic since you captured it. The meanings of the items on the Status Menu are explained as follows:

Rotate   Indicates rotation status as either Left, Horizontal, or Right.
W″×H″   Indicates width and height in inches.
Border   Indicates whether or not a border will print around the graphic.
Pass   Indicates whether the printing pass is 1 or 2.

Viewing with NoMenu

The NoMenu option simply turns off the Inset command menus temporarily. This clears the bottom of the screen, letting you view any portion of the graphic screen covered by the menu. At the Inset Main Menu, type MN (Modify NoMenu). To restore the Inset Main Menu, press any key.

Special Modify commands

There are three special Modify commands, which are available only under unique conditions. You can use them to modify a graphic only when a graphics tag is in place in a WordStar document, and when the tag is the uppermost one on the page.

These special Modify commands change the graphic after it's been tagged to the WordStar document. They help custom-fit the graphic image to its purpose and place in the hardcopy.

Tip: If you have more than one graphics tag on a WordStar document page, and the one you want to modify is *not* the uppermost tag, you can fool Inset by embedding a .PA page break command above the graphics tag.

When invoked under the above conditions, Inset Modify commands act directly on the graphics tag itself. The modifications made control only the graphic printed at one tag location. They don't change the graphics file. Using these commands, you can print the same .PIX graphic differently in different places in the same document.

Invoking the special Modify commands

To invoke the special Modify commands, you must first meet the conditions in the previous section and run Inset with Ctrl−P& or Alt−UI. Along with the Inset Main Menu, a box will appear at the graphics tag location. This box represents the outline, position, and size of the graphic. The special commands are available when you select Modify from the Main Menu. Inset will display a menu with only three commands:

Image   Gives access to all the standard Modify commands except for Clip. You cannot clip .PIX graphics in memory.

Resize   Lets you change the size of an image by modifying its outline. This is accomplished with either natural printer sizes or scaled sizing.

Preview   Accesses Inset's own special preview mode, which shows the layout of both text and graphics.

Controlling the image in memory

The commands available on the Image Menu are Rotate, Expand, Ink, Pass, Border, Status, and NoMenu. (You can't use Clip on images in memory.) Use these options to make the graphic perfect for your needs. They work as previously explained—except that the changes you make affect only the graphics tag. The changes made aren't saved to the .PIX graphics file on disk, but they *are* saved with the WordStar text file.

Resizing a graphic image in memory

The two commands on the Resize Menu allow you to change the size of the graphic image by modifying its outline. This works like scalable soft fonts. You can make the outline bigger or smaller, as needed. Inset adjusts the graphic to fit inside the new outline. The two special size options are:

Natural   Makes the graphic outline bigger or smaller using *natural printer sizes*. This adjusts the image dimensions in multiples only, e.g., twice as wide or four times as high. Natural allows fewer sizes but can give you higher-quality output.

Scale   Changes the graphic size using *scaled sizing*. This adjusts the image dimensions by rows and columns, which gives precise control over the size, but can cause distortion in the printed image (especially in color patterns or detailed patterns). You must maintain the correct proportion between height and width.

With either of these options, use the mouse, the arrow keys, or the PgUp and PgDn keys to adjust the outline box to fit the space set aside in the document. When the outline is made bigger or smaller, press the Enter key. You can always go back and readjust the outline.

Using the special preview mode

Inset has its own special preview mode. Like WordStar's preview mode, you can't modify the onscreen text or graphics. It's meant to show you how and where the .PIX graphic will print in the hardcopy.

1. Before using the Inset preview mode, position the graphics tag at the top of the document screen. This ensures sufficient room for the .PIX graphic to be displayed.
2. Use Ctrl−P&M to run Inset and call the special Modify Menu. Notice that the outline of the graphic appears at the graphics tag. The Inset menu has only three options: Image, Resize, and Preview.
3. Type P to run the Preview mode.
4. Inset will temporarily convert the text screen into a graphics screen. The .PIX graphic will fill its outline onscreen.
5. Check the size, position, and image quality of the graphic. Make a note of any changes you need to make.
6. Press the Esc key to return to the Modify Menu. There you can make any changes necessary to customize the graphic printing. The changes you make will affect only the graphic at the tag you were viewing.
7. Use preview again to check the graphic until it fits your needs perfectly. Then press the Esc key repeatedly until you return to the WordStar document mode. When you save the text file, the modifications to the graphics tag will become permanent.

Previewing the graphic with page preview

The simplest way to check a graphics printing position is with Page Preview. Once a graphics tag is placed in a WordStar document, WordStar automatically displays the indicated graphic whenever you turn on Page Preview. You can quickly see if the graphic is placed correctly.

Tip: For a more precise view of the graphic, turn the Options Grid Display on. This provides a cross-hatch grid overlay to let you pinpoint the graphic's location.

By checking the document in Page Preview, you know whether to move the graphics tag up or down in the text file. Exit Page Preview, make the correction, and view it again.

If you have a VGA or better monitor, the WordStar Page Preview is supposed to display the .PIX graphic exactly as your printer will print it. If you have less than a VGA monitor, Page Preview will display the graphic image as well as it can. You must, however, have a graphics monitor to use Page Preview.

Using Inset's Edit options

Inset has a built-in graphics editor. It's available through the Edit option of the Inset Main Menu. This editor allows you to draw a graphic from scratch or to edit any existing graphic. You can draw with lines, rectangles, circles, or dots. You can also magnify a specific area of a graphic and edit the colors dot by dot. Editing features include Text Mode, Block, Fill, Draw, and Erase.

The Edit Menu features

The Edit features are mainly used to modify, add to, or change the graphic image itself. While you can also use them to draw graphics from scratch, you might find their capabilities limited. Thus, I'll advise you to create all special-purpose graphics on a more sophisticated program, like PC Paint or Lotus Draw. There are ten choices on the Edit menu:

Line   Draws straight lines on graphics and clip art.

Rectangle   Draws rectangles around portions of graphics and clip art.

Circle   Draws circles around portions of graphics and clip art.

Dots   Draws dots and freehand lines in graphics and clip art.

Magnify   Zooms in on any portion of a graphic for "touching up" or modification, pixel by pixel.

Text   Allows you to type text directly into a graphic or clip art.

Block   Allows you to copy, move, or import any portion of a graphic.

Fill   Lets you select the primary background or fill color.

Erase   Allows you to selectively erase portions of any graphic. Remove your mistakes and try again.

Options   These five options control drawing and erasing defaults for such things as line width and background color.

Drawing lines, rectangles, circles, and dots

The straight-line, rectangle, circle, and freehand dot and line drawing features can help you either customize an existing graphic or create one of your own. You need a mouse to use this option effectively. Only a mouse gives you both quick and precise control over drawing. The better the mouse, the better the control. (If you don't have a mouse, use the arrow keys, plus the Home, End, PgUp, and PgDn keys to move the Inset pointer.)

1. At the Inset Main Menu, type E (Edit).
2. If you're not already viewing a graphic, Inset will present the following options: View, Blank, and Convert.
3. To edit an existing graphic, you must first load it into memory with the View command. To draw a new graphic from scratch, you must use the Blank option to erase the screen. To convert onscreen text to a graphic file, select the Convert option.

4. Select either Line, Rectangle, Circle, or Dots, and then press the Enter
5. Use the mouse to position the cross hairs at the point to begin the drawing, or use the arrow keys, plus the Home, End, PgUp, and PgDn keys.
6. With the cross hairs positioned, click the mouse button or press the Enter key.
7. Use the mouse or cursor movement keys to draw. You can reposition the line at any time while drawing it.
8. When drawing a line: You can tell when a line is perfectly vertical or horizontal when it no longer appears broken. When drawing dots and freehand circles: Simply move the pointer and click the mouse button to draw a dot, and hold down the button and drag the pointer to draw a continuous line.
9. When you finish drawing and positioning the line, click the mouse button or press the Enter key. The line, rectangle, circle, dot, or freehand circle will be fixed in place.

Touching up graphics with Magnify

The Magnify command can be used only when a graphic is onscreen. It zooms in on any portion of a graphic so you can touch it up. Before using this feature on graphics printed in color, you need to go through Edit Options to select colors, fill patterns, and line widths to use. Otherwise, Inset uses its default settings.

1. When you select Edit Magnify from the Inset Main Menu, a small box will appear onscreen.
2. Use the mouse to position this box over the section of the graphic needing a touch-up. Then press the Enter key or use the directional keys to move the pointer.
3. The box will get bigger, displaying a magnified view of the portion of the graphic. The box will appear as a pixel-map or grid over top of the image.
4. Use the mouse or arrow keys to highlight the pixel needing change. Then press the Enter key. This will change the pixel to the color, pattern, etc. you've selected.
5. Repeat as necessary to complete the touch-up. If you need to change colors, press the Esc key to exit Magnify. Then select Edit Options and change the colors or background pattern.
6. When finished, exit and save the changes. If you don't want the changes made permanent, exit without saving.

Typing words into a graphic

The Text command lets you type words and phrases directly into a graphic. Different font types and sizes are available, depending on the printer used. Once you type the text in, you can turn it upside-down, or turn it 90 degrees to the right or the left.

1. Run or invoke Inset and view the graphic to which you're adding text.
2. At the Inset Main Menu, type ET (Edit Text).
3. The Edit Text menu will appear below the graphic. You can now select the font, and set its direction, height, width, and italic status. (You can also change any of these settings prior to accepting the text.)
4. When the font is ready to use, press the Enter key.
5. A cross hair will appear onscreen, indicating the place where the text will appear when typed. Use the arrow keys or the mouse to place it where you want and begin typing. Use upper- or lowercase, and any characters on the keyboard. Use the backspace key to delete mistakes.
6. If necessary, use the mouse or the arrow keys to reposition the text on the graphic. Then press the Esc key.
7. You can now accept or undo the text you just typed. The text isn't fixed in the graphic until you accept it, and you can't type other text in a different font size or type until you accept it. The Undo command erases whatever you just typed.
8. Repeat steps 1-7 if you need to use another type or size of font. When finished typing, save the graphic and exit.

This text editor has limited capability. You can use only one type and size of font at a time. If you try to change font type and size before accepting what you've already typed, Inset will change the type and size of the previously typed text.

Cutting and pasting portions of a graphic

Like WordStar, Inset has its own block commands for cutting and pasting. These block commands let you copy or move any portion of a graphic image. You can also import another graphic into the one you're working on. There are three options on the Edit Block Menu. Use any or all as necessary. Their functions are as follows:

Copy   This copies a blocked graphic section to a different location in the same graphic image. The original block remains unchanged, and a duplicate is created at the new location.

Move   This moves a blocked graphic section to a different location in the same graphic image. The original block is deleted. In its place is whatever background color and pattern you've selected. (The Inset default is black.)

Import   This copies a clipped area from a modified and saved graphic, and is used for merging graphic files to create a collage or overlay effect. Build new graphics from pieces of your old ones.

Tip: The imported graphic "pastes in" and prints at whatever expanded size you've set it for. If the imported graphic doesn't fit, then open it separately and change its settings. The easiest solution is to clip it again, and make it bigger or smaller.

Copying and moving

Mark the graphic by drawing a special rectangle on it. Once marked, you can then simply move the rectangle where you want it copied or moved and press the Enter key. You can use either the mouse or the arrow keys to move this box.

1. Run or invoke Inset and view the graphic being worked on.
2. At the Inset Main Menu, type EB (Edit Block).
3. Your options now are to copy, move, or import. Use the arrow keys highlight your choice, and press the Enter key.
4. A cross hair will appear onscreen. Use the arrow keys or the mouse to place it on the upper left corner of the portion being marked. Press the Enter key.
5. Now use the arrow keys or the mouse to draw the box over the block. If you make a mistake, press the Esc key to erase the box and start over. When the rectangle is correctly drawn around the block, press the Enter key.
6. Now, simply move your cursor to where you want to copy, move, or import the graphic image and press the Enter key. These procedures don't become permanent until you save the graphic.

Importing

The Import command allows you to copy a clipped area from a modified and saved graphic file into your current file. When you import a graphic, instead of marking the block to move, you mark the space for the incoming graphic to fill.

1. Load the graphics file and clip the part you want to be imported into your file. Save the .PIX file and clear the screen.
2. Load the file you want to import the graphic into and, at the Inset Main Menu, type EBI (Edit Block Import).
3. When prompted, type in the name of the .PIX file you're importing. A rectangle, representing the image, will appear onscreen.
4. Use the arrow keys or the mouse to position the rectangle over the place where the imported graphic belongs.
5. When ready, press the Enter key.
6. The clipped part of the imported graphic will fill the rectangle. You can now save the graphic, or abandon the changes. The imported image won't become a permanent part of the original graphic until the file is saved.

Selecting a primary background or fill color

The Edit Fill command sets the *fill*, or primary background color. The default fill color is black. Before any copy or move operations, always set the background fill color to match the graphic you're working on.

1. At the Inset Main Menu, load a graphic into memory or blank the screen to draw a new graphic.
2. At the Inset Main Menu, type EF (Edit Fill).
3. Use the arrow keys to highlight your choice for primary background fill.
4. Press the Enter key.

Erasing unwanted portions of a graphic

The Erase commands allow you to selectively erase portions of any graphic. You can also remove the unwanted parts of a clipped graphic. After you clip the graphic, simply erase everything except what is to print.

As with Copy or Move procedures, the portion to erase is marked with a rectangle. Everything inside the rectangle is deleted when you press the Enter key.

1. View the graphic.
2. At the Inset Main Menu, type EE (Edit Erase).
3. A cross hair will appear onscreen. Use the arrow keys or the mouse to draw a rectangle across the portion of the graphic being erased. Then press the Enter key.
4. Repeat step 3 as many times as needed until you've erased all you intend to erase.
5. Press the Esc key to exit.

All erasures made with these steps aren't permanently removed from the graphic until the next time you save the graphic file. So you can escape without saving and the graphic will be unchanged. If you aren't sure how much to erase, then delete and save in stages.

The graphic editor options

The graphic editor has five options to control the drawing and erasing defaults on such things as line width and background color.

Draw Clear Sets the draw and fill border colors used while drawing a graphic. The specific color values are controlled by the palette used.

Erase Clear Sets the color used to fill in after erasing a block from a graphic. The specific color values are controlled by the palette used.

Palette Sets the color palette or spectrum used by the edit draw and erase commands. Each palette is a different group of colors that can be shown onscreen at one time. The palette determines which colors are available. Changing the palette affects printing only when using a color printer.

Width   Sets the line width for both erase and draw. The available values are between 1 and 8. The visual width is determined by the size of the monitor used, and the actual width depends on expanded size of the graphic.

Clear   Clears the monitor screen and sets or resets the graphic mode being used to view or draw graphics. Choices include all modes supported by the installed monitor.

Printing a graphic with Inset

There are six command selections under the Print command on the Inset Main Menu. These are used to start the printing and to fine-control elements of printing.

Go   This command starts printing the selected .PIX file. If no .PIX file is being viewed, Inset prints a graphic screen dump of everything currently onscreen using the setup printer. It also uses whatever Modify, Edit, Print, and Output settings are current. If printing in color, Inset prints with current color and palette settings—what you see is what you get.

Margin   This command sets the left output margin in inches and decimal fractions of an inch. The default is 0.0 inch. You can set negative or positive values. This is for printing with Inset only. It controls the distance that a graphic prints from the left edge of the hardcopy. It's not necessary to reset this margin when printing graphics in WordStar documents. Graphics in WordStar documents are positioned by the location of the graphics tag.

Formfeed   The Formfeed command tells your printer to execute a standard formfeed. The printer must be online, or Inset will lock up your computer.

Down   This command tells your printer to execute a standard linefeed. The printer must be online, or Inset will lock up.

Up   The Up command specifies a reverse linefeed. This command works only if the printer has the capability.

Top   The Top command tells your printer that the current line is the top of the page. Each repetition moves the form or page in order to set the top of form before beginning printing. Depending on the printer, it will send either an incremental or full linefeed.

Aborting the Inset print runoff

There's no command or option for aborting a print runoff once you start it through Inset. In fact, once Inset starts printing a graphic, there seems no way to stop it short of rebooting the computer. Taking the printer offline or turning the printer off has no effect. Inset simply waits until the printer is online again, and doggedly continues printing until the entire graphic is finished.

Controlling print output

There are five commands under Output on the Inset Main Menu. These are for specific control over how the hardcopy prints. They include: Offset, Pitch, Quality, Driver, and Fast Files.

Offset

The Offset command sets the relative column offset or position of graphics when printing them with Inset. The unit of measure is columns and the default setting is 0. The relative offset is the same thing as the page offset. This is the distance from the left edge of the paper. The left margin begins at the page offset. Inset's default left margin is 0.0 inches.

Pitch

The Pitch command sets the printing pitch. Pitch is the number of characters or columns per inch. The default is normally 10 pitch (or 10 characters per inch), but you can specify whatever you want Inset to use.

When printing graphics in WordStar documents, Inset uses the pitch of the current font. The pitch setting controls the width of columns for defining image size in columns. If you use column numbers to position graphics tags, make sure the pitch is the same as your printer's pitch setting.

Pitch affects the resolution and appearance of the printed graphic by widening or narrowing it. Results vary from printer to printer. For example, If you set a graphic's width to 24 columns, and the pitch is 10 cpi, the printed image will be 2.4 inches wide. But if the pitch is 12 cpi, the printed image will be 2 inches wide.

Quality

The Quality command lets you toggle between Draft and Letter (letter-quality) printing. This mainly applies to dot-matrix printers. Laser printers use high resolution printing by default.

Obviously, the quality depends on what kind of output your printer is capable of producing. Draft will print graphics in the draft mode of the printer you're using and Letter will print in the printer's high-resolution mode.

Driver

The Driver command lets you select a different printer without having to change the default printer with SETUP. This is useful if you have more than one printer connected to the computer. The option applies only to graphics printed with Inset. It has no effect on a graphic printed in a WordStar document. WordStar uses whatever printer is tagged to the document.

Fast files

The Fast File command allows you to temporarily toggle fast file creation on and off. The default setting is on, but you can change this with SETUP. When the option is on, Inset creates a fast file the first time you print an image. This file has the same filename as the graphic file, but is given an .FST extension. These files are stored in the same directory as the .PIX files. If you turn this option off, the fast files aren't created automatically when you print the graphic.

- You can print a fast file graphic between 3 – 16 times faster than the first printing of the graphic.
- If you modify the image, or print it with a different printer, then Inset won't use the .FST file for that printing. Instead, Inset will create a new .FST file containing those changes.
- Unless you change the name of the .PIX file when you modify and save it, a new .FST file will overwrite the old version.
- The size of a .FST file depends on the size of the printed image. If you're printing a graphic bigger than a full page, the fast file might take up more space than the original .PIX file. If you're clipping part of a .PIX file, and printing it an inch or less wide, the .FST file should be considerably smaller than its .PIX file.

Tip: Don't permanently stockpile seldom-used graphics on your hard drive. These fast files take up additional space that you could use for something else. Periodically copy them to an archive floppy, and delete them from the hard drive. Copy them back to your hard drive as needed.

Using Inset's built-in help

Inset has a built-in help feature to provide you with information on each feature. For an overview of the Inset help feature, select Help from the Inset Main Menu. For detailed help:

1. Call the menu with the feature you need help on.
2. Press the F1 key.
3. Read the help message, then press any key to return to Inset.

Changing the setup

Inset comes with a utility program called SETUP.COM, which you can use to change the choices you made when you put Inset on the hard drive. While the SETUP program is running, you can change any or all of the settings. This is useful if you've changed monitors or printers since your first installation—or you find you've simply installed Inset incorrectly.

1. Boot your computer and change to the Inset subdirectory of your
   WordStar directory. (At the DOS prompt, type CD \ WS \ INSET and
   press the Enter key.)
2. At the DOS prompt, type SETUP and press the Enter key.
3. The Hardware Configuration Setup Menu will appear, displaying the
   current setup status. Follow the onscreen directions to change any or all
   of the Inset settings. You can, at any time, press the Esc key to Quit
   without making or saving changes.
4. When finished making changes, press the F10 key to save them.

Inset setup options

This section discusses the setup options available to Inset. Where practical,
detailed descriptions are given. The answers you provide here determine the
default settings for how Inset functions.

Selecting a monitor

It's important to indicate the correct type and make of monitor during the setup
procedure. Inset self-adjusts according to the kind of graphics board you've told it
to use. So if you tell it the wrong hardware, the graphics it captures might not look
like you want them to.

If you don't see your particular monitor listed on the Screen Driver Installation Menu, select the type of monitor closest to your own. The three most commonly used graphics modes are described below. Even if you have a special
monitor, it might also use one of the three common types.

IBM Color Graphics Adapter   This is industry-standard CGA. It has four
different display modes. The 80-column and 40-column CGAs are text modes.
Text mode can't display graphic images. The other two are graphics modes.
Medium resolution is 320×200 pixels in four colors. High resolution is
640×200 pixels in two colors.

IBM Enhanced Graphics Adapter   EGA has seven display modes. The
first four are identical to CGA. The additional modes are 640×350 pixels and
640×200 pixels (both with 16 colors), and 640×350 with 4 colors. The
$640 \times 350 \times 4$ mode is a monochrome mode with blinking. To use this mode,
select the EGAMONO screen driver.

Video Graphics Adapter   This is VGA mode. It supports CGA and EGA
modes, plus 640×480 with either 2 or 4 colors.

Selecting the screen mode

This option tells Inset which display mode to use as a default when you invoke it
inside programs other than WordStar. Some programs, like Lotus 1-2-3 and Auto-

CAD, don't tell Inset which display mode to use. So you must use SETUP to tell Inset the mode to use as its override setting.

The choices available depend entirely on the type of monitor and graphics display you've selected. Through SETUP, you can select any screen mode available to your monitor.

Tip: If you're having trouble with a screen mode while using the override pop-up keys Alt−left Shift−I, try setting the screen mode to Current. This tells Inset not to override and use the currently active screen mode.

Selecting a printer

This selects only the printer used by Inset's built-in printing option. Your choice here has no effect on how the graphic is printed by WordStar. When you tag a graphic to a WordStar file and print with WordStar, the hardcopy always goes to the printer selected by WordStar.

Selecting black-and-white or color printing

The default is B&W. Select Color only if you have a color printer, and intend to print graphics in color.

Selecting the buffer size

Selecting 4K buffers sets the number of buffers, or pages (at 4K per page) reserved in memory before using disk space. The default setting is the minimum needed for your computer. A higher number increases the operation speed, while using more memory. If you're using a very high-resolution printer (a laser printer or color printer), try increasing the buffers by 1 or 2.

Selecting a printer port to use

This selects only the printer port used by Inset's built-in printing option. Your choice here has no effect on how the graphic is printed by WordStar. LPT1 is the standard used by parallel printers, and COM1 is the standard serial port. The only reasons to change to a different port are when your printer is connected to a different port or if some other device is using the LPT1 or COM1 ports.

Selecting the width for printing

Select 80 columns for standard 8¹/₂-inch wide paper. 132-column width is for 11-inch paper, or for printing graphics in rotated or landscape mode.

Selecting printing quality

This sets the default for the printer output selection, either Letter or Draft. Letter-quality printing uses the highest quality resolution your printer can print. Draft quality uses a lower quality resolution, but prints faster. Save letter quality for final hardcopy, and use draft for intermediary versions.

Selecting printing pitch

This sets the default for the Output Pitch selection. See *Pitch* under *Controlling print output*, previously in this chapter.

Setting the .PIX directory path

This option allows you to specify a common directory for all your .PIX files. If you don't set a default here, Inset will store the captured graphics files in whatever directory is current at capture time. If you specify a directory here, then all your .PIX files are stored in one place.

WordStar, however, is set to look for .PIX files in the \ WS \ INSET subdirectory. When you issue the command Ctrl−P∗, Inset looks only in this subdirectory—regardless of the current directory or specification in SETUP. Therefore, set the .PIX directory path as \ WS \ INSET. Then all your graphics are stored where WordStar can get them easily.

Setting a temporary directory path

Inset's temporary directory is where overflow files are stored when you're short of disk space. Make sure you name an existing directory or subdirectory. If you've installed Inset as a companion program, the default setting is \ WS \ INSET.

Note: When you install Inset with WSSETUP, it automatically defines the temporary directory as the Inset subdirectory of your WordStar program directory. I recommend that you leave this setting as is. Changing it might interfere with Inset operation within WordStar.

Defining the pop-up keys

The default pop-up keys left Shift−Ctrl invoke Inset when it's used with programs other than WordStar. You press them to make the Inset Main Menu appear. This setup option allows you to define other keys to invoke Inset. The only reason for changing the default pop-up keys is when some other program you work with also uses left Shift−Ctrl as command keys.

Tip: Avoid using these pop-up keys while working with WordStar documents. They can interfere with some mouse drivers, resulting in an invisible mouse pointer when you return to the document. If this happens, use Ctrl−P& to view the graphic, and then exit to WordStar.

Defining a default macro

If you use Inset the same way every time you invoke it, you can create a default macro to execute functions automatically whenever you press the appropriate keys. A default macro is built from a series of Inset commands. It's a fairly complex process, so I'll just give you some basic information:

- The format for an Inset macro is simply what you'd type at the Inset menus to accomplish a specific procedure.
- To select an Inset option through the keyboard, you type the first letter of its name. Use those same keystrokes, in the same order, in defining the macro.
- All letters must be in uppercase, and typed into the space provided for them on the Hardware Configuration Setup Menu.

There are five additional characters you can use to fine-control the macro. They're as follows, with brief descriptions of their function:

Command	Function
;	Same as pressing the Enter key.
^	Same as pressing the Esc key.
#	Pauses the macro execution until you press the Enter key. Allows the macro to pause, for example, in order for a filename to be typed in, and then resumes its function.
{	Moves the cursor one place to the left.
}	Moves the cursor one place to the right.

A macro can save time and frustration if you're a frequent user of Inset. It will perform repetitious tasks at computer speed. However, once you define a macro, Inset uses it whenever you invoke it. In order to use Inset normally, you must use SETUP to remove the macro definition.

Defining the override macro

Inset comes with an override macro that runs when you press Alt−left Shift−I to invoke Inset. If you installed Inset with WSSETUP, this macro is supposed to contain all the available graphics modes available to your graphics board.

Tip: If you're using Inset inside WordStar, the override macro can interfere with WordStar and sometimes cause problems with the mouse driver, forcing you to reinstall it. And Inset might not remain memory-resident permanently. If Inset isn't memory-resident, the Alt−left Shift−I keys call the pull-down Insert Menu instead.

Selecting the keyboard mode

The keyboard mode is used to help Inset work within some programs that interfere with its normal operation. Some programs prevent Inset from receiving the pop-up keystrokes to invoke it. Through SETUP, you can set Inset to "grab" the keystrokes before other programs can get them. There are three different keyboard modes:

Passive   This is the default mode. It assumes that no program interferes with Inset. This should be your choice whenever possible.

Semi-active   If you can't invoke Inset with the passive mode, try the semi-active mode. It's almost as safe as the passive, but adapts Inset to work with programs like Lotus 1-2-3 and Symphony. However, semi-active can interfere with other memory-resident programs (like your mouse driver and WordStar itself if you've made it memory-resident). If this mode interferes with other programs you use, then switch to semi-active only long enough to capture the graphics you need.

Active   When you can't invoke Inset with either of the two modes, try the fully active mode. But use it only long enough to capture the graphics you need. The active mode frequently interferes with other programs, especially other memory-resident programs.

Selecting a different version of Inset

Inset has four different versions: Small, Medium, Full, and Capture Only. You can select between two of them—Small and Full—through SETUP, and use it as the default every time you use Inset.

Full   Loads and uses all Inset commands and options.

Small   loads Inset without its graphic editing capabilities. The Edit Menu and its options don't appear on the Inset Main Menu. You can still capture graphic images and use the other Inset options. The small version uses 15K less of RAM than the full version.

Note: If you've set Inset to use an IBM MONO monitor, it will default automatically to the small version. This is because you can't edit graphics on an IBM monochrome monitor.

You can change between versions without changing the default in SETUP. The keys for running the different versions are given in the table below:

Loading command	Version
INSET/f	Full
INSET/s	Small
INSET/m	Medium
INSET/c	Capture Only

Setting the maximum .PIX size

This option sets the maximum memory size of your .PIX file images. A smaller size will decrease the memory used by Inset. The default .PIX size is 110K. The minimum size is 15K and the maximum size is 447K.

The .PIX memory size determines the maximum resolution of the images you capture. The default 110K is sufficient for most graphic images. Don't increase the maximum .PIX size unless you work with very large or high-resolution images. Those include graphics printed with laser or PostScript C printers.

Turning fast file creation on and off

This option controls whether or not Inset creates a fast file the first time you print an image. It's the same option as the one under the Output Menu. See the section *Fast files*, under *Controlling the print output*, earlier in this chapter.

Removing unnecessary files

When Inset is copied to the hard drive by WSSETUP, the entire program and all its support files are transferred. This includes drivers for every printer supported by Inset, and also every type of monitor. You don't need all of these to use Inset. You need only the ones for the particular printer and monitor connected to your computer. You can delete all the extra ones and use the space on disk for something else.

Deleting unwanted PRD files

Inset comes with a PDF, or printer driver file, for each printer it supports. You need only the PDFs for the printers you use. To delete unused PRD files, use the following steps:

1. At the DOS prompt, type CD \ WS \ INSET and press the Enter key.
2. All Inset printer driver files have a .PRD extension. To list them onscreen, type DIR /P *.PRD and then press the Enter key.
3. The list of available printer drivers will scroll onscreen, pausing when the screen is full, and continuing when you press any key. There should be 67 of them.
4. As you view this list of printer drivers, make a note of the ones that identify the printers you intend to use with Inset.
5. Now use the MS-DOS REN (rename) command to temporarily change the extensions on all the printer driver files you want to keep. Give them the extension .NEW to distinguish them from all the other printer drivers. The format is REN *filename*.PRD *filename*.NEW.
6. Once you've renamed the printer drivers you want to keep, you can safely delete all the others with a single command. Simply type DEL *.PRD and press the Enter key.
7. With the unwanted printer drivers deleted, go back and restore the original extensions to the renamed printer drivers. For each file, type REN *filename*.NEW *filename*.PRD and press the Enter key.

Tip: Before you delete the unwanted printer driver files, make a backup copy of them to a floppy disk. If you add a new printer later, you can install its driver by simply copying it from the backup disk.

Other files you can delete

Inset comes with a screen driver for every monitor it can use. Like the printer drivers, you can delete the extra drivers without affecting Inset. All the screen drivers have an .EXE extension—so you can list them onscreen with the following DOS command:

```
DIR /P \ WS \ INSET \ *.EXE
```

The screen driver names are EGA, VGA, HERC, and so on. You should be able to recognize the name of the screen driver you use by its similarity to the name of your monitor or graphics card. If you aren't sure, don't delete the screen drivers.

You can delete either I20F.EXE or I20S.EXE because Inset uses only one or the other (depending on how you set it up). Delete the capture-only version I20C.EXE if you don't plan to ever use it.

I20F.EXE   The full version of Inset. It's specified by SETUP if you have a graphics adapter card installed in your computer. Delete this if you never use the full version.

I20S.EXE   The small version of Inset. It's selected if you have a mono-chrome monitor without graphics display capability. Delete this if you never use the small version.

I20C.EXE   The capture-only version of Inset. This is used only if you have no graphics monitor to capture simple graphs and charts created from ASCII characters. Delete this if you never use the capture-only version.

Tip: Before you delete the unwanted .EXE files, make a backup copy of them to a floppy disk. If you decide to use a different version of Inset later, you can copy it from the backup disk.

Deleting WordStar graphic files

Heavy use of Page Preview with .PIX graphics uses up much of your hard drive's storage space. This makes it necessary to periodically clean up the hard drive.

The first time you preview a .PIX graphic with WordStar's Page Preview, WordStar builds a special WordStar graphic file containing information about the graphic image. These files have the same filename as the .PIX graphic, but are given the .WSG extension. They're stored in the Inset directory.

Using this WordStar graphic file, WordStar is able to quickly display the graphic on subsequent previews, instead of having to build it each time. This removes the annoyance of having to wait for the image to appear, but it creates a housekeeping problem on your hard drive.

These .WSG files can take up an incredible quantity of disk storage space. Depending on the resolution of the graphic created during conversion, the .WSG file can be enormous. It doesn't take long for them to fill a hard drive. For example, the 161K MONALISA.PIX file created a 565K MONALISA.WSG file on my machine. .WSG files should be in the PREVIEW subdirectory, and can be removed with DELCRT.EXE.

Inset doesn't come with a built-in way to clean out these files when no longer needed. You must delete them manually. You can do this from the DOS prompt, or through the Ctrl−KF DOS window. The following steps tell you how to do it while working on a document.

1. Change to the Inset subdirectory using Ctrl−KL.
2. Use Ctrl−KF to call the Run a DOS Command dialog box.
3. On the command line, type DEL \WS\INSET*.WSG and then press the Enter key.
4. WordStar will delete all the .WSG files and display the message *Press any key to return to WordStar*.

Deleting help messages

Finally, you can delete INSET.HLP if you don't plan to use Inset's built-in help feature. The help feature provides basic information about Inset features while the graphics program is onscreen. You'll want to keep the help feature until you're familiar with Inset.

Without the help feature, Inset uses less memory when it runs, so deleting INSET.HLP could help you use Inset when you're working at the limit of available RAM.

Converting graphics to .PIX format

This section discusses how to convert graphics from other programs to the Inset, or .PIX, format. There are two ways to run the conversion—either through WordStar with Ctrl−P* or from the DOS prompt of the C:\WS\INSET subdirectory.

If you have graphic files from other graphic programs that Inset supports, you can convert them to the .PIX format through WordStar. This is done with the insert graphics tag command, Ctrl−P* (or Alt−IG).

When you attempt to insert a graphics tag for a nonPIX graphic, WordStar displays the Convert Graphic dialog box. This dialog box displays the following message: *The graphic you have chosen is not in WordStar format. WordStar will convert the graphic to .PIX format.* You can either complete the conversion or exit to the document screen. You can exit at any time before the conversion begins by pressing the Esc key.

When you convert the graphic to the .PIX format, you can either use the default settings or select your own from the Convert Graphic Options dialog box. The latter gives you precise quality control over the graphic image produced during conversion. These conversion options, and the formats usable by Inset, are described in following sections.

1. Copy the graphic being converted to the C: \ WS \ INSET subdirectory.
2. To make the conversion, WordStar must be running and a document must be open for writing and editing.
3. Place the cursor where you want the graphics tag to be inserted in the WordStar text file.
4. Use Ctrl−P* to insert the graphics tag.
5. The Insert Graphic dialog box will appear. Below it is the list of available graphics files. Use the arrow keys to highlight the graphic being converted. Then press the Enter key.
6. Whenever the selected file isn't a .PIX file, WordStar will display the Convert Graphic dialog box. (If it isn't a usable graphics format, WordStar will tell you that it doesn't support the format.)
7. The dialog box displays the original filename and directory, plus the converted filename and directory. If you want, you can change the converted filename and directory. But you must give it a .PIX extension.
8. You can use the default conversion settings, or set your own conversion parameters. Use the up and down arrow keys to select your choice.

If you want to use the default settings, use Ctrl−K to start the conversion. When the conversion is completed, you'll be returned to the document screen, with the .PIX tag inserted. There are no further steps.

If you want to use custom settings, use the Tab key to highlight Options, and press the Enter key. The Convert Graphic Options dialog box will appear. Use the Tab key to move from item to item, typing in the setting you want to use. Use Shift−Tab to go back and correct mistakes. When all are set, highlight OK and press the Enter key. When the conversion is completed, you'll be returned to the document screen, with the .PIX tag inserted.

The Convert Graphic options

The number and type of options on the Convert Graphic Options dialog box have a direct effect on the quality of the graphic image produced during conversion. They also determine the length of time required to complete the conversion.

Note: If you change any of the options, the changes are saved to the TOPIX .SET file. They'll be displayed the next time you call the Convert Graphic Options dialog box.

Height The height of the graphic. The default, .00″, uses the height setting from the original file. You can set the height in inches (″), centimeters (cm), or points (pt).

Width The width of the graphic. The default, .00″, uses the width setting from the original file. Like the height, you can set the width in inches, centimeters, or points.

Aspect The aspect ratio is calculated by dividing the width by the height.

Use decimals to indicate fractional portions. The width and height of any graphic should be kept in proportion to one another. Getting the aspect ratio out of proportion can make the graphic taller and thinner, or shorter and wider.

Rotation   Rotation is available for vector graphics only. Set it here in degrees, counterclockwise from the original position. For example, 90 degrees will turn it sideways and 180 degrees will turn it upside-down.

Reverse B/W   Selecting this checkbox causes image inversion. In a black-and-white graphic, black will print white, and white will print black. In a gray or color graphic, foreground and background colors are switched (if explicitly identified). If colors aren't identified, the highest color number on the palette will be switched to the color zero.

Smoothness   Provides edge smoothing for the jagged appearance of raster graphics.

Ignore Background   When an image has a mixed, non-solid background, this option changes it to white during conversion.

Resolution   This controls the clarity of the graphic image created during conversion. Set the vertical and horizontal resolution in dots per inch, or dpi. Though not shown, the default is 300 dpi. The higher the resolution, the longer it takes to create the converted file. (300 dpi takes approximately five minutes.) You can set resolution as high as possible and let your printer sort it out, or set the resolution according to the capability of your printer.

Screen frequency   This option controls the number of gray levels in the graphic. Use the formula gray levels = (resolution ÷ screen frequency) ^{2}.

Contrast   This option controls the relative contrast from lightest to darkest, on a scale of -100 to 100. Increasing the contrast can make your graphics more vivid.

Brightness   This option controls the relative intensity of all colors on a scale of -100 to 100. Increasing the color intensity can make your graphics more vivid, but works only when using a color printer. Otherwise, the effect is similar to changing the contrast.

Colors   The choices are 2, 4, and 16 colors. The default is 16. If your printer can print varied gray-scale graphics, use the default. If not, try 2 or 4.

Process Type   This is the method used to make the conversion. The default is Snap, which matches colors in the graphic to the nearest available color during conversion. Snap produces a quick, high-contrast graphic. Halftone and Dither are good for converting color to black and white. Halftone uses standard diagonal pattern (good for high-resolution printing). Dither uses a more random pattern (best for low-resolution dot-matrix printers). Diffuse works best when the number of colors is reduced during conversion. Diffuse produces the highest resolution graphic, but takes the most time in conversion.

Color Processing   The default is Allow Color. This takes the graphic and converts it as is. Use this selection if you have a color printer. Select Force Gray to use a gray-level palette. Select Force B/W to print all colors as black and the background as white, with no shades of gray.

Formats that Inset can convert

WordStar and Inset can convert and use graphics from 27 different formats, and some 50 different applications. A chart of the different formats, and their filename extensions, is provided below:

Format type	Filename extension
Amiga ILBM	.IFF
ASCII	.TXT
AT&T	.ATT
AutoCAD	.DXF
CALS RASTER	.CAL
CompuServe Graphics	.GIF
Delux Paint	.LBM
Dr. Halo	.CUT
GEM Image	.IMG
GEM Metafile	.GEM
HP LaserJet	.DCL
HP Plotter	.DGL
INSET	.IGF
INSET	.PIX
GoFax Group 4	.KFX
LOTUS	.PIC
MacPaint	.MAC
MacPict	.PCT
CGM Metafile	.CGM
MicroGrafx	.DRW
MS Paint	.MSP
PC Paint Brush	.PCX
TIF	.TIF
Targa	.TGA
Tektronix Plot10	.P10
WordPerfect	.WPG

Troubleshooting Inset

This section discusses common problems encountered while using Inset, and provides possible solutions.

You can't load Inset from the DOS prompt

The Inset drive and directory must be current. This is normally C:\WS\INSET. The PRD file for the printer used by Inset must also be in this directory.

Inset won't run through WordStar

The command Ctrl−P& should run Inset through WordStar. Or you run it through the pull-down Utilities Menu. (You shouldn't encounter this problem if you installed Inset along with WordStar, or through WINSTALL's Add a Feature option.)

- Inset might not have been configured to work with your computer, monitor, and printer. Exit WordStar and run SETUP from the Inset subdirectory.
- WordStar might not have sufficient memory available to load and run Inset. Use Ctrl−O? to check the system status. Turn off auto-hyphenation with Ctrl−OH if it's active. To clear memory used by the spelling checker and thesaurus, exit WordStar and run it again.
- WordStar might not know where to find Inset's program files. Use WINSTALL to check and correct the assignment of WordStar search paths.
- If running other memory-resident programs, exit WordStar and remove them from memory. Once you determine which TSR interferes with Inset, don't use them both at the same time.

Pop-up keys don't invoke Inset

The appearance of the Inset command menu indicates that the program is active and ready to use. If the menu doesn't appear after you press the pop-up keys left Shift−Ctrl or Alt−left Shift−I, it means one of three things:

- Inset isn't loaded and memory-resident.
- The program you're capturing from is interfering with Inset.
- If you hear a beep, your program is in the middle of a DOS function.

If Inset isn't memory-resident, then load it. If your target program is running a DOS function, press the Enter key. If DOS is processing a command, wait until it's complete and try again.

Tip: When using Inset inside WordStar, it doesn't stay permanently memory-resident. You must run it periodically to reload it. Or just use Ctrl−P& to call it. You can check its status with the Ctrl−O? command.

If the target program is blocking Inset, try the alternative pop-up keys. (If left Shift−Ctrl doesn't work, try Alt−left Shift−I; or vice-versa.) If this doesn't solve the problem, run SETUP and try the semi-active keyboard mode. If it still doesn't work, try the active keyboard mode.

If you get some response onscreen when you press the pop-up keys, but the menu doesn't display correctly, Inset might be using the wrong display mode for the current screen. Repeat Alt+Left Shift+I several times. Each repetition, Inset rotates through the available screen modes. One of them should make the menu appear.

With some computers, Inset has trouble determining the presence of an attached mouse, which causes DOS error messages. If you see the message *Mouse installed* and you aren't using a mouse, the NOMOUSE.COM program might solve the problem. The steps for using NOMOUSE are:

1. At the DOS prompt, type CD \ WS \ INSET and press the Enter key.
2. Type NOMOUSE and press the Enter key.

A beep sounds while using Inset

You pressed an invalid key. Try again, and be sure to press the correct keys. The beep might also be telling you that Inset has completed a disk read or write, printing, or clipping functions.

A graphic doesn't print

Inset didn't find the printer. Make sure the printer is on and online, and the patch cables are secure. Make sure the .PRD file for the selected printer is in the Inset subdirectory. Run SETUP and make sure correct printer and port have been selected.

A graphic tagged in a document doesn't print

Check the graphics tag in the document. Make sure it identifies the correct directory path and .PIX file. When WSSETUP or WINSTALL copies Inset to your hard drive, it tells WordStar to look for all .PIX files in the \ WS \ INSET subdirectory. But the .PIX directory path isn't set to anything. So all .PIX files are saved on the current directory, but WordStar still looks for graphics in the Inset subdirectory. Exit WordStar and run Inset's SETUP, and set the .PIX directory path to \ WS \ INSET.

A graphic doesn't print correctly

If the graphic prints too tall and thin or too short and wide, the aspect ratio is probably set wrong. Change it using the Col/Row or Inches options of the Inset Expand command.

If the image still prints incorrectly, try a different line height or line spacing. You can also use the command .LH a to tell WordStar to set the line height automatically.

Tip: Make a habit of using the command .LH a, especially if printing with more than one size font. It allows WordStar to adjust your printer to fit specific printing needs.

If too much white space appears around the graphic, you need to modify it. Use the Clip option on the Modify menu to move the clip lines closer to the actual image. If the graphic appears fuzzy, check the image's screen colors and its settings for printer shades of gray.

You might also be using the wrong Inset printer driver. Run SETUP and check the selected printer driver. If it doesn't match the printer connected to your computer, correct it. This applies only if you're printing the graphic through Inset itself. Try printing the graphic through WordStar and see if it corrects the problem.

If horizontal lines in the graphic stagger left or right when printing it in a WordStar document, try using a different font above the graphics tag. Here too, you might use a different line height or line spacing for the graphic. WordStar recommends 6 lines per inch as the most reliable height.

A dot-matrix printer produces wavy graphics

Use the Modify option, and set Pass to *double*. This should fill in the waviness and make the graphic appear more solid.

A graphic prints in the wrong place

The position of the printed graphic is determined by the position of the graphics tag. Reposition the graphics tag and try again. Use the Page Preview feature (Ctrl−OP) to preview the graphic before printing the document. Turn on the Options Grid Display to get a more precise view of the graphic's printing position.

If the graphics tag is placed correctly, but the graphic still prints out of place, switch to a larger or smaller font above the graphic. (Remember to switch back to the correct font below the graphic.)

If you're printing a graphic image that's enlarged from its captured size, try printing it at its original size. Some printers can't print enlarged .PIX graphics correctly.

Also, view the graphic with Inset, and check how it's clipped. If the balance of the clipping isn't even, it might cause misprinting. Try moving the clip lines or clip the image tighter.

Only part of a graphic prints

The .FST file for this graphic might be damaged. Delete it from the hard drive and try again. If the right side of the graphic is missing, the column width might not be set wide enough. Run SETUP and change the width to 130 columns.

Though intended primarily for wide paper and landscape orientation, this might help on 8½-inch paper. Laser printers present special problems in printing graphics. It's possible to give even a laser printer "too much to handle."

- If the graphic truncates during printing, the laser printer might not have enough memory for the whole page.
- If you're using downloadable fonts, try removing fonts you aren't using in the document.
- If you're not using downloadable fonts, try reducing the size of the image or print fewer graphics per page. Printing graphics puts a burden on laser printers. Multiple graphics, even tiny ones, can overload the printer.
- If the remainder of the page below the graphic prints on the next sheet of paper, you might need to reset the printer. Read the user manual packaged with the printer.

The only satisfactory solutions to insufficient memory in a laser printer are to install more memory or to install a page-formatting expansion board in the computer.

If you have 512K or less memory in the laser printer, you just don't have enough memory to handle graphics printing. It takes a full megabyte of memory to adequately process a page of graphics. Two to four megabytes of RAM is recommended if you print documents using downloadable fonts and multiple graphics.

There are many excellent page-formatting expansion boards available. The JLaser board not only enhances graphics printing, but drastically reduces page printing time. LaserMaster makes the WinJet 800 board, which does all the above, plus enhancing your LaserJet printer to 800 dpi resolution.

Help messages don't appear

If you can't get the Help messages to appear, check the Inset subdirectory for the INSET.HLP file. If it isn't there, use the COPYWS.EXE utility program (on the the WordStar Installation disk) to restore the file.

20
CHAPTER

Using MailList with WordStar

This chapter covers MailList, a companion program that comes with WordStar 7. MailList is a simple program to use and understand. It doesn't require any in-depth explanations. Most of its functions are self-explanatory. You simply run it and use it.

The data files created by MailList, however, are intended for use with merge printing, and merge printing is the most complicated feature of WordStar. Understanding and using merge printing requires a comprehensive knowledge of Word-Star.

Introduction and overview

This section provides an introduction and overview of MailList. The information covers basic use of the program.

MailList is a utility program, and its sole function is writing data files used in merge printing. The resulting data files are identical to ones you can write and edit in WordStar's nondocument mode. The most important difference is that MailList puts a "template" onscreen, with clearly marked places for each item of information. All you do is type the information and press the Enter key to move the cursor to the next item. MailList records the items, and creates the data file record by record.

Running MailList through WordStar

MailList is an option on the Additional Menu, found under the Opening Menu7. It doesn't matter whether you're using control menus, or the newer pull-down menus. Simply select it from the menus, or type the letters AM at the Opening Menu.

Running MailList from the DOS prompt

You can also run and use MailList as a stand-alone program. A copy of the WSLIST.DTA file must be in the directory you boot from. Whenever it runs, MailList always defaults to the WSLIST form and the WSLIST.DTA data file. If you try to run MailList from a directory without WSLIST.DTA, you'll get the error message *Can't find WSLIST.DTA on drive x*. If you then press the Enter key, WordStar will create a new WSLIST.DTA file in the current directory.

Tip: This quirk of the program allows you to keep a separate mailing list in each subdirectory. When you boot WordStar from a directory with a WSLIST.DTA file in it, it uses only that data file. Data added to one such file remains separate from data files in any other subdirectory. But, because all these data files have the same name, you must take special precautions when backing up to floppy disks.

Using the MailList Main Menu

The MailList Main Menu, shown in Fig. 20-1, is both simple and self-explanatory. At the top of the screen is the status line, indicating the name of the onscreen dialog box, and the data file and form being used. There are eight options, each containing a highlighted letter. To select and execute an option, press the key corresponding to the highlighted letter.

```
FORM:C:WSLIST              M A I L L I S T   M E N U          C:WSLIST.DTA
┌─────────────────────────────────────────────────────┬───────────────┐
│                                                       │               │
│   Choose a data file      Locate records by number   │   F1  Help    │
│                                                       │               │
│   Add new records         Sort records               │   Quit        │
│                                                       │               │
│   View and edit records   Use another form            │               │
│                                                       │               │
└─────────────────────────────────────────────────────┴───────────────┘
              Press a highlighted letter.
```

20-1 MailList Main Menu.

Choose a data file MailList always defaults to the WSLIST.DTA file every time you run the program. To use a different data file, you must choose it from an onscreen list.

Add new records A record is the complete list of information for an individual or business on the mailing list. This is all stored on a single line in the data file.

View and Edit Records   Once you've added a new record and gone onto the next, this option lets you go back to add or correct information.

Locate Records by Number   Lets you go to a specific address record by typing in its number.

Sort Records   Allows sorting, or rearranging, of the entire data file using any item on the template as a sort key.

Use Another Form   MailList comes with two different templates, or forms. These are INVNTORY.DEF (inventory lists) and WSLIST.DEF (mailing lists). The default is always the mailing list form.

F1 Help   Calls help messages about the MailList features.

Quit   Exits MailList and returns you to the WordStar Opening Menu.

Choosing and creating different data files

The same command is used to either select a data file or create a new one. A list of available data files appears when you execute this option. To choose one, select it from the list. To create a new one, type in its name and press the Enter key.

MailList always defaults to the WSLIST.DEF form and the WSLIST.DTA data file. You can always create or select another data file with the Choose a Data File option on the MailList Main Menu.

1. At the MailList Main Menu, type C for Choose a Data File.
2. The Choose a Data File dialog box will appear, with the available data files listed below it (see Fig. 20-2). You can either choose an existing data file or create a new one.
3. To select another data file, use the arrow keys to highlight it. Then press the Enter key. To create a new data file, type in $1-8$ letters or numbers and press the Enter key. Don't add an extension. MailList always adds the .DTA extension automatically.
4. When you press the Enter key, the data file is selected and ready to use. You're returned to the MailList Main Menu.

There's no limit to the number of data files you can create. The only limit is the amount of space on your disk drive. You create and use data files on floppy disks as well as your hard drive. To use a different drive, simply precede the filename with the drive name.

Adding new records to a data file

The Add New Records command lets you do just what it says. The following steps briefly describe using it through WordStar's Opening Menu.

1. Run WordStar and, at the Opening Menu, type AM.
2. The MailList Menu will appear. If you don't want to use the default

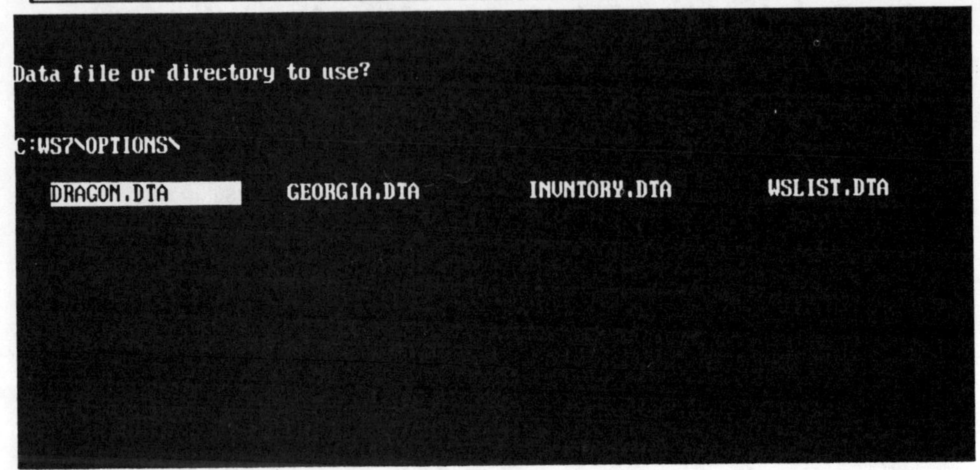

20-2   Choose a Data File dialog box.

form and data file, select another before continuing. These instructions
assume you're using the default.

3. Type A to add new records. A record is the complete set of information
   for one customer or individual in a mailing list.
4. The Add New Records dialog box will display the mailing list template,
   with the cursor on the record number (see Fig. 20-3). If this is a new
   data file, type 1 at the cursor. From now on, MailList will number your
   records automatically.
5. Type the information on the designated lines. Use the Enter key to move
   forward through the items and Shift−Tab to move backward and make
   corrections. Be sure everything is on its correct line.
6. When finished typing the mailing list record, use Ctrl−W to save the
   information to the data file. Then move to the next blank template.
7. When finished adding new records, press the Esc key.

It isn't necessary to type information in every item of the template. MailList
makes sure each record line has the same number of entries—even when some of
them are empty.

Viewing, correcting, and updating a data file

This section discusses viewing, correcting, and updating data files created with
MailList.

```
┌─────────────────────────────────────────────────────────────┬──────────────┐
│  ^Copy from previous record      ^Write/save record in file  │  F1   Help   │
│                                                              │              │
│                                                              │  Escape      │
└─────────────────────────────────────────────────────────────┴──────────────┘
```

Type data and press ←⎯⎤.

```
    Record Number: 00017                                    Date: 00/00/00
           Mr./Ms.: ____________________                          mm/dd/yy
First, Init., Last: ________________ __ ________________   Jr./M.D.: __________
             Title: ______________________________________

           Company: ______________________________________
    Address Line 1: ______________________________________
    Address Line 2: ______________________________________
  City, State, Zip: ________________________ __ __________
           Country: ______________________________________
           Phone-1: ______________________________________
           Phone-2: ______________________________________
User Fields-                Remarks-
1: ________________         ______________________________
2: ________________         ______________________________
3: ________________         ______________________________
```

20-3   Add New Records dialog box.

Viewing and editing records

The View and Edit Records option is used to update and correct the information in your MailList data files. You also can use it to simply browse through the records.

1. At the MailList Main Menu, type V.
2. When the View and Edit Records dialog box appears, the first record in the selected data file will appear onscreen (see Fig. 20-4). You can add to or correct this record—and any other record in the data file. Press the Enter key to move forward through the items, and Shift−Tab to move backward through the items.
3. Use Ctrl−N to go to the next record in the data file. Use Ctrl−P to return to the previous record in the data file.
4. When finished correcting or upgrading the information in any record, use Ctrl−W to write the changes to disk.
5. When finished correcting or upgrading records, press the Esc key to return to the MailList Main Menu.
6. When ready to exit MailList, type Q to return to WordStar.

There are seven commands on the View and Edit Records dialog box (including the three mentioned above):

Ctrl−P   Go to the preceding record in the data file.

Ctrl−N   Go to the following record in the data file.

```
 ^Previous/^Next record      ^Write/save modified record    F1   Help

 ^Erase record               ^Create/change record filter   Escape
```

Type any changes and press ◄─┘.

```
   Record Number: 00015                                      Date: 08/20/91
          Mr./Ms.: ___________________                             mm/dd/yy
First, Init., Last: ____________ __ _______________  Jr./M.D.: ____________
            Title: ___________________

         Company: Writers Guild Association (West)____
   Address Line 1: 9009 Bevery Blvd (Business Offices)_
   Address Line 2: 8955 Beverly Blvd (Register by Mail)
 City, State, Zip: West Hollywood________ CA_ 90048_____
          Country: ______________________
          Phone-1: (213) 205-2540 (business)___________
          Phone-2: (213) 550-1000 (information)________
User Fields-              Remarks-
1: ______________        registered "The Paladyn" _______________________
2: WGA #________          459194________________________________________
3: ______________
```

20-4 View and Edit Records dialog box.

Ctrl−E Erase the record currently displayed onscreen. The erasure doesn't become final until you write the changes to the data file.

Ctrl−W Write or save the changes in the record to storage in the data file.

Ctrl−C Create or change the record filter. This record filter lets you work with a specific group of records. When a filter is being used, only the records selected by the filter can be viewed. See the following section for more information on this.

F1 Press the F1 key to get a help message about this dialog box.

Esc Press the Esc key to exit the View and Edit Records dialog box.

Working with a specific group of addresses

There are times when you'll need to view or update only specific groups of records within your data files. The bigger your mailing lists, for example, the more often you'll want to work with only parts of it.

MailList has a built-in capability of displaying only specific records. This is accomplished by what's called a *record filter*. Each item on the template can serve as a key item in this filter. You specify a certain entry for either an item or a group of items, and then only the records that match these entries will be displayed.

Creating or changing a record filter

1. Select the data file to be viewed through a filter. Then, at the MailList Main Menu, type V to call the View and Edit Records dialog box.

2. Use Ctrl−C to call the Create or Change Filter dialog box.
3. On this dialog box, the template will appear with asterisks in place of the data for each item of information.
4. Press the Enter key to move to any item you want included in the filter. Then type in the information you want to match in that item. Do this in as many items as you need.
5. Use Ctrl−U to accept and start using the record filter. The View and Edit Records dialog box will appear, displaying the first record with the information stipulated by the record filter.
6. Change any information as necessary. Use Ctrl−W to save any changes you make, Ctrl−N to go to the next screen of information, and Ctrl−P to go back to any preceding screens.
7. When through making additions and corrections, save the changes one last time. Then press the Esc key to return to the MailList Main Menu.

Locating a record by its number

The Locate Records by Number command lets you go directly to any record by telling MailList its assigned record number. With it, you can locate any record by its number in the data file. This is also an alternative way to edit records because you can add to or change the record while it's onscreen. Just don't forget to save your changes with Ctrl−W.

1. At the MailList Main Menu, type L.
2. The Locate Records by Number dialog box will appear, showing a blank template onscreen (see Fig. 20-5). The cursor is on the record number.
3. Type in the number of the record you want to locate. Then press the Enter key.
4. MailList will find and display the record onscreen. You can add to or change the record while it's displayed. If you change any record, use Ctrl−W to write the changes to disk.
5. Use Ctrl−N to look at the next record or Ctrl−P to look at the preceding record.
6. When ready to exit, press the Esc key.

Sorting information in a data file

The Sort Records option is used to rearrange the order of the record lines in a MailList data file. This reorganizes the data for different needs. You can use any item on the template form as the key for sorting the information. For example, you could sort a file by name, zipcode, city, or state. Below are guidelines for sorting the information in data files.

20-5 Locate Records by Number dialog box.

- You must sort a data file after adding or deleting records to keep things in the intended order.
- You can create up to 32 different sorting orders, using different combinations of field items as keys. The sort order currently being used will appear at the bottom of the screen.
- Numbers in data items indicate their priority during a sort. The letters A or D in a data field item indicate that its contents are sorted in ascending or descending order.

When you view your mailing list, records will normally appear in the same order in which you added them. Sorting puts the records in any order you want. After sorting, records will appear in the new order until you add, delete, or re-sort the records.

Tip: When you merge print with these mailing lists, the form letters, labels, envelopes, etc., will print in the sorted order. Thus, re-sorting a mailing list data file before printing can change the printing order.

When you're sorting with MailList, it doesn't change the order of the information on the record line itself. What you're rearranging is the order in which the record lines themselves appear in the data file.

Sorting the records

1. Run MailList and choose the data file to be sorted.
2. At the MailList Main Menu, type S (Sort Records).

```
┌────────────────────────────────────────────────────────┬──────────────┐
│  ^Erase order               ^Use this order             │  F1    Help  │
│  ^Key field                 Ascend/Descend              │              │
│  ^Save sort order           ^Choose/Create sort order   │    Escape    │
└────────────────────────────────────────────────────────┴──────────────┘
              Press a highlighted letter or number.
```

```
     Record Number: 1111A *******************************    Date: ********
           Mr./Ms.: ******************                              mm/dd/yy
First, Init., Last: ************ *** 222222222222222222A Jr./M.D.: ************
             Title: ****************************************

           Company: *************************************
    Address Line 1: *************************************
    Address Line 2: *************************************
  City, State, Zip: ********************** *** **********
           Country: *************************************
           Phone-1: *************************************
           Phone-2: *************************************
User Fields-          Remarks-
1: ***************    ***********************************************************
2: ***************    ***********************************************************
3: ***************    ***********************************************************
      system fields: [**] [********]     Sort this field for yymmdd -->[******]
```

20-6   Sort Records dialog box.

3. The Sort Records dialog box will appear, as shown in Fig. 20-6. If a sort filter is attached to the data file, its name will be displayed on the status line.

4. Use the attached sort filter, select another, or change the sort options individually for this one-time sorting.

5. When ready, use Ctrl—U to accept the sort parameters you've selected and begin the sort. MailList will sort the records in the data file as directed.

6. Press the Esc key to return to the MailList Main Menu.

Sorting options

There are eight options on the Sort Records dialog box. These control the nature and order of the data file during and after sorting.

Erase Order   Use the Ctrl—E command to erase or delete the sort order currently selected.

Key Field   Marks the item or field at the cursor position as a key to sort the data file.

Save Sort Order   Saves a newly created sort order to disk. Also saves the existing sort order when changes have been made to it.

Use This Order   Tells MailList to use the selected sort order and sorting parameters, and to execute the sort.

Sorting information in a data file   **347**

Ascend/Descend   Tells MailList whether to use an ascending or descending order while sorting the data file. MailList uses alphanumeric sorting rules. In ascending, numbers precede letters (123abc). In descending, letters precede numbers (cba321).

Choose/Create Sort Order   Tells MailList which sorting order file to use, or whether to create and use a new sorting order file. You can create sorting order files using any combination of key fields and sorting parameters.

Get Help   Press the F1 key if you need information on the sorting options and commands.

Escape   Returns you to the MailList Main Menu.

Choosing or creating a sort order file

A sort order file is a permanent record of parameters and conditions used to sort a data file in a particular way. MailList comes with only a single sort order file, named RECORDNO. This sorts the records by their *record number*—the first item on the template.

It's common to sort lists for different purposes. For example: you might want to work on records in their order of record number, print letters or envelopes by zipcode or state, and print phone lists in alphabetical order. By creating and saving a sort order file, you can use the same set of parameters each time.

1. Run MailList and select the file to be sorted.
2. At the MailList Main Menu, type S to call the Sort Records dialog box.
3. Below the dialog box is a blank template showing the current sort order. This is the set of parameters last used to sort the contents of the data file.
4. Use Ctrl−C to call the Choose a Sort Order dialog box. It will appear with a list of available sort orders.
5. Highlight the sort order you want to use.
6. To create a new sort order, type in a 1−8 character name (using any combination of letters and numbers). Erase errors with the Backspace key.
7. When ready, press the Enter key.
8. MailList will return to the Sort Records dialog box. If you're creating a new sort order file, you must now define the sort order. Use any of the Sort Records options. When you're through defining the sort order, use Ctrl−S to save it to disk.

MailList doesn't save these sort record parameters to an individual file. Instead, they're all saved in the MAILSORT.OVR file in the C: \ WS \ OPTIONS directory. If you want to transfer the sort orders to another copy of WordStar, simply copy and transfer the overlay file.

Appending or dividing data files

There's no trick to either appending or dividing data files in order to create new data files. The data files created by MailList are identical to WordStar nondocuments, so you can open and edit them as nondocuments.

Remember the principle of boilerplate text. Once you've typed anything with WordStar or MailList and saved it to disk, you never have to type it again. You can use any part of a data file in any other data file.

Appending one data file to another

When appending one data file to another, always leave the original unchanged. Change to the C: \ WS \ OPTIONS subdirectory. Open a new nondocument, and save it under an identifying name. Be sure to give it the .DTA extension. Then use Ctrl−KR to read the existing data files into the empty one.

If you want to use only part of a data file, simply open it in a second window, mark it as a block, and use Ctrl−KA to copy the block to the new data file.

Once the appended data file is complete, use the Sort Records option of MailList to reorganize the file and get it in usable order.

Dividing data files into smaller ones

When dividing large data files into smaller ones, always leave the original unchanged. If you have large mailing lists, it's a simple matter to use them to create special-purpose data files. In fact, there are two ways to do it:

- Change to the C: \ WS \ OPTIONS subdirectory. Open a new nondocument, and save it under an identifying name. Be sure to give it the .DTA extension. Open the data file in the second window. Mark the usable portions as blocks, and then use Ctrl−KA to copy the blocks between windows.
- Change to the C: \ WS \ OPTIONS subdirectory. Open a new nondocument, and save it under an identifying name. Be sure to give it the .DTA extension. Use Ctrl−KR to copy the entire data file into it. Then go through it line by line, and delete every record you don't want in it.

When you've finished building the new data file, use the Sort Records option to rearrange the file, and put its information in the order you need it.

21
CHAPTER

Using TelMerge
with WordStar

This chapter provides fundamental and detailed information about the TelMerge companion program. It explains the program and tells how to use it. When possible, everyday uses are given.

Most of the specific information on your modem is supplied by the modem's user manual. The Hayes modem is the industry standard, and TelMerge comes preprogrammed to use this standard. When using a nonHayes modem, you must find the settings and parameters in its documentation.

TelMerge is a telecommunications program. With it, and a connected modem, you can link your computer via telephone lines to the outside world. You can transmit text files, data files, and program files to other computers. You can communicate with other computer users around the world.

You can send e-mail (electronic mail). You can work at home and send your results to mainframe computers using dial-up lines. You can link with online services like CompuServe, Prodigy, and so on. The possibilities are growing all the time.

There are many online services and private bulletin boards to choose from. Once you connect a modem to your computer, you're literally connected to the world. You can dial up and "talk" to any one of millions of computers, thousands of bulletin boards and other services, in hundreds of countries. The possibilities are almost endless.

You can use your PC to reach out to near or distant parts of the world in the same way ham radio operators have done for years. You can talk to and touch the lives of people you'll never meet face to face. Your only limitation is the knowledge it takes to make TelMerge compatible with all the available systems and uses.

Setting up your modem

TelMerge comes set up to use the default switch settings on a Hayes modem. These are the industry-standard settings. You don't have to change them unless your modem uses different factory defaults.

Hayes 300-baud and 1200-baud modems are free-standing and use a serial port and cable from your computer. To use these modems without a serial port, you must have an asynchronous communications adapter or *async card*. You can buy one from any large computer store or mail-order house.

Follow the instructions in the Hayes manual to connect the modem to your computer. These modems have a row of switches, behind the front panel, that come with the settings shown in Table 21-1 for 300, 1200, and 1200B modems. (The Hayes 1200B is an internal modem that plugs into one of your computer's expansion slots.)

If you work in an office environment, it's possible that you have a telephone with a built-in modem. This lets you use the same telephone line for both voice and computer communication. TelMerge can use it if it's Hayes-compatible. It might require special initialization.

Table 21-1   Switch settings for 300, 1200, and 1200B Hayes modems.

Number	Switch setting	Switch function
300- and 1200-baud modems		
1	Down	TelMerge ignores the data terminal ready (DTR) signal
2	Up	Puts result codes (CONNECT, RING, etc.) into English words . . .
3	Down	. . . and sends them to your computer
4	Up	Shows modem commands onscreen while dialing
5	Down	Modem doesn't automatically answer incoming calls
6	Down	TelMerge ignores the carrier
7	Up	Sets modem for single-line phone
8	Down	Turns on modem command recognition
1200B modems		
1	On	Selects the communication port (ON = COM2 port)
2	Off	Sets modem for single-line phone
3	Off	TelMerge ignores the carrier

Installing and customizing TelMerge

To use TelMerge with WordStar, its program files must be in the C:\WS\ OPTIONS subdirectory. If you haven't already installed WordStar, use WSSET-

UP and copy TelMerge along with WordStar to your hard drive. If the TelMerge program files aren't already installed, use WINSTALL to copy them to your drive.

Change to your WordStar program directory. Run WINSTALL, and use the Add or Remove a Feature option to copy the TelMerge program files. Follow the onscreen directions, and have your master disks ready. WINSTALL puts everything where it should be.

Setting up the TELMERGE.SYS file

Before you can use the automatic online phone numbers in TelMerge, you must set up the TELMERGE.SYS file. This file is found in the C: \ WS \ OPTIONS subdirectory (or equivalent).

1. Run WordStar, and change to the C: \ WS \ OPTIONS subdirectory through the Opening Menu.
2. Type N to open a nondocument.
3. Type TELMERGE.SYS and press the Enter key.
4. Go to the end of the file, and find the script template for the online service you intend to use. If you're adding a new service, use the NEW script as a model for creating a new script for the service.
5. When through making setup changes, save the file with Ctrl−KD and return to the Opening Menu. The changes are now in effect for use with TelMerge.

The contents of TELMERGE.SYS

This file contains the control scripts (or pretyped commands) for using TelMerge telecommunications. By typing in the correct information, you can customize TelMerge for your system and the online services you use. The changes take effect after you save the file and start TelMerge. Make your changes to the appropriate areas below:

System The System section controls the default transmission rate, communications port, and other settings for your computer and modem. TelMerge uses the settings from this section unless others are supplied by a SERVICE script or a .TEL file.

Menu The Menu section contains the TelMerge Communications Menu, the list of online services appearing when you start TelMerge. Use it to list only the services you use.

Service The Service section contains logon scripts for each service in the Communications Menu (plus any other scripts you want to store there). Before using a service, you must add to its password or other information. This information comes when you sign up with the service.

Note: When running TelMerge as a stand-alone program from the MS-DOS prompt, a copy of the TELMERGE.SYS must be in the directory from which it's running. The .TEL or individual controls files must also be in this directory. Otherwise, TelMerge won't be able to find them.

Keywords used in TELMERGE.SYS

The following is a complete list of keywords you can use in the TELMERGE.SYS file. See *Using TelMerge keywords*, later in this chapter, for definitions.

ADDLF	FILETY	INIT2	POSTMO
APPEND	FIRST	INTERA	PREFIX
ATDELA	FK	IOADDR	PRINT
ATTEN	FULLS	LABEL	PROMPT
AUTOLO	GRAPH	LINEDE	PROTOC
BITS	HANDSH	LOGFIL	QUIET
CALL	HANGCO	LOGGIN	SEND
CLS	HANGUP	MODEM	SERVIC
DUPLEX	HOLD	NETWOR	STOPS
EMUL	HOST	NUMBER	SUFFIX
END	IF	PARITY	TRY
ENDIF	IFNOT	PAUSE	USEDTR
EXIT	INIT	PORT	USER
WAIT			

The System section

Use the keywords in Table 21-2 to set basic system defaults. The factory-supplied settings work for most systems. If the setting for any keyword here doesn't match your system's requirements, replace it with one of the other choices listed for the keyword.

Use the settings you plan to use most of the time. If an online service needs different settings, use them in the service's script. Settings in a script override settings in the System section.

Note: Text following a { or ; in the TELMERGE.SYS file is a comment. It's for reference only; TelMerge ignores it.

The Menu section

Edit the Menu section to change the list of services on the TelMerge Communications Menu. If you add a service to the menu, you must also add a control script to the Service section.

While editing the Communications Menu, each line to appear onscreen must begin with the word *Say*, and the ¦symbol turns onscreen highlighting on or off.

The line Say¦NEW¦Add new service here is a template for the next service

Table 21-2 System default keywords.

Keyword	Function
Modem HAYES	Specifies a Hayes SmartModem. Other choices: HAYES2400, DIRECT, ANSWER, and ACOUSTIC
Port COM1	Indicates a modem connected to a COM1 serial port. Other choices: COM2, COM3, and COM4.
IOaddr 3F8	Hexadecimal value for I/O address of COM port. Use this to override the default for a COM port if needed. Defaults: COM1:3F8, COM2:2F8, COM3:3E8, and COM4:2E8. 200-3FF are allowed, but many are unavailable.
IRQ 4	Hexadecimal value for IRQ (interrupt request) of COM port. Use this to override the default for a COM port if needed. Defaults: COM1:4, COM2:3, COM3:4, and COM4:3. 2-7 are allowed, but some are reserved or unavailable.
Baud 1200	Specifies a baud rate of 1200. Other choices: 110, 300, 2400, 4800, and 9600. Logging on opens a logfile when you connect to the online service. All messages sent or received during the session are stored in this file.
Print YES	Sends incoming information from a session to your default printer, alternative printer, or a disk file. YES prints to your default printer. NO turns printing off. COM2 or LPT2 send printing to a different device. You can also type a filename to print to a file on disk.
LineDelay 2	Delays the specified number of tenths of a second after sending a line of text. The current setting is 2/10 second.
Emulate VT100	Emulates a mainframe terminal. Other choices: NONE and VIDTEX (VT52).
Graphic NO	Does not display graphics characters from online source. The other choice is YES.
UseDTR YES	Speeds the hang up. Modem switch must be set to use DTR, or data terminal ready.
Append YES	Adds logon of current session to the end of the old logfile, instead of starting a new logfile for each session. The other choice is NO.
Network TYMNET	Specifies the network you're using (if any) Other choices: TELENET and UNINET. Protocol XMCRC selects a file transfer protocol. If you don't include a protocol keyword, Xmodem checksum is used.

you add. Copy it to the line below, then replace the original line with the name of
your new service. Be sure to delete the semicolon from the line describing your
new service or it won't appear onscreen.

The Service section

The Service section contains logon scripts for the services on the Communications Menu. Type in the missing information for each online service to the right of
its keywords. Delete scripts you don't want, or write new script. The first script,
labeled NEW, is a dummy. You can use it as a template for the next script you
write.

If you've already created a .TEL file for a service, use WordStar's nondocument mode to insert it in this section, instead of typing the script from scratch.
Later, you can delete the .TEL file.

When you add a script file, remember to add its label to the Communications

Menu. You can use a completed script to call a service, even if it isn't on the menu. Simply type its three-character label at the Enter your selection prompt.

You can write script files to automate much of an online session, e.g., to send or ask for certain information, or to make several calls in succession. The keywords in Table 21-3 are useful for automating calls (see the TelMerge section of your WordStar manual for details).

Table 21-4 gives brief descriptions of the keywords used in the scripts of the service section.

Table 21-3   Keywords with which to automate TelMerge calls.

Keyword	Function
CALL	Dials the selected service now.
WAIT *word*	Awaits this word from the service after logon.
SEND *word*	Sends this word (or words) to the online service.
PAUSE *secs*	Waits this number of seconds.
QUIET *secs*	Waits this number of seconds after remote has finished sending.
FILESEND *filename*	Sends the specified file.
LOGGING ON/OFF	Turns logging ON or OFF at this point in session.
PRINT ON/OFF	Turns printing ON or OFF at this point in session.
HANGUP	Hangs up phone, gets ready for another call.

Table 21-4   Service keywords.

Keyword	Function
ANSWERBACK *string*	Sends your personal ID code in response to a telex "who are you" request.
BAUD *rate*	Sets the transmission rate used for this online service.
END	Ignores subsequent commands in this script.
HOSTID *string*	Issues up to 30 characters as a network's internal phone number for the service you're calling. An example is HOSTID CPS.
INTERACTIVE *number*	Specifies the phone number of a telex real-time system.
LABEL *string*	Characters you type to start calling this online service.
LOGFILE *filename*	Names the file that records an online session. An example is LOGFILE MCI.LOG.
LOGGING ON/OFF	Turns automatic recording of an online session on or off.
NETWORK *name*	Telephone network used to contact this online service. Examples: TYMNET, Telenet, and UNINET.
NUMBER *number*	Phone number to dial.
PASSWORD *string*	Password required by the service (30-character maximum).
SERVICE *string*	Name of the service you're dialing. It appears on the status line while you're connected (32-characters maximum).
USERID *string*	User identification code required by the online service used (30-character maximum.

Factory-supplied script templates

This section contains sample script templates supplied with TelMerge from the factory. They're found in the TELMERGE.SYS file in the C: \ WS \ OPTIONS subdirectory (or its equivalent, if you've put WordStar in a different directory). The information in each script template defines the parameters used by TelMerge to call up and log on to a specific online service.

Following is the NEW template you can use as a template for new scripts in TELMERGE.SYS:

```
Label        NEW
Service
Number
Logfile
Userid
Password
End
```

Now, following is a list of some of the sample scripts for various online services and companies. You can use them to call and log on to the service. If you don't have a local service number, you might want to call your operator and find out which is the cheapest number to call. Here are the scripts:

CIS

```
Label        CIS
Service      CIS
Number
Userid
Password
Logfile      CIS.LOG
End
```

ESL

```
Label        ESL
Service      ESL
Number
Userid       {01EasyLinkID UserName Password
Baud         300
Logfile      ESL.LOG
Logging      ON
End
```

ITT

```
Label        ITT
Service      ITT
Number
```

Interactive
Answerback
Password
Logfile   ITT.LOG
Baud   300
End

MCI Mail

Label   MCI
Service   MCI
Number
Userid
Password
Logfile   MCI.LOG
End

Official Airline Guides

Label   OAG
Network
Hostid
Service   OAG
Number
Userid
Password
Logfile   OAG.LOG
Baud   300
End

ONTYME Messaging Service

Label   ONT
Network   TYMNET
Hostid
Service   ONT
Number
Userid
Password
Logfile   ONT.LOG
Baud   300
End

RCA Telex and TELEXTRA

Label   RCA
Service   RCA
Number

```
Interactive
Answerback
Password
Logfile          RCA.LOG
Baud             300
End
```

You can also use several WordStar-supplied scripts to access different modes or functions. This one lets you call and log on to the Direct Connect mode:

```
Label            DIR
Modem            DIRECT
Service          TelMerge
End
```

The ANS script template allows you to set up TelMerge in the automatic answer mode:

```
Label            ANS
Service          TELM
Modem            ANSWER
End
```

And the TEL script template calls and logs on to another TelMerge user. Then the F4 Send key lets you send files to the other user with error checking.

```
Label            TEL
Service          TelMerge
Logfile          TEL.LOG
Number
End
```

Running and using TelMerge

TelMerge is a WordStar companion program. It's available through the Additional Menu, on the Opening Menu.

At the Opening Menu, simply type the letters AT. The TelMerge Communication Menu will appear, displaying the online services available to you (see Fig. 21-1). Before you can use them, You must open and edit the TELMERGE.SYS file to define them. These options are as follows:

```
CIS       CompuServe Information Service
ITT       ITT Telex and TIMETRAN
OAG       Official Airline Guides
RCA       RCA Telex and TELEXTRA
DIR       Direct Connect Mode
ESL       EasyLink by Western Union
```

COMMUNICATIONS MENU

CIS CompuServe Information Service   ESL EasyLink by Western Union

ITT ITT Telex and TIMETRAN   MCI MCI Mail

OAG Official Airline Guides   ONT ONTYME Messaging Service

RCA RCA Telex and TELEXTRA   TEL Another TelMerge User

DIR Direct Connect Mode   ANS Answer mode

Enter your selection: █

21-1 TelMerge Main Menu.

MCI	MCI Mail
ONT	ONTYME Messaging Service
TEL	Another TelMerge User
ANS	Answer Mode

To dial a remote service with TelMerge, type one of the three-letter code names on the Communications Menu. Then press the Enter key. TelMerge will retrieve the phone number from its control file and log onto the service for you.

If you haven't added this information to the control file, you can press the F5 key to define and use an individual service file that contains the information necessary to dial out and log on to the desired service or individual. TelMerge will dial the phone, using the information provided from the preset parameters or from the .TEL file you created or selected.

You can also run and use TelMerge as a stand-alone program. Run it from any MS-DOS prompt, providing the proper directory is specified in the path. Use it exactly as you would through WordStar. The only difference is that, when you exit TelMerge, you return to the DOS prompt instead of WordStar's Opening Menu.

1. At any DOS prompt, type TELMERGE.
2. Press the Enter key.
3. TelMerge will load and run the program.

Note: When running TelMerge as a stand-alone program from an MS-DOS prompt, a copy of the TELMERGE.SYS must be in the directory from which it's running. The .TEL or individual controls files must also be in this directory. Otherwise, TelMerge won't be able to find them.

Onscreen function key commands

Following the list of options on the TelMerge Communications Menu is the onscreen template of function key commands. These include:

F1   Get help messages
F5   Select another person to call by creating or using a control file
F8   Go online with your modem
F10   Exit TelMerge and return to the Opening Menu

Creating individual service files

An individual service file is simply a set of parameters you can use to call a specific online service or an individual computer. It serves as a shortcut, so you don't have to edit TELMERGE.SYS or type in the information every time you want to call someone new.

1. At the Opening Menu, simply type the letters AT. The TelMerge Communication Menu will appear, displaying the online services available to you.
2. Press the F5 key to call the Choose/Create Control File dialog box. The names of the available .TEL files will appear below it.
3. Press the Enter key.
4. A prompt line will appear. At the top of the screen is the message *Creating a file to save filing information*. Type in the 1-character to 8-character name of the new control file, and press the Enter key. Telmerge adds the .TEL extension automatically.
5. TelMerge will ask for the telephone number. Type in the area code and phone number; then press the Enter key.
6. TelMerge will ask for the service name. Type it in and press the Enter key.
7. TelMerge will ask for the user ID. If one is required, type it in. If not, leave it blank. Press the Enter key.
8. TelMerge will ask for the password. If one is required, type it in. If not, leave it blank. Press the Enter key.
9. TelMerge will ask for the baud rate. The default is 1200. To accept it, press the Enter key. To use another, type it in, and press the Enter key.
10. TelMerge will ask for the COM port. The default is COM1. To accept it, press the Enter key. To use another, type it in and press the Enter key.
11. TelMerge will ask for the network being used. If one is required, type it in. If not, leave it blank. Press the Enter key.
12. TelMerge will ask for the host ID. This means "Tell the network who to call." If one is required, type it in. If not, leave it blank. Press the Enter key.

13. TelMerge will save the information in the file you named, and use this information to dial the number. If the information is correct and the line isn't busy, the other end will answer and you'll be linked to their computer.

Talking to other computers

You don't need to read this if you use TelMerge exclusively for e-mail through an e-mail service. You can always use the F4 Send function to transfer data. This section will tell you how to talk with mainframe computers and send program files.

Methods of data transfer

There are two general methods for sending and receiving data between computers: ASCII transfer and protocol transfer.

ASCII transfer allows for sending and receiving standard text files. This method doesn't work for files containing print controls, binary files, and program files. Every communications program and subscription telecommunications service supports ASCII transfers. Protocol transfer lets you send text files with print controls in place. It also allows for binary and program files.

A protocol is a set of standard rules or conventions for exchanging data between two computers. Both computers must be using the same protocol for the transfer to work. TelMerge uses the XMODEM checksum and XMODEM CRC protocols.

Selecting a transfer protocol

TelMerge has protocol information installed on the online function keys. There are two sets of online function keys. You must be using Set 2 to select a protocol. When the online screen appears, use the F2 key to toggle between Set 1 and Set 2.

Function key	Protocol selected
F4	The Send option uses the CompuServe A protocol.
F4	If you use any other service, this key does an ASCII file transfer.
F5	This Receive option uses the XMODEM protocol.
F6	This Send option uses the XMODEM protocol.

Talking to mainframe computers

Mainframe computers expect to talk to terminals, not to personal computers. Fortunately, TelMerge can emulate two popular terminals, and therefore fool mainframes. TelMerge might not support some communication controls required by mainframes.

The DEC VT100 is a favored terminal in many businesses. It uses ASCII transfer. This is TelMerge's default emulation. You don't need to add it to your TELMERGE.SYS control file script. The VIDTEX or VT52 is another ASCII terminal. When a mainframe computer requires this emulation, put the command EMULATE VIDTEX in the control file script.

If you encounter logon problems in half-duplex mode, add the following keywords to your service script: DUPLEX HALF and ADDLF NO. The ADDLF NO keyword prevents TelMerge from sending a line feed after every carriage return sent from the keyboard.

Online databases

Online data services, like CompuServe, are really large mainframe computers with local stations distributed throughout the country. When you talk to or through CompuServe, you're using a mainframe computer.

When you send e-mail and text files to an online database, use F4 Send to use ASCII mode and send them without print controls. When making a protocol transfer, the data service usually asks you which protocol you're using.

Talking to another PC

TelMerge is especially good for communication between personal computers and computer bulletin boards using asychronous communications software. Add these services to TelMerge just like any other new service.

Use the F4 Send key to transfer ASCII files. For other files, use a protocol transfer, e.g., XMODEM checksum or CRC. Modify your TELMERGE.SYS file as follows:

1. Open TELMERGE.SYS as a nondocument. Add the new service name to the Communications Menu. (To save time, try replacing a service you don't use.)
2. If you're the receiving computer, create a service entry named RECEIVE. In it, set the modem switch setting for auto-answer to ON. When using TelMerge, select RECEIVE and wait for the sending computer to call and establish communication.
3. If you're the sending computer, create a service entry named SENDER. In it, set the parameters for the computer you're going to talk to. When using TelMerge, select SENDER and wait for the receiving computer to come online.
4. To talk to the other computer, type your message onscreen. The message will transmit as you type.
5. To transmit an ASCII text file, press the F4 key to send. TelMerge will ask for the name of a file to transmit. Type the filename and press the Enter key. (Include drive and path, if necessary.)

6. For protocol transfer, tell the receiver you're about to send a file. When they're ready, press the F6 key to select XM SND. Type the filename and press the Enter key. (Include drive and path, if necessary.)

7. When the transfer is complete, TelMerge will tell you so with an onscreen message.

Receiving an ASCII file is automatic. To receive a protocol transfer, tell the sender to begin the file transfer. When TelMerge says it's ready, press F5 to select XM REC. Type the filename when asked for it. After the file transmission is complete, the sender or receiver must press F10 twice to disconnect.

During an ASCII file transfer, you see the text onscreen as it comes from the modem. If you have logging on capability, the file is automatically stored in the logfile on disk. During a protocol transfer, incoming data is caught in a buffer and written to disk without being displayed onscreen. Instead, the status line displays the name of the file created.

Using your PC for data collection

You can set up your PC to receive data automatically. This is done with the Auto-Answer option. You can then leave the computer unattended, and let TelMerge work for you.

Auto-receiving ASCII file transfers

To set up TelMerge for data collection, add a control file script with the following information:

```
Label       name
Say         Now ready for data collection
Service     TELMERGE
Logfile     COLLECT.LOG Modem ANSWER
Duplex      HALF
End
```

When your modem is in answer mode, TelMerge will treat all incoming calls as a single session. This adds each call to the same logfile. If your callers are using TelMerge, they can add the following script to their SENDING control files to make each file they send create a new file on disk.

```
Label       name of the control file
Say         Sending file to name of receiver
Service     TELMERGE
Duplex      HALF
Number      receiver's phone number
End
```

Being a bulletin-board system operator

When you're receiving files in the Answer mode, this makes you the SysOp, or *system operator*. It's up to you to maintain control over the contents of the directory.

Run TelMerge from a directory with no files in it—one dedicated specifically to receiving files. This defines a bulletin board to use. The main reason for this is protecting files. In both ASCII and protocol transfers, if a caller sends a file with the same name as one already in the directory, the incoming file will overwrite the existing file.

If you expect a lot of incoming calls and many files, be sure your disk has sufficient storage space remaining to handle the traffic. If your disk fills up, TelMerge will disconnect the caller and all subsequent callers won't be able to get through.

The simplest way to avoid this is to make periodic checkups on the directory. Copy the received files to archive on floppy disks. Then delete them from the hard drive.

Talking to another TelMerge user

Protocol transfers between two computers running TelMerge use the CompuServe A protocol. This is the default. When linked with another computer running TelMerge, set up your script as follows:

```
Label      TMERGE2
Say        Now connected to another TelMerge user
Service    TELMERGE
Duplex     HALF
End
```

If you're sending files, you can name the file when it reaches the receiver. You can use the wildcard character * to send multiple files with the same extension, or all the files in a disk or directory. During a PC to PC transfer, whichever user presses the F4 Send key supplies the filename for the other user.

You can tell TelMerge to transfer files directly between computers without modems. Both serial ports must be connected with a special serial cable, and both computers must be using TelMerge. The control file script must be set up as follows:

```
Label      DIRECT
Say        Now set up for direct connection
Service    TELMERGE
Modem      DIRECT
Duplex     HALF
End
```

With the system set up for direct transfer, send the files as though you were making the transfer over a telephone line.

Shortcuts through reprogramming

This section is for advanced users of TelMerge. It tells you how to reprogram TelMerge for nonstandard operations, online services, and hardware/software systems. It also tells you how to create shortcut solutions to time-consuming procedures.

TelMerge comes set up, or programmed, to work efficiently with the common online services most PC owners use. It also comes set up to "talk" through a Hayes or compatible modem. This is done through the script instructions in the TELMERGE.SYS control file.

While Hayes modem compatibility is the standard for North American PC users, there are other modem manufacturers worldwide. Reprogramming TelMerge allows you to use those other modems.

Among other things, you can create shortcuts by reprogramming TelMerge. This allows you to customize it to meet your personal needs, or to execute repetitive tasks automatically. The shortcuts are most useful when using the TELMERGE.SYS file to call online services. The shortcuts include:

- Programming functions keys used with TelMerge.
- Rewriting TELMERGE.SYS to ask for a password, logfile name, printer, or disk output.
- Setting up automated online sessions, which send and receive files without your having to type responses at the keyboard—even exiting from the online service.
- Using the Snap Shot and ShoFil options.

Programming TelMerge function keys

The F7 and F8 keys (on Set 2) are used by TelMerge while it's online with a service. You can reprogram them with functions specific to the service used. These include passwords, commands, or other information the online system needs. You'll find this information in the user manual that comes with the subscription to the service.

An example is given below for defining F7 to check mail on the CompuServe EasyPlex service:

1. Open TELMERGE.SYS as a WordStar nondocument.
2. Scroll through the document until you come to the section beginning with *Label CIS*.
3. At any point after the SAY statement, press the Enter key to add a blank line.

4. Type fk1r,email go_mail on this blank line.
5. Save the file and exit.

The *fk1* stands for the F7 key. The *R* sends a carriage return at the end of the command. When you go online with CompuServe, *Email* becomes the new onscreen label for the F7 key. The *go_mail* and the carriage return are the commands executed when you press the key while logged onto the CompuServe EasyPlex electronic mail service.

Rewriting TELMERGE.SYS

TelMerge uses a built-in scripting language to control what it does while dialing out and going online. You can even use conditional commands like IF, ELSE, and IFNOT to react when predetermined circumstances are met. Before you rewrite TELMERGE.SYS, however, you need to have some experience with the processes and steps of using a particular online service. Only then can you understand what needs automation.

Below is an example of using the scripting language to make TelMerge ask you for a password at the appropriate time and place.

```
SAY          Password?
HOLD         ?
IF           =your password
GOTO         GoodPassword
ELSE
SAY          Sorry. Incorrect password.
EXIT
ENDIF
LABEL        GoodPassword
PASSWORD     !
```

Below is an example of using the scripting language to make TelMerge ask you for a logfile name. Insert the following lines at the correct section of your control file, just after the LABEL line giving the service name.

```
LOGFILE      myfile.log
SAY          What do you want to call this session's logfile?
SAY
SAY          Type a filename and press the Enter key.
SAY          or press Enter now to use filename "MYFILE.LOG."
SAY
HOLD         ?
LOGFILE      !
```

Below is an example of using the scripting language to make TelMerge ask you for printer or print-to-disk output.

```
PRINT         myfile.prn
SAY           Type the name for the diskfile
SAY           or type "P" to use the printer
HOLD          ?
IF            =P
PRINT         Yes
ELSE
PRINT         !
```

Changing the logon script

One of the most convenient things you can do is to set up TelMerge to issue commands automatically. This keeps the amount of typing you have to do during the session to a minimum.

TelMerge issues the commands in a control file in a specific order. If you use a service that needs information in a different order, or input TelMerge doesn't "understand," use the LOGON keyword to customize the logon procedure.

For example, a service requires logon with network ID number, your first name, last name, and your password. Use LOGON *networkid* ¦ *firstname* ¦ *lastname* ¦*password* to automate the process. Each pipe sign, or ¦, in the LOGON command tells TelMerge to issue a carriage return, then wait for a prompt by the service before continuing.

LOGON is one of the last keywords TelMerge checks. Remember to remove the lines containing the network ID and your password from the control file.

Automating an entire session

TelMerge can automatically dial a service and request information or files you need. You can even program it to make several calls in sequence. The keywords in Table 21-5 work together to create automated sessions.

When TelMerge finds a CALL keyword during an automated session, it dials the phone number given in the preceding script, and then executes the following keywords. When it reaches HANGUP, it searches for CALL in any following script. If CALL is found, TelMerge dials the indicated service. If no CALL is found, you're exited to the Communications Menu.

If you press F10 during an automated session, the session cancels and TelMerge hangs up the phone. If you press any key but F10 during an automated session, TelMerge ends the call and switches to normal interactive mode. You can automate the first part of a session, then continue in interactive mode by omitting the HANGUP statement after the last CALL in the control file. Below is an example of an automated TelMerge session:

```
SERVICE       mci
PRINT         yes NUMBER 1 (800) 555-3030
```

Table 21-5 Keywords for an automated session.

Keyword	Description
PREMODEM	
INIT	Modem initialization
INIT2	Additional modem initialization
PREFIX	Dial, the default is ATDT
NUMBER	(or **INTERACTIVE** if interactive telex)
SUFFIX	Wait for carrier reply from modem
ATTENTION	
ATDELAY *n*	Wait *n* tenths of a second
TERMINAL	If on a network
HOSTID	If on a network
USERID	(or **ANSWERBACK** for Telex)
PASSWORD	
LOGON	
FILESEND	In a normal session, TelMerge enters interactive online mode. In an automated session, CALL, WAIT, SEND, PAUSE, QUIET, FILESEND, and HANGUP take effect. Press F10 to hangup the phone, unless there's a HANGUP keyword after the CALL keyword.
HANGCOM	Modem hangs up.
POSTMODEM	

```
BAUD       2400
USERID     dragonrose
LOGGING    on
CALL
WAIT       command:
SEND       dowj
WAIT       query
SEND       //djnews
WAIT       help
SEND       .I/EDP 01
PAUSE      2
QUIET      1
SEND       ^M
PAUSE      2
QUIET      1
SEND       //cqe
WAIT       query
SEND       wstar
WAIT       return
SEND       f
```

PAUSE	2
QUIET	1
SEND	disc
WAIT	command:
SEND	exit

Exiting while online

There are times online when you might need to check a file before sending it. You can do so by exiting a service without having to log off.

1. Use the Edit option by pressing the F9 key.
2. This exits you and takes you to the WordStar Opening Menu.
3. Open and edit the document as necessary. Then save and exit the document.
4. Run TelMerge again from the Opening Menu.
5. Press the F8 key to go online again. Select the service from the menu.
6. Press any key after you reconnect. This skips the automatic logon, because the remote computer thinks you've been online all the time.

Using Snap Shot

The Snap Shot option lets you grab the current screen and either save it to your logfile or store it in buffer memory. The Snap Shot command is on Set 1 of the online function keys.

1. At the TelMerge online screen, use F2 to select Set 1 of the online function keys.
2. Press F5 to take a snapshot of the current screen. This calls the Snap Shot Menu, shown in Fig. 21-2.

```
┌──────────────────────Snap Shot Menu──────────────────────┐
│                                                           │
│   1-5  Save screen in one of 5 memory locations to recall later │
│   ←┘   Write screen to the logfile                        │
│   Esc  Exit Snap Shot                                     │
│                                                           │
└───────────────────────────────────────────────────────────┘
```

21-2 Snap Shot Menu.

3. TelMerge asks you whether you want to save to memory or to the logfile. Type a number, from 1 to 5, to save it to memory. Or press the Enter key to save it to the logfile.

You can use Snap Shot while viewing a file with ShoFil. You can store from 1 to 5 screens in memory, but they'll be lost when you exit the session. If you want to keep snapshots permanently, save them to the logfile. You can always open the logfile as a document and copy them to other files.

Using ShoFil

The ShoFil option allows you to open a file for a read-only session. The file's contents appear onscreen and you can scroll through it. The command to use it is on F8 in Set 2 of the online function keys.

Pressing F8 calls the File To Display dialog box. Press the Enter key to view the logfile. To view another file, type in its drive, path, and filename. Then press the Enter key. The selected file will begin scrolling rapidly by onscreen.

Use the F1 key to pause or continue scrolling. Use the F5 key to take a snapshot of a screen page. Use the F2 key to cancel the ShoFil viewing. Then press any key to return to the online session.

Using TelMerge keywords

The keywords are commands or statements that control actions TelMerge takes during transmission of data or text files. You can use them to fine-tune TelMerge for different needs and purposes. All the keywords are explained in this section.

Tip: While you're working with TelMerge, you can display current settings for keywords by pressing the F1 key.

The order in which keywords are sent

The following list shows the order of keywords as they're sent during a dial-up. Of these, only NUMBER is mandatory; the remainder are optional.

Special-purpose characters

The left brace character indicates a nonfunction comment. All characters on the line are ignored. Use this to insert comments in a control file.

The question mark tells TelMerge to wait for your response from the keyboard. If followed by a number, your response is limited to this number of characters. When used with HOLD, it puts the characters you type in a memory buffer. You can use ! to assign these characters later as an entry for a keyword. (See the HOLD keyword.)

The exclamation mark assigns the contents of the above memory buffer to the preceding keyword in the control file script.

The following special characters can be used in modem keywords: INIT, INIT1, PREMODEM, POSTMODEM, and HANGUP. They can also be used with the logon keywords TERMINAL, HOSTID, USERID, PASSWORD, and LOGON.

A /d causes a delay of one second. A caret (^) sends the next character as a control command; for example, ^E sends Ctrl−E. A double caret sends a caret to the online service or receiver. When the caret is the last character of a string, no carriage return is sent after the string, e.g., Y^ sends Y without a carriage return.

List of keywords

Following is an alphabetical listing of all the TelMerge keywords. Definitions and examples are given.

ADDLF (yes/no)   Tells TelMerge whether to send a line feed following a carriage return from the keyboard. Use it to log on to some half-duplex services like the LEXIS legal service. Without ADDLF NO, an online service might hang up or not respond when you press the Enter key.

ANSWERBACK *ID code*   Sends your personal ID code at a "who are you" request. This is for telex systems only. Telex-based services request your ID to verify you dialed correctly. The answerback code is provided by the service when you sign up.

APPEND (yes/no)   When YES, this command adds information from new sessions to the logfile named in the control file. It allows messages or data to accumulate, instead of starting a new logfile. Use APPEND in automated sessions when making several calls or to avoid renaming .LOG files when you want to save them.

ATDELAY *n*   Pauses before sending the first character. The *n* is in tenths of a second. Some networks require a delay before the first character (usually ATTENTION) can be received. If the online service doesn't respond when you first call, increase *n* to 20 or 30.

ATTENTION *c*   Issues any special character (*c*) required by an online service at the beginning of transmission. For example, ATTENTION ^C would send a Ctrl−C, and ATTENTION ^M would send a carriage return. You can specify a maximum of six characters, but to use more than one, put each ATTENTION on a separate line. This is supplied automatically for preprogrammed online services, and if the NETWORK keyword is used.

AUTOLOG (yes/no)   Toggles the autolog feature on and off. The default is YES. When testing a new control file, you might want to disable autolog.

BAUD *n*   Sets the data transmission rate between modems. The *n* is the baud rate. The default is either 1200 or 2400. TelMerge can use six different baud rates. The lower the baud rate, the slower the transmission. When an online service (CompuServe, Prodigy, etc.) supports alternative baud rates, there are commonly different phone numbers and charges for each.

BITS *n*   Sets the number of bits sent for each character. The default for *n* is 8. The bit rate is already set for preprogrammed online services.

CALL   Used instead of END in automated TelMerge sessions to call an online service. All information for dialing a service should be above the CALL keyword in the control file. When CALL is processed, TelMerge dials the phone number, attempts to log on, and then executes any subsequent keywords in the control file.

CLS   The clear screen command. Wipes the screen and sends the cursor to the upper left corner onscreen.

DUPLEX (half/full)   Determines which computer controls the onscreen character display as you type. The default is FULL. Characters can display on either your PC or the host computer. With DUPLEX FULL, the host computer echoes your characters onscreen as you type them. With DUPLEX HALF, your PC echoes the characters. Most preprogrammed online services already have the proper DUPLEX setting.

ELSE   Used with IF for condition reprogramming of TelMerge. See IF.

EMULATE *terminal*   Lets your PC behave like a mainframe or minicomputer terminal. The choices are VT100, VIDTEX, and NONE. VT100 emulation accepts and displays ANSI standard sequences for cursor movement, colors, and special attributes. These include foreground and background colors, high intensity, foreground and background reverse, and underlining. Some bulletin boards use these sequences for color screens with highlighted text. VIDTEX or VT 52 emulation accepts and displays sequences for cursor movement and printer enable/disable.

END   Tells TelMerge to ignore any subsequent commands and execute the control file. END is similar to the CALL keyword. TelMerge begins at the service label, reads and executes the keyword commands up to the END command, and then dials. CALL is for automated sessions, while END is for interactive sessions.

ENDIF *string*   Tests for specific condition (a string of characters) and proceeds if the specified string is found. See IF.

EXIT   Stops and returns to WordStar. Use with IF or ELSE to end a session if preset conditions aren't met. See IF.

FILESEND *filename*   Sends an ASCII or WordStar file you've specified. In automated sessions, TelMerge sends the file automatically when the FILESEND statement is processed. In interactive sessions (no CALL keyword used), TelMerge sends the file after you log on.

FIRST *character*   Waits for a specific character from the online service before displaying characters onscreen. Some online services send a preliminary series of characters before the prompt you need to read. Use FIRST as a filter to eliminate the preliminary stuff and begin with the first character you want displayed. For example, if you specify P as the first character, your session will most likely begin with *Please log in*.

FK*n*, *label command*   Programs a function key to issue a specific command. The *n* is the key number. The *label* defines the onscreen label for the function key. The *command* is the function to execute. For example: FK1R, EMAIL GO_Mail. In this example, EMAIL defines the label, R sends a carriage return at the end of the command, and GO_Mail is the command to go to the electronic mail menu. Your command can be up to 60 characters long. FK1=F7 and FK2=F8.

FULLSCREEN (yes/no)   Works with EMULATE to improve VT100 and

VIDTEX screen emulation. The default is YES. Removes the status line to allow 24-line display. The status line is temporarily displayed when you toggle F7 logging or F8 printing. Then the line is either overwritten or scrolls offscreen.

GOTO *label name*   Goes to a specific LABEL in the control file. GOTO is always used with LABEL.

GRAPHIC (yes/no)   The default is YES. When active, it specifies that the extended character set be used for graphic display. Some e-mail services and bulletin boards use extended characters to improve screen appearance.

HANGCOM *command*   Sends hangup instructions to the modem. For example, HANGCOM ATH tells your modem to hang up. If your modem uses a different hang up command, use HANGCOM to define it in your control file. See USEDTR.

HANGUP   Used in automated sessions to hang up the phone. To add another call to the automated session, use NUMBER below HANGUP. Then specify any keywords different from the last call. Then use CALL.

HARDCOPY   See PRINT.

HOLD ?   Pauses and waits for user input from the keyboard, and then stores it in a buffer. The buffer temporarily stores up to 80 characters until the end of the session. Use the buffer information as the response to another keyword by typing ! after the keyword.

HOSTID *code*   Issues the host ID code when the online service requires it. The default is no code. The code can be up to 30 characters. It's the network's internal phone number for the service you call. Include this keyword if you're using NETWORK in the control file.

IF, IFNOT, ELSE, ENDIF   These keywords are used for conditional reprogramming of TelMerge. They work together to test for preset conditions.

IFNOT *string*   Tests for a specific condition (a string of characters) and proceeds if the specified string isn't found.

INCLUDE *filename*   Interrupts the current control file script and runs the script in the included file. Use INCLUDE to pass control between multiple files. When the included script is completed, TelMerge returns to the original script at the line following INCLUDE. In effect, this command allows you to use other scripts as subroutines of your new control file. Use as many INCLUDE statements as needed. You can nest up to four files.

INIT *string*   Initializes the modem before dialing. Use this to set an initialization string when it differs from the default set for your modem. The default is INIT ATE1. In this default, AT prepares the modem for a command, E1 echoes input to the screen, and a carriage return follows the string. Add \ d to delay one second.

INIT 2 *string*   Used to add other initialization information. It must follow INIT. For example: INIT2 ATS 7=20. In this example, AT prepares the modem for the command and S tells it to set the number of seconds TelMerge waits for a carrier signal after dialing. The Hayes default is 20 seconds.

INTERACTIVE *phone number*   Defines the phone number of a telex real-time or interactive service. Phone numbers can be up to 30 characters long. Include all dialing prefixes and area codes. The default dialing mode is tone. Precede the number with a P to indicate pulse dialing to the Hayes SmartModem. See the modem manual for information about special punctuation marks. For the Hayes SmartModem, a comma causes a two-second delay. This is useful when dialing out through local PBXs, which usually require a second dialtone.

LABEL *name*   Marks a place in the control file as the destination for a GOTO keyword command. Each GOTO statement must have a corresponding LABEL, or the dialup will fail. LABELS can contain up to 80 characters.

LINEDELAY *n*   Causes the transmission to pause after each line sent with the F4 Send key. The *n* is the time in tenths of a second. Use this keyword if the receiving computer can't keep up with your sending speed. Or lower your baud rate.

LOGFILE *filename*   Assigns the name to the file that records all messages, etc., in an online session. TELMERGE.LOG is the default logfile name. With session logging turned on, everything you send and receive is recorded in the logfile. This gives you a permanent record of all your online conversations. Unless you include the APPEND YES keyword statement in your control file, TelMerge will create a new logfile at the start of each session. The previous version gets renamed with the .SAV extension. If you want to keep a logfile, you must rename or copy it to an archive floppy.

LOGGING (on /off)   Sets the startup status of the logging function. You can turn logging on or off during any online session by pressing the F7 Logging key. When logging is on, a logfile is opened and everything is recorded.

LOGON *string* \ *string* \ *string*   Automates the logon process and much of the online session. It replaces the USERID, PASSWORD, TERMINAL, and HOSTID keywords. It automates the session up to the point of logon. You can automate the rest of the session with the CALL, WAIT, and SEND keywords. LOGON can have up to 80 characters. The *string* stands for what you have to type up to the point of logon. The backslashes separate individual items or fields. Use the pipe symbol to send a carriage return and wait for the next prompt.

MODEM *model*   Defines the type of modem used. The default is the Hayes SmartModem, which automatically dials and answers. Use HAYES 2400 for the Hayes SmartModem 2400. Use ACOUSTIC for acoustic modems, and dial the service manually. If ACOUSTIC is used, AUTOLOG should be set to NO for the service, even if the control file script has the AUTOLOG YES statement. You must also complete logon manually. Use DIRECT for all direct-cable-connection transmissions. Use ANSWER or AUTOMATIC for all PC-to-PC transmissions.

NETWORK *netname* This instructs TelMerge to call a specific network service. For example, NETWORK TYMNET or NETWORK TELENET. Using a network allows communication with an online service through a local phone call, rather than a long-distance call. When using NETWORK, you must also use HOSTID, but you don't have to use ATTENTION or TERMINAL.

NUMBER *phonenumber* This defines the phone number used to call a specific service. The number can be up to 38 characters long to accommodate all long-distance carriers. Include any dialing prefix your PBX system requires (usually a 9) and the area code. Set up the phone number as though you were dialing it manually. The format is 1(706)555-1234 for normal long-distance and 9,,(706)555-1234 for PBX systems. The two commas after the 9 prefix create two one-second delays for a PBX that requires a second dialtone. The dialing default is tone dialing. To use a pulse dialing phone, type P as the first character in the number. Tip: If you have call-waiting and your phone company has a code to disable it, you can include this code in the phone number before the area code. The call-waiting service will be reinstated when you hang up.

PARITY *setting* This selects an error-checking procedure. The default is NONE for most online services, and is set internally for the preprogrammed services. The other choices are ODD, EVEN, ZERO, and ONE. When defining parameters for a new service, change the parity to the setting required by the service.

PASSWORD *password* This defines the password issued automatically to the online service. Passwords are initially issued by the service when you first subscribe. Most allow you to change the password to something of your own choice. (Change your password periodically for security reasons.) The password can be up to 30 characters long. If you don't want passwords included automatically, add the three lines SAY What is your password, PASSWORD ?, and CLS to have TelMerge ask for your password before you log on.

PAUSE *n* Pauses for *n* seconds to allow online service to begin sending. Sometimes TelMerge will send its commands faster than the online service can respond. Use this keyword in automated session when you don't know how quickly the service will respond to keyword commands. Try 3 to begin with, and increase or decrease as needed. PAUSE works with QUIET to ensure that the service finishes sending characters without interruptions from subsequent TelMerge keywords.

PORT *port* Defines the communications port used by your modem. The default is COM1. If your modem uses a different port, be sure to provide this information.

POSTMODE *parameters* Sends a series of characters to an electronic switch after a call is made, and usually restores the default settings of the modem. Use this keyword to initialize the modem for the next use. If a PREMODEM command tells switching equipment to use modem 3, then POSTMODEM can unhook modem 3 to make it available. For example: POSTMODEM ATE1 V1 ^M. In this example, ATE1 puts the modem in echo mode, V1 uses long responses or words instead of single characters, and ^M issues a carriage return.

PREFIX *prefix* Check your modem's manual for specific information about dialing prefixes. This keyword defines a condition for dialing a phone number. The default is PREFIX ATDT. The Hayes SmartModem uses the dial string, which is the prefix, the phone number, and the suffix. The PREFIX statement can be up to 30 characters long. Begin each one with AT, and end each with a dial command (DT for tone dialing or DP for pulse dialing). The command M0 silences the modem's speaker during dialing.

PREMODEM *commands* Sends a series of commands to the communications port before the modem setup commands are sent. A premodem command can have up to 30 characters. It can be sent to systems with electronic switches connecting several modems, phones with built-in modems, or a nonHayes modem requiring special setup for Hayes compatibility. Example: PREMODEM ^Z \ d \ d \ d. Many phones with built-in modems require Ctrl−Z. The \ d issues a one-second pause.

PRINT (yes/no/*filename***/***port***)** Automatically sends the text of an online session to your default WordStar printer. The default is NO. PRINT YES sends a record of your session to the default printer, PRINT *filename* sends the information to a file on disk, and PRINT *port* sends the information to a printer on a different port. Printing is normally set on for preprogrammed Telex services, and printing begins as soon as you log on. Toggle it off or on by pressing the F8 key.

PROMPT *character* This is used to add characters to the prompts TelMerge recognizes. Prompts can be up to 14 characters long. These prompt characters are @, =, !, ?, >, ^, and Q. Use PROMPT to add up to 9 new prompts.

PROTOCOL *protocol* This changes the file-transfer protocol used by a session. The F5, XM REC key on Set 2 defaults to XMODEM checksum protocol. To use the CRC protocol, add PROTOCOL XMCRC to the service script.

QUIET *n* Tells the system to wait until no character has been received for *n* seconds before executing the next instruction in the control file. Use this with PAUSE in an automated session.

SAY *text* Works like the remark command in MS-DOS. Displays the specified text as an onscreen message when you run TelMerge. Each SAY command can contain up to 80 characters and spaces. Create blank lines by using SAY without text.

SEND *text* sends the specified text to the remote service and issues a carriage return. The text is usually requests or commands to an online service. You'll find this information in the user manual for the service.

SERVICE *name* Executes a logon to a named service. It's a description of the information or data service that appears on the status line when you're connected to the service. It can be up to 32 characters long, but keep it short for your own convenience. The preprogrammed online services setup in TELMERGE .SYS are listed below as examples:

Service name	Full name
CIS	CompuServe
ESL	EasyLink
ITT	ITT Telex/Timetran
MCI	MCI Mail
OAG	Official Airline Guides
ONT	ONTYPE Messaging Service
RCA	RCA Telex/TELEXTRA
Telmerge	Any other TelMerge user

STOPS *n*   Sets the number, *n*, of stop bits used by a specific service. This keyword comes internally set for the preprogrammed services, and the default setting works for most services. Check the documentation for the service used for this setting when adding a new service to your control file.

SUFFIX *text*   Issues a post-dial command to the modem. The default is a carriage return. The SUFFIX follows the NUMBER command. For example, M0 is used with PREFIX to turn the modem speaker off before dialing, so use SUF-FIX M1 to turn the speaker on again. The Hayes SmartModem uses the dial string, which is the prefix, phone number, and suffix. See your modem user manual for specific information.

TERMINAL *text*   Defines your terminal type by specifying the equipment you're using. The text can be 1−6 characters. Use this during an automatic logon to a network. Don't use TERMINAL with a preprogrammed NETWORK keyword. Those terminal settings are internally programmed in TelMerge.

TRY *n*   Defines the number of times TelMerge redials a busy number before giving up. The *n* can be a number from 1 to 99. When TelMerge hears a busy signal, it waits approximately 45 seconds before redialing.

USEDTR (yes/no)   This tells TelMerge whether or not to use the DTR switch to hang up the modem. The default is NO. This command can be used only with modems compatible with the DTR switch. The Hayes 2400 modem supports the DTR switch, but requires special initialization. Use INIT2 AT&D3 in the control file. If the modem doesn't hang up when it should, then add USEDTR YES to your control file and set the modem to use DTR. For further information, see HANGCOM.

USERID *text*   Issues your identifying name when you log on to a subscription service. The text is the user identification code issued to you by the service. You must send this code each time you log on to the service. This keyword does it automatically. The USERID can have up to 30 characters.

WAIT *command*   Use this keyword for automated sessions. The computer

will wait for a particular command from the online service before executing the
next keyword in the control file. For example, WAIT *for* tells TelMerge to wait
until the word *for* is received from the online service before proceeding.

Common problems and solutions

This section describes common TelMerge problems and gives their solutions.

Problems with memory-resident programs

TelMerge sometimes has trouble running with TSR programs loaded in memory.
If you have problems using TelMerge, and TSRs are loaded, remove the memory-
resident programs and try again.

Connection problems

The following are common problems encountered while trying to dial out to an
online service:

The modem dials the phone, but there's no answer   The telephone number in the control file might be incorrect. Be sure to include the appropriate prefix
and area code. The prefix is 9 for a PBX and 1 for long distance.

The modem dials and connects, but TelMerge doesn't log on   There
might be something wrong with the control file. The ID or password is wrong, or
the baud rate setting is incorrect. You can also try increasing the character delay.
Set the ATDELAY keyword to 20 or 30.

Transmission is erratic, or cuts off when sending   The end-of-document
marker for this online service might have been unintentionally included somewhere in the text of the document. MCI uses a slash or / to indicate end of a document. Read the documentation for the online service, and find out what the
end-of-document marker is. Then open the document and use global search to
find and replace the offending character. If this isn't the solution, check the LINE-
DELAY keyword on your control file and try increasing it to 10 or more.

When connecting to a service, everything freezes   The PRINT keyword
might be set to YES, but the printer itself is either off or not online. Turn the
printer on and try again. This can also happen if you run TelMerge with memory-
resident programs active. Remove the TSRs from memory and run TelMerge
again.

Problems with the onscreen display

Below are common problems encountered with displaying messages and text on
your monitor screen during transmission:

Nothing you type appears onscreen   The online service being used
requires half duplex. Edit the control file and be sure to add the line DUPLEX
HALF to it.

Everything you type appears twice   The online service being used requires full duplex. Edit the control file and be sure to add the line DUPLEX FULL to it.

The screen fills with random characters   The baud rate you're using doesn't match the one the service is using. Read the documentation for the service you're calling. Then use the correct baud rate in your control file.

Lines of text wrap before the end of the line   Telex services permit less than 80 characters per line. Reformat your document with a right margin of 65 characters and be sure to use a nonproportional font.

File problems

The following is more of a misunderstanding than a problem with TelMerge. It also requires better housekeeping on the hard drive.

The logfile erases each time a new session begins   TelMerge renames the old logfile LOGFILE.SAV whenever you begin a session. It uses the name logfile in every session, and it is specified after the LOGFILE keyword in the control file used to call up the service. If you want to keep old logfiles, you must rename the file after every session. It's also a good idea to copy the renamed files to an archive floppy, and then delete them from the hard drive. If you want to maintain a long, continuous logfile, add the APPEND keyword to the control files for the services whose communications you want to record.

Printing problems

Printing problems don't show up on the sending end of the online conversation. The receiver is the one printing, and thus must get back in touch with the sender to report the problems encountered.

Bold, underline, and overstrike are lost when sent   Because of compatibility constraints, TelMerge strips all print commands from WordStar text files during ASCII transmissions. To retain print controls, you must use a protocol transfer.

Problems sending files created with another word processor   If you're sending files you created with a word processor other than WordStar, and these files contain printing controls or enhancements, you must use a protocol transfer.

During a Telex session, punctuation marks disappear   The character set used for Telex communications is a subset of the typewriter character set. Lowercase characters are customarily converted to uppercase during transmission. Some punctuation marks are stripped, while others are converted to the uppercase symbol on the corresponding key. The service documentation should provide more specific information. If not, call their representative and see if they have a solution.

Alternative communication services

This section gives you some specific information about online services TelMerge is preprogrammed to use. Your best bet is to call the service directly and ask them to send you an information pack. This is an alphabetical list, with no special preference intended.

CompuServe

CompuServe is the largest information service available to most PC users. It offers online information, e-mail, a shopping service, business news, conference calling, United Press International and Associated Press national and international news wires, newspapers like The Washington Post, an electronic brokerage, an airline ticket counter, and much more.

Of special interest to WordStar users is the WordStar Forum, a bulletin board for word processing and desktop publishing. Get help on your problems with WordStar. Talk with other WordStar users, or get tips directly from WordStar's technical staff. There's no extra charge for using the Forum.

CompuServe Information Service
5000 Arlington Centre Blvd.
Columbus, OH 43220
(800) 848-8990
TelMerge name: CIS

Western Union Online Services

Western Union offers EasyLink electronic mail (a store-and-forward system). Also available are FYI (an information service) and a mailgram service. EasyLink telegrams your message when it can't be delivered by a telex network.

Western Union Telegraph
4230 Altha Road
Dallas, TX 75244
(800) 527-5184 (Sales)
(800) 435-7375
TelMerge name: ESL

ITT Telex and TIMETRAN

ITT offers standard telex services worldwide, a store-and-forward message service called TIMETRAN, and a paper mail service. ITT telegraphs your message when it can't be telexed. Also offered is an information service called UPDATE.

TelMerge turns logging and printing on automatically for ITT services. If you don't want to print your sessions, change the PRINT keyword setting to NO.

ITT World Communications
100 Plaza Drive
Secaucus, NJ 07096
(800) 922-0184
TelMerge name: ITT

MCI Mail

MCI Mail offers an electronic mail service, an information service with Dow Jones News/Retrieval, and a courier service. Access to telex networks is also available.

MCI Mail
8th Floor
1150 17th Street N.W.
Washington, DC 20036
(800) 444-6245
(202) 833-8484
TelMerge name: MCI

Official Airline Guides

The Official Airline Guides (OAG) Electronic Edition provides airline schedules and fares for commercial airlines.

Official Airline Guides
2000 Clearwater Drive
Oak Brook, IL 60521
(800) 323-4000
TelMerge name: OAG

ONTYME Messaging Service

ONTYME is an electronic store-and-forward service that provides worldwide call access. You can route messages through the telex networks if you want. TYM-SHARE has another network called TYMNET.

ONTYME Marketing TYMSHARE
2560 North First Street
San Jose, CA 95131
(800) 435-8880
TelMerge name: ONT

RCA

RCA provides real-time telex services worldwide. TELEXTRA is a store-and-forward service. HOTLINE is an information service. RCA Telegram turns your message into a telegram when it can't use the telex network.

TelMerge automatically turns on logging and printing for RCA services. If you don't want to print your sessions, change the PRINT keyword setting to NO.

RCA Global Communications
201 Centennial Avenue
Piscataway, NJ 08854
(800) 526-3969

22
CHAPTER

Converting text files with StarExchange

This chapter covers general and detailed use of the StarExchange utility program. Although this is a simple program to use, first-time users often find it confusing to set up the conversion parameters. Once you've mastered these procedures, however, the rest is easy.

Introduction and overview

StarExchange is a text file conversion utility program. It takes text files created by one word processor and converts them to the format of another. For example: you can take WordPerfect files and convert them to WordStar documents and vice-versa, or you can convert Macintosh text files into WordStar and back into the Macintosh format. This makes WordStar compatible with every major word processing program.

One of the biggest advantages of this utility is that it lets you use WordStar in an office where many others use a different word processor. This puts an end to arguments over which program to use. Everyone can use what they want, and convert the files when necessary to share them.

How does StarExchange work?

First, you run StarExchange. Then you select the type of conversion you want to make, and set the parameters for the conversion. When you start the conversion running, StarExchange does everything automatically. When it finishes, you have the converted files ready to work on with WordStar or another program.

The conversion doesn't change the original text files. Instead, StarExchange creates a new text file in the new format. Once converted to the format of the other word processor, the text files can be opened and worked on in that word processor. The new file might need some minor work to duplicate the exact appearance of the original, but the layout and design are essentially retained.

Program files StarExchange can use

StarExchange can convert the files from more than 50 different application programs. This means that you can use text and data from most word processor, spreadsheet, and database programs.

WordStar accepts any pure ASCII file as a nondocument text file, so it's not necessary to convert these kind of files with StarExchange. Table 22-1 lists the different Word processing programs that StarExchange supports.

Program/environment	Release/version
DOS-based word processing formats	
DEC WPS PLUS (DX)	3.0 and earlier
DisplayWrite	2.5
First Choice	3.0 and earlier
IBM Writing Assistant	1.01
MASS-11	8.0 and earlier
Microsoft Word	4.0 thru 5.5
MultiMate	3.6 and 4.0
MultiMate Advantage	All
MultiMate Advantage II	All
Nota Bene	3.0
PFS: Write	A, B, and C
Professional Write	2.2 and earlier
Samna Word	IV Plus and earlier
SmartWare	1.5 and earlier
Volkswriter	3, 4
Wang PC (IWP)	2.6 and earlier
WordMARC Composer	Plus and earlier
WordPerfect	5.1 and earlier
WordStar	7.0 and earlier
WordStar 2000	3.5 and earlier
XyWrite	III+ and earlier
Macintosh-based formats	
Microsoft Word	4.0
WordPerfect	2.0 and earlier
MacWrite II	1.1

Table 22-1   Word processing formats supported by StarExchange.

Table 22-1   Continued

Miscellaneous formats

ASCII	n/a
Intelligent ASCII	n/a
DCA/FFT	All
DCA/RFT	All
Navy DIF	All
Microsoft RTF	1.0 and earlier

Spreadsheet formats

Enable	3.0
First Choice	3.0 and earlier
Framework	III and earlier
Lotus 1-2-3	3.0 and earlier
Lotus Symphony	2.0 and earlier
Microsoft Excel	2.0 thru 3.0
Microsoft Works	2.0
Mosaic Twin	1.0
PFS: Professional Plan	1.0
Quattro	PRO and earlier
SuperCalc 5	All word processing
SmartWare II	1.5
VP Planner 3D	1.0

Database formats

	dBASE	IV and earlier
	Data Ease	4.0
*	dBXL	1.3
	Enable	3.0
	First Choice	3.0 and earlier
*	FoxBase	2.1
	Framework	2.0
	Microsoft Works	2.0
	Paradox	2.0 thru 3.5
	Q & A	3.0
	R:Base	3.1 & earlier, System V, Personal
	Reflex	2.0 and earlier
	SmartWare II	1.02 thru 1.5

---

* If you want to convert dBXL or FoxBase files, use dBASE as the conversion program to represent these files.

Automatic translation during conversion

Normally, you tell WordStar what program the source text file was created with. If you don't know what program was used, StarExchange can diagnose the file and determine the format with the automatic translation feature.

Running StarExchange from the DOS prompt

Assuming you installed WordStar in the C: \ WS directory, at the DOS prompt type CD \ WS \ CONVERT and press the Enter key. Then, at the C: \ WS \ CONVERT prompt, type CONVERT and press the Enter key.

A quick start for using StarExchange

The following is a quick-start set of instructions for those of you who don't need detailed explanations:

1. Copy the file being converted to the directory where you need it, run WordStar, and change to this directory.
2. Start StarExchange through the Opening Menu by typing AS.
3. When the StarExchange Main Menu (shown in Fig. 22-1) appears, type 3 for System Setup. This calls the Setup Options Menu.
4. You must now select the program format for the conversion (the format to which the text file converts). Use the arrow keys to highlight the

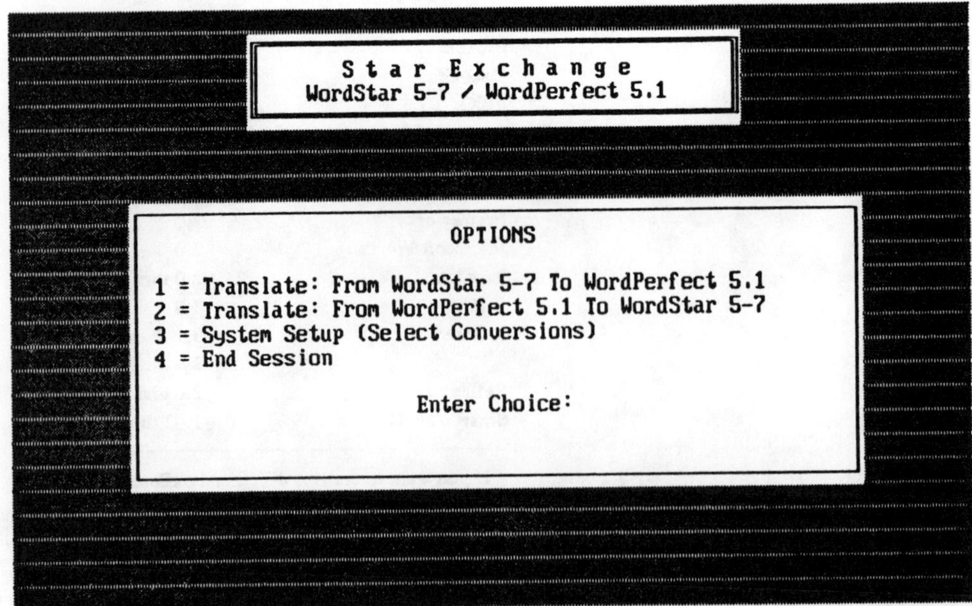

22-1 StarExchange Main Menu.

program name. Use the left and right arrow keys to move the program to the Conversion A and Conversion B boxes.

5. When finished setting up the conversion options, press the Esc key. You'll be returned to the StarExchange Main Menu.

6. At the StarExchange Main Menu, type 1 to select Conversion A, or 2 to select Conversion B.

7. StarExchange will now ask you to queue your documents for translation, which means it wants to know what files to convert. And the word *queue* means you can convert a batch of files at once. Type them in one by one, and press the Enter key. The current directory will display at the bottom of the menu. If the files aren't in this directory, precede the filename with the directory path.

8. When all the files are queued for conversion, press the F10 key. StarExchange will begin converting the files in the order of the queue.

9. When all the files are converted, the new files are stored in the current directory. Type 4 to exit StarExchange and return to the WordStar Opening Menu.

10. You can now work on the converted text files with WordStar.

Setting parameters

There are five conversion parameters to choose from on the Conversions Menu:

System Parameters   Settings that affect the internal system work area, keyboard type, character filter, spreadsheet delimiter, and margins.

Conversion A Parameters   Settings used for the Conversion A program (usually WordStar).

Conversion B Parameters   Settings used for the Conversion B program (the program you're converting from).

Edit Character Filter   Character filter that fine-tunes a conversion by replacing a character in the source text file with a specific character in the converted file.

Edit Typestyle Filter   Filter that allows you to substitute any typestyle or font in the source text file with another character in the converted file.

Selecting a program format

The most important part of working with StarExchange is selecting the correct set of parameters to make the conversion. Fortunately, it's not difficult.

1. At the StarExchange Main Menu, type 3 to select System Setup and choose the parameters for making the conversion.

2. The Conversions Menu will appear onscreen. The conversion boxes on the menu show the programs and other file formats available for

conversion. Normally, WordStar is in Conversion A box, and the other program is in Conversion B.

3. Use the up and down arrow keys to highlight the name of the program that created the file. Then use the left or right arrow keys to move the name into the conversion box. (Be sure WordStar remains in the Conversion A box.)
4. Change any other necessary parameters.
5. When ready, press the Enter key. This saves the setup and returns you to the StarExchange Main Menu.

Tip: If you want, you can select Auto Translate. Then you won't ever have to change the settings for converting program files to the WordStar format. Auto Translate scans a file, identifies its format, and makes the conversion automatically. Auto Translate is especially useful when you don't know what program was used to create a file, but you know it's not in WordStar format.

Setting system parameters

The different parameters you can change through the System Parameters setting, shown in Fig. 22-2, are as follows:

System Work Area Directory   Determines where the temporary work files are stored during conversion. Although StarExchange deletes these temporary files after each conversion, they need approximately $1^1/_2$ times the size of the text file being converted. To set this parameter, type in the name of an existing drive or directory.

Keyboard Type   The default is US/Group1. Change this only if you're using a different language keyboard.

Character Filter File   This selects an existing filter to use during conversion. Leave it blank if you don't want to use a filter.

Spreadsheet Delimiter   This specifies characters or keys StarExchange should insert between columns of converted information from spreadsheet or database files. You can use commas, tabs, or spaces. Use commas when creating a data file for merge printing. Use tabs if the data is to go in tables.

Spreadsheet Top Margin   The default is 1″. This setting determines the top margin of a converted spreadsheet file when loaded into WordStar. Type the value as a number, followed by the unit of measure (cm or inch).

Spreadsheet Bottom Margin   The default is 1″. Determines the bottom margin of a converted spreadsheet file when loaded into WordStar. Type the value as a number, followed by the unit of measure (cm or inch).

Setting conversion parameters

StarExchange stores a separate set of parameters for each program it supports. Some parameters determine how converted files get named and stored, and are

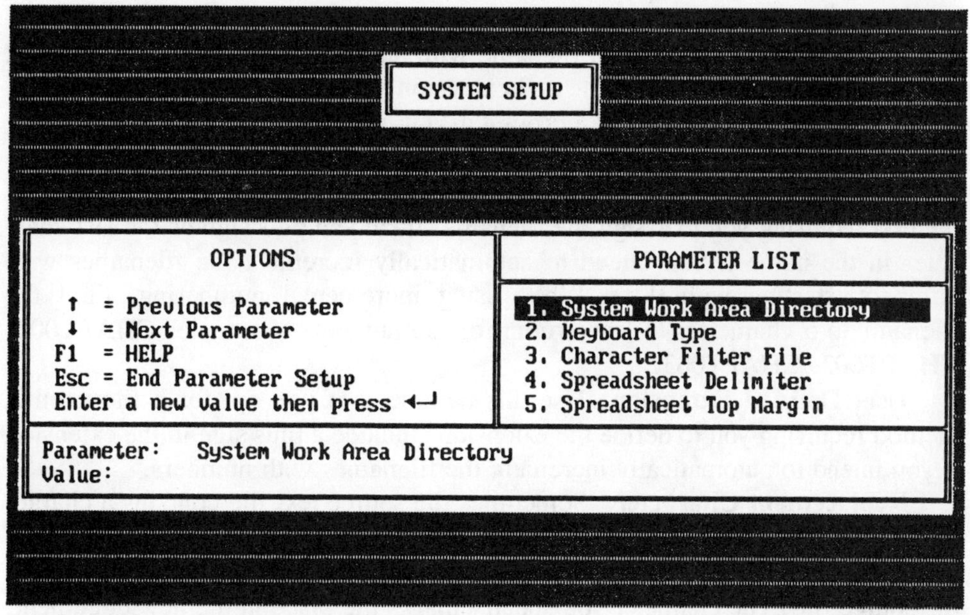

22-2   Parameter List in the System Setup Menu.

standard for all supported programs. Others apply to specific programs, and can be changed with this option.

The first time you use StarExchange, the default settings are standard values. Whenever you change any conversion parameters, they become the new defaults. The parameter changes affect only the selected program. You might want to keep written notes of the changes you make in the event you don't get the results you intend.

1. To set conversion parameters, go to the Conversion Menu. Press F3 to specify the Conversion A program. Press F4 to specify the Conversion B program.
2. When the System Setup Menu appears, use the up and down arrow keys to move through the list of parameters. Each time you change a value, press the Enter key to save it.
3. When finished with parameter setup, press the Esc key.

The standard parameters are shown as follows, and are available for most application programs. There are no available parameters for spreadsheet or database files, because you can't convert to those formats.

Output Directory   This important parameter controls where converted files go when StarExchange finishes its conversion. Type in the name of the drive and directory you're working in. If you don't want to keep changing this parameter, create a directory especially for receiving converted files. Then you'll always have them in the same place.

File-Naming Method This controls how the converted files are named. There are five options: original filename with an extension you specify, original filename and extension, filename and extension you define; filename you define with an original extension, and a prompt asking you to type in a filename during conversion.

User-Defined Filename Use this parameter if you selected a file-naming method requiring you to assign the filename. Include a plus sign as the last character in the name if you intend to automatically increment the filenames with numbers (starting with 001). When using incremental numbering, limit the filename to 5 characters to leave room for the numbers. Example: CHAPT001, CHAPT002, CHAPT003.

User-Defined Extension Use this parameter if you opt for a file-naming method requiring you to define the extension. Include a plus sign in the extension if you intend to automatically increment the filenames with numbers.

Replacement Character Sometimes the source text file contains a character that can't be translated during conversion. This parameter defines a special character inserted in a converted file to replace any nontranslatable character in the source file. The character you specify marks the place in the new document. You can use Ctrl−QF to find each occurrence for correction while working on the document. Replacement characters are represented by their ASCII numbers.

Input File Type This is useful when you have a database file you want to use with WordStar. When you choose Data File as the input file type, StarExchange converts the file to an ASCII comma-delimited file. You can then use it as a data file for merge printing.

Editing the character filter

With this option, you can fine-tune conversion by creating a character filter file. This file contains information for replacing a character or characters in the source file with a character or characters in the converted file. This becomes necessary when the destination program doesn't contain characters supported or used by the original program.

This feature requires you have intimate knowledge of both the source program, and WordStar. You must know if there are characters in both which are not shared by the other. The purpose of the Character Filter is to compensate for the lack of one or the other program.

If you want a filter file used during conversion, you must specify the drive, filename, and extension in the Character Filter File parameter. This is discussed in the subsection *Setting system parameters*, earlier in this chapter. Below are the steps for editing a filter file:

1. At the StarExchange Main Menu, type 3 for System Setup, and call the Conversions Menu.

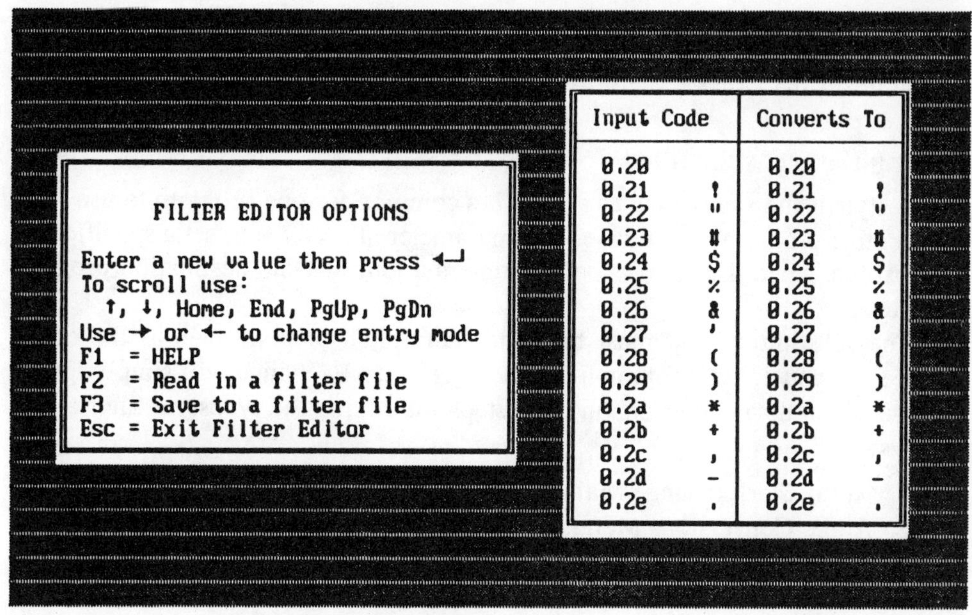

22-3 Filter table in the Filter Editor Options Menu.

2. At the Conversions Menu, press F5 to display the filter table, shown in Fig. 22-3.

3. In the filter table, the values in the Input Code column represent characters in the source document. You can't change the input code values. The values in the Converts To column represent the actual replacement characters you can change and use.

4. In the Converts To column, use the arrow keys to move the cursor to the character you're replacing.

5. In the beginning, the characters in both columns are identical. To change a character, type either a new character or its ASCII number. The object is to replace characters the end-user program can't use with ones it can.

6. When you're finished the character filter, press F3 to save it.

7. At the Save File prompt, type in a filename and press the Enter key. (Use any name and extension you want. Precede it with drive and subdirectory names if you don't want it to go to the current drive/subdirectory.)

8. Press the Esc key twice to return to the StarExchange Main Menu.

Once you have a filter file, you can reopen and edit it. You can also use an existing file as a template for a new one by making changes and saving it to a new filename. The steps for editing an existing file filter are as follows:

1. At the filter table, press the F2 key to read in a filter file.

2. At the Read File prompt, type in the name of the file being edited.
3. Make all the necessary changes and save them.
4. Press the Esc key twice to return to the StarExchange Main Menu.

Editing the typestyle filter

A typestyle is the same thing as a font. It's common for one program to use fonts that another program doesn't use. This parameter allows you to set a specific font to substitute when the conversion encounters a font that the destination program can't use.

The substitution font must have the same pitch or point size as the one it replaces. If you select a font in a different size, StarExchange will simply ignore your selection during conversion. The steps for editing the typestyle filter are as follows:

1. At the StarExchange Main Menu, type 3 to call the Conversions Menu.
2. At the Conversions Menu, press the F6 key. This calls the Choose a Direction to Edit dialog box (see Fig. 22-4).
3. At the Choose a Direction to Edit dialog box, press 1 or 2 to select the direction of the conversion.
4. In the Typestyle Filter Options dialog box (see Fig. 22-5), the top window lists the available options, the middle window the fonts supported by the source and target programs, and the bottom window

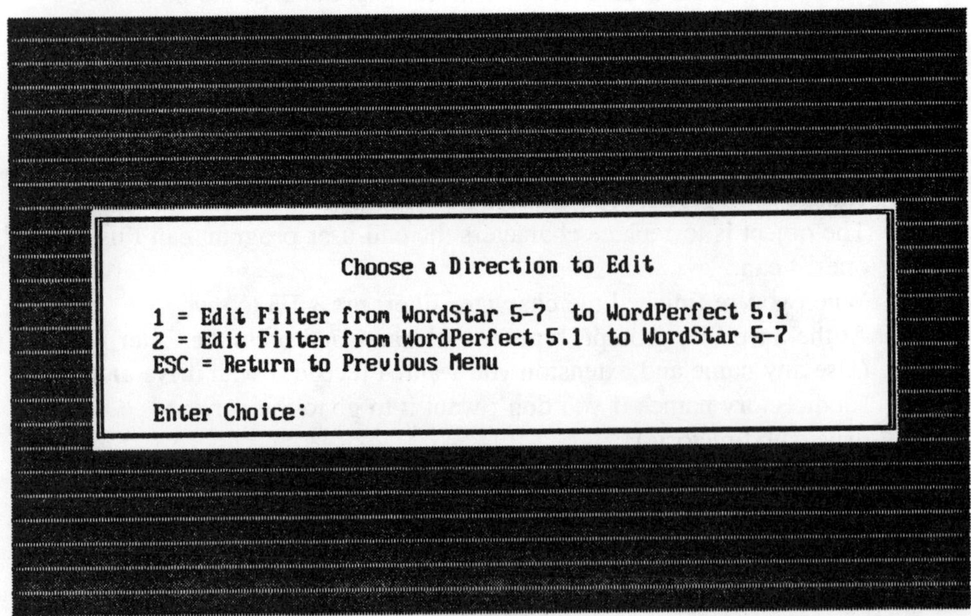

22-4 Choose a Direction to Edit dialog box.

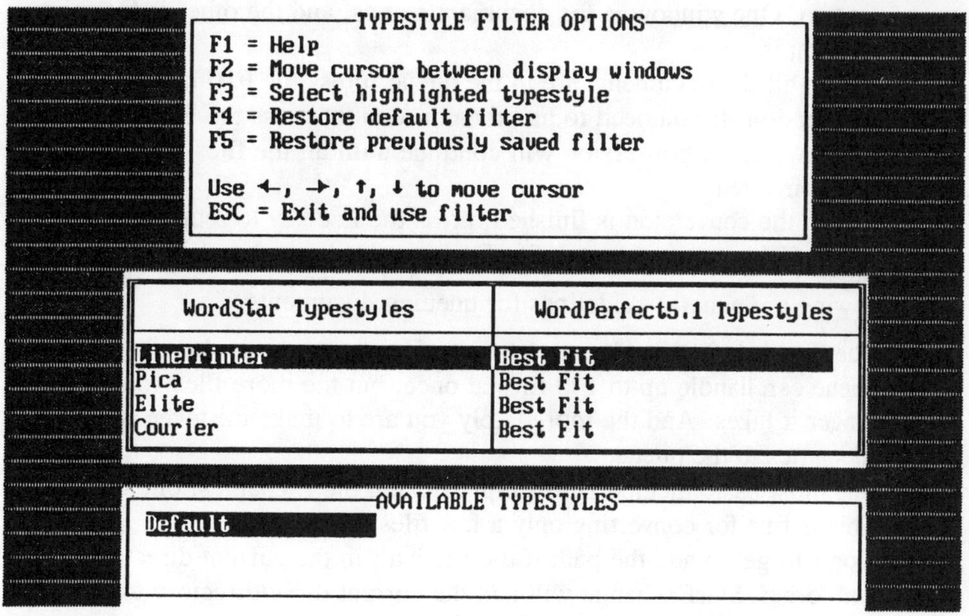

22-5 Typestyle Filter Options dialog box.

the available fonts for the target program. Select a substitution font from the third window by highlighting it. Press the F1 key to get help, F2 to move between windows, F3 to use the highlighted font, F4 to restore the StarExchange default font, and F5 to display the previously saved filter changes and allow you to make further changes.

6. When through editing the typestyle filter, press F10 to save the changes.

Queuing documents for conversion

When you have all the parameters set properly, you're almost ready to start the conversion. The next step is to queue the documents for translation, which simply means telling StarExchange which files you want converted. Do this by typing them into the Input Queue dialog box.

1. At the StarExchange Main Menu, select the type of conversion you want to make. Your choices are Conversion A and Conversion B. Type 1 or 2 to set the direction of the conversion.

2. At the Input Queue dialog box, type in the name of the file you're converting and press the Enter key. If necessary, include the path.

3. The input queue has room for 100 filenames. The program named onscreen is the source, or the one from which you're converting. Tip: When you're using the Auto Translate option, the Input Queue will split

in two. One window is for document names, and the other is for source
programs.

4. When all the documents are in the queue, press the F10 key to start the
   conversion. If you need to halt the conversion, press the Esc key.
   Otherwise, the conversion will continue until all the files in the queue
   are converted.

5. When the conversion is finished, press the Esc key to return to the Main
   Menu. Then press 4 to exit StarExchange and return to WordStar.

The following are general guidelines for queuing documents.

- The first rule is "Don't convert more files than you can handle." The
  queue can handle up to 100 files at once, but the more files you add the
  longer it takes. And the more likely you are to make mistakes adding the
  filenames to the queue.
- The most basic method is to simply type in the filenames, one by one.
  This is fine for converting only a few files.
- Don't forget to add the path if the file isn't in the current directory. If
  you forget, StarExchange will add the current drive/directory to the
  filename when you press the Enter key.
- To queue all text files in a directory, use the correct path, followed by the
  . wildcard specification.
- To queue documents with similar filenames or extensions, use wildcard
  characters for the shared characters, for example, *.TXT or
  CHAPTER.*.
- All documents in a queue must have been created by the same program.
  The only exception is when you're using Auto Translate. It can handle
  multiple formats during one conversion.

Using automatic directory assistance

The fastest way to add documents to the conversion queue is with a feature called
automatic directory assistance. To use it, press the F2 key while in the Input
Queue Menu. This calls up a submenu where the filenames are displayed
onscreen. Just follow the onscreen directions to move the highlight and select files
for the conversion.

Deleting text files from the conversion queue

If you make any typos and don't catch them before you add the filename to the
queue, the only way to correct them is delete the document from the queue and try
again.

1. To delete files at the Input Queue Menu, press the Del key.

2. The Delete Options Menu will appear. Follow the onscreen directions to delete either highlighted filenames or the entire queue.
3. When finished deleting, press the Esc key.

Coping with typing mistakes

StarExchange won't verify the existence of a file until it tries to convert it. If it doesn't find the file as named, you'll get the error message *Input open failure*. Your options are to:

- Press the Esc key and abort the conversion process. You can then delete the offending filename and type it correctly.
- Press the F2 key and retry. This gets you nowhere.
- Press the Enter key, skip the file in question, and continue the conversion process.

StarExchange doesn't automatically erase the queue after conversion. If you need to convert other files, you must delete the filenames from the queue. StarExchange does, however, erase the entire queue when you exit and return to WordStar, so the queue is always empty when you run StarExchange.

Using Auto Translate

The Auto Translate option on the Conversions Menu lets you tell StarExchange to do all the work for you. It works on not only unidentified files, but all file formats StarExchange can handle. When all the parameters are set and the files for conversion selected, you're ready to start the conversion process.

Tip: Before you begin the conversion, be sure you have sufficient space on the target disk. During conversion, StarExchange creates temporary files on disk, and deletes them when the conversion is completed. So during conversion, StarExchange requires about $1\frac{1}{2}$ times the combined file space of the selected files.

1. At the StarExchange Main Menu, select the type of conversion you want to make by typing either 1 or 2.
2. Add the filenames to the input queue.
3. When ready, press the F10 key to start the conversion. Unless interrupted, the conversion will run until all the files in the queue are converted. If you need to interrupt for any reason, press the Esc key.
4. When the conversion is complete, the message *Press any key to continue* will appear. When you press a key, you'll be returned to the StarExchange Main Menu.
5. Type 4 to exit StarExchange and return to the WordStar Opening Menu.

Once the files are converted to the WordStar format, you can open them as WordStar documents or nondocuments. Treat them exactly as though they are WordStar text files.

Using the Directory Assistance menu

The Directory Assistance menu gives a visual display of the available files in the source directory. The display is an easy way to select files and add them to the Input Queue dialog box. All you have to do is follow the onscreen instructions, using the arrow keys and function keys. A function key template shows you the commands installed on the function keys—and tells you what they do. The options are:

Directory Information Line Shows the path StarExchange is using. The path includes drive, directories, and filename.

Directory Edit Window Lets you change the drive, directory, and filename of the file to convert. To change the directory, press Ctrl—Backspace and delete the current window. Then type in the new directory name and filename.

File List Window On the left side of the Directory Assistance menu, this option lists the files in the current directory and any subdirectories. Use the arrow keys to move the highlight through the onscreen list. To add a filename to the queue, press the F10 key. Press the Esc key to close the list.

Document Viewing Window Displays the contents of the selected file onscreen.

File Information Line Indicates the file format and cursor position of file shown in the document viewing window.

Message Line Provides status information or instructions for completing a task.

Function Key Template Shows function keys 1—10, and the commands assigned to them. For some commands, you must use the Ctrl key with the function key.

Using the document viewing window

The document viewing window lets you browse through a text file. If you're not sure which file you need, you can find it with this feature. You can't write or edit files with this option.

1. At the Input Queue dialog box, press F2 to call the Directory Assistance menu.
2. Highlight the file you want to view.
3. Press the Tab key to display the file onscreen. Exactly how the file appears depends on its format and type. Most word processing formats appear in their original format. You can only view text files with this option. Use the arrow keys to move through the document. Use Zoom to enlarge the window. Use Search to locate specific text.
4. When finished browsing through the file, press the Esc key. This closes the document.

Zooming in on viewed documents

The Zoom option magnifies the document viewing window so it fills the entire screen. Press F2 to zoom in on the document for a better view. To switch to a different document while zooming, press the plus or minus keys. These will switch you to the next or preceding file in the directory. When finished using Zoom, press F2 again.

Searching for text in viewed document

The Search option lets you look for specific text in a viewed document. While in the document viewing window, press F9 to begin the search. The search prompt will appear onscreen.

- The arrow after the prompt indicates the direction of the search. Use the up or down arrow keys to set the search direction.
- The Case prompt reveals whether case sensitivity is on or off. When case sensitivity is off, StarExchange ignores case as a parameter during the search. Use PgUp to turn it on and PgDn to turn it off.
- There's room to type up to 40 characters in the Search window. Type a phrase, word, or part of a word. You can't use wildcard characters. StarExchange doesn't always find phrases when they're broken by wordwrap.
- To initiate the search, press the Enter key. To find the next occurrence, move the cursor past the found text, and press F9 and Enter again.

Converting spreadsheet and database files

StarExchange has the ability to convert entire spreadsheet or database files, or selected lines or blocks of them. When you view one of these files, the function key template has additional commands for selecting individual lines or blocks of text. To convert only part of a spreadsheet or database file, define the desired portion in one of the following ways:

- Select individual record lines
- Mark a specific block of data or record lines
- Mark nonadjacent or random range of rows and columns throughout the spreadsheet or data file

Unless the source files are truly enormous, these commands replicate functions that are done more easily and quickly with WordStar cut-and-paste functions. This is especially true if you find yourself spending much time searching for data and marking it for conversion. It's usually simpler to convert the entire file, open it in a second window, and cut and paste the data where you need it.

Marking individual rows or record lines

Press the F3 key to mark one row (in a spreadsheet) at a time, or one record line (in a database) at a time. Use the up and down arrow keys to move the highlight up or down to extend the highlighted area.

Marking blocks of data

The following are the steps for marking a rectangular block of data in a spreadsheet or database file:

1. Place the cursor at the upper left corner of the desired block.
2. Press the F4 key to begin the block.
3. Use the arrow keys to move the cursor to the lower right corner of the desired block. As you move the cursor, the highlight will extend to cover the block.

Marking nonadjacent rows and columns

When cutting information from a spreadsheet or database file, you might want to select only specific rows or columns of data instead of an entire block. You can do this by using Ctrl−F3 to define a horizontal range, and Ctrl−F4 to define a vertical range. These two commands work together. Define the ranges, and the selected area will be defined by the intersection of those two ranges.

Tip: It's simpler to convert the entire data file, open it in a second window, and use the WordStar Ctrl−QF block-marking commands and Ctrl−KA to copy the information between windows.

To define the horizontal range, move the cursor to the first row of the range and press Ctrl−F3. If the range includes more than one row, move the cursor up or down to define all the rows you want to include. To anchor the end of the range, press the spacebar. This allows you to move the cursor without extending the highlight. Repeat these steps until you've marked or defined all the horizontal ranges. To define the vertical range, move the cursor to the first column in the desired range, and press Ctrl−F4. Then use the same steps as defining the horizontal range.

When you've defined both horizontal and vertical ranges, the marked area (intersection of the ranges) will be displayed in reverse video. If you find that you've marked rows or columns you don't want, you can deselect them the same way you selected them. When you're ready, start the conversion.

Working on converted text files

It's unlikely the line length or font size in the source document will be the same as those you use in WordStar. You'll need to reformat some or all of the paragraphs.

As a safe bet, use Ctrl−QU to realign the entire text file when you first open it. This should correct most minor problems.

If you've used the character replacement filter, you should search the document for replacement characters. Remember that these are markers that StarExchange substituted for nontranslatable characters it found in the source files. Use Ctrl−QF to locate them one by one, or Ctrl−QA to replace them globally.

DisplayWrite files might present special problems. If they're stored in RTF (revisable for text) format, use the DisplayWrite Convert Documents utility program to change them to text files before converting them.

MultiMate files also might present special problems. Large documents converted into MultiMate format can exceed the maximum number of format lines, number of pages, and so on. These documents will be split into separate files during conversion. You might have to rewrite the files to establish chapter or section breaks between portions of the document.

Features supported by StarExchange

StarExchange recognizes and uses 26 standard word-processing features during text file conversion. They're listed below:

Boldfacing
Italics
Superscript and subscript
Overstrike
Underlining
Soft carriage returns
Hard carriage returns
Regular tabs
Decimal tabs
Titles
Hard hyphens
Soft hyphens
Right and left margins
Top and bottom margins
Indentation
Forced page breaks
Automatic or soft page breaks
Line spacing
Headers and footers
Footnotes
Nonprinting comments
Printing pitch and font
Stop codes

Transferring files between PCs and Macintoshes

Macintosh conversions can identify and convert files in the MacBinary format or a standard format, also called *data fork*. These conversions are supposed to be invisible to the user in that the Macintosh does most of the work for you. It doesn't depend on Output File Type parameter settings. Almost all file transfers from Macintosh to MS-DOS computers will result in either MacBinary or standard file formatting.

If you're converting a file from Macintosh to WordStar, you must transfer it from the Macintosh disk to an MS-DOS disk, and vice-versa. The three basic methods for moving a file between an MS-DOS computer and a Macintosh are Apple File Exchange, SuperDrive, and direct transfers.

When converting a WordStar document file to a Macintosh word processing format, you must consider whether it's into a MacBinary or standard format. When converting WordStar documents to Macintosh standard format, use the Macintosh Tagger program to tag the files. When converting WordStar documents to MacBinary format, it isn't necessary to tag the files.

The terms *tag* and *tagging* are StarExchange terms, not Macintosh terms. In Macintosh terminology, the process being described is similar to changing the creator or type for a file.

Apple File Exchange and SuperDrive

The Apple SuperDrive is now a standard device in all Macintosh computers sold. The drive has built-in capability for reading MS-DOS disks, and can transfer MS-DOS files to a Macintosh disk. The process is executed with a utility program named Apple File Exchange, or AFE. The program is a standard part of Macintosh Systems 6.0 through 7, and is readily available.

When using AFE to transfer a converted file to a Macintosh, use StarExchange's system setup and select Standard as the file type in the Output File Type parameter.

Tip: A product named DOS Mounter by Dyna Communications makes an MS-DOS disk look exactly like a Macintosh disk when you put it in a SuperDrive.

Direct transfers

There are many different combinations of hardware and software you can use to make direct data transfers between an MS-DOS computer and a Macintosh. These include:

- Modem or network connections using standard telecommunications software.
- Direct serial or parallel connections using standard telecommunications software like ProComm, Hayes SmartCom, or CrossTalk on the PC and MacTerminal, and Microphone or Red Ryder on the Macintosh.

- Connections using dedicated file-transfer software or hardware combinations like LapLink Macintosh, MacLink Plus PC, or pcAnywhere.

Before making a direct communication transfer, make sure your Macintosh software allows the Mac to receive files in the MacBinary format. If working on a Macintosh several years old, you might not be able to use MacBinary. If you have a new system, there should be no problems. The newest Mac communications programs allow you to use MacBinary with no problems. Most MS-DOS communications programs can send the MacBinary file using XMODEM protocol. And virtually all specialized systems can receive and send it.

- If your software allows MacBinary file transfer, use the StarExchange system setup to specify MacBinary as the output file type for the Macintosh format. When a file is sent to a Mac disk as a MacBinary file, it's ready to use without tagging.
- If your software doesn't support MacBinary files, use the StarExchange system setup to specify Standard as the output file type for the Macintosh format. When transferred to a Mac disk, it will probably need tagging for the word processor being used.

Macintosh file types

MS-DOS files are created with a single stream of bytes and miscellaneous DOS information (like date and time). MS-DOS word processors and other programs can open almost any file, regardless of filename or system information.

Macintosh files are created with two streams of data, called the *data fork* and the *resource fork*. These two streams include information associating a creator and type with the file. Macintosh computers use this information to display icons, and to allow starting a program by double-clicking on its icon. If a Macintosh document doesn't have the correct creator or type, the file can't be opened—not even by the program that created it.

MacBinary When a Macintosh file is in an MS-DOS disk or computer, using the MacBinary format preserves the special information, plus the separate data and resource forks. This format groups filename, creator and type information, and data and resource forks into a single stream of bytes. Most Macintosh telecommunications programs can send and receive files in this format without loss of information.

Standard When the transfer hardware and software can't handle MacBinary, the conversion can produce only the data fork of the Macintosh file—thus the other information is missing. This is the Standard format. A file produced in this format can't be opened by a Macintosh word processor because of the missing information.

Error messages

This section lists and describes StarExchange error messages that might appear onscreen while you're using the conversion program. They indicate mistakes you've made or problems the program is encountering. Where possible, I've provided solutions to the problems. The messages are alphabetically listed.

Access denied The file cannot be opened for viewing because it's locked for some reason. This is a system security or access problem. The file might be protected, locked out on a network, or someone might be currently using it.

Application load failure, EXE corrupted One or more program files needed by StarExchange might be damaged or didn't copy correctly during installation. You can reinstall StarExchange with WINSTALL by using the Add or Remove a Feature option. Reinstall the conversion format with the damaged file. If you know the specific .EXE file that's damaged, you can reinstall it with the COPYWS utility program on disk 1 of your WordStar master disks.

Application load failure, EXE not found A StarExchange conversion file is missing. You can reinstall StarExchange with WINSTALL by using the Add or Remove a Feature option. Reinstall the conversion format with the missing file. If you know the specific .EXE file that's missing, you can install it with the COPYWS utility program on disk 1 of your WordStar master disks.

Application load failure, insufficient memory This companion program requires a minimum of 384K of RAM. Check the available memory from the WordStar Opening Menu by typing the letters FU. This calls the Status dialog box. If you're using other memory-resident programs like Inset, SideKick, or SuperKey, remove them from memory and try again. If you don't have at least 640K of RAM, you need to upgrade your system.

Command file processing error StarExchange can't use the work area. Check the System Parameters option. Make sure the drive letter (including the colon) and directory are correct. Make sure there's enough room on the target disk. (You need at least 1 1/2 times the size of the largest document for the work area.)

Disk read error StarExchange can't read the source document. The disk might have an error. Copy the file to another disk or directory.

Disk write error StarExchange can't complete the conversion by writing the new file to the target disk because there isn't enough room. Delete files or use another disk. Then repeat the conversion.

Input file open failure StarExchange can't find the file as you've listed it in the input queue. The filename, drive name, or directory path might be incorrect. If you find a typo, delete the file from the queue and try again. Or, too many files might be open for your current computer system setup. Check the CONFIG.SYS file. The FILES= statement must be at least 30.

Insufficient memory for conversion Your computer doesn't have enough memory to hold the files during conversion. You must have at least 384K of RAM.

RTLINK failure, RTLINK.COM not found   The RTLINK.COM program file is either damaged or missing. Use COPYWS to decompress and copy the file to your C: \ WS \ CONVERT subdirectory (COPYWS A: C: \ WS \ CONVERT RTLINK.COM). You can eliminate the path in this command, but don't forget to leave a blank space between C: and RTLINK.COM or COPYWS won't accept it.

RTLINK failure, general RTLINK failure   One or more of the RTLINK files have been damaged or deleted. Use COPYWS to decompress and copy the files to your C: \ WS \ CONVERT subdirectory (COPYWS A: C \ WS \ CON VERT RTLINK.COM and COPYWS A: C: \ WS \ CONVERT SCC_____??.RTL).

RTLINK failure, SCC_____??.RTL not found   The SCC_____??.RTL file can't be found. Copy it from the master WordStar disks.

Run-time error R6001, null pointer assignment   You've probably chosen the wrong conversion format for the file you're trying to convert. Use the system setup to check format and parameters. If you change formats, try again, and still get the error message, try using Auto Translate and let StarExchange determine the format. If the format is correct, reopen the source document and edit it. Scroll to its end, save, and close it. Then run StarExchange and try again.

Unable to create output file   StarExchange can't create the converted file on the target disk. You need at least 1$^{1}/_{2}$ times the space of the largest file to make the conversion file on the target disk. If you can't delete any files on it, use another disk. Also, check the CONFIG.SYS file and be sure the FILES= line is at least 30. Finally, make sure you're using a valid MS-DOS filename, including drive and directory path.

Unable to load application definition files   One or more of the .DEF or definition files is damaged or missing from the C: \ WS \ CONVERT subdirectory. Use COPYWS to recopy the .DEF files from the WordStar master disks to the hard disk. Then rerun StarExchange and try again.

Unable to read source document   StarExchange can't read the source document. Press the Esc key to abort the conversion. Then exit WordStar by typing X. At the DOS prompt, type TYPE FILE.LOG and press the Enter key. FILE.LOG should contain a message telling you the probable cause of the error. Also, check the original document for errors in the program that created it. It possibly wasn't saved correctly. Or it wasn't correctly copied to the disk or directory you're working from.

23
CHAPTER

Working with WordStar's notes

You can find a quick start set of instructions for WordStar notes in Chapter 9, *Using the Onscreen Format Menu*. This is a complicated feature, with five different kinds of notes and a wide variety of uses. This chapter is necessary to cover the subject in complete detail.

What are WordStar notes?

Through this Notes Menu, you can select the type of note you want to use (from a list of five different kinds) and attach it directly to your document. Each note can be up to 40K in size—enough room for fifteen pages. If you find yourself writing notes this big, however, you need to reevaluate the scope and nature of your document.

WordStar has five different kinds of notes you can attach to your documents through the Onscreen Format menu: footnotes, endnotes, annotation, nonprinting comments, and index entries. These are all available through the Notes Menu, and are described as follows:

Footnotes   Creates references to material in the body of a document. They're numbered sequentially, and automatically print at the bottom of the page.

Endnotes   Creates references to material in the body of a document. They're numbered sequentially, and print in a separate section at the end of the document.

Annotations   Similar to footnotes and endnotes, except you define and set the reference symbol appearing in the text instead of using sequential numbers.

Nonprinting comments   This option embeds a hidden comment in the body of the text file. Use this to make personal, hidden notes about the contents of the file you're working on.

Index codes   Embeds a special indexing code in the body of the document. The text in the note merges into the index when you run the Index generator program from the Opening Menu.

There are five utilities options for working with WordStar notes after you've written and attached them to your documents. These are:

Ctrl−OND   Use this to reopen any existing WordStar note of any type, and rewrite or correct it. The cursor must be on the beginning of the embedded note symbol. This feature works best if you have the command tags display toggled on.

Ctrl−ONV   Use this to change a WordStar note from one type to any other type. Thus, you can convert a footnote to an endnote, a comment to a footnote, etc. The cursor must be on the beginning of the embedded note symbol. This feature works best if you have the command tags display toggled on.

Ctrl−ONU   This is a variation on the command to align the rest of the document; it aligns the rest of the text in the note. Here, the alignment changes only text in the WordStar notes. Use this when you've changed layout and design settings and you need to make the notes fit the new settings.

Ctrl−ONG   This is a variation on the global search command; use it to go to a note. The search looks only for text stored in WordStar notes. Selecting this calls the Find Note dialog box, where you can select the type of note you want to find. Next, the Go To Note dialog box appears. Type in up to 65 characters, and use Ctrl−K to start the search.

Ctrl−ONL   This is a command to spell check the rest of the notes; it's a variation on the command to check the rest of the document. Here WordStar checks the spelling only in the embedded notes. This command is a bit awkward to use. It's best used to correct spelling in your WordStar notes after you finish writing or editing them. Then you don't have to go back for global spell checks.

Ctrl−ONN   Use this to set or reset the starting number values for footnotes and endnotes. You can also specify whether footnote numbering starts over on each page or is continuous throughout the document. The best place to use this option is at the beginning of the text file.

Using footnotes, endnotes, and annotations

Footnotes, endnotes, and annotations are used mainly in research papers, thesis papers, dissertation papers, and other technical documentation. They're all reference notes, and are used for citing or attributing source materials for documents. Use them also for making statements or explanations outside the body text of the document.

The three kinds of reference notes are virtually identical. Their differences are only minor mechanical ones:

- Footnotes are numbered sequentially. They print at the bottom of same page as their reference number.
- Endnotes are also numbered sequentially, but they print in a group at the end of the document.
- Annotations are not sequentially numbered. Instead, you assign each a special reference symbol. WordStar prints them like footnotes, at the bottom of the same page as the reference symbol, but it's acceptable to put them at the end of the document.

Reference notes work hand-in-glove with quotations and excerpts included from other sources. Whenever you quote someone in your document or use an excerpt from another source, you must use a reference note to tell the reader where the quotation came from. You must also reference specific ideas that come from other sources, even if you've paraphrased or summarized them.

A research paper requires a careful balance between your own thoughts and the supporting materials you borrow from other sources. It's perfectly acceptable to borrow material from other writers and documents to enhance your own material.

You must, however, always give full credit to other writers when you use their words. This is called *citing* or *attributing* the reference material. If you don't give credit where credit is due, you're plagiarizing—which is the same as stealing.

A shrewd, sensible use of reference material is essential to research and technical writing. The object is to take the best parts of other works, and use them to help build something new. Or you take quotations from other writers, and use them to support your own premise or theory.

Inserting a footnote

A footnote is a reference, explanation, or comment placed below the body text on a printed page. It refers to something supporting or related to the subject being written about.

1. Place the cursor at the end of the quotation or subject being referenced.
2. Use Ctrl−ONF to call the Notes Menu, and open a footnote window.
3. If necessary, use Ctrl−OM to resize the window.
4. WordStar automatically inserts the number for the footnote. After the number, type the text of the footnote. You can use Ctrl−KR to paste in boilerplate text from another file.
5. Use paragraph tags, fonts, and style or layout commands to format the footnote.
6. When ready, use Ctrl−KD to save the footnote, close the note window, and return to the document mode (or use Ctrl−KQ to abandon the footnote without saving it).

7. When you return to the document mode, you'll see either the number of
    the footnote or the first 15 characters in brackets inserted at the cursor.

Inserting an endnote

An endnote is a reference, explanation, or comment placed at the end of the body
text of a printed document. It refers to something supporting or related to the subject being written about.

1. Place the cursor at the end of the quotation or the subject being
    referenced.
2. Use Ctrl−ONE to call the Notes Menu, and open an endnote window.
3. If necessary, use Ctrl−OM to resize the notes window.
4. WordStar automatically inserts the number for the endnote. After the
    number, type the text of the endnote. You can use Ctrl−KR to paste in
    boilerplate text from another file.
5. Use paragraph tags, fonts, and style or layout commands to format the
    endnote.
6. When ready, use Ctrl−KD to save the endnote, close the note window,
    and return to the document mode.
7. When you return to the document mode, you'll see the endnote's
    number or the first 15 characters in brackets inserted at the cursor.

Using annotations

Annotations are explanations made outside the main body of the document. If you
say something complex, complicated, or confusing—which a reader can take
more than one way—you can then "step aside" to furnish further comments or
information. In other words, you can comment on source materials to clarify,
interpret, or evaluate main points.

Don't overuse annotations. People often use them to make their writing, or
themselves, appear more important. Annotations work best when kept brief and
few. You're better off keeping your explanations in the body text of your document.

Inserting an annotation

An annotation is like a footnote. It's a reference, explanation, or comment placed
below the body text on a printed page. Use it to comment or explain a reference or
citation made in the document.

Annotations aren't numbered sequentially. Instead, you give each a special
symbol or character in place of the number. This makes them stand out from footnotes. You can thus use footnotes and annotations together, or endnotes and footnotes together.

You can use any character on the keyboard as the annotation symbol. You can also use the extended character set. Insert these by holding down the Alt key and typing their character number on the numeric keypad.

1. Place the cursor at the end of the quotation or the subject being referenced.
2. Use Ctrl−ONA to call the Annotation Mark dialog box.
3. At the Annotation Mark dialog box, type in the letter or symbol you want to use to mark the annotation. Then press the Enter key.
4. This opens the annotation window. If necessary, use Ctrl−OM to resize it.
5. WordStar inserts the annotation symbol you just typed. After the symbol, type the text of the annotation. (You can use Ctrl−KR to paste in boilerplate text from another file.)
6. Format the endnote as desired.
7. When ready, use Ctrl−KD to save the endnote, close the note window, and return to the document mode.
8. When you return to the document mode, you'll see either the symbol of the endnote or the first 15 characters in brackets inserted at the cursor.

Standard footnote and endnote formats

It's important to learn, and properly use, the different formats for attributing your reference materials. The format differs depending on who you're doing research for—and where it's being published. This section describes some standard formats for footnotes and endnotes. Use whichever format you require.

When you select Footnote, Endnote, or Annotation from the Notes Menu, WordStar opens a special notes window at the bottom of the screen. It is here that you type the text of the reference note.

While in this notes window, all WordStar writing commands and options are available. You simply type and edit the note as though you've opened another document window. You can also use the spelling checker and thesaurus.

When finished typing or editing the note, save the note, close the note window, and return to the document mode using Ctrl−KD. The new or edited note will automatically be embedded in the text file. What you see depends on whether command tag display is on or off. When it's on, you'll see the first 15 characters of the note between brackets. When it's off, you'll see only the note number or annotation symbol.

Bibliographic footnotes and endnotes

In a bibliographic footnote, the first reference cites complete bibliographical information about the source of the quotation. In following references, the footnote contains only the note's number, the author's last name, and a key word from the title if you're quoting more than one work by the same author.

WordStar automatically inserts a superscript number for the footnote. Indent the first line one tab stop (five spaces, or .5 "). Type the author's name (first, middle initial, last). Underline book and magazine titles. Use commas between main items, except before parentheses. Use parentheses to enclose book publication details or magazine publication date. End each footnote with a period outside the parentheses.

When you use the bibliographic format for footnotes or endnotes, you must also include a bibliography at the end of the document. The bibliography is an alphabetical listing of all the books, periodicals, and so on that contain reference material cited in the document. To learn how to do this, read the section *Bibliography lists*, later in this chapter.

Parenthetical citations

The parenthetical citation method is an internal way to give proper attribution to referenced sources. Many authorities consider this the most up-to-date way to cite someone else's work. Another name for this is *parenthetical annotation*, and is the required format for most master's theses and doctoral dissertations.

Enclose the sources for your references in parentheses, and place them directly in the body text of the document, instead of in footnotes. This system also requires a bibliography—a list of references or works being cited. This list belongs at the end of the document.

Two of the most popular parenthetical formats are those recommended by the Modern Language Association of America, or MLA, and its counterpart for scholars, The MLS style. In most cases, both of these are identical to APA style (see next section).

APA style references

The APA style is a specific form of attribution used by the American Psychological Association (APA), commonly used in behavioral and social sciences. The APA style uses the word *references* rather than *bibliography* to refer to the alphabetical list of works at the end of the document.

Make the first line of each note flush with the left margin. Indent all other lines in the note by three spaces. Use either single or double spacing. Several examples of APA references (from the APA Publication Manual) follow:

Liptz, A. (1979). *Prisons as social structures*. Los Angeles: Scholarly Press.

Klein, D.F. & Wender, P.H. (1981). *Mind, mood, and medicine: A guide to the new biological psychiatry*. New York: Farrar, Straus & Giroux.

Pinker, S. (1980). Mental imagery and the third dimension. *Journal of Experimental Psychology: General, 109*, 354-71.

When referencing more than one work by the same author, list them in order of their publication date, with earliest first. Repeat the author's name for each entry.

APA style citations

The APA style of in-text citation uses an abbreviated format of the items in the reference list, where the full publishing data appears. The elements of APA citation are the author's last name, the year of publication, and the page number (when the reference is to a specific passage) in the source material. Enclose these between parentheses, like this:

(Michaelsohn, 1992, p.333)

When mentioning the author's name in the text of the document, you need use only the date, or the date and page number. Enclose these between parentheses, like (1992) or (1992, p.333). You can use this type of citation for short, in-text quoted material; longer, block quotations, and paraphrased information.

The MLS documentation format

Most research papers in the Humanities now use the MLS format. Its main features are parenthetical citations in the body text, a list of cited works (bibliography), and (when needed) explanations in endnotes. The parenthetical citation in the text normally includes:

- The author's last name. When citing two authors with same last name, include their initials.
- The location of the resource material in its publication. In single volume works, the page numbers alone are sufficient.
- In multivolume sources, give volume numbers as well.
- For literary works, give act, scene, line, chapter number or title, book title, or stanza.

The parenthetical statement goes at the end of the sentence containing the reference material, inside the punctuation. Leave a blank space after the last character in the sentence. Type the opening parenthesis, the last name of the author, a blank space, the page number of the quotation, and the second parenthesis. The sentence's punctuation comes after the parenthetical citation.

The MLS bibliography corresponds to the APA reference list; both are located at the end of the document and both contain an alphabetical list of all cited reference sources.

Bibliography lists

The key to successful parenthetical citation is the list of cited reference sources at the end of the document. Every parenthetical reference must correspond to and match a record in the bibliography or reference list.

In APA and MLA styles, sort the list of cited works alphabetically by author. Format the first line of each record flush with the left margin. Indent the remaining lines five spaces (or the approximate space with proportional fonts) from the left margin. When using more than one work by the same author, list them in the record alphabetically by their title. Include the author's name only with the first title.

The three basic elements of MLA

MLA bibliographical entries or records often have only three elements, separated by periods:

(Stendhal. Red and Black. New York: Norton, 1990.)

The above elements are the name of the author, the title of the book, and publication data. Don't sequentially number MLA entries.

Author's name   Give the last name first, then the first name or initials. This lets you arrange the bibliography alphabetically by the authors' last names.

Book title   Underline the title.

Publication data   Include the place of publication, the publisher, and the copyright of the edition being cited. You may abbreviate the publisher's name as long as it's clear who the publisher is.

Some bibliography entries require more than the three basic elements. Two examples with more elements (the first a literary work from an anthology and the second an article from a daily newspaper) are given below:

Bond, Nelson. "The Voice from the Curious Cube." *100 Great Science Fiction Stories*. Ed. Isaac Asimov, Martin Harry Greenberg, and Joseph D. Olander. New York: Doubleday, 1978. p. 172-175.

White, Joseph. "Deficit dilemma: Is the Cure Worse than the Disease?" *Atlanta Journal-Constitution* 14 June 1992, Section G:1.

Some recommended style manuals

The following is a list of useful sources of information on writing research papers and reference notes:

The Associated Press Stylebook
The Associated Press, 1992

The Chicago Manual of Style
University of Chicago Press

Harbrace College Handbook
John C. Hodges and Mary E. Whitten, with Suzanne S. Webb
Harcourt Brace Jovanovich
Chapters 33–34

A Handbook For Scholars
Mary-Claire van Leunen
Alfred A. Knopf

The McGraw-Hill College Handbook, 2nd edition
Richard Marius and Harvey S. Wiener
McGraw-Hill
Chapters 35-39

MLA Handbook for Writers of Research Papers
Modern Language Association of America

The MLS Style Manual
Modern Language Association of America

Embedding nonprinting comments in a text file

WordStar 7 offers two different ways for embedding nonprinting comments in your text files. These are useful for placing hidden notes to yourself that can be read only by opening the text file with WordStar. The first method uses the Notes dialog box. The second is simply a dot command you type in wherever you want it.

There are times when you'll need to make comments that don't print with the document. Below are the steps for inserting a nonprinting comment through the Notes Menu.

1. Place the cursor at the point where you want to embed the nonprinting comment.
2. Use Ctrl−ONC to open the nonprinting comment window.
3. If necessary, use Ctrl−OM to resize the comment window.
4. Type the comment as you want it. Use any WordStar writing and editing features you need.
5. When finished writing the comment, use Ctrl−KD to save and close the comment window. You'll be returned to the document mode.
6. The comment is embedded in the body of the text file.

If command tag display is on, you'll see the first 15 characters of the comment, enclosed in brackets. If the display is off, you won't see anything. These comments don't add length to the document. You can delete them as a single character.

If you want to insert a one-line embedded comment, you can do so with a dot command. Like all dot commands, this nonprinting comment takes up a line of its own in the text file. This is simpler to use than the Notes Menu, and you can use Ctrl−QF to search for them.

1. Place the cursor at column 1 of any blank line.
2. Type two periods and then the words of your comment. Use any characters you want.
3. When you get to the end of the line, press the Enter key.

You can see these comment lines whenever the dot command display is on. They don't print with the hardcopy, and don't add length to the printed document. To remove them, delete the entire line.

The Modify Notes options

There are three options on the Notes Menu you can use to modify notes you've already embedded in the body of a text file. These allow you to edit or change the text in the note, change the note to a different type, and realign the text in the rest of the notes.

To edit any WordStar note, the command tag display should be on. This is mandatory for nonprinting comments and index markers, as they aren't visible if the tag display is off.

1. Place the cursor at the beginning of the marker in the text file, and use Ctrl−OND.
2. WordStar will open the note for you to change or correct it.
3. Make any changes or edits you want. Then use Ctrl−KD to close the notes window, or press the Enter key to close the Index Entry dialog box.
4. WordStar will return to the document mode.

Endnotes, footnotes, annotations, and nonprinting comments open in a separate window. All WordStar writing and editing features are available.

Index notes open in the Index Entry dialog box. Use Ctrl−F to move forward and Ctrl−A to move backward along the command line. Delete with Ctrl−T, and the Backspace or Delete keys.

Cut-and-paste functions with notes

Though not listed as an option on the Notes Menu, you can cut and paste the contents of WordStar notes and use them in other documents.

Cutting and pasting text from boilerplate file

You can cut and paste the contents of any text file into any WordStar notes window. The only limit is the 15-page maximum length allowed for WordStar notes.

Tip: If you attempt to insert a text file longer than 15 pages, you'll get a file error message. Everything beyond the page maximum limit will be truncated.

These cut-and-paste capabilities are especially useful if you've stored footnote, endnote, or annotation information in separate files. Then all you have to do is copy in the text you've already typed.

1. Place the cursor at the point in the text file where you intend to embed the WordStar note.
2. Open the notes window for the note you want to paste into.
3. Use Ctrl−KR to call the Insert File dialog box, and select the file to paste in from the onscreen listing.
4. Use Ctrl−K to complete the command and insert the selected file.

Saving WordStar notes to disk

You can save the text of any WordStar note to a boilerplate file for permanent storage. All you do is open the note, mark its text as a block, and then use Ctrl−KW to write it to disk.

You can write each WordStar note to a separate file, or use the append option of the Copy To Another File dialog box to write them all to a single file.

I strongly recommend that you save footnotes, endnotes, and annotations to boilerplate files as soon as you write them. You can delete WordStar notes from the text file as a single character. This makes them especially vulnerable to accidental deletion or loss.

24
CHAPTER

An introduction to merge printing

This chapter introduces WordStar 7's merge printing. Merge printing combines WordStar files into form documents. You must have at least a basic knowledge of WordStar for this information to make sense. The different elements of merge printing, introduced in this chapter, are explained in greater depth in chapter 25, *Merge printing, in depth*.

If you've used merge printing with any earlier version of WordStar, the changes and additions to version 7 should be easy to grasp. Everything you already know still applies. You just have to learn how to use the new features.

How to learn merge printing

The best way to learn merge printing is as a hands-on experience, i.e., learn by doing. Don't be afraid to make mistakes. It's the best way to learn.

Merge printing is easier to use than to explain because the parts are more complicated and confusing than the whole. So it helps to understand what it is, and what it does, before trying to use it.

WordStar has merge printing tools to create any kind of form documents you need. Try the simpler features first and then work your way through the more difficult ones. Learn to make a simple mailing list, and then write a master document to print a form letter or mailing labels.

You don't have to learn every feature or use every option every time. Just learn the basics and the tools you need to get your work done. Don't worry about the rest. Don't be intimidated because merge printing seems complicated or because the procedures are new. It's a relatively easy feature to use.

419

Merge printing isn't difficult to use if you have a working knowledge of WordStar. There is, however, no quick way to get started with merge printing. Below are the three basic steps in the process:

1. Writing the mailing list or other data file
2. Creating the form letter or other master document
3. Printing the form letter or other master document

The elements of merge printing

Merge printing is the joining of information stored in a data file into a template to create a single document during printing. This printing utility allows you to assemble custom documents from building blocks so you don't have to type each document individually. It's most commonly used to create repetitive documents like form letters, mailing labels, contracts, and any other kind of standard form.

The basic elements of merge printing are the same, regardless of the type of form documents being produced:

- Data files
- Master documents
- Boilerplate or variable text
- Dot commands to tell WordStar and the printer what to do

What is a data file?

A *data file* is a text file written in either the nondocument mode or with the Maillist companion program. It holds things like names, addresses, phone numbers, serial numbers, inventory information, and any other useful data or boilerplate text to be inserted into a form document. The information that the data file contributes to the merge printing process changes from document to document.

What is a master document?

A *master document* is the template for the merge printing process. It's a standard document file containing the basic shell of the form document, with blank places left for the boilerplate text to be inserted during printing. The master document part of the merge printing doesn't change from document to document.

What about those special dot commands?

WordStar has many dot commands that are used specifically with merge printing. With them you can fine-control the process by telling WordStar the names of data files and boilerplate text to use, the generic names of data in the files, and what to do during printing.

What is boilerplate text?

The term *boilerplate* is an old printing name for text you can use over and over again without ever changing it. This can be something as simple as a return address copied into every letter you write, a disclaimer statement, copyright notice, or licensing agreement. Or it can be something as complicated as tables and lists of information, standardized descriptions, or entire passages of text. Boilerplate text can be stored in an archive or a text file of its own.

Another term for boilerplate text is *variable information*, because it varies from copy to copy. The actual text or data in the data files is divided into lines and columns. Each line is a data record. The items in a data record are the individual pieces of boilerplate text, and they stack to make data columns. Each column has a name to identify it, known either as a *variable name* or a *generic name*. Some common generic names are: name, address, city, state, and zip code.

It doesn't matter what a generic or variable name is, only that it be consistently used to represent the text in the data file or boilerplate file.

How merge printing works

During the merge print runoff, WordStar draws normal text from the master document and sends it to the printer. When a variable name is found in the master document, WordStar searches the data file for the text the name identifies. When found, it inserts the data into the document being printed. All of this takes place without visible pause. In most cases, it requires no further input from the keyboard.

An easy-to-remember comparison

Think of merge printing as a railroad switchyard. You can assemble many different trains at the same time in a switchyard. Using an automated queuing process, you can bring the individual cars together, one by one, to make a train. The switchmaster has his instructions and knows which cars are to be gathered to make up each train. When the process is complete, every boxcar, tanker, or pullman in the train is in the right place, each with a specific purpose and destination. The switchyard and switchmaster are the master document, and the individual cars are the pieces of boilerplate text.

Merge printing uses special commands to guide each print runoff. These commands assemble each hardcopy just like a switchmaster assembling a train. The data and boilerplate text used during the merge printing process can come from any or all of the following sources:

- Data files written with WordStar using the nondocument mode
- Data files written with the Maillist companion program or with any program producing pure ASCII files

- Data files purchased directly from a third-party vendor
- Instructions or data you type on the keyboard when prompted by WordStar
- Embedded commands at the top of the master document text file
- The body of the master document itself
- Boilerplate text files containing entire paragraphs or sections of text

Uses for merge printing

Form documents are an important part of most businesses, which use form documents to communicate with clients, suppliers, and customers in the outside world.

Merge printing eliminates having to send the same mimeographed letter to everyone on a mailing list—or sending one of those form letters where a space is left blank and typed in later. Gone forever is the expensive practice of typing personalized letters one at a time. Merge printing can genuinely customize documents according to the individual or company receiving them.

The primary function of merge printing is the insertion of text from one source into a document as it's sent to the printer. There are unlimited uses—some common, some obscure. This chapter describes only some of the more common uses.

Printing form letters

Since its invention, merge printing has mainly been used for printing form letters. It lets you print personalized form letters for each client or customer in a mailing list. A form letter can be:

- A complete document, minus gaps where data, names, addresses, and personalized information is inserted during printing
- A conditional printing template, containing dot commands telling WordStar where to find boilerplate text to be inserted
- A combination of the above two categories

Printing mailing labels and envelopes

Mailing labels and addressed envelopes are the second most common use of merge printing. The same data file that contains the data for a form letter can be used for mailing addresses (which you can print either on adhesive labels or directly on the envelopes).

Whatever type of printer you have, there are mailing labels available for it. These range from boxes of tractor-fed labels for a dot-matrix or daisywheel printer, to sheets of labels especially designed for a laser printer.

Many printers have optional bins or devices for feeding the envelopes directly

to the printer. This lets you make the form letter or document look even more personalized.

Printing form contracts or agreements

Standard contracts and agreements are the third most common product of merge
printing. It's possible to keep all such documents stored in master documents on
disk, and to make all necessary changes either before or during printing. You
never have to retype them again.

The traditional solution before merge printing came along was to either cus-
tom-write each contract as needed, or to stock preprinted copies of every variation. But no contract or standard document can cover every contingency. So
contracts or agreements were printed with blank spaces to be filled in, and standard sections or paragraphs were simply marked out when they did not apply.
This often resulted in blanks without enough space, and untidy documents with
many paragraphs crossed out.

Reassembling divided documents

Merge printing can join several text files, making a single continuous document.
By merge printing data files to ASCII, you can join them and then sort them in
whatever order needed. Thus, you can assemble minor files into a variety of different documents. You can nest or insert them inside of major files during printing, or print individual files one after the other.

It's very common to divide any long document, like a novel, screenplay, thesis paper, or dissertation, into files no longer than a section or a chapter. This
makes them easier to work with for a variety of reasons:

- It takes less time to load smaller files into memory, and to save them
  back to disk.
- Short documents are easier to move around in, and keep track of where
  you are.
- Each chapter or section can be printed and proofread individually.

When you've finished writing the whole document, however, you want a single
document, with everything in the right order and the pages numbered sequentially. There are two ways of doing this: you can use Ctrl−KR to read all the individual files into a single document file, or you can use merge printing to join the
files in a single hardcopy as they're going to the printer.

Chain printing

Chain printing sends a series of files to the printer, one after the other. Create a
master document containing only a chain of dot commands indicating the names
of files to be printed. When a master document is merge printed, WordStar reads

the chain of dot commands and prints the files in the order listed. When one file completes printing, the master document directs the next to the printer, until the end of the list is reached.

You can chain together text files or data files from any drive or directory in your computer. There is also a dot command to pause printing, and this lets you change disks while printing a chain document.

Conditional printing

Conditional printing merges data or text into a document only if predetermined conditions are met. If you're announcing a sale that applies only to customers in a specific area, it would be a waste of time and money to send copies to customers outside that area. You can specify city, state, or zip code as a condition for printing, and have a mailing go only to people living in the specified area.

You can use any field of information as a condition for printing. The only limitations are your creativity and specific needs.

Nested printing

Nested printing merges one text file into the middle of another during printing. Use the file include dot command in the text file where you want the file to be inserted. When merge printing reaches the embedded command, it will stop printing the master document long enough to find the other file and print it before continuing with the rest of the master document text.

Use this feature to assemble different versions of a form letter for different customers. Create a master document with standard opening and closing paragraphs. Then write a variety of alternative paragraphs to be included among the standard paragraphs.

Multiple file nesting is also possible. This allows you to nest or merge one file inside another, then merge yet other files inside the nested file in the same print runoff. Multiple file nesting is limited to a maximum of seven levels.

25
CHAPTER

Merge printing, in depth

This chapter is a more in-depth discussion of the merge printing process. It contains explanations of the different elements of merge printing that were introduced in the previous chapter: data files, master documents, variable information, and dot commands.

Data files

This section describes how to write and use data files as a resource for mailing lists, form letters, and standard contracts. Each term is defined, and a sample data file is given. All WordStar data files are written in exactly the same way and follow the same set of rules, so you can use the same format for writing any kind of data file.

In the context of merge printing with WordStar, a *data file* is any text file containing names and addresses, prices and values, or other similar information— stored in an orderly fashion for easy retrieval.

You can write data files in WordStar's nondocument mode, with the MailList companion program, or with any other program that produces ASCII text files. You can't write data files in the document mode, because it embeds special word processing commands that interfere with the merge printing routine.

Until now, you might have been keeping address records on a card file system. Each card contains the same basic information about every person or company in the mailing list: title, first name, middle name or initial, last name, street address, apartment number, city, state, zip code, company name, organizations a member of, and so on.

425

In such a filing system, this information is contained on a single card in the file. In a data file mailing list, it's written on a single *data record*. Each of these records is further divided into individual items, or *fields*. When these records are "stacked" in a data file, they make data columns—each containing the same type of information. The columns of data are "fenced off" from one another with a special character that's set aside for that purpose. This character is called the *delimiter*, and is almost always either the comma or the tab.

Using alternate characters as delimiters

WordStar comes from the factory with the comma installed as the delimiter character. This is an industry standard, and is followed by most personal computer software. Some people prefer changing the delimiter to the tab because it aligns data files into visibly distinctive columns. There's nothing wrong with this, providing you remember to make the change in all your merge printing data files.

You can define any unique character as the delimiter. By unique, I mean that the character must be reserved for use as the column marker inside the data files, and can't be used in its normal value in the data records. For this reason, you must limit it to characters other than letters and numbers.

While you can define any character as the delimiter, only one character can be the delimiter in any version of WordStar. If you share data files with other WordStar users, you must all agree to use the same delimiter. To change the delimiter character, use the utility program WSCHANGE.

Note: The most common mistake people make in writing data files is forgetting to insert delimiters between columns or items in a data record. Inserting an extra delimiter character is the second-most common mistake. This is an easy mistake because the delimiter is usually the comma, and the comma is also a punctuation mark.

Don't casually change delimiter to some other character. If you change it inside WordStar, you must remember to change it inside all your data files—including those created or used by other programs.

As far as I'm concerned, the only other character safe to use as a data column delimiter is the tab. The sole benefit of using the tab is the fact that it aligns your data in neat columns that can be easily read—either onscreen or in hardcopy.

In order to use the tab as the delimiter, you must embed a ruler line at the beginning of the data file. Next, set the tab stops on that ruler so that there's only one tab per column, and the columns are far apart so none overlap. Be sure to count your tabs. Remember that each is now acting as a delimiter character.

Elements of a data file

Think of a *data file* as a grid with information listed in horizontal lines and vertical columns. These lines and columns create x and y coordinates. The computer reads the coordinates as directed by the master document and copies the data to the hardcopy.

A *data record* is a single line of information in a data file. This line holds the different pieces of information for one specific item. For instance, a person's name, his address, phone number, and business affiliations would be one data record for a mailing list.

Data columns are created as you write the data lines. Because the information in each data record is in the same order, the data is stacked up in columns. Each column contains all the information of a specific type on that data record. This creates an information resource for WordStar during merge printing.

A data field is a single piece of information in any data record or data column. Unfortunately, the term *field* is used so many different ways that it's usually confusing to the new user. For the purpose of writing a data file for merge printing, I'll use the term *data item* instead.

Keeping columns in order

It's vitally important to keep every item of information in a data file in its proper column. There's a place for everything, and everything must be in its place. Merge printing is unforgiving.

Each column holds a specific kind of information, and the only thing separating columns is the delimiter character. So if you put even a single delimiter out of place, all the columns will be scrambled from that point on.

The data columns in every data file must be perfect. They must be in exactly the same order, and each line must have exactly the same number of columns. Every column must be accounted for in every record line—even when a column item is left blank. The columns must be in exactly the same order as the variable name line at the top of the data file.

Writing a data file

The steps for using the nondocument mode to write a mailing list are as follows:

1. At the Opening Menu, type N to open a file in the nondocument mode.
2. Enter several blank lines to give yourself some room to work in. (Make sure to delete any empty lines left over when you finish writing the data file.)
3. Begin typing the first item of the first data record line at column 1 and line 1 of the data file. Type each item of each record in exactly the same order as the variable names at the beginning of the master document file. Each record line must have exactly the same number of items as there are variable names, and each item must be separated by the correct delimiter. End each record with a carriage return.

4. A record line is complete only when the last item is typed and all the delimiters are in place.

5. Go back periodically and check each record to make sure it has exactly the same number of items.

6. It can take a long time to write a data file in the nondocument mode. Save the file regularly as you're writing it.

The following are rules to follow when you're writing a data file with the previous steps:

- Never leave blank lines between data record lines. Always keep the lines stacked tightly.
- Every record line must have exactly the same number of delimiter characters. When in doubt, count them onscreen.
- If the comma is used as the delimiter, avoid using it inside the data items themselves. If you must use a comma in a data item, enclose that entire item in quotation marks. This tells WordStar to print the comma verbatim. It's much easier to put your punctuation in the master document rather than the data file.
- Don't use quotation marks in any other way inside the data file. If you want quotation marks to print, put them around the variable names in the master document.

Tip: Don't print your merge-print document to test the accuracy of the data file. Test print the master document to ASCII, and open the file to check for errors. When you find an error, make a note of what and where it is, and then return to the data file and correct it. Keep test printing to ASCII until you've found and corrected all your mistakes.

You can always go back and add new lines (records) to a data file. Just remember to open the data file as a nondocument. Use Ctrl−QF to find the point where the new line belongs. Issue a carriage return to clear a blank line, and type in the new record line. Remember to give it exactly the same number of columns as the rest of the line.

A sample data file

Below is CUSTOMER.DTA—a sample mailing-list data file. It contains the account numbers, names, street addresses, cities, states, and zip codes for customers of a picture framing supply company.

```
2309,Dragonrose Enterprises,Box 315,Bowman,GA,30624,WordStar
2310,Gladstone Gallery,124 Valley Way,Del Mar,CA,92014,WordStar
2311,Finlayson Frames,333 Barber Lane,Abbeville,SC,24141,WordStar
2312,The Frugal Framer,6 Cherry Street,Asheville,NC,28801,WordStar
2313,Frames R Us,357 California Avenue,Elberton,GA,30310,WordStar
```

2314,Nouveau Gallery,21 Flatiron Blvd.,Asheville,NC,28801,WordStar
2315,Moore Art Supplies,104 N.Polk St,Tullahoma,TN,37388,WordStar
2316,Framer's Supply Co.,519 S. Broad St.,Bowman,GA,30624,WordStar
2317,Stiefel Frames,301 Colonial St,Knoxville,TN,37920,WordStar
2318,The Art Store,2121 University Place,Athens,GA,30905,WordStar
2319,Bonnie's Designs,25 Emily Way,Asheville,NC,28805,WordStar

This mailing list has all the essential elements of a data file. Each record is on a line of its own and has exactly the same number of columns, and all the items are arranged in exactly the same order.

Master documents

Once you have a data file for your mailing lists, inventory, and so on, the next step is to write a master document to use the data in form letters, contracts, and the like. This section details the steps involved in writing and using these master documents. A *master document* is a text file that serves as a template for printing repetitive documents. It always contains the following components:

- Dot commands at the beginning of the document that list the order of the variable items in the corresponding data file.
- Variable names to indicate where the variable text is inserted during printing.
- The body text of the form document.

The master document file contains the body text of the letter, minus the variable text to be inserted from the data file. Variable names mark the places where the variable text (the data items from the data file) is to be merged during printing.

WordStar prints the body text until it encounters a variable name. At that point, it merges the variable text into the document being printed and then continues with the body text until the next variable name—all the way to the end of the document. When printing a series of form documents, WordStar then begins printing the next.

A command file is a master document that contains only dot commands and no body text. The dot commands tell WordStar the names of the files to be merged, joined, appended, or nested.

The master document contains the four basic things WordStar needs to complete the merge printing job: an embedded command block, variable names representing variable text, and the body text.

The command block

The command block is the group of dot commands placed at the very beginning of the master document. Some of these are the same dot commands you would place at the beginning of a normal document, but most are specific to the merge-printing process. They're put together in a block at the beginning of the file so you can see them all at a glance.

There's a specific order in which these commands need to be arranged. Some commands must always come before others. If you get these out of order, it will confuse WordStar by sending the wrong instructions during merge printing. A sample command block is given below. You can use it in a master document that uses the sample data file given in the previous chapter.

```
.op off
.df subscrib.dta
.rv ACCT#,NAME,STREET,STATE,ZIPCODE,PRODUCT
.sv DATE,November 2, 1991
.av SIGNATURE
```

This is only a very basic command block. Notice how it has a very definite structure. WordStar looks for merge printing information in this order. Your command blocks can be much more complicated than this, depending on the kind of merge printing you're attempting. Each command in this command block is defined in the following sections:

.OP This command tells WordStar to toggle page numbering off. When printing form letters or mailing labels, you never want the standard page numbering left on. Otherwise, WordStar will sequentially number every page or label it prints. If you must have page numbers in your form letters, set it with a footer or header.

.DF This command tells WordStar the name of the data file to be used during merge printing. It can be in any drive or directory in your computer, if you specify the drive and subdirectory as a prefix to the filename.

.RV This command contains the variable names in the order that they're listed in the data file. The variable names must be in the same order as the data file items, spelled identically, and all delimiter characters must be in place.

.SV This command tells WordStar to set a variable that isn't stored in the data file. In this case, it's the date, which is typed in after the variable name. You can set more than one variable on an .SV command line, but it's simpler to set each on its own line. This lets you keep track of them at a glance.

.AV This command tells WordStar to pause printing at the variable name, and lets you type in a variable that changes from copy to copy of the form document. In this case, SIGNATURE is the variable, and the variable name is placed in the signature block of the letter. This lets you type in a different signature for each hardcopy.

These command-block commands are explained in more depth under the subsection *The command block* of the section *Dot commands*.

A sample form letter

A sample master document, a form letter, is shown in Fig. 25-1. You can use the sample data file from the previous chapter with this master document. Use them together, if you want, as a training exercise. The same basic format can be used for writing any form letter.

This sample master document is typical of form letters used daily in different kinds of businesses. The letter contains all the elements necessary for telling WordStar how to merge print a form letter using a data-file mailing list. Notice the command block in place at the top of the file.

```
.op off
.df SUBSCRIB.DTA
.rv ACCT#,NAME,STREET,STATE,ZIPCODE,PRODUCT
.sv DATE,November 2, 1991
.av SIGNATURE



                                              Dragonrose Software
                                              Box 315
                                              Bowman, GA 30624


&DATE&
&NAME&
&STREET/o&
&CITY&, &STATE& &ZIPCODE&

Dear &NAME&:

We received your warranty registration card in the mail. Congratulations on your
recent purchase of &PRODUCT&. Dragonrose Software is confident it will open a new
world of software use for you. We know you will be satisfied with &PRODUCT&. Many
of your neighbors in &CITY& have also purchased &PRODUCT& and have confirmed their
satisfaction with it.

We have added you to our mailing list for upcoming Dragonrose releases and
&PRODUCT& updates.



Sincerely,



&SIGNATURE&
```

25-1 Sample master document.

Variable names

Insert a variable name in the master document by typing it exactly as it appears in the .RV line in the command block, and enclosing it between ampersands. Ampersands tell WordStar "this is a variable name." Avoid using ampersands to substitute for the word *and* in the body text of the master document.

WordStar looks for ampersands in pairs. If you omit one from a variable name, WordStar will consider the ampersand to be part of the body text—and print it verbatim. If you misspell a variable name in the body of the master document, WordStar will also consider it to be body text and print it.

WordStar has eight predefined variable names you can use in any master document. Data to fill these variables come directly from the WordStar program. These variable names are as follows:

Variable	Inserted information
&#&	Current page number.
&_&	Current line number.
&@&	Today's date. The date is drawn from the computer's real-time clock.
&!&	Current time. The time is drawn from the computer's real-time clock.
&:&	Current drive.
&.&	Current directory.
&*&	Current filename.
& \ &	Full path of the current file.

You can also use these symbols, minus the ampersands, to insert the same information into headers and footers, for any document. They're also the hotkeys for macros available through the Macro Menu. To execute the macros, use Ctrl—M then type the symbol.

Tip: The format for date and time inserted by the Macro Menu (and by the variables &@& and &!&) can be set with WSCHANGE.

The body text

Type the body text of the text file as you would any other. Type it according to the particular style of the document you're writing. Use the same margins, tabs, line spacing, whatever. When you come to a place where variable text is to be inserted, type its variable name and then continue with the document.

At the very end of the form letter, use .PA to insert a page break. Use only a single carriage return after this command. If there are any blank lines below the page break, then delete them. This command tells WordStar to start printing the next copy of the document on a new page.

If you leave out this page break, WordStar will begin printing the next form letter on the same page, immediately after the last carriage return. If you leave any blank lines below the page break, WordStar will space down that far before beginning to print the next copy of the form document.

Test printing the form document

The best way to test print any form document is to merge print it to ASCII. (This prints a copy to a file named ASCII.WS in the current drive and directory.) Then you can open that file in the document mode and scan through it for mistakes. This should help pinpoint mistakes in the master document, the data file, and any other variable files you've used.

Doing this provides two major benefits. First, the printing is completed as fast as your drive can receive it—so you don't have to wait on your printer. Second, you don't waste a single sheet of paper or a single mailing label. This might not seem important, but test printing to hardcopy can waste a lot more than time.

Handling missing data record entries

If you have a record in your data file that doesn't contain one or more of its data items, then you need to create a blank item. For instance, if you have a record in a mailing list for a person who doesn't have a listed phone number, the data record for that person might be:

Frank Smith,411 Maple Dr.,Baltimore,MD,,

Notice that the blank item is marked with commas. This is very important, especially if the missing item is in the middle of the record. If you didn't include the commas, the rest of the variables for that record would be placed in the wrong place in the master document.

If the data file has a blank item, WordStar won't print anything in the space reserved for it in the master document. If the text indicated by the variable name is the only text on a line, as in an address, the hardcopy will have a blank line at that point.

The simplest way to avoid these problems is to phrase your master documents so missing data items don't leave gaps. Another way is to always use the .AV command to add variables for which there's no convenient alternative in the data file. It takes longer to print a runoff when using .AV, and someone has to remain at the computer to type in the information, but it's a way to deal with nonstandard data. The third way to handle missing data entries is to use /O with variable names, which stands for *omit*. This tells WordStar that there are record lines with empty data columns—and to omit the entire line when no data is available to fill it. The following are rules for using this command:

- You type /O (a slash followed by the letter O) as a suffix to the variable name with one or more blank entries in its data column. It goes inside the ampersands, and can be in either upper- or lowercase.

- It's common for some addresses on mailing lists to have more lines than others. The /O lets you use an extra line where needed without leaving a blank line for other records.
- When used, the /O key tells merge printing to close up the address block on the hardcopy. Without it, WordStar would leave an entire blank line.
- For /O to work, the variable name must be on a line by itself in the master document. For this reason, it normally works best with items like apartment, suite, or box numbers. Don't try to use this after a variable in the body text.

A checklist for writing master documents

When writing master documents, always keep the following points in mind:

- Be sure to put the .DF command above the .RV command to which it refers. This is very important! WordStar looks for this order. Failure to do this will ruin the printout.
- Before you put names for variables in the body of the document, be sure they're all identified in the command block.
- When typing variable names in the body of the document, never forget to enclose each between a pair of ampersands. If you forget even one, anywhere in the document, all your merge printed documents will be wrong.
- Remember to end the master document with the .PA page break command, with no blank lines following it.
- When the master document is exactly the way you want it to be, save it one last time and close the file with Ctrl−KD. It also never hurts to make a backup copy of the file on an archive disk.

Variable information

This section describes in detail the use of variable names in all phases of merge printing, data files, and master documents. They're an extremely important aspect of the merge-printing process, and it's necessary for you to understand them fully.

During merge printing, WordStar searches the data file for two types of information—record lines and items within each record. When retrieving the latter of these, WordStar must be told how to recognize categories of data on the record lines. Categories of information are identified by their location in the line, and by their variable name.

A *variable name* is an arbitrary title or designation that represents a column of data in a data file. It can be anything you want it to be. Use any combination of letters and numerals. Your average mailing-list data file will use the variable names NAME, ADDRESS, CITY, STATE, and ZIPCODE. For convenience, restrict yourself to letters and numbers, and use names of 10 characters or less. Be consistent throughout your data files and master documents.

Placing variable names in the master document

Variable names are used in two different places in the master document. They're in embedded commands that supply information to the finished document, like the .DF command line. They're also in the body text of the document. Enclosed between ampersands, they mark the spot where variable text is merged during printing.

Assigning variable names

Variable names are assigned to variable information in one primary place—in the .RV command line in the command block of the master document (where they must be spelled the same and be in identical order to how they're listed in the data file). Variables can also be assigned with the command block's .SV and .AV commands, where they represent data not found in a data file.

A variable name merely represents text that's drawn into the file from some other source, e.g., a data file. When WordStar encounters this representation in the master document, the computer searches the record column identified by the variable name. Whatever is found in that column for the correct record WordStar merges into the current hardcopy being printed. For the same spot in the next form document, WordStar will merge the information from that same column in the next record line.

You can change variable names without affecting the merge print runoff, providing you also change it throughout the data files and master documents being used. Changing even a single character is the same as giving it an entirely different name. If you change it in the .RV command line, you must also change it in the body text.

Placing variable names in body text

In the body text of a master document, variable names are substituted for information that's to be grabbed from the data file.

- Variable names in the body of the master document must be enclosed between a pair of ampersands (e.g., &name& and &address&).
- This ampersand pair is the tag, telling merge printing it must fill that space with data or text from a designated data record and column.
- Merge printing won't print this variable name or the ampersands. (To print the master document verbatim, deselect the Interpret Merge Variables option on the Print dialog box.)
- Merge printing will print ampersands when they're used normally in the

document as an alternative to the word *and*, but it's best to avoid their use to prevent confusion.

Warning: Never leave blank spaces between the ampersands and the variable names they enclose. WordStar will interpret this as a normal use of the ampersands and print them verbatim.

Sample variable names

Following are sample variable names for variable information stored in a data file, and a sample data file to correspond with the names.

&NUMBER&,&LASTNAME&,&FIRSTNAME&,&DOB&,&BONUS&

355,Alguire,James,"November 28, 1965","29,000"
356,Brooks,Michaelsohn,"August 15,1941","23,000"
357,McIntosh,Bonnie,"September 15,1955","36,000"
358,Pitts,William,"November 2, 1948","43,000"
359,Sheridan,Shadow,"October 30, 1955","36,000"

In the master document body text, information from a data column must be referred to with the appropriate variable name (for instance, 356 with &NUMBER&) for the text it represents to appear in the printout.

Picking the data columns to use

You must identify all the data columns, in the correct order, in the .RV command line. But it isn't necessary to use every column in every data file to merge print a document. You can pick and choose among the columns of information available.

WordStar only uses a data item from a specific data record when its variable name appears in the body text of the master document. So your data files can contain many different kinds of information. And one data file can print many different merge documents.

You can maintain permanent data files, adding or changing data to suit your needs. Then simply adapt the master document to use the modified data file.

Rules of thumb for variable names

- When you come to a place in the master document where you need to place a variable name, type an ampersand, the name, and the second ampersand.
- If you're going to use the same variable names in many different master documents, it's well worth the trouble to create a macro for each of them. Then you can insert them with two keystrokes instead of having to type them from scratch.
- A variable name can be up to 40 characters long, and be any

combination of letters and numerals, either upper- or lowercase. Most people find it inconvenient to use variable names longer than 10 characters.

- Never leave blank spaces in a variable name. If you want to separate characters for visual effect, use punctuation marks, hyphens, underlines, or slash marks instead of blank spaces.
- Never use a number or hyphen as the first character in a variable name.
- When typing the .RV command line at the beginning of a master document, remember to specify the variable names for every data column in the data file. They must be spelled the same and appear in the same order. Do this even if you're using data from only a few of the data columns.

Changing the variable name delimiter

A delimiter is a character used in a special way to mark the beginning and end of special text. In the data file, the standard delimiter is the comma. In variable names, the standard delimiter is the ampersand. When used in pairs to enclose text, it tells WordStar "this is a variable name."

The delimiter doesn't have to be the ampersand. You can change it to almost any other character by using the customizing program WSCHANGE. WordStar will then look for the new character as the delimiter. If you change the delimiter, you must also change it in all your master documents.

Don't change the delimiter unless absolutely necessary. Once you change it, your master documents will become incompatible with other versions of Word-Star. And your version of WordStar will become incompatible with other master documents. Whatever delimiter character you use, you must be consistent with it throughout all your files that are used for merge printing.

Special variable commands

The commands and configuration keys described in the following sections are used for defining special variable information for merge printing. Some control the size or format of the space into which the data prints. Some execute complex functions. Some are complicated to use. Some aren't. None are truly difficult. All these commands are based on previously given WordStar and merge printing information, and require practice to master.

Variable-space formatting

The command .SV *variable name = defined space* allows you to set aside a particular type and size of space for inserting text during merge printing. This helps ensure a consistent layout when text items in the data file aren't consistent in size or number of decimal places.

Its three basic steps are to first give a variable name to the variable space, then define the format to which the inserted text is to conform, and finally to tell WordStar where to use the specially formatted space by placing its variable name in the body of the master document.

Variable-space formatting uses the .SV command to give even finer control over the way the printed document looks. When the data is inserted during merge printing, it's made to conform to the space assigned to it, with the alignment you've preset. This is especially valuable for inserting variable data in tables or charts.

Unless you maintain absolute control over data files, the data in columns can wind up in many different sizes. Sometimes it's impossible to avoid this. The purpose of variable-space formatting is to control irregularly sized text when it's inserted from a data file.

Variable-space formatting allows you to use any defined format with any variable in the master document. Inserted data can be printed flush left, flush right, or centered. To define a variable-space format, follow these steps:

1. Embed the command .SV in the command block. Leave one blank space after the command, and give the format a number or letter as a variable name. For example: .SV 5 or .SV A (you can use any letters except O, L, R, C).
2. Type an equal sign after the name, as in .SV 5= or .SV 7=.
3. Type the letter L, R, or C for the kind of formatting you want to use (L stands for flush left, R for flush right, and C for center). The number of times you type the letter sets the number of spaces in the format. Each character represents a single space. For example, to set a 15-space centered format, you could use the following command:

   .SV 7 = CCCCCCCCCCCCCCC

4. When you want to apply this format to a specific variable in the master document, include the number 7 in the variable name, for instance, &NAME/7&.

During merge printing, if any item is too big to fit into the defined space, WordStar will cut off the excess characters.

Masking variable spaces

Any characters, including blank spaces, that are different than the formatting letters (L, R, and C) in the .SV definition will be printed verbatim. You can use this to substitute or insert characters or spaces into printed data. This is called *masking* because the characters in the format definition mask, or take the place of, characters in the variable data being inserted.

The most common masking character is the space. It's the only character you can put ahead of the first character in a format definition. All other characters must go after the first letter of the space definition. To tell WordStar that blank spaces are being used for masking, the entire .definition must be enclosed with quotation marks, as shown here:

.SV 5 = " LLLLLLLLLLLLLLL "

If the variable data to be printed in this defined space is 1234567890, then Word-Star will print:

(one space)234567890(six spaces)

The leading space in the formatted definition has masked over the first character of the data being inserted. The last six Ls are replaced with blank spaces because the definition covers 15 spaces—and the data is only 10 characters long.

Note: Masking works only with left- and right-justified format definitions. When the letter C is the first one in the definition, other spaces and characters to the left of the C are printed verbatim instead of being masked.

Variable-number formatting

Variable-number formatting is a modification of variable-space formatting. The command .SV *variable name = defined space* allows you to set aside a particular type and size of space for inserting numbers during merge printing. This helps ensure a consistent layout when numbers in the data file aren't consistent in size or number of decimal places.

Using variable-number formatting is a three-step process. First you give a variable name to the variable-number format, then define the format to which the inserted numbers are to conform, and finally tell WordStar where to use the specially formatted space by placing its variable name in the body of the master document.

By predefining the size and type of variable-number formatting, WordStar controls the look of variable numeric items in the hardcopy. Special characters serve as wildcards in the command line, and are replaced with information from the data file. There's also an option to use the .MA math dot command to calculate and insert math results during printing.

Embed the command .SV in the command block. Space over once after the command and give the format a number or letter variable name, followed by an equal sign. Then type a definition character a certain amount of times. The number of characters determines the number of spaces in the variable-number format. Each character represents one space. Numbers are always right-justified in these spaces, which keeps the number columns aligned correctly.

The special characters used in variable-number format definitions, and the specific functions of each, are as follows:

9 If there's no numeral in the data item for this space, a 0 is printed. Thus, if the number in the data column is 19.48 and the defined format is 99999999.99 then 00000019.48 will be printed.

Z   If there's no numeral in the data column for this space or if the numeral is a leading zero, then a blank space is substituted. For example, if the format is ZZZZ.ZZ, 17.62 would print as (space)(space)17.62.

*****   If there's no numeral in the data column for this space in the data being inserted or if the numeral is a leading zero, an asterisk is printed before the decimal and a zero is printed after the decimal. Thus, the number 48 in the format ********.** would print as ******48.00.

$ This inserts a $ to the left of the first numeral being printed, and substitutes for a numeral unless there's a leading space in that position. If there's no numeral and no leading space, a blank space is inserted. Thus, the number 19.48 in the format $$$$$$$$.$$ would print as $19.48. Note: When using this character in the definition, you must have one more dollar sign in your number format than the largest number you expect to have inserted as variable data.

—   This indicates negative numbers. It places a minus sign to the left of the first character in the data being inserted. If the dollar sign is inserted before a number, the minus sign is inserted to the left of the $. If there aren't numbers for every space in the format, the numbers will close up to fill the empty spaces. Thus, if the number 19.48 is inserted in the format −$$$$$$$$.$$, it will print as −$19.48. Note: When using this as a definition character, the number character must be one space or character larger than the biggest number being merge printed.

.   This marks the decimal position in the definition. If the number being merge printed has more decimal places than the defined format, the extra numerals will be cut off and not printed.

,   This is normally used in the defined format and doesn't print if there are no numerals to its left.

( )   Parentheses enclose negative numbers or substitute blank spaces. They must be the first and last characters in the definition. Note: When using parentheses in a definition, you must have two more spaces than the largest number you expect to merge print.

Inserting results of math calculations

The math command .MA *variable name = equation* can calculate an equation during merge printing, with values drawn from the data file, and then substitute the results in place of its variable name. The catch is that you must know how to write a mathematical equation to use this command.

Place this command in the command block of the master document. You can use as many .MA commands as are needed. Each variable defined by the command must have a different name.

- Each command, on a line by itself, defines a single variable item.
- The equation is typed on the line after the command.
- The symbols, format, and syntax of the equation are identical to the ones used by the Math Menu, called with Ctrl−QM.
- To use data values from a data file, substitute variable names in place of numbers in the equation.

During merge printing, WordStar uses the equation to calculate a new variable number from data stored in the data file. The results of this calculation are inserted in the hardcopy in place of the variable name defined by the command.

Tip: Because of the complexity of this command, the only way to check the accuracy of your equations is to test print the merged document to ASCII. Then check the results to see if your answers are correct.

Writing some simple math definitions

The only difference between equations for the .MA math command and those from the Math Menu is the use of variables drawn from data files in place of fixed numbers. In the equation, the variable names are substituted for variable information. Just like variable names in the body of the master document, the variable names in the equations must be nested between a pair of ampersands. Below are three sample .MA equations:

```
.MA sum = &value1& + &value2& * &value3&
.MA total = &value1& − &value2& − &value3&
.MA amount = &value2 / &value3& + &value1&
```

The .MA command relies on other embedded commands to tell it where to find information assigned to variable names in the equation. Data files are the major source of the information to be used in calculations. Remember that data files are identified by the .DF command at the beginning of the master document. The math dot command can also use information provided by .AV and .SV commands.

Displaying your own messages

In addition to .AV, there are two other commands to display messages onscreen during printing. Whenever WordStar encounters one of these commands during printing, it reads the message typed on the line and displays it without interrupting printing.

The embedded command .DM *message* is used to display a message onscreen during printing. This command can be inserted anywhere in the master document. You can use the same message repeatedly or embed as many messages as you want—one per line. WordStar processes each as the page is being sent to the printer.

A .DM command can be up to 240 characters long. The recommended length of a message is 65–80 characters, to ensure the whole message fits onscreen.

Tip: Use this command to display the version of a form letter currently being printed by using a variable name from the data file on the message line. For example, *.DM Now printing letter to &NAME&* would insert the name of the customer for the current version of the form letter. This command must go below the .DF command line.

You can use the display message command in combination with other dot commands to tell you what to do to satisfy merge printing conditions. Below are sample commands used to display onscreen messages with this command:

```
.DM Now printing letter to &NAME&
.DM Now printing Chapter 19
.DM Load envelope in printer, Press P
.DM Insert next disk in Drive B
.DM Take a break . . . I'll be printing awhile.
```

The command .CS *message* is the one to use when you're displaying several messages during a single printing. It tells WordStar to clear the previous message from the screen so the new message can take its place.

Dot commands

Merge-printing dot commands are more of the same kind of embedded commands you learned how to use with WordStar's document mode. With WordStar, *embedded* means a command has been typed or inserted into the text file so that, even though it looks like normal text and can be deleted, copied, or moved, it doesn't print in the hardcopy. Instead, WordStar reads it as a command and executes its functions.

Dot commands are very simple. Every dot command takes up a line of its own, and must begin at column 1. WordStar doesn't consider the words or numbers in a dot command line to be printable text. Dot commands controlling page layout and design become active as soon as you embed them. Dot commands controlling printing and merge printing are executed only as the file is being sent to the printer.

Warning: Be careful not to let periods used as punctuation fall on column 1 as you type your documents (although this should happen only if a space is accidently inserted before a period). Whenever WordStar finds a period in column 1, it's treated as the beginning of a dot command and everything else on that line is treated as part of a command. The text on that line won't print in the hardcopy.

Merge-printing dot commands are special because they take effect only during the merge printing runoff. The normal printing routine has no effect on them. They serve only to gather and control variable text and then merge it into the hardcopy.

Dot command format and syntax

With dot commands, *format* means the content and purpose of the command; *syntax* refers to the order in which text is typed and the commands are placed.

Every dot command uses the same basic format. This must be followed precisely. The way you type it defines the command—in effect telling WordStar what to do with the file on which you're working. If the format and syntax aren't correct, the dot command either won't work at all or won't work the way you want it to.

- A dot command takes up its own line in the text file, called the *command line*.
- The command line must always begin on column 1. Otherwise, WordStar treats it as normal text.
- A dot command line must begin with a period and end with a carriage return to keep it separate from text that doesn't belong to the command.

Some dot commands stand alone and perform the same function regardless of where they're placed in the text file. Some dot commands work as a supplement or corollary to others. Thus one command defines, identifies, or locates something—and the next uses the information supplied by the previous command.

The function of a dot command takes effect on the command line, and continues down through the text file until countermanded or toggled off by another dot command—or until the end of the file.

The command block

The *command block* is the name given to the group of dot commands embedded at the very beginning of the text file. With standard documents, these embedded commands control the design and layout of the document. They do so by setting values for margins, line spacing, and so on.

With few exceptions, merge printing dot commands also belong in this command block. Some work best and some work only if they're in the command block. Others are placed there so you can check them at a glance—or change their settings consistently.

Command blocks can be used as variables just like any other text. Once you have a command block set exactly like you want it, you can use it again in other master documents. You can also open the original document in a second window and copy the block from the old file to the new. The simplest way is to mark it as a block of text and write it to a file of its own. This way you create an archive of command blocks that you can read into your new master documents (with Ctrl−KR) when you create them. For safety's sake, store copies of your command blocks on separate floppy disks.

Basic merge printing dot commands

The special embedded dot commands in the following sections are used for directing the merge-printing process.

Note: When working with dot commands, remember that it doesn't matter whether the letters of the command are in upper, lower, or mixed case. WordStar makes no distinction. For your own convenience, be consistent in whatever case you use—in the event you need to use a global find-and-replace command to alter your dot commands throughout the master document.

Identifying the data file

The command .DF *filename* tells WordStar the name of the data file it's to use for merge printing. Type this on any line below the commands used to set up the layout and design. Leave a blank space after the two letters of the command, and then type the full name of the data file, including its extension.

- Specify a data file in a different disk or path by prefixing the filename with the drive or path.
- The .DF command must always be paired with a .RV command, and it must be on the line directly above that .RV command.
- The paired commands can be placed anywhere in the body of the master document, but it's recommended to put them in the command block.

You can use more than one data file to merge print a form document. Be careful not to confuse WordStar as to the specific data or file being used. Either identify the data columns in each with different variable names, or embed the command lines directly above the paragraphs using the different data files.

Identifying variables to be read

The dot command .RV *name,name,name* is the command that tells WordStar the variable names that correspond to the data columns of variable information in your data file.

- The command does not work alone. It must always be paired with a .DF command, which identifies the data file being used. It must always be on the line directly below the .DF command.
- The variable names in the command line must exactly match those in the data file being used. They must be spelled the same and be in the same order.

Make sure to type in the variable names of the data columns exactly as they are in the data file. Separate the variable names with commas (or other delimiter, if you've changed the default) and don't leave any blank spaces between the names and the commas. Be sure to end the line with a carriage return.

Adding variables during printing

The dot command .AV [*prompt*], *variable name* is the command to pause printing and allow you to type in additional text not available from a data file or variable file. You can use it to insert any word or phrase. It's commonly used to type in a different date or signature line, or to create form letters for customers not in a data file.

The *prompt* is just an onscreen query for a particular response. In this case, it's the text or message displayed onscreen when the printing pauses. It's usually either a variable name given to the specific use, or a message telling you what to do. It's common to phrase it as a question. Use up to 65 characters in the prompt, but "short and to the point" is the best rule of thumb. The *variable name* part of the command identifies the variable to be inserted.

The .AV command interrupts the automatic printing of form documents. This means that you must remain at, or return to, the keyboard during the printing of every copy of the form document. Printing doesn't resume until you type in the requested data and press the Enter key.

If you don't include a prompt in the .AV command, when the master document processes the command, it will prompt you with just the variable name followed by a question mark. For instance, when WordStar comes across the following .AV command:

.AV PHONENUMBER

the merge printing will pause, and WordStar will display the following prompt onscreen:

PHONENUMBER?

Limiting the inserted characters

You also can set a limit to the number of characters to be typed in response to the onscreen prompt. This is used to prevent a line of text from overprinting the right margin.

To set the limit, type a comma after the variable name, followed by the number of the maximum characters allowed. When the prompt appears onscreen during merge printing, the cursor will stop moving after you type in the maximum set number of characters. The following command, for example:

.AV ZIPCODE,10

would prevent anyone from typing in more than 10 characters for a zip code—catching a typographical error before it prints in the hardcopy.

Prompts with custom messages

Write an .AV command to display a message of your choice onscreen, instead of just the variable name. Enclose this message between quotation marks when you type it on the command line. It must go before the variable name. For example:

.AV "Type the name as: Last, First, M.I.",NAME"

would cause merge printing to pause at the variable name, and display the following message onscreen:

Type the name as: Last, First, M.I.

Form letters without a data file

You can use the .AV command to create and print form documents without first creating a data file—or adding the information to your data file. This is actually one of the earliest forms of merge printing.

1. Set a .AV command for every item of variable text: name, address, city, state, zip code, phone number, and so on.
2. Write a master document with the variable names in place.
3. Start merge printing the master document, and tell WordStar to print the number of copies needed to get the job done.
4. Type in the information for each copy as WordStar prompts you for it.

This isn't as convenient as a fully automatic merge printing, but it does let you print form documents for people not in your data file mailing list.

Setting a specific variable to print

The .SV *variable name,variable information* command tells WordStar to insert specific variable information given in the dot command at a place identified by the variable name.

This is used to insert variable text not found in the data file or a variable file. You specify the complete information in the dot command itself. Merge printing looks only at the command line for the information to be inserted.

Embedding the command in the document

To use the command, begin it at column 1 on a blank line above the variable name in the body text. For simple convenience, I recommend that you place all .SV commands in the command block.

1. Type a period, SV, a blank space, and the variable name as it's to appear in the body of the master document.
2. Type a comma, and then the exact information to be inserted in the hardcopy by the command. Do not leave a blank space after the comma, or the blank space will also be inserted during the merge printing.
3. Now type the variable name, enclosed between ampersands, where you want the data text to be inserted during merge printing.

This command can be no longer than 240 characters. Use as many .SV commands as needed, and place each on a line above the variable name it defines. Two sample .SV commands are as follows:

    .SV PARTY1,Fred Lewis
    .SV PARTY2,Tony Sterrett

If these two commands are placed in the command block at the beginning of the master document, when the following sentence appears in the text:

    This contract is between &PARTY1& and &PARTY2&.

it will actually print like this:

    This contract is between Fred Lewis and Tony Sterrett.

Assembling separate files into a single hardcopy

An extremely valuable feature of merge printing is its ability to merge the contents of entire files into a single printed hardcopy. This allows you to assemble entire documents from their component sections.

The .FI *filename* command tells WordStar to read the identified file during a merge printing and copy its contents into the document being printed.

The dot command must be embedded in the master document at the exact point where the contents of the file are to be inserted. Use as many .FI commands as are needed. WordStar sets no limit because each .FI command is processed individually before the next is begun. When the inserted file is printed, it begins printing at the line position of the .FI dot command.

The most common use of the .FI command is to join the sections of a large document into a complete hardcopy, which requires a master document containing only dot commands and command instructions.

1. Open and name the master document like any other.
2. In the command block, set up all headers, footers, and page numbering you intend the complete document to use.
3. Now embed an .FI *filename* command line for every section of the complete document. If your files are in different drives or directories, simply preface the filename with its path.
4. Streamline this process by giving all sections the same filename and identifying them by the extension. If you were assembling the chapters in a book, for example, your .FI command lines would be as follows:

    .fi CHAPTER.01
    .fi CHAPTER.02
    .fi CHAPTER.03
    .fi CHAPTER.04
    .fi CHAPTER.05

5. To create the complete document, simply merge print this master document. WordStar will join the files in the same order as they're listed in the master document.

Beginning each section on a new page

To ensure each section of a document begins printing on a new page, embed the .PA dot command between the .FI command lines. For example:

```
.fi CHAPTER.01
.pa
.fi CHAPTER.02
.pa
.fi CHAPTER.03
.pa
.fi CHAPTER.04
.pa
.fi CHAPTER.05
```

After WordStar finishes printing the first file, it will issue a form feed and then begin printing the next file at the top of the following sheet of paper.

Swapping floppy disks while printing

If you're using files on different floppy disks, the .FI command has a key to permit swapping disks during the merge print runoff. To use the key, simply type a comma after the filename, then type the word CHANGE or simply C.

This command is useful when the complete document is too large for all its sections to fit on a single floppy disk. When WordStar finishes printing all the sections on one floppy disk, it will pause to let you swap the floppy disk. The command also tells WordStar to expect a different disk, and to read its file allocation table. When WordStar encounters the CHANGE specification during merge printing, the following message will appear onscreen:

Insert disk with the file (*filename*); then press RETURN

At that time, take the old disk out of the drive, put the new one in, close the door, and press the Enter key. If you make a mistake on the command line, or put the wrong floppy disk in the drive, the following error message will appear onscreen:

* * * Cannot change disk in drive A:, request ignored

What happens at this point depends entirely on which drives you're using.

Merge printing documents to disk

It isn't necessary to print a hardcopy of the complete document with merge printing. You always have the option to merge print the compiled document to a file on disk. You might want to do this as a test before sending the file to the printer. In fact, it's always best to test print merge printing to a file on disk—because merge printing can waste a lot of paper.

1. Start the merge printing normally.
2. At the Merge Print dialog box, advance the cursor to the Redirect Output to Port command line.
3. To merge print the document to a file in the current directory, type in the filename you want to use. To merge print the document to a file in a different drive or directory, preface the filename with the path.

Nested printing with File Include

WordStar allows you to nest files during merge printing with the .FI command. This means that the .FI command can also be embedded in files being merged by the .FI command in the master document (a .FI inside of a .FI).

You can use multiple levels of nesting, but there's a definite limit to what WordStar can handle—no more than seven levels. Nested printing becomes progressively more complicated for each level of nesting depth. This can noticeably hinder or slow the printing speed. If you're also swapping disks or switching directories, it can become even more pronounced. Even worse, the more levels and complexity you use, the easier it becomes to make mistakes and ruin your printout. The best rule of thumb is "keep it simple."

Merge printing multiple copies

There are three different ways to print multiple copies of merge printed form documents. One is with the Merge Print dialog box, the second is with a dot command, and the third requires tractor-fed paper. Remember that multiple copies of a merge printed series can use a tremendous amount of paper. Before printing multiple copies, carefully assess your need.

Tip: Each line in the data file prints one form document. This includes the first line, which is only the variable name identification line. Most merge printings begin with page two to avoid printing a dummy copy of the form letter. To have a dummy copy for your files, begin merge printing from page one.

Setting the number at the Merge Print dialog box

Whenever you start merge printing, you have the option of printing multiple copies. Just move the cursor to Number of Copies and type in the number desired. When you tell WordStar to merge print multiple copies from the Merge Print dialog box, WordStar will complete the entire series of merge print form documents before beginning the second, third, and following copies.

The Repeat Print dot command

To use the .RP command, the master document must also contain both .DF and .RV commands. The command is followed by the number of times you want to repeat the printing. The default repetition value is 1, so you don't have to type a number value to get it to repeat once.

1. Embed the dot command line on a blank line below the .DF and .RV command lines.
2. Type a period, the letters RP, a blank space, and then the numeral value of the number of repetitions desired.
3. End the line with a hard carriage return.

This command automatically prints copies every time you merge print the document.

Reformatting during merge printing

Because variable information comes in all different sizes, merge printing can drastically vary the length of a line of text in the hardcopy. If you're printing documents with fully justified margins, inserted text can undo the justification. The only way to prevent this is to use either print-time reformatting or output justification. These options are executed with dot commands. Use either in the command block, or combine the two.

Print-time reformatting

The .PF dot command tells WordStar to reformat every paragraph of a document as it's being sent to the printer. There are three ways to customize this command—by specifying on, off, or dis (for discretionary). The discretionary specification works only with conditional merge printing.

Embed this dot command either in the command block or directly above and below the paragraphs requiring reformatting. Reformatting during printing takes longer than simple merge printing, so limiting the command to specific paragraphs will speed up the printing. Paragraphs receiving variable text will be reformatted; other paragraphs will be printed verbatim.

- To turn print-time reformatting on, type .PF ON or .PF 1 at column 1 of the line above the paragraph needing reformatting. (If this is the entire document, then embed the command once in the command block.)
- To tell WordStar to stop print-time reformatting, type .PF OFF or .PF 0 on a blank line below the paragraph needing reformatting.
- When using conditional merge printing, use .PF DIS to tell WordStar to reformat the paragraph at its own discretion. This means the paragraph is reformatted only when necessary.

Output justification

The .OJ dot command normally toggles full justification on and off, depending on its sequence in the document. When used with print-time formatting, it can set paragraphs to print alternately in full or ragged-right justification. Thus, you can print fully justified documents from ragged-right text files, or ragged-right documents from fully justified text files—without permanently reformatting the source text file.

To turn output justification on, embed the .OJ ON command above the text to receive the formatting. To turn the output justification off, embed the .OJ OFF command below the text receiving the formatting. When you use Ctrl−OJ to insert the justification command, it automatically toggles it to the opposite of the current status.

Glossary

^   The caret is a symbol that often represents the Ctrl key. When seen in this book, it will almost always mean "Hold down the Ctrl key while typing the letter or letters that follow."

.   This is an abbreviation that stands for all files and all extensions. You can use it in any MS-DOS function where you want to manipulate all the files in any drive or directory. For example, the command COPY A:*.* B: tells MS-DOS to copy all files from drive A to drive B.

abort   This means to cancel a command or leave a function before it begins or completes its execution.

active   This word describes the window, menu item, dot command, print control command, etc. when its command function is in effect. Anything is said to be active when it's highlighted. This refers to the text, window, or menu item. Text is active when you're in the write-and-edit mode and the cursor is on the text. When using multiple windows, you can tell which window is active because the cursor is in that window. (If you have only one window open, then it's always active.) Menu items become active when you call the menu. Then each item becomes active as you highlight it. *See also* highlight and selection cursor.

active printer   The printer currently connected to a serial or parallel communication port, and ready to be used for printing. This is normally the same thing as the default printer, the one WordStar expects to use unless told otherwise.

alignment   The horizontal position of text on a line within that line's left and right margins. Also, the justification status, which determines how the text fills the line. Right-aligned text is right justified, left-aligned text is left justified, and center-aligned text is center justified. *See also* justified and ragged.

alphanumeric   This is a contraction of the words alphabetic and numeric. It refers to characters that are either letters of the alphabet or numerals.

Alt   Many programs use the Alt key as a special function key, allowing you to combine it with other characters to execute commands or features. It works like the Shift and Ctrl keys. To use it, hold it down and then type or press other keys.

annotation   This is a note or comment added to a document. It can be in either hidden (nonprinting) or printable text. If hidden, you can either display it onscreen or not. Hidden annotations are good for making notes to yourself or to someone who will later edit your documents with a word processor. Printable annotations are a good device for making remarks. *See also* hidden text.

ANSI character set   The American National Standards Institute's 8-bit character set. It contains 256 characters. The ASCII character set is a subset of this one.

applications program   This is another term for software, and is also referred to simply as *program*. An application program is designed and written to perform a particular kind of work. As such, it's *applied* to a specific task. Programs that perform standard tasks like accounting, bookkeeping, invoicing, calculations, data manipulation, and word processing are application programs.

archive file   A collection of useful bits and pieces of information stored in a glossary or file that can be inserted or copied into a text file to avoid having to retype it. Once you type anything in a text file, you never have to type it again. You can store it on disk and reuse it later by calling it from the disk.

arrow keys   These are the cursor-movement keys on your keyboard, and can be found either directly to the right of the letter keys or in the numeric keypad. These move the cursor in the direction the arrow points, in increments of one space or one line. By holding down these keys, you can move the cursor continuously.

ascending order   The ranking of sorted text beginning with the lowest selected value and moving to the highest.

ASCII   This is an acronym for American Standard Code for Information Interchange. This is a standard 8-bit information code used with most computers. ASCII allows you to transfer standard information from program to program, and computer to computer. ASCII characters include the first 128 characters of the ANSI character set.

ask instruction   This is a WordStar merge printing instruction. When you put it in a main or master document, it tells WordStar to prompt you for text that must be typed into the form document being printed.

asynchronous communication   This is a way of transmitting data from one device to another, in which each transmitted character is preceded by a start bit and followed by a stop bit.

automatic style sheet   A style sheet is a specific set of paragraph style tags. A distinct style sheet is created by copying the WSSTYLE.OVR file to a text file archive directory, then editing and creating paragraph tags for a specific kind of document. If you boot up WordStar from that directory and just start typing, these default settings will automatically be used until you change the settings.

Backspace   The Backspace key deletes one space backward at the cursor. This isn't the same as the left arrow key, which simply moves the cursor.

background printing   This means to send one file to the printer, while continuing to work on another file or with another program.

backup disk   A backup disk is a copy of a program disk, or a disk created to hold backup copies of data or text files. It's a very good idea to make backup copies of all program disks and use them instead of using the master copy. These backup disks are also called working disks.

BASIC   This is an acronym for Beginner's All-purpose Symbolic Instruction Code. There are many different versions of BASIC available for different microcomputers and different applications.

batch file   This is a text file that functions as a program file. In the file are MS-DOS commands that can be executed in strings or in series to perform complicated DOS functions. Batch files must always have the .BAT extension. This tells MS-DOS that it's a batch file, so it will know to process it as a program file. You execute batch files simply by typing the filename at the DOS prompt and then pressing the Enter key. These files are simple to write, and are extremely useful for managing your computer system.

baud   This is a unit of measurement for data processing speed. Baud rate is a measurement used in rating data transfer with modems. The most commonly used baud rates are 300, 1200, 2400, 4800, and 9600. The higher the rate, the faster the modem is transferring and receiving data.

binary file   Any file containing characters in machine-readable form.

bit   A bit is the smallest unit of information that a computer can recognize. This is usually a single binary character. All information processed by any computer is written in bit form.

bitmap   An image stored as an array of bits.

block   It's common in word processing to think of portions of a text file as a block. Once you mark a block of text by highlighting it, you can copy, delete, move, and reformat it. Think of a text block as a building block. From these you can build a text file.

block marking   Some word processing programs have special symbols to mark the beginning and end of a block of text. With WordStar 7, you use the function keys or the mouse to extend the highlight over a text block.

block move   To mark a portion of a text file as a block of text, then delete it and insert it elsewhere in that text file. This can be done with either Ctrl−KV, or the delete and unerase commands.

body text   The words and paragraphs in the main body of the document. This excludes headers, footers, page numbers, footnotes, endnotes, chapter titles, and section heads. When using the outlining feature, this refers to text not marked as a heading or subheading.

boilerplate text   *Boilerplate* is an old printer's term for text used over and over again without ever being changed. It can be something as simple as a return address copied into every letter you write. Or it can be something as complicated as tables and lists of information or entire passages of text to be inserted into everything you write. Boilerplate text can be stored in a file of its own. *See also* archive file.

boot   This generally means to start up a computer or a computer program. The word comes from the phrase "pulled up by the bootstraps."

buffer   A buffer is memory space that's set aside for storing and manipulating computer data. Computers, programs, and printers use buffers for temporarily holding data that might be used elsewhere. Buffer space can also be set aside on a working disk, where a file too large to hold in memory can overflow while it's being worked on. This is how some word processing programs manipulate large text files. They create temporary buffer files to store the text file as it passes through memory.

built-in font   Any font permanently stored in the read-only memory of a printer. Also known as a *resident* or *hardware font*.

bug   A flaw or problem with hardware or software. The term was first used when a moth crawled inside a mainframe computer relay and caused the entire system to malfunction. Attributed to Commodore Grace Hooper, a pioneer in both computer hardware and software.

byte   In computer memory or disk storage, it's a unit of measurement equivalent to one character. There are eight bits to a byte, and 256 possible combinations—because there are 256 ASCII characters.

calling macro   Any macro that, during its own execution, calls or invokes another macro. This is used to combine macros so they execute as one, or in a sequence.

Caps Lock   The Caps Lock key toggles the uppercase lock on and off. It works the same way the Shift Lock key on a typewriter works.

cartridge font   Any font contained in a cartridge that physically plugs into your printer. Cartridge fonts are normally associated with laser printers, but many 24-pin dot-matrix printers can also use them.

character   A character is any single letter of any alphabet, a punctuation mark, a special symbol on the keyboard, any numeral, or any other individual symbol that the computer can read, write, or store. It's anything you can type onscreen by pressing a key.

checkbox   In WordStar, a small square box that appears in a dialog box. When the checkbox is selected, an X appears in it. A checkbox represents any option that can be set or unset.

choose To use an arrow key or a mouse to pick a command, menu item, or option in a menu item.

click The single press and release of a mouse button.

clip art Any set of stored graphic images used to illustrate word-processing and desktop-publishing documents. These can be created by the user, come as part of a DTP program, or be purchased from third-party suppliers. Clip art can be entire files, or individual images cut and pasted into a document.

Clipboard In Windows, a temporary storage location used to transfer data or text between documents, and between programs. *See also* buffer.

clock speed The internal "heartbeat," or speed of a computer. Every computer has a built-in clock to regulate the internal operation of the system. In computers, specific functions must be carried out at specific intervals. If they don't the system will crash. The higher a clock speed, the faster the computer is running. Adding a faster clock will speed up processing functions, providing the computer's circuits can handle the increased speed.

close The opposite of opening a file to work on it. This removes a document from memory and closes the window in which it displayed. When you close the last window, WordStar returns to the Opening Menu.

clone A functionally identical or generic copy of another system or device, as in IBM clones. It refers to hardware that successfully runs the same software and performs the same functions as an original manufacturer's equipment.

CLS This is the DOS command used to clear the screen of any superfluous display. For example, when you run a directory it will remain onscreen. If you type CLS and press the Enter key, everything will disappear from the screen but the DOS prompt and the cursor.

collapse The opposite of *expand*. This refers to an option in the outlining companion program. When document headings are marked with the outlining options, you can "collapse" the document to show only the headings in the form of an outline. In other words, the body text becomes invisible.

columns A vertical division of text on a page. In page layout, this refers to vertical pillars of text printed between the margins on a page. Regular, full-length text is one column. You can also print in newspaper and side-by-side tabular columns. Words or numbers typed in newspaper columns begin at the left-hand side of the column, move to its right edge, then wrap down to the next line as you continue typing. WordStar does not display newspaper columns side-by-side in the document mode. To view them as they'll print, use Page Preview with Ctrl−OP.

column number The text in a file is divided into lines and columns—like a grid system with x and y coordinates. The cursor position is designated as line x and column y. This is the only way you can know exactly where you and the cursor are in any given document. The page, line, and column number are always displayed on the status line.

COM port *See* serial port and parallel port.

command This is a specific instruction to tell a program, computer, or any peripheral device what to do and how to do it. In MS-DOS, a command is a short program that tells DOS how to do a specific task. Computers, and all their appliances, cannot do anything unless you tell them, each step of the way, what you want them to do—every single time you want them to do it. That's what is meant by giving a command.

command area The space on any dialog box where you type in, or insert from a list, specific text or instructions to be used in executing a command.

push button In WordStar 7, an icon or graphic image of a button. When you click on this button, it carries out or cancels the selected action. Two common command buttons are Cancel and OK. All in all, it is a silly attempt to make an onscreen image look like something you can press with your finger.

command-driven A program, like classic WordStar, that accepts commands typed in from the keyboard. Command-driven programs can be more difficult to learn because they require you to memorize a series of interrelated commands. Once you learn the commands, though, you can use the program faster because your hands never have to leave the keyboard. Contrast with *menu-driven*.

command menu An onscreen list of commands and options you can choose from and execute. The command menu is the medium through which you issue instructions to WordStar. There are two different kinds of command menus to choose from: classic and pull-down.

communications settings In WordStar, these are special settings used to specify how to send information using a serial device like a modem or printer.

conditional operators Merge printing allows you to preset conditions that determine whether or not specific data gets printed in a document during merge printing. They can even determine if a form letter gets printed at all. These conditional operators are instructions included in a main or master document. They tell the print routine to check data in a mailing list (or other data file) to see if it meets the defined conditions. If the conditions are met, the text is printed.

confirmation message A message displayed by WordStar when you've initiated a destructive action. It asks if you want to proceed. One appears, for example, when you're about to delete a file or copy a file to an existing filename.

conventional memory The first 640K of RAM that MS-DOS uses to run a program.

copy This can be either a term or a command. As a term, it means to duplicate computer data by drawing it from memory or disk and making a duplicate of it at another place in memory, or on another disk. COPY is also an MS-DOS internal command used for copying files from one disk to another disk, directory, or filename.

crash A software or hardware breakdown or failure.

crop A term derived from photography. It means to cut off or eliminate portions of a picture or artwork that detract from its usefulness in a document. The remainder can be resized to fit the available space set aside for it.

Ctrl key The Control key is used universally as a key for initiating computer commands. It works like the Shift and Alt keys; you must hold it down while typing or pressing other keys.

Ctrl−C This MS-DOS command is used to stop or interrupt a command while it's running. For example, when using the DOS commands DIR or TYPE to display a file too large to fit on a single screen you might see what you're looking for and want to stop the rest of the display. Sometimes it will stop a command immediately, and sometimes it must wait for the first interrupt point before it can break in and halt the command.

Ctrl−S This MS-DOS command is used to temporarily halt a screen display that's scrolling past. For example, when using the DOS commands DIR or TYPE to display a file too large to fit on a single screen you can use Ctrl−S to stop the display for viewing. To exit from the scrolling display, use Ctrl−C.

current directory/drive In WordStar, this is the directory and drive that's currently specified as the target and source for text files.

current page The page of the document where the cursor is blinking. This is where words appear as you type, copy, or move them.

cursor The small blinking box on the monitor screen that indicates the next location for text or data entry and deletion.

Cut To move text from a document into a temporary storage area called a buffer in WordStar.

cut and paste The process of using copy, move, delete, and insert commands to write and revise a document by combining text files or parts of text files. Think of using scissors and rubber cement to dissect and reassemble a document.

data instruction The first paragraph of a data document or data file. It names the data file. *See* header record.

data file A file that's used by a program as a source of information. For example, in merge printing generic information is drawn from a mailing list data file and inserted into a form letter.

data record A paragraph in a data file that contains the information specific to a single copy of a form document. In a mailing list, it would be the name, address, zip code, phone number, etc., corresponding to a single addressee. A data record can also hold information that conditional printing uses to determine whether printing conditions are met. The individual pieces of information in a data record are called fields or items.

debug To solve the problems or work out the flaws in a system or a program. To get things working as they should.

default   The standard values that WordStar is preset to use if no other setting is substituted. Also, any action occurring automatically unless different directions are given.

default button   The command button in some dialog boxes preselected as the safest or most normal action. This button is more solid looking when the dialog box appears, and executes if you press the Enter key.

default drive/subdirectory   The drive or subdirectory that applications will go to when they need to run commands or routines. It's the drive or subdirectory that the programs were booted from. Don't confuse this with the current drive and directory. Those are where an application is presently hooked into for specific tasks or purposes.

default printer   The printer that WordStar is preset to use automatically when you start a print runoff. Only one printer at a time can be the default. The default printer is set up using the utility program PRCHANGE. This printer must also be active and online before WordStar can use it.

delete   To erase words or paragraphs from the text file. The next time the file is saved to disk, the text will be removed from the version on disk. What you delete is temporarily stored in a special memory location called the unerase buffer in WordStar. From there, you can reinsert it elsewhere or save it in a boilerplate file.

Del key   Pressing the Delete key will delete or erase one space forward. Hold it down to delete continuously.

descending order   The ranking of information in a sort that organizes the text in a range from highest value to lowest.

destination directory   The directory to which a file is copied or moved.

device   A device can be either hardware or software, depending on point of view. It is something to which data can be sent, or from which data can be received. Different kinds of devices are disk drives, printers, keyboards, monitors, computers, and RAM disks.

device driver   A program or set of instructions for running a device so WordStar and the system can use it. For example, WordStar has a large set of printer drivers it can use to tell it how to use each of the specified printers. And you must use a mouse driver to tell your computer how to use a mouse.

dialog box   A box appearing onscreen that either requests or provides information. Many dialog boxes contain options you can use to customize the command or function being executed. Some dialog boxes contain warnings or explain why a command can't be carried out as specified.

DIR   The MS-DOS command to give to display a list of the files in the current drive or directory.

direct formatting   Assigning format tags to text with an Alt command instead of using a command menu. This is the same as speed setting.

direction keys   *See* arrow keys.

directory   A list of the files stored on a disk. It holds the names of the files, the size of the files, and the dates and times the files were last saved.

directory path   *See* path.

Directory tree   A graphic display of the directory and subdirectory file structure on a disk. The name of each directory identifies its relative location. In recent versions of MS-DOS, you can call this representation by typing TREE and pressing the Enter key. Directories are shown as a branching structure that resembles a tree, where the bottom-level directory (the trunk) is the root directory.

disk   An electromagnetic device for the permanent storage of computer files. It uses the same metal oxide base as the tape in a stereo cassette. There are hard disks and floppy disks—hard disks are internal and fixed, and can store a large amount of information; floppy disks need to be inserted into disk drives and can hold only a fraction of the information that a hard disk can.

DISKCOPY   This is an MS-DOS copy program that can be used to make duplicate copies of disks. It will copy the contents of one disk to a blank disk of the same type. If the blank disk isn't formatted, DISKCOPY will format it before copying the files to it.

disk drive   A mechanical device used to store and retrieve data files and text files from floppy disks. This machine uses magnetic disks as the storage medium. Files are written to it, and read back, using the same basic technology as for recording or playing back music with magnetic tape.

document   This is a word processing term for a standard text file.

document dictionary   A personal dictionary you make and use to correct the spelling in a specific kind of document. This is good for storing words and special terms that are peculiar to a single document, or single type of document. It should be stored in archive under a different name, then copied into the WordStar file PERSONAL.DCT when needed to check that kind of document.

document window   A window inside a program that contains a document created or edited with that program. When you run WordStar and open a document, you have one window open. You can open other documents in additional windows.

DOS   This is an acronym for *disk operating system*. This is the DOS in MS-DOS, which was written by Microsoft. A computer can't run programs and carry out basic commands unless it has a set of instructions that tell it exactly what to do. When you boot up your system, part of DOS is loaded directly into memory, where it resides to tell the computer how to work. The rest of DOS remains on disk, where its commands are available when needed.

DOS prompt   This appears when no program is running or when you open a DOS window from inside of a program. It consists of the letter of the active drive, followed by a colon (although you can modify it to display more information), and appears by itself on the monitor. At any DOS prompt, you can type and execute MS-DOS commands.

Double-click When using a mouse to command WordStar, you can select options or files with a click of the mouse, and execute them with a double-click. Tap the mouse button twice rapidly on the item to be executed.

download To transfer computer data or text from one system to another; as in downloading from mainframes to microcomputers or from UNIX to MS-DOS.

downloadable font *See* soft font.

drag A common movement while using a mouse. It's executed by holding down the mouse button and moving the mouse. You can mark blocks of text by clicking on the beginning and dragging the mouse cursor over the text to the end of the block.

ELSE instruction A conditional statement in merge printing. It's often used with IF statements to make exceptions that determine whether or not selected text will be printed in a form document.

embed To place a command or remark in a text file so that it will show onscreen and serve a desired function, but not appear in the printed document.

EMS memory A type of expanded memory available to systems conforming to the Lotus-Intel-Microsoft expanded memory specification (LIM EMS).

emulation mode An operational status in which a device can imitate the function of another device. For example, most dot-matrix printers contain the Epson instruction set. Therefore, such a printer can emulate the printing characteristics of an Epson printer.

End The End key moves the cursor to the bottom of the screen.

endnote A reference or attribution note placed at the end of a document. It can also be used to add information about a subject being discussed in the document.

endnote text The words you type into an endnote.

endnote window WordStar's term for the window you can open while working with endnotes. It's where the endnote text is automatically stored. You must save (Ctrl−KD) or abandon the note window to return to the main document.

Enter The Enter or Return key works like a carriage return. The term is commonly misused to refer to typing something at the keyboard, to fill out an electronic form, or to write something like an invoice in accounting software. Words are typed or written, not *entered* or *keyed*.

EPT port A port requiring a special expansion board and special software. Only certain printers, like the IBM Personal Pageprinter, use this kind of port.

error messages Error messages are displayed onscreen whenever MS-DOS detects that something is functioning as it should. Within the limits of a small message, it will tell you what is wrong.

Esc The Escape key lets you escape from certain functions.

expand This refers to the companion program outlining feature. It's the opposite of collapse. When you collapse a document in the outlining mode, the body text becomes invisible and all you see are the headings, thus you see just the outline of the document. When you expand the document, the body text reappears.

expanded memory RAM above the conventional 640K of memory that's readily available for programs to use. It's allocated in 16K blocks.

extended memory RAM above the conventional 640K of memory that's not readily available to MS-DOS or MS-DOS software. Computers with 8086 or 8088 microprocessors can't use extended memory.

extension A suffix added to any filename. It's separated from the filename with a period followed by 1−3 arbitrary characters. The purpose of the extension is to lengthen a filename, or to make it more specific to your purposes. You can use the same filename over and over again with different extensions. Properly used, filename extensions provide quick reference to the contents or types of files.

Fax Derived from the term *facsimile*, and originally called a telecopy. Fax machines scan a printed page and convert its image into code transmittable over a telephone line. The receiving machine receives and reconverts the code to print a copy of the original. Widespread use of these machines has created the verb form "to fax," as in "fax me that report."

Fax board An expansion board to be installed in a computer. (There are also externally connected versions.) It transmits a fax copy directly from a computer fax file, permitting a better image than a fax machine (which must optically scan its image). Fax boards can transmit directly to fax machines, or to other computers having fax boards.

Fax modem A combination of a fax board and a standard modem. These are gaining popularity because they require only a single expansion slot or external port.

Fax file A text file or document that has been converted to a special graphics format so it can be easily transmitted by a fax board. Fax files can be transmitted directly to a fax machine or to other computers having fax boards. When received by other computers, they're printed on whatever printer the receiver has.

field A computer term for a particular item in a data file, or any selection on a menu. In a mailing-list data file, a field is a specific piece of information in a record, such as a name, address, phone number, or zip code.

file A file is a collection of related information that's treated as a distinct unit saved to a disk by the computer, and given its own distinct name. A file on a disk can be compared to a file folder in a desk drawer. There are three basic types of computer files: program files, data files, and text files.

file format The structure or arrangement of data or text stored in a file.

filename   A filename is a set of characters (letters, numerals, or symbols) used to identify a specific file. There are fixed rules for naming a file. MS-DOS filenames can be up to eight characters long, followed optionally by a period and a three-letter extension. There are some characters that are reserved for special use; MS-DOS won't accept a filename with reserved characters.

folded text   A phenomenon that occurs periodically with WordStar; it's a glitch in the display of a document's text. Words, sentences, or an entire page can become "folded" and no longer appears onscreen. Text on either side of the fold will close up to fill the gap. This can usually be corrected with a screen wipe executed with the Ctrl−|command.

font   A set of characters from a particular typeface that are distinguished by an attribute, like italic, bold, light, demi, etc. An example would be semi-bold Times Roman. (Semi-bold Times Roman is the font; Times Roman is the typeface).

font cartridge   A piece of hardware that's physically plugged into a printer. Inside the cartridge, fonts are stored on ROM chips. The printer can read the fonts and their printing instructions, and use them while printing documents.

font size   The height of the font, usually measured in points. In printing, fonts are commonly referred to in terms of their size and name, as in 14-point Helvetica or 12-point Times Roman.

footer   A word, phrase, or number that appears at the bottom of every page in the section, chapter, or other division in the printed document.

footnote   A reference or attribution note placed at the bottom of the page that contains the passage being referenced. It can also be used to add information about a subject being discussed in the document.

footnote text   The words you type into a footnote.

footnote window   WordStar's term for the note window that opens while you're writing or editing footnotes. WordStar literally opens a window at the end of the page, where the footnote text is automatically stored. This keeps the current footnote onscreen while you write it. You must save or abandon the footnote in order to return to the main document.

format   This is one of those unfortunate terms used so many different ways that it can be confusing to new users. The two main definitions are as follows: In word-processing programs, formatting controls character attributes, paragraph style, and page or document layout and design. These control the appearance of text in a document, or the way text is printed on the paper. In MS-DOS, formatting is what you have to do to a blank disk to prepare it for use by the computer. This process physically writes tracks, sectors, and their coordinates onto the disk. You can then copy files to specific locations, and their location coordinates are recorded in the file allocation table (FAT).

form document   As in a form letter or form contract, it's any printed document created by merging varying information from a data file into a master document. You can use the same letter over and over again, and change particulars in it like name, address, phone number, and so on.

function keys   These are special keys on the keyboard (F1 through either F10 or F12) that are assigned different functions by either the user or a specific program. After a function is assigned to a key, pressing that key will execute the function.

global search   A procedure that has the computer look through an entire text file to find specific characters or strings or characters in that file. You can limit the search with the following modifications: a required confirmation, the direction of the search, either whole or parts of words, and capitalization status.

global replace   Also global search and replace. A procedure that uses the computer to look through an entire text file for specific text, and then replaces each instance of that text with some other text. You can limit the search and replace with the same modifications as a search, see above.

graphics mode   A display mode that shows the onscreen format as it will look when printed. Boldface looks bold, italic is slanted, underlined has a line below it, etc. This is what you get with Page Preview. WordStar's default display is the text mode.

graphics resolution   The quality level at which graphics are printed. The higher the resolution, the finer the quality of the printed graphics—and the slower the printing. The standard graphics resolution of laser and inkjet printers is 300 dots per inch. Dot-matrix printers are much less. The standard commercial lithograph Webb press (used for printing books and magazines) prints at 1500 dots per inch.

gutter   The inner margins of facing pages, or the blank space left between columns on a printed page. The term comes from the V shape in the middle of an opened book, similar to the gutter running down the sides of streets or the troughs attached to the eaves of houses.

handshake   This is an electronic link between computers; between a computer and its devices; or between a program like WordStar, the computer, and disk drives. When you run WordStar and access a disk drive, you establish a handshake relationship between WordStar and that drive. The technical definition, however, is the "go ahead" signal sent between computers or devices to indicate that communication is possible. It's commonly sent by a local computer to a remote computer or terminal. XON/XOFF is the standard software handshaking method.

hanging indent   This is when one line of text, usually the first in a paragraph is aligned on the left margin, and the rest of the lines are indented so as to hang under the first line.

hardcopy   A copy of your text file actually printed on paper.

header   Text that's printed at the top of every page in a printed document.

header file   Don't confuse this with a header. This is a file containing a header
with information used in printing form documents. A header record is a list of
field names that correspond to both names used in a master document and to
the columns of information in a data file. During merge printing, the computer reads both files and then substitutes text from the data file into the document being printed from the master file.

header record   A list of field or column names that's stored in the first paragraph of a data file. These names represent categories of information. The
names in this record must be in the same order as the columns in the file.
When a name from this record is placed in the body of the master document,
merge printing will match it with its column in the data file and draw information from it to insert in the form document.

heading   A title in a text file for a chapter, section, subsection, etc. A heading is
usually on a line of its own, and is often in a different font type or font size
than the body text.

hidden file   Any file marked with its display attribute changed to Hide. This tells
MS-DOS and WordStar not to show its filename in any listing of files. The
most common hidden files are the MS-DOS system files IO.SYS and
MSDOS.SYS, which are kept hidden and read-only to keep them from being
viewed and modified by a careless user. Hidden files can also be used to
copy-protect software. A "pirate" copy of a program won't contain hidden
files, and thus won't work properly.

hidden text   Special character tagging that removes the printing codes from text.
Hidden text shows onscreen but, like a dot command, won't print in your
hardcopy. You can use hidden text to insert comments, annotations, and place
markers to the electronic document. You can see these remarks onscreen, and
use global search to find them. WordStar offers two different ways to insert
hidden text in a document: through the Notes Menu as a nonprinting comment, or by the traditional method of typing two periods on column 1 of a
blank line, followed by the comment.

highlight   An inverse video display onscreen that indicates command choices,
text selected for special formatting or handling, and features that are currently
active. Anything that's highlighted onscreen indicates that an icon, filename,
or text has been selected and will be affected by the command or routine
being executed.

high-memory area   Usually called HMA, it's the first 64K of the extended
memory in your computer. This area is reserved for use by some programs.

Home   The Home key moves the cursor to the left side of the line of text.

icon   A symbol used as a graphic representation of a command or function.
Clicking on the icon with your mouse will execute the represented function.

IF instruction   A conditional printing instruction used in merge printing. It tells
WordStar to check the text in the data columns of a data file to see if it meets

specified conditions. If the conditions are met, the text will be used to print the form document. IF instructions can also be used in macros.

illegal Any word, character, or command that isn't allowed for use in a given program—usually because it's been reserved for special use in that program or because it hasn't been given a value at all. MS-DOS has certain characters, filenames, and extensions that are illegal for use in naming text files.

import To merge data from another program into a WordStar document file as it's being sent to the printer.

inactive window Any open window, whether displayed or not, in which you're not currently working. Its most notable characteristic is the absence of a blinking cursor.

incremental spacing WordStar uses incremental spacing to adjust the distance between words on a line when a paragraph is fully justified. This aligns text neatly against the right margins, but often leaves wide gaps between words on a line. (Auto-hyphenation can help reduce this somewhat.)

indent Moving text in from the left or right margins. Also, the distance the text is moved.

index code The three characters, .i., that mark terms for inclusion in an index. The Library Index routine will read these codes and use them to generate an index of the document.

index entry A word or phrase preceded by the index code. When the Library Index routine generates an index from the document, the word or phrase will be included in the index.

Insert Can be either a command or a function. As a command, it will take text from a glossary or the buffer and put it into the document at the insertion point. As a function, it's simply the mode for typing new text into a document at the insertion point. The text to the right will move over to make room for the new text.

insertion point The current cursor position at the time of typing or pasting in text. Text is always inserted at the cursor.

justified The alignment of lines of text within a paragraph. The most common is left justified, where the text is lined up against the left margin, printing a smooth left margin and a ragged right one. Right justified lines the text up against the right margin, printing a smooth right margin and a ragged left. Center justified puts each line in the center of the space between the set right margins, and prints both margins ragged. Full justified adds incremental spaces between the words to make each line exactly the same length so that both margins are smooth.

kerning Refers to adjusting the space between letters and words.

key code As in style tags or Alt commands. When you define a style tag, you give it a one- or two-letter key sequence as a name. You can execute this style tag by pressing the Alt key and they typing its key code letters.

layout The physical arrangement of words and artwork on a printed page. Elements of layout include number of columns, gutters between columns, size of page, font type and size used, margins, line spacing, and anything else having to do with the appearance of the page. Same as design.

leader characters Characters used to fill the space between columns as a means of leading the reader's eye to the information in the next column. This is most often used in a table of contents to lead the eye from the heading across the page to the corresponding number. In WordStar, the default leader character is the period, and is tagged to tab stops, so that periods are automatically inserted when you tab with Ctrl−P. You can change the leader character to any character by using the utility program WSCHANGE.

left arrow The direction key that moves the cursor left.

line editor A line editor is any program that allows you to create ASCII text files, and they're called *line* editors because most allow you to edit or enter only a single line at a time. Most people use line editors to write and edit computer programs. MS-DOS has a built-in line editing program called EDLIN, which can be used to write and edit batch files. Word processing began as line editors, but was difficult to use. For convenience, more and more word processing features were added until these programs became the advanced word processing programs of today.

line feed To feed paper through a printer one line at a time. This command is automatically inserted by wordwrap during paragraph alignment. Can be inserted manually with the command Ctrl−PL.

line number The vertical cursor position on a page in a document. The line numbers start over once you pass the bottom of the page. You can show the line number on the status line by turning on the display through the main menu options.

list box Inside a dialog box, this is any listing of available choices, for example, the list of all available files in a directory or the options used to make a command function more specific to the the task being ordered.

load To copy a program file or text file from disk storage into computer memory.

LPT port Same as *parallel port*.

macro In WordStar, a series of commands or string of actions tagged to a simple keystroke sequence. By typing the keystroke sequence, you can execute the string of commands together. You can assign macros to special keys, called hotkeys, or to longer descriptive names.

mark In WordStar, mark means to cover a block of text with the inverse video highlight so it can be copied, moved, or deleted.

master disks This is another term for the factory-made program disks that you buy as a software package. Whenever possible, you should avoid using the master copies to run the program. Make working copies of the disks and use them instead. Even if your master disks are copy protected, you're legally entitled to use copying software to make copies for personal use.

memory-resident software   Also called *TSR*. A program that loads into memory and is available for use when another program is running. These are programs that can be used "inside" of another program, usually as some form of desktop tool like a calendar or calculator.

menu   A list of programs, commands, options, or items that can be selected and executed. You normally select a menu item by highlighting it with the arrow keys or by clicking it on with the mouse. You execute it by pressing the Enter key or by double-clicking the mouse.

menu bar   The horizontal bar below the status line that contains the list of all the pull-down menus available to call and use.

merge   As in merge printing, to join one or more text files—or the data in data files—into a text file to produce a larger document during the printing run.

monospaced font   A typeface or font set in which all characters take up the same space, regardless of individual character size or shape. Compare to *proportional font*.

network   Any group of computers connected by cables and using software that links them electronically to share equipment (like printers) and exchange information.

network disk drive   A disk drive in a network of computers that has been set aside for use by everyone hooked into the network. Network drives are commonly used to store data used by all or to hold messages sent from one user to another.

normal distribution   A function that approximates the distribution of many random variables (as in the outcome proportion of a particular sorting of a large number of independent repetitions of an experiment in which the probabilities remain constant from trial to trial).

Num Lock   The Number Lock key toggles the numeric keypad on and off. When toggled on, you can use the arrow keys on the keypad to move the cursor.

open   To copy the contents of a text file or graphics file into memory and display it in an open window.

onscreen   Anything that appears on the computer monitor screen.

option   A choice on a menu or dialog box. As a choice on a menu, it runs another program or executes a major function of an active program. As an item on a dialog box, it allows you to adjust the function of the command with which it's associated. Dialog boxes generally have several kinds of options, including exclusive option buttons and nonexclusive checkboxes.

option button   An icon, or graphic representation of a small, round button inside a dialog box. These offer an "either or" situation, as you can select only one option button in any group of buttons.

overwrite mode   When typing text into a file, you usually have the option of being in the insert mode or the overwrite mode. When in the overwrite mode, everything you type will write over existing text in a file, replacing it with what you're typing. In almost every case it's best to stay in the insert mode.

parallel interface   A linkage between the computer and a printer in which multiple bits of information are sent to the printer in groups. Same as a *Centronics interface*.

parallel port   A communication outlet on the back of your computer where you plug in the cable to the printer. This port is usually LPT1. WordStar supports parallel ports LPT1 through LPT3.

parameter   Specific information describing the limits of a device, system, or program. In MS-DOS, it's often called a key and allows you to fine-tune the execution of a command or program. In the command DIR /p, the /p parameter tells MS-DOS to pause the directory listing when it fills the monitor screen. Many MS-DOS commands have such keys.

paste   This is an editing or rearranging function. In WordStar, you use it to copy or move a marked block or to insert text from the Unerase buffer.

patch   An alteration to a program, either temporarily or permanently, in order to make that program perform an additional function. It also means to physically connect hardware together with patch cables or a patchboard.

path   The directions to a specific directory or file stored on a drive in your computer. The syntax includes the drive name, the directory and any subdirectories, plus the filename. My best advice is to keep your directory tree as simple as possible and avoid creating subdirectories whenever possible.

pels   *See* pixels.

peripheral   A secondary piece of hardware added to a computer system to enhance capabilities or perform desired functions.

pixel   The smallest graphic unit onscreen. These are the actual dots of colored phosphors that light up when irradiated by the electron gun in the back of the monitor. Pixels are also used as the unit of resolution for a monitor. (The more pixels per square inch, the higher the resolution and the finer the image possible.) Also known as picture elements, or pels.

PgDn   This is the Page Down key. It moves the onscreen text one screen page down. A screen page is the 21−24 lines of text that appear onscreen when you open a document file with WordStar.

PgUp   The Page Up key moves the onscreen text one screen page up.

point   To move the mouse cursor onscreen until it rests on the item or option to be selected, activated, or executed.

point size   A unit of measurement for the height of a printed character. A point equals $1/72$ of an inch. Point size is normally given as an indentifier along with the font name, as in 12-point Times Roman.

pointer   The onscreen cursor that marks the location of mouse actions. The shape of the pointer varies from program to program and commonly changes shape to indicate a different mode is active, but an arrow is usually the default. Desktop publishing programs have a different pointer for every mode of operation. Graphics drawing programs have many different pointers.

port   Derived from the nautical term for places that ships sail into for loading or unloading cargo, this is a communications plug on a computer or device used to attach a cable that transfers data or text between devices. For example, a parallel port is used to send information from the computer to the printer.

print queue   A list of files that have been sent to a particular printer. The computer, or network controller, processes the files in the order received and sends them on for printing. Derived from the word *queue*, or long braided ponytail.

printer driver   A file containing information an application program uses to tell a printer how to print documents. Thus, it controls how the printer, the computer, and a program like WordStar interact. A printer driver provides WordStar with information about fonts, layout and design, and basic printing instructions.

proportional font   A font in which the space each character occupies depends on the character's width. This makes the characters fit together better in words, and allows for more text to print within the given margins. The process of adjusting the space between proportional font characters is *kerning*. Compare to monospaced font.

protected mode   The operational capability of a computer to address or use extended memory.

queue   *See* print queue.

RAM   Acronym for random access memory. RAM is composed of computer memory chips into which a program is loaded for use. It's also used to perform necessary tasks while the computer is running. The data in RAM chips is erased every time the computer is turned off or a new program is loaded into the computer.

raster font   Any font created as a graphic bit-map image. Available only in a fixed size. Raster fonts are used mostly for onscreen display, but some dot-matrix printers use them and they're built into some laser printers. Being fixed in size and shape, they require less processing and thus print faster.

read-only file   Any file whose attribute status has been coded to lock out changes or to prevent deletion. This is what is done to a file when you protect it with the option on the Opening Menu. A read-only text file can be opened and viewed, and copied to any other drive or directory. But it can't be edited, changed, or deleted. Data files and program files can be marked read-only to prevent unwanted modification.

return   The Return is another name for the Enter key, which works like a carriage return.

right arrow   The right arrow cursor key moves the cursor right.

ROM   This is an acronym for read-only memory, computer memory chips that can be read but not modified or erased for new use. ROM contains information that directs the computer's functions, and software can be permanently written into ROM chips to dedicate the system to a specific function or program.

root directory   The lowest or base directory on every disk. Every formatted disk has a root directory. The directory tree grows out of the root, branching into directories and subdirectories.

sans serif   Literally meaning "without serifs," those short lines stemming from and at an angle to the upper and lower ends of the strokes of a letter. Helvetica fonts are noted for their attractive simplicity and lack of serifs.

scaled point size   Refers to fonts whose point size can be varied up or down on demand. Scalable fonts contain instructions on how to make the shape of the font, and they're drawn in the size needed.

screen font   A raster font that's designed to replicate a printer font onscreen. The rendition isn't always accurate, simply because there are too many different printer fonts to conveniently store their screen counterparts in your computer. There are hardware and software solutions available to make onscreen fonts look exactly like the printed ones.

scroll   To move text or graphics up or down onscreen without moving the cursor, in order to see parts of the file not visible.

scroll bars   In WordStar, this is the graphic bar running down the right-most edge of the monitor screen. The scroll bar contains a small box and two scroll arrows. By clicking on the arrows or the scroll bar, you move the document up or down. You can also scroll by clicking on the box and dragging it up or down, and thus move many screen pages at a time.

Scroll lock   The Scroll Lock key toggles the scroll lock on and off.

SCSI   Pronounced "scuzzy." It stands for small computer system interface, and is a peripheral control port or technology for handling up to seven devices (like disk drives). It uses high-speed data transfer, up to 4Mb per second, to connect multiple peripherals, while using only one expansion slot in the computer.

select   To highlight an item or option on any menu or dialog box. You can move the highlight with the arrow keys or by clicking on the item with the mouse. Selecting does not execute the function of the option. Do this by pressing the Enter key or by double-clicking the mouse.

selection cursor   The mouse cursor or pointer that shows you where you are in a window, menu, or dialog box.

serial interface   A communication method between a computer and printer in which the computer sends single bits of information or data one after the other. Same as *asynchronous* and *RS232 interface*.

serial port   A communication outlet from a computer (usually COM1) where the cable for a serial printer or other serial communication device is plugged in. The most common other device is the modem.

serifs Those short lines stemming out of the upper and lower ends of the strokes of a letter. Serifs are used to make a font fancier or more attractive. Used properly, they make words easier to read. Roman fonts are noted for their attractive serifs. *See* sans serif.

server *See* network disk drive.

share A partition of a network disk drive.

Shift key You hold down the Shift keys while typing other letters to get the uppercase versions of those letters. Shift can also be used like the Alt and Ctrl keys; you hold it down and type another key to initiate a command or function.

sneaker net The human alternative to a local area network. It's made up of people who carry floppy disks from one computer to another.

soft font A font stored in a file that's copied to the printer's memory whenever it's needed to print a file. The file is either stored on a floppy disk or copied to your hard disk.

software Any and all instructions to the computer. A related series of instructions to execute a specific task is called a program. The two major types are system software and application software. MS-DOS is system software. WordStar is application software.

soft return A word processing control code inserted into a text file to mark the end of a line. When the document is printed, a soft return is converted into the return code that tells the printer to begin printing a new line. Soft returns are determined by the right margin, and are changed when the right margin is changed (and affected paragraphs reformatted).

solid color The color on a monitor when all the pixels are emitting the same color. Monochrome monitors have only a single color, usually green or amber.

sort The arranging, organizing, and categorizing of text according to selected or specified characteristics. Text can be sorted alphabetically, numerically, or alphanumerically.

source directory The directory in which the files to be copied or moved are sorted.

spacebar The key you use to insert blank spaces to a line of text.

spike A temporary, sudden, sharp rise and fall in the voltage of an electric power source. The term comes from the visual image or wave form the surge makes on an oscilloscope.

spool To hold all or part of a text file in memory in order to free the computer for other activities. Also called *background printing* or *print buffering*.

standard settings Same as *default settings*. These are the values that a program contains when it's shipped from the factory, and are the settings that a program uses if no others are specified. There are standard settings for every feature of WordStar, everything from margins and tabs to line spacing.

subdirectory   Any directory that's split off from another directory. All directories are subdirectories of the root directory.

surge   A sudden temporary increase in electrical current.

switch   *See* parameter or key.

System menu   *See* Control Menu.

system time   The time that's used by the computer's internal clock to mark a file in a directory. This time is either supplied at bootup by the real-time clock, or typed in by the user.

Tab   The Tab key performs preset tab movements.

task   A running program. Multitasking is when several programs run at once, allowing you to switch between them on demand.

terminal emulation   The ability of hardware and software to simulate the function of a remote terminal. By linking your computer with other computers via cables or telephone lines, it can serve as a terminal in a network. Terminal emulation allows your computer to display received data and to use features of the remote computer.

text file   A file containing only ASCII characters, plus any print controls and hidden word processing commands. These can be either document or non-document files.

text flow   How text reacts when it encounters a graphic or picture. Standard practice is to have the text flow or wrap around the picture. But text can print over a picture, using it as background.

TSR software   The current jargon for memory-resident software. It's an acronym for terminate and stay resident.

tweak   To change slightly, usually in reference to a value or function.

typeface   A group or set of fonts with the same general appearance or representative features. The Times typeface contains fonts with serifs and variable character widths. The Helvetica font family contains sans serif fonts and variable character widths. Most typefaces are the registered property of their designer, and their use is licensed and covered by copyright laws.

vector fonts   A pattern of dots connected by lines that can be scaled or printed in different sizes. Typically used by plotters. Also known as *stroke fonts*.

volume label   A name used to identify a disk. A disk can be named during the formatting, with either the /v parameter or the MS-DOS label command. It can be up to 11 characters long, with blank spaces allowed.

wildcard character   A wildcard character is used to represent another character in a global search and replace or any directory search. MS-DOS reserves the asterisk and the question mark for use as wildcards in filenames or text searches. The asterisk stands for all characters while the question mark stands for individual characters. For example, *.DOC tells MS-DOS to display all files with the .DOC extension.

window   Any rectangular onscreen space set aside to display a program or document. Depending on the software, multiple windows can be opened as separate viewing areas. WordStar 7 allows two documents to be opened at once in separate windows. When you boot WordStar and open a document, the text will appear in the full-screen window. You can open either documents or nondocuments in the second window, work on both at once, and copy or move text directly from one to the other. You can also change the window size to full screen, half screen, or a specific number of lines.

wordwrap   An onscreen layout feature that breaks off text from the end of a line when it passes the right margin, and moves it down to the next line at the left margin. This eliminates the need for hard carriage returns to end a line of text. Just type until you reach the end of the paragraph. Carriage returns are used to end a paragraph and to insert blank lines onscreen.

workspace   The area of a window that displays the program being worked with or the document being written or edited.

WSCHANGE   This is the WordStar customization utility program. Use it to customize and set up WordStar to work exactly the way you want. Its primary function is to set the default or startup values for most WordStar features and options. You can also use it to customize how WordStar works with your computer and your printer.

Index

Other Bestsellers of Related Interest

MICROSOFT® MONEY MANAGEMENT
—*Jean E. Gutmann*

Written especially for first-time Windows users, *Microsoft® Money Management* is a complete guide to effective financial record-keeping with Microsoft Money—the new money management software for Windows that's perfect for individuals and small businesses that don't need a full-fledged, double-entry accounting package. With this user-friendly guide, you'll become a pro in no time as you take advantage of the expert hints and proven techniques not found in software manuals. 272 pages, 132 illustrations. **Book No. 4172, $17.95 paperback only**

BATCH FILES TO GO: A Programmer's Library—*Ronny Richardson*

Ronny Richardson, respected research analyst and programmer, has assembled this collection of ready-to-use batch files featuring over 80 exclusive keystroke-saving programs. These fully developed programs—all available on disk for instant access—can be used as they are, or altered to handle virtually any file management task. 352 pages, 100 illustrations. **Book No. 4165, $34.95 paperback only**

VISUAL BASIC POWER PROGRAMMING
—*Namir C. Shammas*

With *Visual Basic Power Programming*, you'll have a programmer's toolbox complete with routines for file management, text and graphics manipulation, calculations, scientific plotting, and much more. Shammas's book goes beyond introductory books by telling you how to "put the program to work" and taking a modular approach in which each chapter can stand alone. The code contained in the book is provided on disk for easy use. 400 pages, 160 illustrations. **Book No. 4149, $29.95 paperback, $$39.95 hardcover**

NORTON UTILITIES® 6.0: An Illustrated Tutorial—*Richard Evans*

Richard Evans shows you how to painlessly perform the most dazzling Norton functions using the all new features of Norton Utilities 6.0. He also reviews the best from previous releases, providing clear, easy-to-follow instructions and screen illustrations reflecting Norton's new developments. You'll also learn about NDOS, a new configuration and shell program that replaces COMMAND .COM. 464 pages, 277 illustrations. **Book No 4132, $19.95 paperback, $29.95 hardcover**

BUILD YOUR OWN 386/386SX COMPATIBLE AND SAVE A BUNDLE
—2nd Edition—*Aubrey Pilgrim*

Now, with the latest in Pilgrim's best-selling Build Your Own series, you can assemble an 80386 microcomputer at home using mail-order parts that cost a lot less today than they did several years ago. Absolutely no special technical know-how is required—only a pair of pliers, a couple of screwdrivers, and this detailed, easy-to-follow guide. 248 pages, 79 illustrations. **Book No. 4089, $18.95 paperback, $29.95 hardcover**

VISUAL BASIC: Easy Windows™ Programming—*Namir C. Shammas*

Enter the exciting new world of visual object-oriented programming for the Windows environment. *Visual Basic* is chock-full of screen dumps, program listings, and illustrations to give you a clear picture of how your code should come together. You'll find yourself referring to its tables, listings, and quick-reference section long after you master Visual Basic. As a bonus, the book is packaged with a 3.5-inch disk filled with all the working Visual Basic application programs discussed in the text. 480 pages, 249 illustrations. **Book No. 4086, $29.95 paperback only**

INSIDE AMI PRO™ 2.0: Professional Tips & Techniques—*Maria A. Hoath*

Whether you create letters, memos, contracts, advertisements, newsletters, or books, *Inside Ami Pro 2.0 Professional Tips & Techniques* will show you how to produce high-quality printed documents more efficiently and safely with the latest version of Ami Pro. Hoath provides more than 300 tips and 250 actual screen printouts, and all the professional advice you need to gain the level of proficiency you want. She outlines all the improved features of Ami Pro 2.0. Including brand-new functions, menu changes, and enhancements to old features. 608 pages, 270 illustrations. **Book No. 4078, $24.95 paperback only**

MACINTOSH SYSTEM 7: The Complete Sourcebook—*Gordon M. Campbell*

Campbell shows off some of the exciting new features of System 7 and offers tips for upgrading your hardware and software. This is your best guide to the first major development in the Macintosh since its introduction in 1984. With this book by your keyboard, you can count on clear skies and smooth sailing, for either upgrade or installation. 320 pages, Illustrated. **Book No. 4074, $32.95 paperback only**

HARD DISK MANAGEMENT WITH DOS 5 —3rd Edition—*Dan Gookin*

Updated to reflect all the new features of DOS 5, this handsome volume is a powerful tool for breaking down and reorganizing jumbled files and data into manageable units using a creative combination of partitions and subdirectories. This fully updated and revised edition will not only save the experienced user from hard disk chaos, but it will also save the first-time hard disk user from experiencing the headaches and frustration caused by poor hard disk management. 424 pages, Illustrated. **Book No. 4072, $29.95 paperback, $39.95 hardcover**

FOXPRO®: The Master Reference —2nd Edition—*Robin Stark and Shelley Satonin*

Design and run powerful, customized databases in no time using all the exciting new features of FoxPro. This alphabetical guide to every FoxPro command and function covers all versions through 2.0—more than 350 entries in all. Its innovative three-part indexing system leads you quickly to all commands, functions, and examples found in the book. 512 pages, 135 illustrations. **Book No. 4056, $24.95 paperback only**

ADVANCED BATCH FILE PROGRAMMING—3rd Edition—*Dan Gookin*

Now updated to cover DOS 5.0, this book includes enhanced coverage of bath file commands, material on several new code compilers, and an expanded reference section. In addition, you'll get a number of sample programs, complete with line-by-line explanations—all of which are included on disk. 528 pages, 125 illustrations. **Book No. 3986, $29.95 paperback only**

WRITING AND MARKETING SHAREWARE: Revised and Expanded —2nd Edition—*Steve Hudgik*

Profit from the lucrative shareware market with the expert tips and techniques in *Writing and Marketing Shareware—Revised and Expanded Second Edition*. If you have new software ideas, but are not sure they'll be competitive in today's dynamic PC market, this detailed guide will show you how to evaluate and sell them through shareware distribution. Plus, to get you started in the right direction, a 5.25″ disk—featuring a shareware mailing list management program and a database with over 200 shareware distributors and 100 magazine review contacts—is available through a special coupon offer. 336 pages, 41 illustrations. **Book No. 3961, $18.95 paperback only**

Order Form for Readers Requiring a Single 3.5″ Disk

This Windcrest/McGraw-Hill software product is also available on a 3.5″/720K disk. If you need the software in 3.5″ format, simply follow these instructions:

- Complete the order form below. Be sure to include the exact title of the Windcrest/McGraw-Hill book for which you are requesting a replacement disk.

- Make check or money order made payable to *Glossbrenner's Choice*. The cost is **$5.00** (**$8.00** for shipments outside the U.S.) to cover media, postage, and handling. Pennsylvania residents, please add 6% sales tax.

- Foreign orders: please send an international money order or a check drawn on a bank with a U.S. clearing branch. We cannot accept foreign checks.

- Mail order form and payment to:

  Glossbrenner's Choice
  Attn: Windcrest/McGraw-Hill Disk Replacement
  699 River Road
  Yardley, PA 19067-1965

Your disk will be shipped via First Class Mail. Please allow one to two weeks for delivery.

Windcrest/McGraw-Hill Disk Replacement

Please send me a replacement disk in 3.5″/720K format for the following Windcrest/McGraw-Hill book:

Book Title ____

Name ____

Address ____

City/State/ZIP ____

If you need help
with the enclosed disk . . .

This disk contains macros, batch files, boilerplate text, and patches you can use to enhance WordStar 7 and increase your writing productivity. These various files are intended to complement the material presented in *Commanding WordStar Release 7.0, 2nd Edition* (Windcrest book 4154), © by Windcrest Books, an imprint of TAB Books.

Simply use these files with your version of WordStar 7. The macros are contained in a separate subdirectory, A:\MACROS.